Guide to Laos and Cambodia

Guide to
Laos and Cambodia

John R Jones

Bradt Publications, UK
The Globe Pequot Press Inc, USA

First published in 1995 by Bradt Publications, 41 Nortoft Road,
Chalfont St Peter, Bucks SL9 0LA, England
Published in the USA by The Globe Pequot Press Inc, 6 Business Park Road,
PO Box 833, Old Saybrook, Connecticut 06475-0833

British Library Cataloguing in Publication Data
A catalogue record for this book is available from the British Library
ISBN 1 898323 22 4

Library of Congress Cataloging-in-Publication Data
Jones, John R.
  Guide to Laos and Cambodia / John R Jones.
  p.cm.
  Includes Index
  ISBN 1-56440-815-9
  1. Laos – Guidebooks.   2. Cambodia – Guidebooks.   I. Title.
  DS555.25.J66 1995   95-17762
  915.9404'4 - dc20   CIP

Illustrations   Jane Keay
Maps *Inside covers:* Steve Munns   *Others:* Hans van Well
Photographs   John R Jones
Front cover   sunset, Mekong River, Luang Prabang
Back cover   dancer, Royal Cambodian Ballet, Phnom Penh

Typeset from the author's disc by Wakewing Ltd, High Wycombe HP13 7QA
Printed and bound in Great Britain by
The Guernsey Press Co Ltd, Guernsey, Channel Islands

ACKNOWLEDGEMENTS

Immeasurable thanks must go to all my interpreters throughout Laos and Cambodia. Without their help this guide would not have been possible. In Vientiane they included Sisana Vongsak, Meun Somvichit, Kaysone Siphandon and Som Saochanthala. Am Pablia was extremely helpful with the travel arrangements. I am greatly indebted to Claude Vincent, Céline and Soumana Loire of SODETOUR, Vientiane, and Christian Piantoni of Fimoxy-Sodetour in Hong Kong who provided me with much of the tour information. A special thanks to Becky Bale at Phoenix Travel Services, Hong Kong, who provided friendly assistance with general and tours information. Hoth Phanivong, director of Lao Travel Service, Vientiane, gave me vital assistance with the visa information; he deserves my warmest thanks. Outsama Souvannasing, marketing manager of Raja Tour, Vientiane, provided me with helpful information on itineraries throughout Laos; I send him my thanks and best wishes. I have pleasure in thanking Bodhisvane Vayakone and Vilay Phiahouaphanh of Diethelm Travel (Laos) Ltd, who supplied me with masses of information on the country. I am very grateful to Rob Stewart for the information on Vang Vieng and to Walter Pfabigan of BURAPHA for information on Lao Pako. I am indebted to Tommy Rebbick for updates on Skanska's progress with the roads and to Bob Stewart for introducing me to the Tad Leuk Waterfall area. The publisher of *Dok Champa* (the in-flight magazine of Lao Aviation) deserves special thanks for back copies which contained valuable information on the country. Thanks also to Lao Aviation representatives Khemphone Phachanthavong and Chang Hu for flight information.

I am greatly indebted to Ngin Sareth of Phnom Penh Tourism who provided me with many valuable maps and temple plans and gave vital assistance on many aspects of tourism in Cambodia. Chou Ta-Kuan deserves thanks for information on Cambodian culture and architecture. Zhou Daguan, who provided valuable information and plans of Angkor Wat, deserves a special warm thanks. My thanks to staff and management of Apsara Tours, Phnom Penh, and Diethelm Travel Cambodia Ltd. Kouch Virya, the assistant director of Aroon Tours, together with Chith Pok and Or Anthony (Yuthana) provided me with valuable tour information; I extend to them my gratitude. Without my faithful friends and interpreters Kromamun Bongsprabandh and Wiphousana, who accompanied me on my trips in Cambodia, I wouldn't have got much done; they are thanked most warmly for their kindness and friendship.

In Phnom Penh, I couldn't have got around to the extent I did if it wasn't for my cyclo driver friends Samoeum, Mao and Ratha. I would like to extend a special thanks to Kheang, my friendly guide at Angkor. Pak Sokhom, Ministry of Tourism, was extraordinarily helpful and also deserves special thanks.

I also have pleasure in thanking representatives from Mekong Travel (NY), Paul Cummings, managing director of Orbitours, Sydney, who sent me some hard-to-get information, Visami of Impex International, Manila, Kuan of Lam Son International, Bangkok, David Lomas, video expert Explore Worldwide (UK) and representatives from Lao America (USA), Inter-Lao Tourisme, Diethelm Travel (Bangkok), Lao Investment Promotion Corporation and Sai Travel (Tokyo).

Immeasurable thanks to freelance journalist, Pat Yale, who helped update some of the hotel information, provided some valuable advice to backpackers and made many useful comments. My mother-in-law, Margaret Jones, deserves a special mention for all her valuable support in the project. I must acknowledge my indebtedness to Jane Keay for her superb drawings from my photographs which have added considerable interest to the guide Without the help of Siân and Ian with the word processing, this guide would have been a few months late being published. I thank them most warmly for all their hard work. A very special thanks to Hans van Well for his work as editor and for his maps, plans and drawings.

Last but by no means least, I would like to thank my lovely wife Alison who helped with the careful editing of the text and for giving me her loving support right through the project.

THIS BOOK IS DEDICATED TO THE FRIENDLY PEOPLE OF LAOS AND CAMBODIA AND TO THE MEMORY OF MY DEAR MOTHER, KATHLEEN JONES.

THE AUTHOR

John R Jones is a professional travel photographer, writer and biologist who has contributed pictures and articles for publication worldwide. He graduated from London University with a master's degree in hydrobiology and also holds degrees in botany and zoology. Although various assignments have taken him to over 50 countries in the world, he has particular fondness for the east, as evidenced by his previous books *Vietnam Now* (Aston Publications) and the first ever English-language *Guide to Vietnam* (Bradt Publications) which was first published in 1989. Since then he has written a highly successful new *Guide to Vietnam* (Bradt Publications, October 1994) which is intended as a companion volume. He has made fourteen trips to Indochina and is a regular contributor to the *Vietnam, Laos and Cambodia Broadsheet*.

If you would like to help with future editions of this book, I would be extremely grateful. I would be pleased to hear about hotels and restaurants not listed and would appreciate your comments about those that are. Any interesting information that you would like to share with future readers would be gratefully appreciated. If you have any valuable suggestions, comments or even disaster stories, all would assist future travellers to get as much as possible out of their Indochina adventure.

Please write to me at 'The Green', Llanidloes, Powys SY18 6ES.

Thank you very much.

John Jones

CONTENTS

Wat That Luang Neua

KEY TO MAP SYMBOLS

⌀ ⌀ ●	URBAN AREA, TOWN, SETTLEMENT etc
■ ●	BUILDING or PLACE of INTEREST
═══	ROAD
=====	ROUGH ROAD (FOOTPATH in Town Maps)
+++ ▬▬	RAILWAY
～～	RIVER ; DYKE or CANAL
～～	SHORELINE
⋈⏸⋉	FALLS
✕	BRIDGE
⁓⁓	CONTOUR (Heights in metres)
—··—	NATIONAL BOUNDARY
⊔⊔⊔⊔	NATIONAL BOUNDARY of Featured Country
▲ △	MOUNTAIN or PEAK (Heights in metres)
Ω	CAVE(S)
⚘	WOODLAND or PARK
⊕	AIRPORT
⛴	FERRY TERMINAL or PIER
--(F)--	FERRY ROUTE
⊕	HOSPITAL or Medical Centre
⬭	STADIUM or Sports Complex
✉	POST OFFICE
£$	$	BANK
MKT	MARKET
STA	STA	RAILWAY STATION
B	BUS STATION or STOP
T	TAXIS
G	GARAGE or FILLING STATION
+	CHURCH
Mon.	MONUMENT

Section One
Preparation

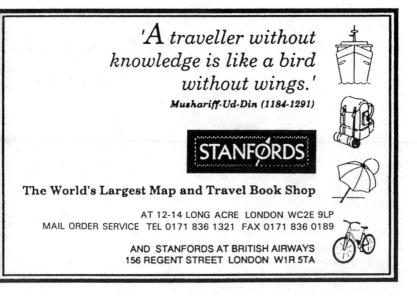

Chapter One

Health and Safety

HEALTH

Vaccinations required

You are allowed to enter both Laos and Cambodia without vaccination certificates against cholera, typhoid or hepatitis. Those entering from a country where there is yellow fever require a vaccination certificate.

Although not an entry requirement, it is advisable (according to the School of Tropical Medicine) to be vaccinated against cholera, typhoid, polio, tetanus, hepatitis A and the little-known Japanese encephalitis.

Experienced long-haul travellers these days are also vaccinated against rabies and hepatitis (gamma globulin). Tuberculosis and diphtheria are fairly common, so if you are not vaccinated already against these, it is advisable to get this done.

Give the School of Tropical Medicine a ring if you are unsure about what to do about vaccinations – Liverpool 0151 708 9393 or London 0171 636 8636.

Medical insurance

Because the standard of emergency treatment in these countries is not as high as it is in the West, it is advisable in addition to normal medical insurance, to take out a policy which covers evacuation. The specialist in this form of insurance is SOS Assistance Far East Ltd, PO Box 1080, Robinson Road, Singapore 9021; tel: (65) 226 3937; SOS 24-hour emergency line: (65) 226 3936. There is an office in Ho Chi Minh City which is at Interlink Resources Pte Ltd, 135 Nam Nghi Street, District 1; tel: 230 499; fax: 290 583. The other alternative is to contact the SOS Vietnam Operation Centre; tel: 230 499/441 182. In the UK, contact Worldwide Travel Insurance Services Ltd; tel: 0622 722231.

Also offering this service are Eurasie Travel, 86 Pasteur Khan Daun Penh, Phnom Penh; tel: (855) 23 27144/27374; fax: (855) 23 27374. The price is US$45, and the service may be taken out when booking one of their tours.

Included in membership of SOS are the following:
- 24-hour telephone access to the SOS network.
- 24-hour telephone medical advice.
- Emergency medical evacuation and/or medically supervised repatriation.
- Hospital admittance deposits.
- Dispatch of doctors and medicine.
- Interpreter access.

- Emergency message transmission.
- Legal assistance and bail bond services.
- Baggage retrieval assistance.

Some medical problems

Heat exhaustion

One of the main problems you will come across in Laos during the very hot period (April onward in lowland areas) is heat stress, dehydration and sometimes in severe cases, total exhaustion. Make sure that you get a steady intake of salt, put plenty on your food. It may not be good for your arteries but if you lose too much through your skin by sweating you can become very ill indeed. Symptoms of heat exhaustion include muscle cramps, loss of balance, headache, vomiting and in extreme cases total disorientation and even temporary blindness. Always carry a good supply of salt tablets. Dissolve plenty of them in water and take immediately if the symptoms persist. No matter how careful you are this is something which can happen to anyone exposed for long periods to hot climatic conditions. It is accelerated if you have diarrhoea since you will not be absorbing your body's salt requirements. Take extra precautions then. If you cease to sweat under very hot conditions, it is possible that you are suffering heat stroke. This is an EMERGENCY SITUATION, if you are in Vientiane call the emergency number **3590**. An ambulance should quickly come to your rescue.

Symptoms of heat stroke

Your face will become very red, your head will start to pound, you may become disoriented. In extreme cases you could faint. If you think you have heat stroke get into the shade immediately. If you are near your hotel room, get into a cold bath of water and completely immerse yourself. Don't do anything energetic, never take alcohol. See a doctor as soon as possible.

People sometimes mistake the symptoms of heat stroke with prickly heat. If you have just flown into Laos on an international transfer flight, stay in the shade as much as possible until your skin gets used to the excessive heat. If it begins to itch, this is one of the symptoms of prickly heat. As long as you cover your skin with water at regular intervals, your sweat glands will soon adapt and the prickly feeling will go away. The message here is to avoid long exposure in the sun, especially just after a long flight. Wear a hat and use a sunscreen.

Malaria

The most common malaria parasites transmitted by mosquitoes in Indochina are the protozoan species *Plasmodium vivax* and *Plasmodium falciparum*. The latter is particularly widespread in the Tonlé Sap area. For up-to-date information about what type of prophylactics to use, contact the School of Tropical Medicine or the Malaria Reference Laboratory in London; tel: 0171 636 7921. A loop tape will give you the current update for South East Asia. Equip yourself with Buzz-Bands, which are manufactured by Traveller International Products, or another product called Buzz-Off which burns slowly through the night releasing a vapour harmful to mosquitoes. Pyrethrum coils can be bought cheaply in Bangkok which serve the same purpose. Avoid being bitten in the open by using insect repellent sprays such as Autan, or eat plenty of garlic.

The School of Tropical Medicine has confirmed that *Plasmodium falciparum* has developed resistance to fansidar and choroquine. Action Aid workers in Laos take one 100mg tablet of doxycycline daily if they are working off the beaten track. You should check with the experts before you decide what type of prophylactic to use as some prophylactics can cause dangerous side effects. Because of this, in some countries such as Taiwan, South Korea and Japan, choloquine, which is still widely prescribed in the west, is banned. Foreigners who work on long projects in Laos don't take any form of prophylactic drug. Highly experienced travellers will also tell you that taking any malarial prophylactic drug for long periods is just not on. The best form of prophylaxis is to avoid being bitten by mosquitoes in the first place. Personally, if I am in a high risk area, I plaster myself with insect repellant spray, eat plenty of garlic and at night spray the room (hut) with a concentrated insecticide a few hours before retiring. I wear buzz bands, burn two insect repellant coils and ensure my mosquito net has absolutely no holes. Paranoid you may think but it works!

Plague
The WHO have reported several outbreaks of this in Indochina. Avoid contact with fleas which are the carriers. Spray suspect mattresses with pyrethrum spray and use flea powder on your body.

Hepatitis
It is a good idea to have a jab against this because it can be easily caught drinking contaminated water and eating vegetables washed in local water. It is best to buy soda water (*soda kroch chmar*), used boiled water (*dteuk*) and to avoid ice. Condensed milk and coconut milk are safe to consume. Cola is readily available. Vegetables should not be eaten raw but stir fried. It is probably worth having the new three-part jab. This is quite expensive but well worth having because it offers long term protection.

Hepatitis B and HIV
Both viruses are transmitted through blood products and sexual intercourse. Avoid both and carry a sterile needle pack (and condoms). See Medical Kit.

Rabies
This is fairly common in Indochina so try to avoid dogs. Never run from a savage dog, try to scare it off somehow. These days the rabies vaccine is perfectly safe and there are no side effects. Keep away from cats which will pester you everywhere.

Dengue fever (Breakbone fever)
This is caused by a parasite which can be transmitted by mosquitoes. The symptoms are similar to those experienced from malaria: high temperature, severe headache and copious sweating. There is no suitable prophylactic except avoiding being bitten by mosquitoes. It is not fatal but it can last for a few weeks.

The World Health Authority have reported five strains of it in Laos. Medical authorities say that children are more susceptible than adults. Again, avoid getting bitten. For some reason the disease is not carried by the night biting variety of mosquito, *Culex pipiens*, but a species which is active during the day, *Aedes vulgaris*.

Japanese encephalitis

This nasty disease can cause blurred vision and, in extreme cases, loss of eyesight. The vector is the mosquito. A vaccine is available against this virus which can easily be obtained in the Far East. Many clinics in Bangkok carry stocks. If you go for a course of vaccinations, carry your own supply of sterile needles as a precaution against AIDS. You will need to be in the area for a considerable time to get complete immunity. The first vaccination must be followed by another seven days later. The third vaccination must be administered three or four weeks after that. The best prophylactic is, again, to avoid being bitten if you are not prepared for the hassle involved in attaining complete immunity. You are at greatest risk during the rainy season.

A UK clinic, Bridge the World, Chalk Farm Road, London NW1 (tel: 0181 444 4070) now offers vaccinations.

In Laos it is extremely rare. The World Health Authority say that outbreaks only occur during the monsoon season.

Eye infections

Trachoma is common in Cambodia. To avoid getting it carry your own towel and use this all the time instead of one provided by your hotel. Better still, take disposable paper towels, then there is no risk of prior use by anyone else. If you contract this disease, contact a doctor for antibiotic eye-drop treatment

Liver fluke diseases

These are more common in Laos than most places in Indochina. The areas badly affected are the southern provinces bordering the Mekong River. Fish may be infested with larval forms of Liver Fluke which can be passed on to humans by eating raw fish. The Laotians love fermented raw fish which in rural communities is carried around for a lunchtime snack in bamboo tubes. They call this delicacy *paa daèk*. Avoid eating it, I'm sure your hosts will understand if you refuse. There is also a slight chance of contracting opisthochiasis by swimming in the river, especially in the south. Larvae of another type of fluke causing schistosomiasis are also found here. The larvae enters the blood stream by burrowing through the skin. Symptoms of the disease include irritating rashes on the skin which completely vanish after a few days but reappear a few weeks later. Blood in the urine is a sure sign that the disease has really taken hold. Without treatment the disease can affect body organs, the spleen, liver and central nervous system in particular.

Bilharzia (*schistosomiasis*)

This condition is contracted through bathing in water which contains a particular type of nematode worm. The larval form of this worm penetrates through the skin causing 'Swimmer's Itch', followed several weeks after by pains in the abdominal region. A sure sign that you have it is the appearance of blood in the urine. It can easily be cured by the use of Praziquantel.

Other worm infestations

Eggs of round-worms and thread-worms are sometimes ingested with food. Once in the intestines they hatch out and in the case of round-worms, can enter the blood stream. This could lead to severe problems if the infestation is a large one. Some types of round-worm remain in the intestine and visible confirmation of their presence will be given in your faeces. Cestode worms can attach themselves to the lining of intestines and begin to bud, forming long segmented structures which (if there are enough of them) can cause a blockage in the intestines. Both types can be killed by taking Mebendazole which is also marketed under other trade names. Another good tip is to avoid walking around in bare feet because there are types of hook-worms in Indochina which lay their eggs in the soil. These hatch out into larvae which can penetrate the skin through the soles of the feet.

Fungal infections
In a very humid climate, athlete's foot is common; this can be prevented by using anti-fungal powders and creams. To reduce the chance of infection on other parts of the body, wear loose cotton garments to reduce sweating.

Cuts
These take much longer to heal in tropical countries. Take along a good antiseptic cream, wash the damaged area well with water and cover with Newskin, followed by a plaster.

Snake bites
There are many varieties of poisonous snake in the area. Most tourists won't come across them and even those who travel to remote areas are likely to scare them off before being attacked. The deadly krait can kill a person in about 30 minutes. Bamboo viper, which are the same colour as green vegetation, are more common in Preah Vihear. Cobras are more common in Stung Treng. Bright green Hanuman snakes with yellow eyes are common in the Angkor region. If you get bitten, it is important to remain calm so that the poison doesn't spread through your system too quickly. Rather than use a tourniquet apply a crepe bandage tightly around the bitten limb. Anti-venoms are available in most hospitals but only if you know exactly what variety of snake bit you. The least thing you are likely to do is to attempt to catch the culprit so that it can be taken along for identification. Remember that you aren't safe in sea water either, some of the most poisonous snakes in Cambodia live in sea water off Koh Kong and Kampot. Remember that if an antivenin is available that it can be dangerous to administer it unless signs of envenomation can be seen. Doctors advise against sucking wounds and administering aspirins. Do not give the victim alcohol.

Bee and wasp stings
There are species of bees in Indonchina which are much larger than western species. They carry huge stings which can be very nasty. Watch yourself if you travel around on small canals as hanging nests are common and you could just get your head tangled up in one. They are by no means lethal – locals will very often grab hold of a nest with their bare hands and stuff it into a sack for transporting to one of their hives. Some people are, however, very allergic to stings. They should include an antihistamine in their medical kit.

Stings from sea creatures
Stone-fish with sharp dorsal fins and Scorpion fish can sometimes be encountered in shallow water. Wear plimsolls in the water to avoid getting stung.

Beware jellyfish, which can inflict multiple injuries. Jellyfish stings, which are caused by hundreds of nematocyst threads, can cause severe discomfort. Only people with severe allergies to the poison are likely to die. Irritation can be lessened by use of antihistamine creams. Fish venom can be inactivated by bathing the limb in water which is uncomfortably hot.

Diarrhoea

You are a very lucky person indeed if you have never suffered from diarrhoea while travelling. The usual causes are poisoned food, inadequate water treatment or eating vegetables which have been washed in impure water. Travellers should avoid eating cream cakes and ice-cream in particular, vegetables which have not been thoroughly stir-fried and uncooked food. Ice should never be taken with drinks and purified bottles of water should be carried everywhere. Avoid buying unsealed bottles of water on the street in Phnom Penh and around Angkor. Many vendors just fill up bottles with any clear water they can lay their hands on and sell on to tourists. If you are very thirsty and you don't like the look of what is available, try a coconut. There is nothing safer than coconut juice which is fresh out of a nut.

An extra warning should be given about salad vegetables since many locals use human faeces and bat droppings as fertiliser. If they are not washed properly, goodness knows what you could go down with. Avoid oysters and mussels which are generally eaten raw; they are OK if they have been thoroughly charcoal-roasted. When you sit down to a meal in a good restaurant, you will generally be given a damp cloth. Avoid wiping your lips since bacteria and viruses can easily enter through mucous membranes. If you do contract the dreaded runs, don't eat anything for a 24-48 hour period, as this only feeds the culprits! During this period, it is very important to drink plenty of water. Only take anti-diarrhoea drugs as a last resort (if, for example, you have a plane to catch or you have to make a long bus journey). These drugs, such as kaolin and morphine, just slow peristalsis in the alimentary canal, ie they slow down the rate that the faeces will be expelled. Lomotil and Imodium are good to stop you running to the toilet every half an hour but they won't kill the offenders. Some travellers who are totally obsessed by their bowels take a spoonful of Pepto-Bismol every day. Since this does nothing but coat the lining of the intestines, its net effect is similar to the other drugs. The native method of dealing with mild diarrhoea is to consume only the liquid from rice congee which is left after the rice has boiled. Whether this works or not I don't know. Blood in the stool is an indication of amoebic dysentery which needs the prescribed drug, metronidozole, to clear up.

Always maintain a high degree of personal hygiene, wash your hands frequently with plenty of soap and use antiseptic wipes on your journeys.

Medical kit

This is the most important part of your luggage so always carry it in hand luggage when flying. Ready-made kits containing all you require are available at extortionate prices from medical supply laboratories. It is much cheaper to make up your own, especially if you have a sympathetic family doctor who will prescribe a few extras. If you have special requirements, take them with you.

- A good supply of bandages, plasters and cotton wool.
- A bottle of Germolene New Skin made by Beechams. This is good for germproofing the skin after acquiring minor cuts.
- A pain-killer such as codeine phosphate or soluble aspirin.
- Tiger Balm which is good for stopping insect bites from itching which will lead to infection. Minor back aches and muscle pains can also be treated. You can purchase this anywhere in Indochina.
- An eye ointment containing choramphenicol.
- Anti-diarrhoea tablets for emergency travel, eg kaolin, lomotil or imodium. Metronidozole, if you can get a doctor to prescribe it.
- Rehydration packs are extremely useful if you suffer from extreme loss of fluid. A supply of sugar and salt is essential if you want to make your own. Use one teaspoon of salt to eight of sugar in one litre of water.
- A broad spectrum of antibiotic such as septrin, if you can get it prescribed.
- A fungicide dust powder for minor fungal infections. A good one is Micronazole.
- Clove oil to stop toothache.
- Malarial tablets as prescribed by the School of Tropical Medicine.
- Sterile needles in case you need injections (absolutely essential now because of AIDS). A kit can be purchased through MASTA, tel: 0171 631 4408.
- Small scissors and tweezers.
- Emergency dental kit which can be purchased at any dentist.
- Sun screen.
- Antiseptic cream.
- Antihistamine cream.
- Water sterilisation tablets if you are travelling in remote areas.

Other essentials related to general health
- Insect repellent, Diethyl Toluamide.
- Flea powder because of the risk of plague.
- Medical shampoo (carbaryl for lice infestations).
- Mosquito repellent devices.
- Condoms (if you are likely to succumb to temptations).

Useful addresses

Vaccinations
British Airways Vaccination Centre, 9 Little Newport Street, London WC2H 7JJ; tel: 071 287 2255/3366.
Thomas Cook Vaccination Centre, 45 Berkeley Square, London W1; tel: 071 499 4000.
PPP Medical Centre, 99 New Cavendish Street, London W1; tel: 071 637 8941.

For last-minute vaccinations:

British Airways Medical Centre, Terminal 3, Heathrow Airport; tel: 081 759 7208 (Open 08.00-20.00 7 days a week).

There are also vaccination centres throughout the country.

MASTA, Keppel Street, London WC1E 7HT; tel: 071 631 4408. This is the
address to contact if you want advice on traveller's health. They also stock
Medical Equipment packs which include sterile syringes.

USPHS, 330 Independent Avenue, SW, Washington DC 20201. They give free
advice on vaccinations and traveller's health.

CDH, Commonwealth Centre, Chifley Square, Corner Phillip and Hunter
Street, Sydney, NSW 2000; tel: 239 3000. Traveller's health.

Department of Health, Bledisole State Building, Civic Square, Auckland;
tel: 774 494. Traveller's health enquiries.

HWC, 3rd Floor, 55 St Clair Avenue East, Toronto, Ontario M4T IM2;
tel: (416) 966 6245. Traveller's health enquiries

Useful books on travellers' health:
The Traveller's Health by Dr Richard Dawood. Published by OUP.

The Traveller's Handbook edited by Melissa Shales. A WEXAS Publication.
This has an excellent section on travellers' health.

The Tropical Traveller by John Hatt. Pan Books. A little out of date but it
explains health problems in a very basic way.

The Traveller's Health Guide by Dr Anthony Turner. Published by Roger
Lascelles.

Highly recommended is the 1995 Cadogan Healthy Travel Guide, *Bug Bites
and Bowels* by Dr Jane Wilson Howarth

SAFETY
General safety information
Theft
Although Laos and Cambodia are generally less dangerous than many other
countries, it is still worth being on your guard, especially against snatching of
valuables. It seems that you are more likely to have your rucksack stolen
complete than to have something stolen from it. As elsewhere, people are
basically honest; don't let your visit be spoiled by one of the few.

Violence
It's been reported that fights are not uncommon, although not normally
involving tourists. Sexual harassment is also relatively rare but, again, there's no
harm in being careful. Beggars aren't known for turning violent.

The police
I've heard of instances of harassment, often in the form of 'fining' a car or mini-
bus driver for some (imagined?) misdemeanour. It is presumed that we tourists
pay for these ultimately, in fares.

This is not to say that the majority are susceptible to bribery: in the main, the
police are relatively straight.

Drugs
Some drugs, particularly marijuana, are occasionally available in various
locations, often without apparent repercussions. The standard advice must be
followed, however: don't.

Other dangers

Cambodia is littered with unexploded mines. One reliable source estimates that there are at least four million in in the country. NEVER WANDER OFF THE BEATEN TRACK, TAKE SOUVENIRS OR TOUCH ANYTHING SUSPICIOUS. Read *War of the Mines: Cambodia, Landmines and the Impoverishment of a Nation* by Paul Davies, published in 1995 by Pluto Press. Cambodia has more disabled people than anywhere else in the world, an estimated 1 in 236 has been the victim of 'antipersonnel' mines which maim but do not kill. There are a staggering 300-700 amputations carried out every month.

Be very careful when visiting Angkor, don't get carried away and wander off the beaten track. *In 1994 an estimated 1,000 land mines and well over 7,000 unexploded shells were cleared from around the Angkor Wat Temple Complex alone!*

Restricted areas and restrictions on travel

Foreigners are advised not to travel by bus, boat or train out of Phnom Penh. Since the train ambush on July 26 1994 in which three Westerners were abducted and later killed, any tourist attempting to buy a train ticket is immediately reported to the authorities; immediate deportation will follow. Bus and car trips are presently allowed on the overland route to Vietnam, for visits to Tonlé Bati, Phnom Chisor and other temples in Takeo Province such as Angkor Borei and Phnom Dar. Tourists are also allowed to travel to the Oudong stupas, 40km from the city, and the Killing Fields of Choueung Ek, 15km away. For 1996, as long as the political situation remains stable, a permit has been granted to Apsara Tours to fly tourists to Sihanoukville and the remote province of Rattanakiri. Diethelm Travel Cambodia Ltd can also arrange this although it is not widely advertised.

All visitors are strictly advised to use the air service to Angkor as overland travel on this route is extremely dangerous. Although there are five flights daily to the region, these can be and are sometimes cancelled with very short notice indeed. Due to its historical significance and the large number tourists that visit, the region is heavily patrolled by the Cambodian military. Visitors should not be alarmed about this as it is for their own safety. Incidents such as the murder of an American tourist and her guide in January 1995 are extremely rare but still immensely sad.

UNDER NO CIRCUMSTANCES SHOULD TOURISTS ENTER ZONES KNOWN TO BE KHMER ROUGE TERRITORY. THESE INCLUDE CAMBODIA'S STUNG TRENG PROVINCE BORDERING LAOS, PREAH VIHEAR, NORTHERN SIEM REAP, ODDAR MEAN CHEY, BATTAMBANG, PURSAT, KOMPONG SPEU AND PARTS OF KAMPOT.

It should also be stressed that no area outside Phnom Penh is 100% safe. Even in the capital itself care should be taken, especially at night in deserted streets.

Chapter Two

Equipment

Luggage

If you are travelling independently, avoid suitcases. Choose ultra-light canvas stuff-bags or a light-weight backpack. Avoid rucksacks with external frames because it is advisable, when travelling on public transport, to pack the whole thing into a canvas sack. This can create hassle when you want to take something out but it also makes it more difficult for a thief. If you are carrying cameras, there is nothing better than 'Camera Care' pouches which can be carried on a belt around your waist. Smaller pouches can be purchased for carrying film or important travel documents, which is very useful when you are going through customs at airports. Since they can be sealed with draw-strings, they are superbly secure. Travelling extra light will certainly give you the freedom to be more adventurous.

Toiletries

Good quality toilet soap is available but it is far better to bring your own since you will have to pay about four times as much for it when you arrive. Ordinary local soap is adequate but far from luxurious. Don't forget a good supply of toilet paper and antiseptic wipes. Use the bin provided, not the toilet; many sewage systems in the area simply can't cope with masses of paper. Women will need to take tampons since they will not be generally available. Take along a small quantity of washing powder, toothpaste, dental floss and a small hand towel.

Clothes

Inexperienced westerners will carry enough to clothe their entire family. If you think that it is not essential, do not take it. You will certainly not need things such as suits and ties since the locals are not snappy dressers.

I would personally recommend:-
- Three T-shirts/blouses made of cotton.
- One cotton long-sleeve shirt for keeping mosquitoes off in the evening.
- Three pairs of cotton socks.
- Cotton underwear.
- Two pairs of light cotton baggy trousers (skirts or dresses) with zips on all pockets and sewn-in security pockets inside. These can be used for money and passport. (Put the passport inside a plastic bag in case you get very wet.)

- Light walking shoes. Flip-flops are useful to guard against hookworm, athlete's foot and spiny animals on beaches.
- Avoid taking a cagoule – cagoules of any type tend to be too hot. Throughout Indochina people generally use thin plastic sheeting with holes cut through it for their arms. An umbrella is useful, particularly if you are carrying expensive cameras.
- One hat for protection against the sun.

Useful addresses

The Survival Shop, Survival Aids Ltd, (TRH9), Morland, Penrith, Cumbria CA10 3AZ; tel: 0800 262 752. This shop is excellent for lightweight rucksacks, rucksack covers, clothes and footwear.
The Traveller's Shop, 14-18 Holborn, London EC1N 2LJ; tel: 071 242 3278.

Photography

There is no problem bringing in large quantities of film. Remember that if it is not in your hand luggage, it will be X-rayed by an antiquated machine which will cloud the emulsions. Always ask for a hand search, never let your precious film go through this machine. Print films such as Fuji, Agfa, Kodak and Konica can be bought in Vientiane, Phnom Penh and at Angkor. Be aware that film in market stalls may often have been subjected to extremely high temperatures.

Fuji slide film since 1993 and Kodak Ektachrome since 1994 has been readily available in Phnom Penh. Some is also available at Angkor at inflated prices. It is far better and cheaper to take along films purchased in the West. They will also be fresher and will not have been subjected to hot conditions. If you are travelling from Hong Kong or Singapore you may be able to purchase film more cheaply than in the USA or UK. These days, there won't be much in it, especially if you buy in bulk from discount stores.

Avoid taking auto-everything cameras to Indochina, they have too many features which are likely to go wrong. It is far better to take non-sophisticated work-horses such as Nikon FM2s which are totally mechanical (ie do not rely on batteries). Range-finder Leicas are also ideal. When in high humidity areas, tape over flash and motordrive sockets when not in use. Never put your camera near an air-conditioning unit or a heater in a car. Always keep the cap on the lens when not in use. The optics can act like magnifying glass and concentrate the rays of the sun on one spot, the result could be a warped shutter or worse. Keep films away from aerosol sprays and out of direct sunlight. Canisters will protect films against high humidity. Drying capsules are useful to protect film and cameras from high humidity but remember that they won't work unless they have been previously heated. Take plenty of slow film, around Angkor you may need faster ones since the sky is often cloudy.

Section Two
Laos

That Luang Stupa

Part One
The Country and its People

LAOS –
PROVINCES

Chapter Three

Geography

Landlocked in the centre of the Indochinese peninsular, 70% of Laos' 236,230km² (91,428 square miles) is high mountain territory. Its border stretches for 5,088km (3,162 miles), much of which it shares with Thailand (1,754km – 1,090 miles) and Vietnam (2,130km – 1,324 miles). In the south it borders troubled Cambodia for 541km (336 miles). In the north, the land frontier is shared with Burma's Myanmar Province (238km – 148 miles) and China's Yunnan Province (425km – 264 miles).

A provincial boundary map drawn up in 1990 shows that Laos now contains sixteen provinces (*khoueng*), the same number it had in 1971. Close examination however reveals that there have been substantial changes in boundary demarcation. In the north, Luang Prabang Province has been split down the middle into Oudomsay and Luang Prabang, Houa Khong (adjacent to Burma's Myanmar) has been divided into Luang Nam Tha and Bokeo Province. In Central Laos, Vientiane Province has totally absorbed the old Borikane Province which now ceases to exist. Further south, Khammouane Province has now been divided into two and the northern half called Borikhamsay. There have been some pretty drastic changes further south as well, the old Wapikhamthong Province has disappeared and its territory absorbed by Saravane, whose old southeastern portion now constitutes the new province of Sekong. Bordering Cambodia, Champassak Province has grown considerably and now covers the old territories of Se Done and Sithandone. All are divided into districts (*mùong*) which are again divided into cantons (*tasseng*).

Topographically the country can be divided into two distinct regions.

The northern and central region

These are the least accessible regions of the country because they consist mainly of folded mountain ranges which run from northwest to southeast. Some of these reach only 1,000m but in many places drop off steeply into V-shaped valleys. Many show the effects of water erosion because they are composed largely of limestone and sandstone. Among the north-central group of mountains, many of which extend to over 2,000m, is Phou Bia which, at 2,819m, is the highest mountain in Laos. This lies in south-central Xieng Khouang Province, an immensely attractive area composed predominantly of green, rounded hills. Further north is Mount Khe (2,125m) which overlooks the Plain of Jars on the

Tran Ninh Plateau. Tourists are reminded to tread carefully here because of the immeasurable numbers of bombs which were jettisoned by B52 bombers heading back to their bases in Northern Thailand.

To the east is the Annamite Chain, which forms an enormous spine extending along the border with Vietnam. Several peaks in this range reach over 2,000m. In south-central Laos there's Mount Keo Neua (2,286m) which can be seen from Ha Tinh in Vietnam. Further north, parallel with Tran Ninh Plateau, is Mount Xai Lai Leng (2,711m) which is a part of what the Vietnamese call the Giang Man, the 'Hanging Curtain'. Further west in Laos this merges with the Pu Sao range (2,620m). Much of the spine is composed of basalts, which over millions of years have become superimposed on crystalline and igneous formations dating from well before the Palaeozoic period. Most are surfaced with sandstone or clay. High mountain ranges to the north, particularly those in Phôngsali Province, tend to average between 1,800 and 1,900m. These have presented a formidable barrier to population migrations and make access difficult for tourists across strict ethnic boundaries between Laos and Vietnam. Others extend along the 213 mile Laos/China/Burma border through Phôngsali, Luang Nam Tha and Bokeo Provinces. Much of this is off-limits to tourism because of the numerous poppy farms minded by the H'mong, Yao and Lahu minorities which extend deep into the 'Golden Triangle'.

South, on the western side of the Mekong, is remote Sayaboury Province, the domain of the Htin, Iko, Khmu and Kri where very few Westerners have ever set foot. Mountains here overlooking the river valley generally don't reach more than 1,100-1,200m. Only one, which can be seen from Muang Xaignaboury, is over 2,000m.

A belt of mountains stretches from west to east, north of the Nam Ngum reservoir. Through this, National Highway Number 13 heads for Luang Prabang from Vientiane. Only two roads were ever built through this highland barrier, the other is a dirt track which extends from Muang Pakxan to the Tran Ninh Plateau.

Opposite the provincial capital of Muang Khammouan across the Cammon Plateau are the attractive limestone peaks which extend along the Annamite chain into Vietnam's Quang Binh Province. This is caving country, where streams disappear into deep chasms. The highest mountain here reaches 1,492m.

The southern region

This is mountainous towards the east where the Annamite Cordillera heads for the Cambodian border. Between here and the Mekong Basin are the rolling hills of the fertile Bolovens Plateau. Parts of this area, which is steeped in history, is savanna country. The rich, red soils which extend into Vietnam's Central Highlands contain high deposits of aluminium which has never been mined. The French built many coffee plantations in the region which, although reduced in number, continue to be farmed by many of the minorities. The alluvial lowlands extend through much of the western part of southern Laos and serve as one of the country's 'rice-bowls'.

The river system

The rivers, particularly the Mekong, are the communication and economic lifeline of the country. These conduits are greatly affected by the country's climate, which consists of a six-month cycle of wet and dry season. When the

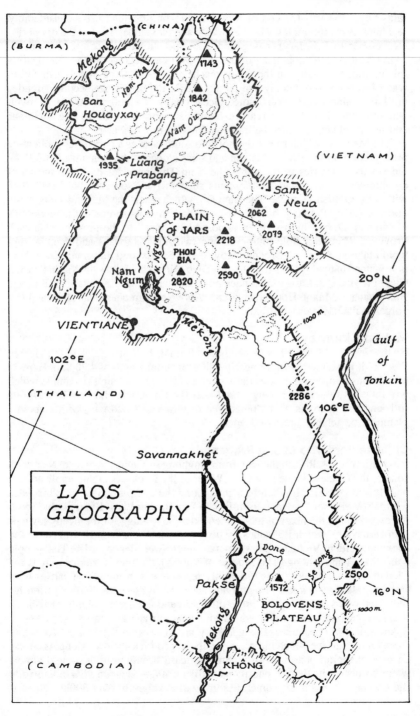

LAOS –
GEOGRAPHY

rains begin towards the end of May, the Mekong begins to rise considerably, reaching its maximum level between June and November. During the dry period (November to February), navigation on some stretches becomes difficult; in March and April (the hottest, driest period) it can become impossible. During this period, especially on the upper reaches of the Mekong and its tributaries, water levels drop so quickly that 50 ton and 20 ton barges can become stranded until the rains return once more. Occasionally the monsoons can be over-generous and flooding can reach calamitous proportions. Cities like Vientiane and Savannakhét may then be immersed in one foot of water.

The Mekong, which runs from north to south, acts as a huge drain, collecting precipitation off the Khorat Plateau and steep slopes of the Annamite Cordillera. One of its tributaries in the north, the Nam Tha, provides the main means of communication to isolated settlements such as Ban Nou and Ban Pawi, deep within the Golden Triangle. The Nam Ou, which enters the Mekong some 15km north of Luang Prabang, runs for over 400km from its source in the mountains of Yunnan. During high water it is possible to travel to the heart of Phôngsali Province. This incredible journey along twisting waterways and deep valleys would take you through Muang Ngoy to Hat Sa. Beyond this small town there is a water channel which runs to the Dien Bien Phu Valley in Vietnam's Lai Chau Province. In Laos it continues north through Muang Khoua, Pak Ban and Ban Khana to Muang Hounxianghoung. Above here frequent waterfalls and fast gorges make navigation difficult.

Mekong journey
By the time the Mekong has reached Laos from its birthplace high in the Tibetan Plateau, it has already run for nearly half of its total length of 4,200km. Here its tumultuous rampaging is essentially over and it begins a long slow amble which will take it 1,600km to Không Island near the Cambodian border. To travel its full length in Laos is an unforgettable experience which can, with elaborate planning, be achieved fairly cheaply.

Chinese border to Luang Prabang
Navigation is possible all the way from Jinghong in Yunnan Province. Nearer its source, the Chinese name Dza Chu (Water of the Rocks) is highly applicable. It has slowed considerably before it runs along the 270km border which isolates Burma's Myanmar Province from Bokeo Province in Laos. Running due south it flows through the heart of the Golden Triangle heading for the sleepy town of Ban Houayxay, which it reaches by turning towards the east. From here to the Mekong Delta in Vietnam, it is known as the 'Lower Mekong'. The Thai people call it Mae Nam Khong (The Mother of Waters), the Laotians refer to it as the Menam Khong. To both it is the highly respected highway which carries their freight, passenger barges, pirogues and sampans. It provides vital irrigation for their rice fields, brings them fertile alluvium and a constant supply of fish. To the speedboat drivers which whizz along its surface at speeds in excess of 85km/h, it is a constant challenge. They are always on the lookout for white foam on the surface which indicates deadly jagged rocks below. Along its course an ever changing panorama of picture postcard beauty unfolds around almost every corner. In its depths, enormous catfish (*Pangasianodon gigas*), known to the Laotians as *pla buck,* sometimes grow to a weight of over 300kg. There is

always the remote chance of sighting the very rare Irrawaddy dolphin (*Orcaella brevirostris*) which the Laotian people believe may be a reincarnation of their ancestors. They are as sacred as the river itself.

The 300km stretch between the Golden Triangle and Luang Prabang contains some truly awesome scenery. Tangled webs of impenetrable greenery lead the eye to rolling hills and high mountains beyond which are the homes of the H'mong, Yao, Lahu, Lisu and Akha. Totally isolated from the Western world, they tend to their poppy fields and refine heroine from raw opium – some of which will eventually end up on the streets of the world's capitals. Nearer the river, the Khamu look out from their stilt settlements and pan for gold in the muddy waters. At the remote town of the Muong Pakbéng, clusters of pirogues are moored along the wooden quay, rows of dilapidated wooden houses extend up the hillside.

Much nearer to Luang Prabang, beyond the small settlement of Ban Lat Han, the river rounds a steep bend. On the Laotian side it runs along a 350m cliff which contains the remarkable sacred temple sanctuary of Tam Ting. This is a popular day excursion from the old capital. Nobody really knows how the hundreds of small Buddhas seen in this holy place originally got there more than 400 years ago. Close by one of the Mekong's largest tributaries, the Nam Ou, completes its long journey from the mountains of Yunnan. Between here and Luang Prabang large sandbanks are exposed when the water level begins to fall in January. Many locals then journey to the area to try their hand at digging and panning for gold. This can be very profitable – even if the Thai traders who buy it do take a large slice of the profit.

Luang Prabang to Vientiane

The river meanders slowly along wide stretches and begins to accelerate as it heads for narrower gorges. Steep rocky slopes then hem it in on either side and during the wet season cascades of water tumble hundreds of metres into its depths. Boatmen greatly fear these gorges which are at their most deadly during the hottest dry period, between mid-March and mid-April. Overloaded barges risk being ripped to pieces on the sharp rocks hidden a few metres below the surface. The most feared of all is the 500m Keng Luang stretch of white water which, over the years, has claimed many a life. Further south the river has become more tranquil as it heads for the old French garrison town of Pak Lay. Here it still has another 170km to go before it gets to Vientiane. Beyond Chiang Khan the scenery on both sides of the river provides a remarkable contrast. On the Lao side, it is green and lush, on the Thai side it is brown and barren. Because of the massive deforestation, the soil is badly eroded. Alternating broad and narrow stretches follow. About 20km before reaching Vientiane, the river narrows considerably. This site at Pa Mong has long been chosen for a massive hydroelectric project; part of the ambitious plans of the Mekong Committee which are responsible for administering the hugely expensive Mekong Project. Despite being formed as early as 1957, warfare and political turmoil had created an impasse of insurmountable dimensions. Originally it was intended that the Pa Mong Dam would be a 250m wall of concrete capable of holding back a sheet of water which would cover 3,700km^2. If it had gone ahead, over 250,000 people would have lost their homes in the attempt to tame the river.

Vientiane to Không Island

About 19km below Vientiane the wind of change, which has been blowing in ever increasing velocity across the Indochina peninsula, has allowed the building of the massive Mittaphap Bridge (Bridge of Friendship). This effectively ends Laos' isolation. Opened by King Bhumipol Adulyadej of Thailand in mid-April 1994, it is another important step forward in continuing the Pacific Rim economic boom. Further east, the Nam Ngum tributary pours into the Mekong where it is nearly 1km wide. Along the upper reaches of this river one of Laos' most important industrial economic achievements materialised in the 1970s in the form of the 150MW capacity Nam Ngum Dam.

Near Muang Paksane, two other tributaries, the Ngiap and the Xan, join it as it meanders gracefully towards the small town of Ban Baksa. Towards Muang Khammouane, a humped limestone panorama becomes visible on the Laotian side. This is part of the Cammon Plateau which merges further west with the formidable Annamite Cordillera separating Laos from Vietnam. Rapids are few and far between along this stretch, which eventually leads to Savannakhét. This can be reached from its twin town, Mukdahan, by ferry boat. Eventually there are plans to replace the ferry with another bridge, providing better road access to the Lao Bao crossing point into Vietnam. Midway between Savannakhét and Paksé the river enters a dangerous stretch known as the 'Khemmarat Rapids'. During periods when the Mekong reaches its peak holding capacity, the water here can accelerate to an alarming 4.5 metres/sec. In March and April it is impossible to navigate as sharp rocks, previously submerged under deep water, appear at the surface. Nearer Paksé it is joned by the Mae Nam Mun, which originates in Thailand's Khorat Plateau. Nearby are the Pha Taem cliffs where it is possible to see prehistoric rock paintings between 1,000-2,000 years old. Thirty kilometres further south the Mekong is joined by the Se Done tributary near the town of Paksé.

About 130km from here the river begins to accelerate appreciably and divides into a network of gushing cataracts below the large island of Không. Over the centuries the eroding effects of the water has created hundreds of small islands. This is one of the favourite scenic attractions for Thai tourists, who flock here in their thousands to see the spectacular Pha Pheng and Somphamit Falls. These formidable barriers to river travel put pay to the dreams of French explorer Francis Garnier who, during the Mekong River Expedition of the 1860s, had been convinced that he would have been able to sail all the way to China. Here the 12th longest river in the world comes to the end of its 1,600km journey through Laos and enters the troubled lands of Cambodia.

Climate

Laos experiences a wet season from May to October. Rainfall from the southwest monsoons is fairly uniform throughout the country except at the highest elevations. One of the wettest places is the Bolovens Plateau, which can get as much as 4,060mm (160 inches) annually. Travellers in July and August could experience almost continuous rainfall, except perhaps in the Luang Prabang area which has the lowest rainfall in the country (1,270-1,525mm – 50-60 inches). As November approaches the cold, dense air of the winter northeastern monsoons settles on most of the Indochina peninsula. Showers become far less frequent and by mid-November the air is very dry. Now until

February Laos experiences a cool dry climate when the temperature varies between 15°C (60°F) and 21°C (70°F). During March and April, temperatures can soar as high as 38°C (100°F) or even higher. It can be extremely tiring for tourists during this period especially if they have a hectic itinerary.

It is also worth noting that during the winter period, temperatures can drop as low as –1°C (30°F) at high altitude. Tourists should come prepared if they intend going into the mountains.

Flora and fauna

Around two thirds of Laos is mountainous. Here you will find dense tropical forests which are said to cover about 150,000km² (58,000 square miles). Much of this is impenetrable jungle territory, the home of species of plants and animals which are rarely seen by the Western world. In the northern forests you are likely to see bar-backed partridge, red-headed trogans, rufous-throated fulvetteas and magnificently coloured pheasants. Further south on the Tran Ninh Plateau in Xieng Khouang Province, bird species commonly seen in Central Vietnam make an appearance. These include white-crowned forktails, many species of babblers and pittas. Towards the border with Lai Chau Province in Vietnam, in the remote highlands of Phôngsali Province there have been rare sightings of imperial pheasants. Minorities in this area regularly hunt green peafowl which are considered a delicacy. Many species of monkeys are common in the north which are hunted with blowpipes. Tiny roe deer here are becoming rare because of over-hunting. Large boars roam the forests and can be very dangerous if in large groups. In Luang Nam Tha Province, H'mong and Yao are known to hunt striped foxes for their fur. The pelts of this rare animal have been sold in the markets of northern Thailand for high prices. Flying squirrels in the northern jungles are also hunted to near extinction. Judging from the live animal market held at Saravane in the south, nothing is safe in this area. Hunting parties regularly head for the Bolovens Plateau where they trap birds such as barbets, babblers, warblers and silver pheasants. All are destined for the bird markets of Bangkok, many end up in cooking pots. Here you can buy deadly kraits, huge pythons and even cobras. Many of these end up in snake farms in Thailand, some become the focus of attention in travelling circuses. For sale you may see the horns of deer (*cervidae*), numerous forms of beetles (*coleopterans*) and tortoise shells which are all eventually ground down and used in Thai traditional medicine. There is also an increasing market in butterflies which are sold live to Western butterfly farms. The Kalima is fairly common on the Bolovens Plateau together with large phoenixes and fairy butterflies. People in the region even capture deadly crocodiles in the Don River for export to the numerous crocodile farms across the Mekong. Monkeys are popular since they can be sold as meat or for pets. Black squirrels (*Ratufa gigantea*) and gibbons can often be seen at the Saravane market where they are squashed into tiny cages where they can hardly move. One of the species which, thanks to extensive publicity, is no longer exploited by Mekong fishermen is the endangered Irrawaddy Dolphin (*Orcaella brevirostris*). Grants are now available to fishermen who are prepared to cut their nets rather than risk drowning one of these magnificent animals.

A large part of the Bolovens Plateau and Xieng Khouang Province is covered in sparsely wooded savanna. Towards the western fringe of the country this merges with dense forest belts where huge trees such as *Saraca* species and

Aglaia form the highest canopies. Some of these grow to 30m in height. Other smaller species make up the second level canopies. These include varieties of *Cinamomum, Magnolia* family, *Bacaurea* and *Sauropus.*

In the wetter areas, parts of the Bolovens Plateau (western region) for example, many species of orchid flourish. These epiphytes occur right along the Annamite spine. Many such as the vanilla orchids, sword-like orchids and fishbone orchids are very beautiful. Creepers are common through the forested zones, often growing so densely that they prevent the light from falling onto the forest floor.

In north-central Laos there is a large evergreen woodland belt which, although interrupted in places, extends from Khammouane Province through Borikhamsay into Xieng Khouang. It is said to be extremely dense in parts of the Cammon Plateau. Bamboo, as in Vietnam, is mostly seen in the northern parts of the country where in many places it has become too dense to penetrate. In some areas, large forests of it have been destroyed through slash and burn agriculture. This practice has also denuded large land masses in the north which has resulted in erosion problems. Deforestation in Laos has not reached such catastrophic proportions as those seen in neighbouring Thailand where logging has been largely banned. Minorities continue the trends handed down to them by their forefathers.

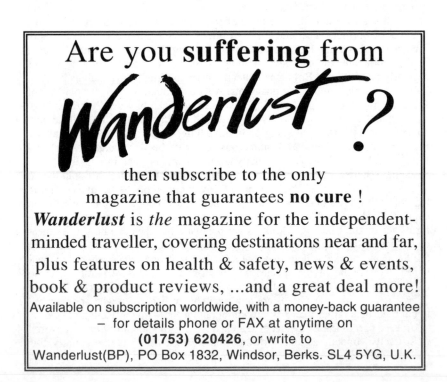

Chapter Four

A Brief History

Archaeological evidence suggests that primitive man had come to northern Laos by 500,000 BC. As nomads and hunters, Hoabinians became widely distributed by 10,000 BC. Bronze tool finds suggest that between 2,000 and 500 BC the highest concentration of the population was along the valley of the Mekong River. Recent discoveries suggest that the Plain of Jars was colonised between the 8th and 5th centuries BC and that iron forges were in use from around the end of that period. Sometime between the 5th and 6th centuries AD people from the Indian subcontinent came to live in the Champassak region in southern Laos. The area was inhabited by a large number of Khmer during the reign of Jayavarman I. At this time central and upper Laos were under the jurisdiction of the Kingdom of Chenla. Towards the end of his rule, upper Laos came under the suzerainty of 'Water Chenla'. A rather nebulous period follows when due to lack of written records, historical facts are a little thin on the ground.

The most extensive population migration into the area occurred during the second half of the 13th century. Large numbers of Tai, forced to leave what is now China's Yunnan Province because of continual pressure from the Han Chinese, fled into the valley of the Mekong. Here they came under the yoke of the court of Angkor. By 1279 the Kingdom of Sukhotai had been formed by King Ramkhamheng and established sovereignty over the northern Kingdom of Lan Na (Chieng Mai) and the central Kingdom of Vieng Chan-Vieng Kham (Vientiane).

By 1353 Fa Ngum had captured Muong Swa (Luang Prabang) assisted by Khmer troops provided by his father-in-law, King Jayavarman Parameswara. He made this the capital of his new kingdom, Lan Xang (the Kingdom of a Million Elephants). Here he lived with his Khmer wife, a former princess of the court of Angkor. He was a very religious king and invited monks from all over the country, together with many he had met while in exile in Cambodia, to visit him in his new capital. The Khmer monks brought Pali scripts and a sacred Buddha which had originated in Ceylon. This, the Phra Bang Buddha, became the most important religious object in Lan Xang. When he died in 1373, his son Oun Hueun became king when he was only 17 years old under the name of Phaya Sam Sén Thai. During his popular reign many Buddhist temples and monastic schools were built. He was a clever man who had the uncanny knack of making a profound impression on anyone he met. Using his social graces to the full he had soon established important contacts with his neighbours, Annam and Siam.

Trading routes between the allies were quickly established and through a fortuitous marriage to a princess of the court of Sukhotai, Muong Swa soon became a business mecca.

This peaceful reign was followed by a period in which relations with Annam became embittered. King Lan Kham Dèng (1417-28), who had gone to the rescue of the Annamese when they had been threatened by Chinese aggressors, sided with the opposition. Retaliation was not fast and furious as would have been expected because they were too busy fighting the Cham to seek revenge. When they overthrew the Cham Empire in 1471 they turned on the Lao. The Kingdom of a Million Elephants was overthrown and the Laotian King Sao Tiakaphat (1438-79) fled from the country. His son, Thène Kham (Souvanna Ban Lang), became king in 1479 after winning a great victory against the aggressors. The next century was a troubled period, during which battles raged between the Burmese and the Thai over the northern Kingdom of Lan Na (Chieng Mai). During this period King Phothisarat (1520-48) had been more concerned about converting more of his people to Theravada Buddhism than extending the area of his domain. Circumstances however changed when the king of Chieng Mai, Thai Sai Kham, was murdered in 1543. Since he had no son, Phothisarat, who was the son of a Chieng Mai princess, became the obvious choice. Despite severe opposition from many quarters he accepted the throne on behalf of his 12 year old son Sai Setthathirat. Opposition mounted as soon as his son became the new monarch. King Phrajai of Ayuthia attempted to take the throne but was thwarted. When Phothisarat returned to Lan Xang, a Shan Prince, Mekuthi, captured the Lan Na Kingdom.

Conflict with the Burmese

In 1558, Sai Setthathirat sent an army to attack the Burmese, defeating Mekuthi. Their stay was shortlived – days later they were driven out by a superior Burmese force. In 1560 the capital was moved from Xieng Dong-Xieng Dong (Luang Prabang) to Vieng Chan (present day Vientiane). An important alliance was also made with the Kingdom of Ayutthaya. The Burmese invaded the Kingdom of Lan Xang in 1563 and took Vieng Chan. Setthathirat was powerless to prevent them taking his queen and heir-apparent back to Burma. Soon after the Burmese retreat in 1565 many important religious buildings were built in the new capital. These included Wat Phra Kéo in 1565 and That Luang in 1566. In the former he installed the priceless Emerald Buddha. Other vicious attacks by the Burmese occurred between 1569-70. In 1571 Sai Setthathirat died under mysterious circumstances while on an expedition in southern Laos. He was succeeded by his son, Sen Soulintha (1571-75), whose reign marked the beginning of 20 years of insurrection, civil war and Burmese dominance. Following the bitter years of anarchy, Nokèo Koumane (No Muong, 1591-98) ascended the throne and temporarily became master of Laos.

Conflict within the kingdom

A period of civil war followed, during the reign of King Thannikarath (1603-22). It began when his son, Opayavarat, deposed his father and proclaimed himself monarch in 1621. Over the next 15 years the kingdom was ruled by a succession of seven kings. The struggle for the monarchy ended in 1633 when Soulinga Vongsa became king. During his long, glorious reign (1636-90), Laos experienced a new age of peace and prosperity. It was during this period that the first Europeans arrived in Lan Xang. Recorded in the annals of Laotian history are the arrivals of Gerrit van Wuysthoff, a Dutch merchant, in 1641 and Jesuit Priest, Father Giovanni-Maria Leria, in 1646.

Following Soulinga Vongsa's death civil strife broke out yet again during a torrid struggle for succession. During the competition for the monarchy, Laos became divided. At first a high ranking mandarin, Tian Thala, had seized the throne but six years later he was executed under the orders of the provincial governor of Nantharath. This prompted Soulinga Vongsa's grandsons, Kitsarat and Inthasom, to flee to Luang Prabang. Sai Ong Hue (son of Soulinga Vongsa's brother) returned from exile in Annam and in 1698 mounted the throne of Lan Xang in the name of Setthathirat II. In 1705 he ordered that the sacred Phra Bang Buddha should be removed from Luang Prabang to Vieng Chan for safe keeping. Two years later Kitsarat seized the throne of Luang Prabang and sent an ultimatum to Sai Ong Hue proclaiming sovereignty over lands to the north of the Thuong River. Soon after, his territory was further reduced when Soi Sisamouth Phuthanekun (nephew of Soulinga Vongsa) became ruler of Champassak. More conflict in the north followed when Inthasom captured Luang Prabang. Right up to his death in 1730, Setthathirat II was forced to witness the steady decline of the Kingdom of Vientiane. Constant racking of the countryside by rivalry between princes had done nothing but create chaos.

Interference from Annam, Burma and Thailand

Annam, who had assisted in the overthrow of Luang Prabang, then began to exercise its rights. When King Inthasom of Luang Prabang refused to pay tribute to the Vietnamese a small military force was sent. This was defeated, but three years later, in 1753, the Burmese were more successful and a huge army led by Alaungpaya took Luang Prabang. Fortunately for Inthasom, history took another turn and Burma was invaded by China. Seeing his chance, he was quick to retake the city, which had been left under guard of a weakened force. By 1760 Siribunyasan (Ong Boun) had succeeded his father but the Kingdom of Vientiane was now but a fragment of its former self. Suryavong, who had become king of Luang Prabang in 1771, entered into an alliance with Thailand in 1774. Vientiane was, however, allied to Burma. In 1778 King Taksin of Siam took Champassak and then Vientiane only one year later. The country's most sacred images, the golden Phra Bang and the Emerald Buddha, were carried off to Bangkok. When Nanthasen became the new king of Vientiane in 1781, Rama I returned the golden Phra Bang but not the Emerald Buddha, which he stubbornly said had originally belonged to the Lan Na Kingdom of Chieng Mai. In 1804 Nanthasen's death resulted in his brother, Anuvong, the viceroy, becoming the new king. By 1819, Anuvong had extended his territory to include Champassak; but his ultimate ambition was to obtain hegemony over the lands of Siam. To do this he needed a vast army, so he approached King Mangthathourath, who had been crowned king of Luang Prabang in 1815. He was rudely rebuked. Determined not to give up, he attempted to gain favour with Emperor Gia Long of Annam; this was unsuccessful too. Stubborn to the point of stupidity he set off with his own meagre force and managed to penetrate far into Siamese territory, where he was routed during a battle which lasted seven days. Retaliation was hard and fast and Vieng Chan fell to a superior Siamese force in 1827. Not only was the city devastated but the sacred Phra Bang was again carried off, together with many of the cityfolk. Anuvong fled into the jungle and then to Hue, where he pleaded with the Emperor to furnish him with a force large enough to retake Vieng Chan. This he did but most of the army deserted before they got there. What remained was insufficient to deal with the Siamese so the king was forced to flee once more; this time to the Kingdom of Xieng Khouang. It was a bad move since King Chao Noi almost immediately handed him over to the Siamese rather than risk their wrath. This proved to be a fatal mistake because Chao Noi was summoned to the court of Hue by Emperor Minh Mang who ordered his execution in 1828. The people of this little kingdom which surrounded the Plain of Jars were treated very harshly by the Vietnamese. They were forced to wear Vietnamese clothes, pay high taxes and pay tribute to the court of Hue. When a new enemy, in the form of the French, appeared on the scene, the Vietnamese soon lost interest in Xieng Khouang and left Chao Noi's son to rule under the title of 'Imperial Mandatory Prince'. In 1867 the Phra Bang Buddha was returned to Luang Prabang by King Mongkut. In the same year the French Mekong expedition, headed by Doudart de Lagrée, arrived in Luang Prabang. Meanwhile French personnel of another type had their eyes firmly fixed on the complete conquest of Indochina. Most of Laos at this time was still under Siamese control but, as the French conquest began in Vietnam and the country became a French protectorate in 1883, the Siamese began to fear that they, as well as Laos and Cambodia, might be high on the colonialists' list.

French Colonial Expansion

One of the first steps towards colonial conquest of Laos was to persuade the Siamese to allow them to install a French vice-consulate in Luang Prabang. Only five months after the vice-consul, Auguste Pavie, arrived in February 1887, Luang Prabang was attacked by Chinese and Black Thai bandits. He, together with King Oun Kham, fled down the Mekong River. This small incident did nothing to pacify the French eagerness to go ahead with the conquest of Laos. In order to gain an advantage over the Siamese who controlled the country, French gunboats provoked an incident by clashing with the Thai on Lower Mekong territory. Afterwards they sailed all the way up the River Menam to Bangkok to demand redress from the Thai king. Convinced by the British that it was the only way to avoid a full scale conflict, the Thai king accepted the French ultimatum and Laos became a French protectorate. A *Résidence-Supérior* was installed in Vientiane and a vice-consul took office in Luang Prabang. Laos was thus added to the Union of Indochina which had been formed in 1887 and Vientiane became the capital of French Laos.

French Rule

By 1895 the French had divided the country into Upper and Lower Laos to ease the administrative burden. Tax increases followed in 1896, and three years later provincial boundaries were reorganised by the *Résident Supérior*. New tax laws were introduced in May 1914 which provoked a revolt by Lu and Chinese-Tai minorities in Houaphan and Phôngsali Provinces. The result of this was that the whole of the northeastern territories were placed under military administration. By November 1919 a revolt by H'mong tribesmen, which had started a year

Laotian kings

Name	Reign	Kingdom
Fa Ngum	1353-1373	
Phaya Sam Sén Thai	1373-1417	
Lan Kham Dèng	1417-1428	
Sao Tiakaphat	1438-1479	
Souvanna Ban Lang	1479-1485	
La Saen Thai	1486-1496	
Somphou	1496-1500	
Visun	1500-1520	
Phothisarat I	1520-1548	
Setthathirat I	1548-1571	
Sen Soulintha	1571-1575	Lan Xang
Voravongsa	1580-1582	
Sen Soulintha	1582-1583	
Nakhone Noi	1583-1591	
No Muong	1591-1598	
Thannikarath	1603-1622	
Opayavarat	1621-1622	
Phothisarat II	1622-1626	
Mone Keo	1626-1627	
Soulinga Vonsga	1633-1690	
Muong Chan	1690-1691	
Ong Lo	1691-1695	
Nantharat	1695-1698	
Setthathirat II	1698-1707	
Soi Sisamouth	1707-1713	
Phuthanekum	1713-1737	Champassak
Sayakuman	1738-1791	
Sotikakuman	1749-1771	Luang Prabang
Suryavong	1771-1789	
Nanthasen	1781-1804	Vieng Chan
Anturuttha	1791-1815	Luang Prabang
Anuvong	1804-1828	Vieng Chan
Manoi	1813-1819	Champassak
Mangthathourath	1815-1836	Luang Prabang
Chao Noi	1819-1828	Champassak
Chao Houy	1828-1840	
Soukaseum	1836-1850	Luang Prabang
Chao Boua	1850-1852	Champassak
Chantarath	1851-1870	Luang Prabang
Youtti Thammathone 1	1856-1858	Champassak
Kham Souk	1863-1900	
Kham Souk	1894-1904	Luang Prabang
Sisavang Vong	1904-1946	

earlier in Yunnan, spread into northeast Laos. By 1934 more riots were sparked off by anti-French demonstrations on the Boloven Plateau (another minority stronghold). In December 1937, France and Thailand signed a friendship treaty to enhance trade along the Mekong River. By 1941 the Japanese had occupied French Indochina. Thailand at this time took Sayaboury Province. To compensate them for this, the Vichy French allowed the Kingdom of Luang Prabang to become part of the French protectorate. In March 1945 the French were ousted from Laos by the Japanese *coup de main*. Although the loyalty of King Sisavang Vong was clearly on the French side, under duress he was forced to proclaim that Laos was an independent country. His prime minister, Prince Phetsarath, who was ardently against the return of French Colonial rule, set up the Lao Issara Movement immediately the Japanese surrendered in August 1945.

The Lao Issara Government was formed on October 12 1945. Despite the opposition from the Lao Issara (Free Laos) Movement, the French reoccupied the country by April 1946. A lavish ceremony took place in which Sisavang Vong was reinstated as King of French Laos. Many members of the Free Laos movement were forced into exile in Thailand, where Prince Phetsarath continued to support his comrades in Laos under the title of 'Regent'. After a radical change in Thai politics took place in 1947, many of the movement's supporters returned. By 1949 many of the movement's demands had been met and guerrilla activity had ceased. An amnesty treaty (The Franco-Lao General Convention) was signed on July 19 1949, establishing Laos as an independent associate state. Although it still had many supporters, who later formed the nucleus of the Revolutionary Pathet Lao Organisation, the Lao Issara Government was officially dissolved on October 24 1949. Prince Phetsarath's half brother, Prince Souphanou Vong, continued to oppose the colonialists. As leader of the former Lao Issara guerrilla forces, he was already an ally of the Viet Minh. It was inevitable that he would become a prominent figurehead in the Pathet Lao Organisation which was given official political status by a manifesto read out at the Congress of Free Laos Front in 1950. Meanwhile, in neighbouring Vietnam, the Viet Minh had launched a full scale offensive against the French. Eager to make sure that the same thing wouldn't happen in Laos, the French gave Laos full sovereignty under the Franco-Laotian Treaty signed on October 22 1953. By December 1953, the Viet Minh launched a full scale offensive into northern Laos. Here they fought hand in hand with Pathet Lao Revolutionary troops against the combined army of the French and Lao Royal Government. Phôngsali and Houaphan Provinces were soon under their control despite extra opposition in the form of a H'mong 'secret army', which was said to be funded by the American CIA.

After the astonishing victory gained by the Viet Minh against the French in the battle of Dien Bien Phu (May 7 1954) and the convening of the Geneva Conference (July 1954), Laos was at last assured 'freedom and neutrality'.

Rise of Communism
With the French threat permanently removed, the Pathet Lao military established a political voice in the form of the Lao Patriotic Front (Neo Lao Hak Sat), which was formed in January 1956 under the presidency of Souphanou Vong. By November 1957 the Lao Patriotic Front had been integrated into a

united government and Phôngsali and Houaphan Provinces had been reinstated into the State of Laos. In the May 1958 elections the Lao Patriotic Front won seven of the 21 seats, a fact which led in June to the suspension of the United States aid package to the country. Eisenhower had always feared that if Laos ever became communist this would would trigger a communist explosion which would quickly spread throughout the whole of Asia. By July 22 1958 the Souvanna Phouma government was forced to resign. When the new right-wing Phoui Sananikone government came into office on August 18 1958 there was a notable absence of members of the Lao Patriotic Front Party. As part of the government's national clean up tactics, Pathet Lao leaders, including Prince Souphanou Vong, were arrested in Vientiane on July 28 1959. Three months later King Sisavang Vong was dead and had been replaced by King Savang Vatthana (October 29 1959). After only four months in office, in December 1959 the Phoui Sananikone government was forced to resign. A period of unrest followed during which Souphanou Vong escaped from jail along with other members of the NLHS (Neo Lao Hak Sat). By the beginning of January 1961, following the August coup d'état against the right wingers and the counter-coup by General Phoumi Nosavan, Vientiane was controlled by the government of Prince Boun Oum. Souvanna Phouma had formed the Khang Khay government which controlled a large chunk of northeastern Laos around the Plain of Jars region. Here he put Captain Kong Le in charge of his troops. As a bastion of communism, the government and the military were naturally funded by the Soviet Union, whereas Prince Boun Oum got his military aid from the new Kennedy administration, which was determined to prevent the spread of communism. By May 1961 members of the various political factions, Souphanou Vong (NLHK ie Pathet Lao), Souvanna Phouma (Neutralists) and Boun Oum (Rightwing) met to discuss the formation of a second coalition government at the Geneva Conference. This was formed on June 23 1962.

Minor skirmishes between the neutralist forces led by Kong Le and Pathet Lao forces broke out in early 1963. Trouble escalated, and when a peaceful compromise could not be reached in April 1964 a right wing coup d'état followed. Heavy fighting resumed around the Plain of Jars region resulting in a defeat for Kong Le's troops. When news of this was received in the United States, reconnaissance flights began almost immediately over the Pathet Lao bases. In June 1964, the Royal Lao Air Force began bombing the Plain of Jars. In January 1965 there was another attempted coup, led by General Phoumi Nosavan; when it failed he was forced to flee into Thailand. By October 5 1965 the Pathet Lao military had become known as the Lao People's Liberation Army.

The following year chaos was created when an abnormally high flood threatened many lives and destroyed countless rice crops. In June, parts of Vientiane were several feet under water. In September 1966 the National Assembly was dissolved by King Savang Vatthana. Two years later, due to fierce fighting between Royal Lao government troops and the Lao People's Liberation Army (LPLA), half a million people were left without homes. The problem had been exacerbated in eastern Laos by the American bombing of the 'Ho Chi Minh Trail' which had started as early as 1964. By 1969 an estimated half a million tons of bombs had been dropped. When Nixon became President on November 5 1968, the fireworks really started. By 1973 all parts of the trail which extended into Laotian territory had been pulverised beyond belief. Over half a million sorties had been flown and an estimated two million tons of bombs dropped on the country. It is interesting that Pathet Lao bases nearest to the trail (Sam Neua area) had been built in caves which gave them maximum protection against the bombs. These had similar facilities to the tunnels of Cu Chi which had been used by the Viet Cong during the Vietnam War. Many were turned into hospitals, accommodation, some served for weapon storage, others were even used as entertainment centres.

When the cease-fire came into effect on February 21 1973, much of northeastern Laos was left looking like a moonscape. By April 5 1974 a third coalition government had been formed in Vientiane under the premiership of Souvanna Phouma. The Lao People's Liberation Army leader, Souphanou Vong, became head of the Joint National Political Council. As the Viet Minh were coming to the end of their victorious march on Saigon in April 1975, the Pathet Lao (The Lao People's Liberation Army) were advancing on Vientiane. By August they had achieved their goal and by the 23rd the 'Revolutionary Administration' had taken power. One of America's worst nightmares had become reality. Souphanou Vong had achieved his greatest ambition and his army could be finally renamed the 'Lao People's Army'.

The People's Democratic Republic
On December 1-2 1975, the third coalition government was dissolved. King Savang Vatthana abdicated, putting an end to the 600 year old Lao monarchy. The Red Prince Souphanou Vong became the President of the People's Democratic Republic of Laos. Instead of being discreetly retired, the ex-king became special advisor to the Laotian politburo. In March 1977 he was arrested and accused of resistance activity. It is believed that he and his queen were sent to a re-education camp in the Vieng Say area where he died sometime in 1979.

In February 1979, the Lao Front for National Construction was formed to replace the Lao Patriotic Front. This was followed in May by the formation of the 'Lao Socialist Party'. On January 10 1984, the Neutralist Prince, Souvanna Phouma, died, aged 82. Relationships between Laos and Thailand had worsened by the end of 1976, following the Bangkok military coup d'état. Rumours had been circulated that Thailand was financing rebel activity amongst the H'mong in the northeastern part of the country. As a result of this, the border between the two countries had been opened and closed on several occasions. In June 1984 military exchange occurred between the two countries because of a border dispute. On September 19 1986 a treaty was drawn up between Laos and Vietnam which strictly delimited their territorial boundaries. On October 29 1986, Souphanou Vong resigned as President of the LPRP because of ill health. By August new exchanges had occurred between Thai and Laotian forces over another border dispute. On September 11 1987, Phoumi Vongvichit became the new President of the LPDR. In December 1987 and January 1988 there were heavy clashes between Thai and Laotian troops in the Sayaboury-Phitsanulok region. In order to promote friendship between the two countries the Commander-in-Chief of the Thai Army visited Vientiane on October 28-30 1988. This resulted in the setting up of the Border Committee in Bangkok on December 28 1988 – an attempt to prevent further bloodshed. Relations with China improved after the visit of Li Ping, their Prime Minister, to Vientiane on

December 15-17 1990. On February 15 1991, a national conference on transport and road communication took place to discuss the building of the road through Southeast Asia's last frontier. This was followed by very dramatic events in March which took place as a result of the Fifth Congress of the LPRP. Shocked faces looked on as the Party Secretariat was abolished and three eminent Politburo officials retired, President Souphanou Vong among them – he was replaced on August 15 1991 by Kaysone Phomvihan, who had been chairman of the LPRP since 1956. With his new radical thinking policies, which leaned away from Socialism towards Capitalism, Kaysone Phomvihan, was ahead of his time. The wind of change which had begun to blow gently in Vietnam as early as 1984 had finally arrived in Laos. What the Russians called *perestroika* and the Vietnamese call *doi moi*, the Laotians aptly named *chin thanakan mai*, the 'new thinking'.

Sadly President Kaysone Phomvihan died, aged 71, in November 1992. He was replaced by Nouhak Phousavanh. The elections which took place in December 1992 saw a 90% turn out and changed nothing. During 1993, monetary support for the new way of thinking flooded in from various sources. The USA was the greatest contributor then but since the opening of the Thai/Laos 'Friendship Bridge', funds have become more available from Thailand. In 1995, Japan has considerably stepped up its economic aid and now provides Laos with more monetary assistance than any other country.

Memorial to the War of Resistance, 1964-1973

Chapter Five

Economy

The first significant study of the Laotian economy was carried out in 1967 and was based on statistics collected in 1964. Analysis showed that the Gross Domestic Product (GDP) was US$65 per capita per year. In 1964, to assist with currency stabilisation, the Foreign Exchange Operations Fund (FEOF) had been set up with the assistance of a consortium from the United States, United Kingdom, Australia and France. By 1965 money had also become available from Japan. In the same year the United States had assisted with the setting up of the Agricultural Development Organisation (ADO), which provided vital financial help for farmers. By 1967 there had been a marked improvement in financial institutions, the Development Bank of Laos now replaced the National Credit Bank of Laos (formed in 1956) and was available to lend money to stimulate economic enhancement. An Economic and Social Development Plan was announced on March 31 1969. Known as the Plan Cadre de Dévelopment Economique et Social (1969-74), its purpose was to improve those circumstances which could ultimately lead to improved industry, trade, development and local finance. Industry was still extremely undeveloped, very few skilled workers were available and managerial staff practically non-existent. Although it was known that Laos had rich resources of gold, oil, coal, zinc, salt, copper, iron and phosphorous, only tin was mined in the Royal Lao Government areas. Over two-thirds of the country was covered in forests, but in 1969 much of it was unexploited. Laos has rich sources of valuable teak and secondary products such as benzoin (used in the perfume industry), sticklac (used in lacquer manufacture) and cardamom were available from the dense forests. Military skirmishes in upland areas prevented mass harvesting. Land utilisation was extremely poor, only 8% of the total land mass was arable. Rice production in Royal Lao Government-controlled areas in 1964 was a mere 537,000 tons – families lived at subsistence level and were dependant on extra imported rice donated by the state. Those living in areas suitable for growing cotton, tobacco and coffee were the lucky ones. In unpoliced zones, particularly in the north, opium provided villagers with their material needs. Smuggling along the boundary with Thailand, Burma, Vietnam, China and Cambodia was rife.

In the early 1970s, Laos had already begun to realise the potential of hydro-electric power. This was mainly due to the elaborate survey and feasibility study which had been instigated by the United Nations Economic Commission for Asia, in which a dam had been proposed to be situated north of Paksé on the Se

Done River. The Nam Dong Dam, south of Luang Prabang, had also been suggested, together with a larger dam on the Nam Ngum River (north of Vientiane) which had received financial backing from the World Bank. Because it made sound economic sense, money had been donated by a consortium of countries including France, Japan, Denmark, Thailand, Canada, Australia, New Zealand and the Netherlands. The proposed Pa Mong irrigation and hydro-electric project, just north of Vientiane, was still a developer's dream. Road communication was practically non-existent despite an artery being opened up between Vientiane and Luang Prabang and another between the capital and Savannakhét in 1968. New industries began to appear in Vientiane in 1969/70, including an ice-cream factory, one for producing bricks and other very small concerns which manufactured nail, wire, washing powder and candles. To encourage more investment, a tax incentive scheme was launched by the government in February 1970.

It is also worth pointing out that in 1971 two separate economies existed, one in the areas under the control of the Royal Lao Government and another administered by the Neo Lao Hak Sat (NLHS), which was better known as the Lao Patriotic Front (LPF). Very few statistics are available on the latter.

By 1971, the money raised from exports was less than one-tenth of that required to pay the import bill for essential commodities such as petroleum products, machinery, food, transportational aids and equipment needed for agricultural development. International aid came from a wide source, the USA being the greatest contributor (US$74 million/year). All of this quite naturally went to the Royal Lao Government controlled areas. When monetary aid suddenly dried up in 1975, the result was economic chaos. To make matters worse, most of the Laos elite had fled from the country leaving very few people sufficiently educated to sort out the mess. Agriculture in the next few years was to receive additional blows by severe droughts which considerably reduced the rice harvests.

By May 1978 the government had decided to introduce a recovery package which included a massive programme of agricultural collectivisation together with nationalisation of larger businesses. The collectivisation policy backfired however and was suspended in July 1979.

In January 1981, a Five Year Plan was announced, which proposed that agriculture should be modernised, that the state should invest more heavily in industry and that important infrastructure such as communication and transport should be radically updated. A team was appointed to seek new ways of improving exports. By April 30 1981, the Third Party Congress of the LPRP had fully endorsed its proposals. During this period a certain amount of free enterprise was encouraged. Soon after the 10th anniversary of the founding of the LPDR had been celebrated, the Second Five Year Plan was announced in January 1986. The wind of change was blowing fiercely throughout the land. The radically new, foreign and private investment policy was loudly applauded and quickly ratified by the Fourth Party Congress. This attempt to revitalise the country's economy was in fact the Laotian version of Vietnam's *doi moi* (renovation, or new thinking). The policy was widely welcomed and even at the village level it led to a gradual improvement in the standard of living. The privatisation of farms meant that highly productive agricultural zones around Vientiane and Savannakhét thrived. Rice production on the Mekong flood plain increased by around 30% during the 1986/88 period, helped considerably by the weather which was particularly favourable. Double cropping became the norm and growers, now able to trade freely in the local markets, became more prosperous. Previously owned agricultural land, which during the collectivisation phase of development had been confiscated by the state, was returned to its rightful owners. Many of the Lao elite who had fled the country in 1975 returned to reclaim their family villas.

Life went on as normal in the highly mountainous regions in the North. Despite being condemned repeatedly for their 'slash and burn' agricultural techniques, highlanders continued to deforest large areas. Valuable timber such as teak, which in controlled areas was the second highest export earner, was cut down so that far less valuable crops such as coffee, tea, tobacco and upland rice could be cultivated. This point was high on the agenda when the first national agricultural conference took place in Vientiane between June 1-12 1988. New restrictive policies were introduced to curb the massive deforestation, which was currently running at 300,000 hectares/year. Instead of raw timber being exported, forestry experts demanded that the wood should in the future be processed in Laos.

The most valuable crop of all, opium, continued to be produced in large quantities despite the anti-narcotic legislation passed in 1971. This, the vital lifeline of many H'mong, Lolo, Akha and Lahu communities continued to be smuggled into Thailand and China through many remote border areas. Re-education programmes by anti-narcotic squads, largely financed by the USA in 1987, were only partly successful in their bid to encourage the use of crop substitutes. One of the most important economic developments of the decade was the signing of an agreement by Thailand and Laos to build a friendship bridge across the Mekong on February 17 1989. This brought them one step nearer to a trade alliance which was further cemented by the visit of Crown Princess Sirindhorn to Vientiane early in 1990. Following the royal visit, the Thai government announced that Laos had been given the go-ahead to import 363 items which had previously been on a restricted list. Relations continued to improve between Laos and China after the visit of Chinese Prime Minister Li Peng, 15-17 December 1990. Money flooded in from Peking to help fund the road and education expansion schemes.

Following an agreement between the USA and Laos to allow free access to officials searching for MIA's and the stepping up of their Counter-Narcotics Co-operation programme, US monetary aid was resumed. Further financial support came from signing the ASEAN Co-operation Treaty, UNESCO, United Development Programme (UNDP) and the Asian Development Bank (ADB). A massive famine brought on by a severe drought during 1992/93 prompted The World Food Humanitarian Programme run by the United Nations to donate over US$1 million in emergency funds. As there had been an unconditional withdrawal of Thai and Laotian troops from disputed border territory, two new Thai banking organisations set up shop in Vientiane.

Determined to attract greater foreign investment (a policy which no doubt would have been endorsed by the Third Five Year Plan, if it had reached fruition), the Laotian government decided to adopt a very liberal policy. Foreign ownership in a new venture could be 100%, provided that this complied with their 15-year rule. After this period, the situation had to be reviewed and a new permit applied for. During 1993, this attracted foreign investment in the textile industry from Thailand, France, Hong Kong and Malaysia. Shrewd businessmen, eager to avoid export restrictions, relocated to the Laotian capital bringing with them an export deal which topped US$38 million by the end of the year.

With the opening of the Thai/Laos 'Friendship Bridge' in April 1994, more Thai financial institutions set up in Vientiane, bringing the total to seven. By now over 400 foreign investment licenses had been granted by the Laotian government, mostly to Thai businessmen in service industries, agriculture, textiles and timber processing. Japan, the USA and Taiwan had invested heavily in the electricity generating potential of the country, which was also backed by the Export-Import Bank of Thailand which realised that, in this field, Laos outshone its Indochinese neighbours. Energy experts had little doubt that this would pay off heavily even if the major Pa Mong Dam project (to be built on the Mekong, just north of Vientiane) were not given the go-ahead by the various members of the Mekong Committee. Other dams are proposed, such as the Xeset in the south and the Nam Tuen, near Tha Khaek, which have already received financial backing from another industrial giant, Daewoo from South Korea. More than a casual interest has been expressed by Japanese mining companies in the rich mineral deposits just waiting to be unearthed on the Xieng Khouang and Bolovens Plateaux. As the road network continues to improve, courtesy of Sweden's Skanska Company, new trade arteries are being opened up leading straight through the centre of the 'Golden Quadrangle'.

As far as tourism is concerned, Laos continues with its soft courting policy even though the government realises that this could be their greatest foreign currency earner. Despite the significant improvements which have brought inflation down to an all time low of 6%, Laos still has a US$500 million foreign debt and accepts foreign aid packages amounting to US$170 million a year. Its GDP is still only US$240 per capita per year and even top government officials earn little more than US$50 per month.

Buddha Collection, Pak Ou

Chapter Six

The People

ETHNIC GROUPS

According to the census completed on March 7 1985, the total population of the country was 3,584,803. For convenience the majority can be divided into four distinct ethnic groups.

Lao Lum

This group of valley dwellers constitutes the Lao majority. The 1985 census showed that they comprised 56% of the total population. They are mainly concentrated along the fertile Mekong River Valley in the provinces of Vientiane, Savannakhét and Luang Prabang. The Lao of the Plains are wet rice cultivators. Only the Lao elite (upper class) tend to be highly educated and become doctors, teachers, government officials and lawyers. The village Lao are often very poor and are administered by a headman (*pho ban*) who is generally one of the better-off members of the community. The most highly respected person in every village is, however, the keeper of the *wat* (temple).

The Lao Tai

The only census to estimate the number of tribal Tai in Laos took place in the 1960s, when they constituted 13% of the total population. They are found mostly on the high plateaux and upland valleys of central and northern Laos. Included in this group are the Red Thai (*Tai Deng*), Black Tai (*Tai Dam*), the White Tai (*Tai Neua*), the *Phu Tai* and the Lu seen in the north of Houaphan Province. The Lu (or, more strictly, the Muong Sing) are descendants of those seen in Yunnan in China. In this area over two thirds of the population belong to this group and are administered by a head called the *chao fa*. Other Lao Tai live in communities called muong which are headed by the tribal chief, the *chao muong*. All the commune chiefs (*ly truong*) are responsible to him.

The Lao Theung

These are the people of the mountain slopes. Ethnolinguistically they belong to the Austro-Asiatic language group. The 1985 population census showed that they comprise about 34% of the total population. The southern upland groups of Lao Theung include the Oi, Alak and Loven. Few are highly educated but some (eg Sithone Kommadam, an ethnic Loven) have held high positions in the Lao People's Liberation Army. Many of the Loven live on the Bolovens Plateau where their wealth is gauged by the number of gongs and buffalo they own. Unlike many other tribal groups, the Loven do not have an overall leader but rely on the collective efforts of the richer members of the community (*lem*). The northern upland groups of Lao Theung include the Khmu and Lamet.

Lao Sung (Lao Soung)

These high mountain dwellers belong to the Sino-Tibetan language group. According to the 1985 census, they comprise about 9% of the total population. The most prominent members are the Meo (H'mong) and the Yao (Man). The Meo in Laos have strong linguistic and cultural ties with their neighbours in Vietnam, Thailand and southern China. Many grow opium poppies in fields above an altitude of 1,000m and many keep livestock, grow rice and corn and have become socially well organised. Like the Yao, they communicate using various dialects of the H'mong-Yao language which has evolved over thousands of years. They live in communities called *muong*, and are administered by a chief (*chao muong*) who is responsible for organising the trade with their ethnic neighbours, the Ho in Yunnan. He is also responsible for helping to resolve marriage disputes, for determining migrational patterns and settling quarrels. Meo communities are mostly concentrated in the provinces of Xieng Khouang, Luang Prabang and the Xam Neua (Sam Neua) area of Houaphan Province. The Yao are mainly scattered in small settlements on the border with Thailand (Bokeo Province), between Yunnan and Luang Nam Tha Province and in northern Phongsali Province.

Over the years the H'mong have developed a reputation as fearless fighters. Well documented in their eventful history are the exploits of Ba Chay, who led them against the French (1918-22). Others, such as Van Pao, are awarded legendary status – he because of the aid he gave to the Americans, organising a massive 'secret army' which was largely funded by the CIA. During the 1970s thousands of H'mong died fighting the Lao People's Liberation Army (LPA); many became refugees and were forced to live in Thailand. Attacks on them escalated between 1976 and 1977 when it was rumoured that they were sprayed with deadly 'yellow rain'. Right into the nineties there are still occasional reports of conflicts between the H'mong and the troops of the Lao government.

Other tribal groups

Well represented are the Akha (Tibeto-Burman group) who live in the northern highlands, particularly on the border with Thailand. They still believe that illness is caused by 'spirit affliction' (*neu gu la-eu*) and a person can get extremely ill from 'soul loss' (*la ba ba-eu*). They practise spirit purification and when someone is buried, a spirit priest conducts the ceremony.

Also seen in smaller numbers along the Lao-Thai border in the north are the Lahu. All are devoutly religious and have holy days which are set aside for paying homage to their gods, spirits of the mountain and valley (*hk'aw ne law ne*) and spirits of the house (*yeh ne*). Unlike their Thai cousins, none of the Lao-Lahu have become Christians, but they still believe in a supreme power (*g'ui sha*) which rules over all their spirits. There are also small numbers of Lolo in the north which, like the Akha and Lahu, speak the Tibeto-Burman dialect.

Other inhabitants

In Laos there are also a small number of Chinese who have settled mainly in Paksé, and Vietnamese who are fairly common in Savannakhét. In addition, there are also substantial numbers of Thai and small populations of Indians, Pakistanis and Khmer, who mainly live in Champassak Province.

RELIGION

There is no concrete proof of when Buddhism was first introduced into Laos. It is believed that Fa Ngum (1353-73) was the first king to be converted to the religion. During his reign, the Phra Bang, the most sacred Buddhist statue in the country, was presented to him by Khmer monks. This became the symbol of Lan Xang and has continued to be highly revered up to the present day. During the reign of his successor, Phaya Sam Sèn Thai (1373-1417) many religious buildings were constructed. This continued under successive rulers and received extra prominence during the reign of King Phothisarat (1520-48). The Royal Capital had by then been moved to Vientiane, where he ordered the construction of many Buddhist wats. The *Sangha* (monastic order) had evolved to the point where even the king bowed to the superiority of the chief abbot (*Sangha-raja*). Phi worship was suppressed when Sai Setthathirat (1548-71) became monarch. He built Wat Phra Kéo and That Luang in the holy city of Vieng Chan (Vientiane). In the latter he enshrined Lan Xang's symbol of religious sovereignty, the hallowed Emerald Buddha made from green jasper, which he had guarded with his life from Burmese invaders. During the period which has been frequently described as 'the golden age' of Laos, King Soulinga Vongsa (1633-90) founded many monastic schools. As a result Buddhist doctrines became more widespread.

Following his peaceful reign, Laos became a war ravaged land. Two of its more prized religious treasures, the golden Phra Bang Buddha and the Emerald Buddha, were stolen by the Thais and exhibited at Bangkok in 1778. (The Emerald Buddha still stands in Bangkok's Royal Palace, having never been returned because the Thais have always believed that it originally belonged to the Kingdom of Chieng Rai).

The immensely important Wat Si Saket was built in Vientiane by King Anouvong in 1818, and still stands to the present day. When the Yunnanese pillaged the city in 1873, they burnt That Luang which was subsequently rebuilt by the French. This Great Stupa, and that at Wat Xieng Thong, built in 1560 at Luang Prabang, still remain the most magnificent temple edifices in the whole of Laos.

The Tripitaka and other religious books

The Tripitaka contains sacred texts and includes the teachings of Lord Buddha. In Laos it was translated from Pali into Tham, the sacred language of Laos Buddhists. Together with the Jatakam, which records the lives of the Buddha, it has pride of place in all monasteries. A third book, the Paritta, is also widely studied by Theravada monks. The Laotian versions of the Panchatantra and the Rāmayāna, which stem from Hindu doctrines, are also very popular.

Karma

Every Theravada Buddhist endeavours to attain the perfect peace known as nirvana. According to karma doctrine, what one does in one life determines the path of an individual in another. The more merit one gains the more one improves his or her karma. Any traveller in Laos becomes immediately aware of how intimately bound up with everyday life this doctrine is. Laotians are generous to the extreme, humility is an important part of their psyche; most have family members who have become monks or nuns in their youth. They will very often go without so that they can present gifts and offerings to members of the *Sangha*. Whatever town or city you are in, it is worth getting up extremely early in the morning to see the promenading of monks on their daily alms rounds. People will literally queue up to attend to their food needs. No thanks is expected and none given. To do good, what the Laotians call *hed boun*, is just something they do every day. Children in every school are taught to tread heavily along the Eightfold Path, not to think evil thoughts, to meditate, speak correctly, to behave, to have a purpose, to have the right vocation, to try hard and to have the right understanding. Many go to school at local wats, where the monks will teach them not to steal, and to eschew opium smoking, alcohol or any illicit practice. A few will be persuaded to join the *Sangha* brotherhood where they will become totally detached from the outside world.

On your journey through the country you will come across scores of beautiful Buddha figures. The sights and sounds of deeply spiritual people unpretentiously practising their beliefs will remain in your memory for ever. The daily ritual of visiting a wat has profound significance. Paying reverence to Lord Buddha places a person one more rung up the ladder of perfect beatitude on the way to an eternal state of everlasting peace. Don't be afraid to enter a sanctuary, even if there is a religious service in progress, everyone is more than welcome. Exercise extreme politeness and dress respectfully. Photography is allowed but always remember where you are, light up a joss stick, leave a small donation; it's always greatly appreciated.

Like Burma, Laos is certainly a land of a million Buddhas. You will see them everywhere, on doors, on walls, on ceilings, on floors, in caves, in sanctuaries and in the most humble of dwelling places. Wherever you are take a close look. At Wat Phra Kéo in Vientiane can be seen numerous sitting Buddhas, the so called Bhumisparcamudra. With his right hand resting on his right knee he is 'calling the earth to witness' by touching the ground with his left fingers. Some fine examples are seen in the main sanctuary of Wat Xieng Thong in Luang Prabang. There is also an excellent example on the main shrine in the Pak Ou Caves up river from Luang Prabang. If you examine every individual Buddha here, you will come across over 30 different *mudras*. Commonly seen is the Dhyanamudra; the Buddha is in a seated position with the right palm held open over the left one which is also open. The Buddha is in a deep state of meditation, his legs are crossed, the right one being on top of the left (so called virasana yogic posture).

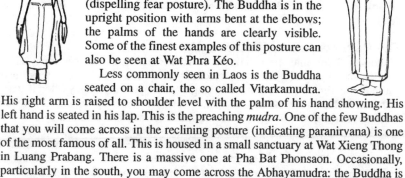

Some Buddhas stand upright with their arms and fingers pointing directly towards the ground. This is the so called 'Buddha calling for the rain' posture, which is the most common seen in Laos. Another 'attitude' or *mudra* commonly seen is the Abhayamudra (dispelling fear posture). The Buddha is in the upright position with arms bent at the elbows; the palms of the hands are clearly visible. Some of the finest examples of this posture can also be seen at Wat Phra Kéo.

Less commonly seen in Laos is the Buddha seated on a chair, the so called Vitarkamudra. His right arm is raised to shoulder level with the palm of his hand showing. His left hand is seated in his lap. This is the preaching *mudra*. One of the few Buddhas that you will come across in the reclining posture (indicating paranirvana) is one of the most famous of all. This is housed in a small sanctuary at Wat Xieng Thong in Luang Prabang. There is a massive one at Pha Bat Phonsaon. Occasionally, particularly in the south, you may come across the Abhayamudra: the Buddha is standing, holding the back of his right hand against his chest making the palm clearly visible, his left arm pointing directly at the ground. In this posture he is dispelling fear. On your wanderings through the country, never touch these sacred figures, which are as precious to Laotian people as life itself.

Religion and the state

The monastic brotherhood, the *Sangha*, is headed by the *phra sangha-raja* who is the religious head of all the province's Buddhist leaders (*chao khana khoeung*). It is the provincial religious leader who is responsible for appointing the head (*chao khana muong*) of the district (*muong*). The head of the *Sangha* is appointed by the state after consultations have been made with the provincial religious leaders, but the *Sangha* is totally divorced from any involvement in the country's politics. Many writers have reported that during the 30 years of bitter struggle between the Pathet Lao and government forces (1945-1975) both sides attempted to get the support of the *Sangha*. When they failed, harsh measures were often adopted to bring it under government control. Between 1976 and 1980, the Royal Lao government placed many restrictions on Buddhism but during the 1980s the situation became more relaxed. Many members of the Lao elite, including Politburo officials, attend religious ceremonies.

Today the largest Buddhist order in Laos is the Mahanakay, which has countless representatives in the central and northern provinces. The Thammayut is the largest Buddhist order in the south.

Tribal religion and *phi* worship

The *phi* are the spirits which many Laotians believe have control over many parts of a human's existence. If a person is taken ill, the *phi* bonze must be called to perform an exorcism ceremony. This is part of everyday life in most communities of Lao Tai, Lao Theung and Lao Soung and is commonly practised by the lowland Lao Lum, with the exception of the Lao Lum elite. Every rural village has a *phi* altar at its wat which is the responsibility of the cult master.

In many minority villages an abnormal form of death is greatly feared. They believe that if one should die during a fight with a neighbour, for example, a spirit called a *phi phetu* will be released which will never rest and will go on tormenting other people forever. Many communities will attempt to appease *phis* by offering presents at the *phi* altar. This is very important just before a harvest or a marriage. There is also belief in *phi-pops,* evil people who are capable of feats of black magic. To be cursed by a *phi-pop* is to invite certain death.

The Basi ceremony (Soukwan)

Visitors to Laos may be privileged to be invited to a Basi ceremony. This religious ceremony is a form of welcoming that Laotian hosts bestow on their guests. Sometimes it is performed during a 'goodbye party'. Very often it starts with the performance of the *lamvong,* a folk dance during which attractively dressed young girls will gyrate to the music of a *khene* while they perform graceful arm and leg movements. Many villagers may join in with other bamboo harmonicas, two stringed fiddles, drums, xylophones and an instrument called a *khuong vong.* This is a horseshoe shaped structure which holds 16 small gongs made from bronze. Guests will be invited to participate in the proceedings.

The religious proceedings follow, during which a much venerated member of the community conducts prayers. According to an ancient Lao superstition, the human body is composed of 32 organs, each of which is looked after by a spirit called a *kwan.* In his prayers he is inviting wandering *kwan* to return to people's bodies to restore harmony and promote good health. Offerings (*phakwan*) in the form of a highly decorated tree of rice cakes, banana leaves, bread, flowers and luxuries are presented to induce the *kwan.* Once they have been received, members of the community will pass around all the guests and tie pieces of string around their wrists. Now the knots have been tied, the wandering *kwan* are held securely in place. The ceremony goes a long way to promoting friendship between the foreign guests and their hosts.

Soo Khuan ceremony

This is very similar to the Basi ceremony. In Lao the word *soo* means to call something back, *khuan* is a spirit. The ceremony therefore is involved in calling back the spirit or soul. It has great religious significance and is intended to restore a person's self confidence by giving them courage and eliminating all fears.

The much venerated old man who performs the ceremony is called *mor phorn* or *mor khuan.* During his repeated chanting, he is calling the spirits. The participants sit cross-legged around a *kong khao khuan* tray. Pieces of white string are tied around the wrist of the departing/arriving person. The tray, sometimes also called the *soo khuan,* is made up of a basket (*kong*), a spirit (*khuan*) who has been called to the feast, rice (*khao*), eggs and peeled chicken (*khai khuan*). The person who is being honoured must not remove the string for three days. When it is finally removed, it must not be cut but carefully unknotted. The devout well-wishers will then have succeeded in heightening the person's self confidence and bestowing on him/her their love and friendship.

Chapter Seven

Culture

FESTIVALS AND FEAST DAYS

H'mong New Year

Celebrated in Phônsavan and surrounding areas in Xieng Khouang Province. This minority festival attracts other ethnic groups. A local tradition is that young men can ask the girls they fancy to marry them during the festivities by presenting them with a cloth ball called a *makoi*.

New Year Festival (Boun Pimai)

Travellers in Laos will realise how devout the people are if they arrive just at the end of the hottest period (in April). Mid-April is the beginning of the new year according to their calendar. At the end of the old year there are many processions in cities, towns and villages throughout the country. Like any spring festival it celebrates the renewal of life and the return of prosperity. Offerings of fruit, flowers and food are presented at local altars. Many traditional rites are practised, such as sweeping houses to rid them of evil spirits. Buddhas throughout the country are washed by priests and ordinary people. Along the countries waterways votive mounds made from stone and sand are built in prominent positions. They also appear in temple courtyards where highly coloured streamers bearing the signs of the zodiac flap in the wind. These are also seen on many of the capital's buildings and on peoples' homes. On many parts of the Mekong, serpent boats crewed by 30 oarsmen race against each other.

In the olden days when the King was in residence at Luang Prabang there were spectacular elephant parades, candle processions and a great feast would be held in honour of the priests. The King himself would go along to Wat Xieng Thong to present offerings and to wash the Buddhas. These days everyone enjoys a holiday from April 15 to 17 inclusive. Children are given presents and attend wat ceremonies dressed in brand new clothes. If you are lucky enough to be in Luang Prabang at this time, you may see the Miss New Year beauty competition. The winner (*Nang Sang Khan*) joins the colourful New Year parade, which consists of immaculately dressed girls in traditional costumes carrying different coloured umbrellas, fruit and floral offerings. A spectacular man-made elephant decorated with flowers is carried around on one of the floats. In the evening there are mask dances and firework displays. The most important religious event of this festival is the enthroning of the golden Phra Bang Buddha in Wat Mai which is followed by a washing ceremony performed by monks.

Vixakha Bouxa
Sometimes called Boun Bang-Fay, this is the main Buddhist festival. Occurring on the 15th day of the 6th lunar month it celebrates the birth, enlightenment and death of Lord Buddha. Festivities take the form of puppet shows, dancing and jubilant processions. Visits will be made to local wats where there will be services throughout the day and far into the night. In many cities there will be candle-lit processions in the evening followed by firework displays. In the past, a pre-Buddhist fertility rite was practised but, due to its licentious nature, it was banned by the Laotian government. As part of the general festivities in the past rockets were built from bamboo and fired into the heavens in an attempt to prompt the thunder-god into releasing the first rains of the season. If you want to see the rocket festival now you have to cross the Mekong to the northern Thai town of Yasothon.

Vien Thiene
A candle-lit festival takes place in the north generally in May.

Khao Vatsa
This is a serious religious festival during which priests recite the *patimokkha* before disappearing into retreat for a three month period. There are processions of bonzes in most towns and cities. During the next three months (the height of the rainy season) they are forbidden from wandering from one monastery to another. It takes place during the July full moon.

Ho Khao Padap Dinh
Otherwise known as the Feast of the Dead, this festival honours Buddha's commandment to remember the dead and present them with gifts. People everywhere will pray that their ancestors will never be forgotten. Many gifts are presented to the members of the *sangha*. This usually occurs in the 9th month of the lunar year (August or September).

Ho Khao Slak
This is another religious festival and occurs during the tenth lunar month. Members of the *sangha* are again presented with gifts and children throughout the country are given new toys, fruit and sweets. It also honours the dead.

Bouk Ok Phansa (Boun Ok Vatsa)
This important festival, which takes place in Vientiane during the 11th lunar month, celebrates the end of the rainy season and Buddhist Lent. The evening before, small highly decorated rafts carrying candles will be released along the Mekong. The next day pirogue crews will race against each other. Homes are decorated to expel evil *phi* who have come to reside during the rainy season.

That Luang
This generally occurs in November. Hundreds of monks promenade between the national shrine (That Luang) and Wat Si Muang. In the evening there will be a

candle-lit procession which will circumambulate the Great Stupa. During the week that follows there will be numerous parades, dancing, festivities and a carnival-like atmosphere.

Mokha Bouxa (Magha Puja)

This falls in the 12th lunar month and commemorates the calling together of the disciples of Buddha before his *parinibbana* (death) and his passage into an eternal nirvana. It is a time for prayer and presentation of offerings. This festival is usually only celebrated in the capital and at Wat Phou in Champassak Province.

Cart racing festival

There is a cart racing festival in Phônsavan in Xieng Khouang Province on December 2.

Important dates in the Laotian calendar

January 1	The Lao Lum invite their families to a Basi ceremony at their homes to celebrate New Year's Day.
January 6	Pathet Lao Day. This public holiday honours the anti-French guerilla movement. There are parades in most cities.
January 20	Army Day. This is a public holiday.
March 8	Woman's Day. This is a public holiday.
March 22	People's Party Day. Another public holiday.
May 1	Labour Day. This is a special day which honours all Laotian workers. Everything closes down and there are parades in the main cities.
June 1	Children's Day. People throughout the country honour their children.
August 13	Lao Issara Day. This commemorates the movement which opposed French jurisdiction. It is a national holiday.
August 23	Liberation Day. This commemorates the people's uprising to 'liberate' Vientiane from the US-backed government.
October 12	Freedom from the French Day. This celebrates the formation of the Lao Issara Government on October 12 1945.
December 2	Independence Day. During this national holiday there are military parades in most cities.

THE ARTS

Dance and theatre

The mohlam khu

This is a form of traditional music drama during which a man will court a woman using love songs. It involves question and answer dialogues. Both performers are in a very melancholy mood.

The mohlam dio

This popular form of folk theatre uses a singer to relate communist doctrines, political propaganda and religious thought.

The mohlam luang
This is Laotian musical drama, another aspect of its folk theatre.

The mohlam chote
This interesting form of folk theatre involves two people of the same sex who argue about a particular subject. One may relate a story and the other will follow with an alternative version.

The lamvong
This folk dance is performed by delicate maidens to the accompaniment of a bamboo harmonica called a *khene*. Graceful arm and leg manipulation mimic tales from the Laotian version of the Rāmayāna and Panchatantra.

Silhouette puppetry
This is very similar to the Thai version. Shadow plays will be carried out behind a screen during which cut-out puppet figures will be manipulated to re-enact a religious theme. Stories are very often taken from the Mahabharata and the Vedas. The puppets are supported on sticks and performances will be backed by a verbal commentary.

Music
Laotian music is very simple compared to that of its neighbours Vietnam and Cambodia. When sung it is always memorised; improvisation is common. Even orchestral music is not formal, there is no system of musical notation and the melody is usually created using song or played on a flute.

The main Laotian instrument is the harmonica, which is believed to have originated there. The Laotian harmonica is made from bamboo and is called the *khene*. This is said to be ideal for performing the heptatonic (seven-note) scale. It is the usual form of accompaniment except for religious music, when an orchestra called the *seb gnai* is used. This utilises large drums and wind instruments similar to Western clarinets.

The other type of orchestra, the *seb noi* uses *khenes* of varied lengths, flutes called *khuy*, the *so* which is a two-stringed instrument and the *nangnat*, a form of xylophone. The music is considerably enriched by the *khong vong*, which is a semi-circular instrument made from cane with 16 cymbals arranged around its periphery.

Crafts
Most households in the north have looms. Over the decades, this well-practised art has produced some enormously attractive designs which are now copied for the tourist market. Few visitors will leave the country without a skirt or scarf made from cotton or silk. Many have gold or silver braiding and feature the unique style of Laotian embroidery. Silver belts are also a popular buy which can be worn with almost any evening dress. Objects fashioned from the gold collected from the Mekong sandbanks can be bought at Luang Prabang. There is also plenty of choice in wooden sculptures and delicately carved pirogues. Laotian musical instruments also make attractive ornaments, particularly the bamboo *khene*, which can be purchased very cheaply. For the connoisseur of ethnic art there are many objects for sale made from wicker and bamboo by the Yao, H'mong and Lahu tribes.

Architecture

Much of the wooden religious architecture which was the pride and joy of Lan Xang has not survived. Visitors will however be impressed by what remains. The doors through which you enter many pagodas are highly ornate and the design sometimes shows a distinct Thai influence in the north and Khmer influence in the south. These often open into the ordination hall (*sim*) which contain the main altar and Buddha statues. This is the most lavishly decorated area. Nearby is a small chapel (*hor song pha*) and a library (*hor trai*) which is a depository for sacred manuscripts and books. Most of the larger wats have an open pavilion (*sala*) which often houses a sacred bell. Architecturally plain but highly functional are the monks quarters (*kuti*).

There are distinct differences seen in the style of wats in different parts of the country. The most magnificent are to be found in the ancient capital, Luang Prabang. Roofs here are very low and are characterised by a steep upward sweeping portion which is topped by curved pointed dragon spires (*dok sofa*). Many, such as Wat Xieng Thong, have over ten of these structures, indicating that they were built by a king. Others, such as Wat Mai Suwannaphumaham, feature multi-tiered roofs which still retain the northern style. The original builders of these religious masterpieces had a fine eye for detail as well. Visitors will be mesmerised by the dazzling opulence of the gold votives, the multi-enamelled, highly colourful mosaics and the intriguing gilded reliefs seen on many of the walls.

In Vientiane the roofs are much higher, the *sims* rectangular and the doors more prominent. Here you will see the Sacred Stupa of That Luang which, with its lotus bud four-sided golden spire, must surely rank as one of the most unusual structures in the whole of Indochina.

Further south in Champassak Province you will see one of the most bizarre palaces ever built, at Paksé. Looking more like a multi-tiered wacky wedding cake than a building, this extraordinary structure was once the dream home of Prince Boun Oum.

Wat That Luang Neua

LANGUAGE

The most common language is Lao, which in many aspects is similar to Thai. Lao script is said to be a simplified version of old Siamese and contains some multisyllabic words which are similar to Khmer and Indian dialects. If you are interested in the language it is recommended that you obtain a copy of *Learning Lao for Everybody* by Klaus Werner. Most good bookshops in Bangkok will have a copy. In Vientiane it can be purchased at the Rain Tree Book Store, PO Box 456, 25 Pang Kham Road (tel/fax: 856 212031).

When travelling in Laos it is useful to know some French. Many of the Lao elite also have a good knowledge of Russian.

A few useful Lao words and phrases

How are you?	*Sa-bâi-du*
Thank you	*Khàwp jai*
I want a ticket	*Yàak dâi pû*
Where is?	*Yuu sâi?*
Do you have?	*Mú baw?*
Do you have a room?	*Mú hawng baw?*
toilet	*hàwng nâm*
hotel	*hóhng háem*
bus	*lot méh*
boat	*heúa*
market	*talàat*
post office	*pai sá nii*
doctor	*mãw*
hospital	*hóhng pha-yáa-baan*
one	*neug*
two	*sãwng*
three	*sãam*
four	*sii*
five	*hâa*
six	*hók*
seven	*jét*
eight	*páet*
nine	*kâo*
ten	*síp*
eleven	*síp-ét*
twelve	*síp-sãwng*
twenty	*sáo*
forty	*sii-síp*
fifty	*hâa-síp*
one hundred	*neung hâwy*
one thousand	*neung phán*

See also Appendix One for a glossary for use in Laos.

Part Two
Practical
Information

Chapter Eight

Getting to Laos

VISAS
Obtaining a tourist visa

You must first decide how you intend to enter Laos; the options open to you are by air, by land from Vietnam and across the Mekong River from Thailand. Before you apply for a visa read carefully the relevant section later in this chapter. You will be required to fill in three identical application forms and present three passport photographs of yourself to the agency concerned. Don't forget to STATE YOUR INTENDED ENTRY POINT on your applications. Before you leave the office make sure that the agent concerned has clearly understood your request.

In Thailand
Through a Bangkok travel agent

Make sure you don't go to a 'cowboy' agency. Because of trouble in the past since Laos opened its doors to tourism in 1989 the government has drawn up a hit list and refused to issue some agents with a 'certificate of approval'. To help you choose one which is not on the 1995-6 hit list, only approved agencies are listed. This also guards against agencies which have simply changed their names once they have been discredited.

The following are recommended.

Diethelm Travel, Kian Gwan Building 11, 140/1 Wireless Road; tel: 2559 150; fax: 2560248.

East-West Travel, 46 Soi Nana Nua, Sukhumvit; tel: 2530681.

Exotissimo Travel, 21/17 Sukhumvit Soi 4; tel: 2535240; fax: 2547683.

Inter Companion Group, 86/4 Rambuttri Rd, Banglamphu; tel: 28229400; fax: 2827316.

MK Ways, 57/11 Withayu Road (Wireless Road); tel: 21221532; fax: 2545583. Highly recommended.

Pangkaj Travel, 625 Sukhumvit Soi 22; tel: 2582240; fax: 2591261.

Siam Wings, 173/1-3 Surawong Road; tel: 2534757; fax: 2366808.

Spangle Tour, 205/1 Sathorn South Road; tel: 2121583; fax 2867732.

Thai-Indochina Supply Company, 79 Pan Road, Silom; tel: 2335369; fax: 2364389.

Transindo, 9th Floor Thasos Building, 1675 Chan Road; tel: 2873241; fax: 2873245. Highly recommended.

Vista Travel, 24/4 Khaosan Road, Banglamphu; tel: 2800348; fax: 2800348.

If you use an agent not listed here or in the back of this book ask to see an approval certificate.

The Lao approved Bangkok agencies offer a wide range of services. When you purchase your visa you will usually be required to pay for a tour. The only way around this problem is to say that you do not intend going anywhere other than Vientiane. In order to obtain as much flexibility as possible when you get to Laos, only book a short tour in Bangkok. You can then change your itinerary arrangements when you get there because you will still receive a 15-day tourist visa. This will also work out cheaper than booking all your itinerary with the Bangkok agent who must pay the Lao agent a commission on services booked.

When you book your visa you will be asked what category of service you require for your tour. This will determine what Lao agency in Vientiane you will be assigned to. For example, a customer booking a first class tour will be assigned to Diethelm Travel Laos, Namphu Square, Thanon Settathirat.

Booking the minimum two-day tour with them could set you back US$250 which includes the first night's accommodation but no flight or other transportation (except for your tour of Vientiane) (this could cost up to US$360 for a three-day tour).

A customer booking a budget tour may be assigned to: Raja Tour, 2nd Floor, Anou Hotel, Thanon Hengboun. The minimum two-day tour with them (including the cost of the visa) will work out no more than US$130. (Top price US$210 for a three-day tour.)

Both the above will of course depend on how many people book the tour in the first place. If you are travelling in a group of five, you could get away with paying just US$100 for your two day tour (US$135 for three days). In either case, when you purchase your visa STATE YOUR METHOD OF ENTRY. Allow seven days for visa processing.

Booking direct with a Vientiane agency

Booking direct will give you a visa authorisation arrangement. This means that when you arrive at Bangkok, armed with this permit you will be able to proceed to the Laotian embassy to have your passport officially stamped. The Laotian Embassy in Bangkok is at 193 Sathon Tai Road; tel: 286 0010.

To get your visa authorisation, first pick a reputable agency in Vientiane from the list in the Vientiane directory. Write to them at least three months before you intend to travel. They will reply with details of a three-day tour giving you the price and method of payment required. They will normally require you to pay a 25% deposit. Their office will require personal details for your visa:

1. Name in full
2. Nationality
3. Passport number
4. Arrival date
5. Flight number

By this method you obtain a 15-day tourist visa more cheaply than going through Bangkok or International agencies.

Some examples valid during 1995-6 period:

Diethelm Travel
Setthathirath Road, Namphu Square, PO Box 2657, Vientiane, Lao PDR; tel: 856 21 213833/215920; fax: 856 21 217151/216294; telex: 804 4351 DIET LAO LS.

Day 1 Arrival Vientiane, transfer to hotel.
Day 2 At leisure, with accommodation and breakfast.
Day 3 Breakfast at hotel, end of their services.
Prices: 1 PAX = US$204; 2 PAX = US$142/PAX; 3-5 PAX = US$124/PAX.
Hotel used - Anou or Lani Guesthouse
The one quoted is one of the cheapest available.

If paying by credit card, Diethelm Travel Laos Ltd charge 4% on Visa and nothing on American Express. They have a charge of 2% if you pay using travellers cheques. Your contact is Vilay Phiahouaphanh. Full payment will be required two weeks before travelling.

Diethelm is thoroughly reliable and highly recommended.

Lao Travel Service
08/3 Lane Xang Avenue, PO Box 2553, Vientiane, Lao PDR; tel: 856 21 216603/216604; fax: 856 21 216150; telex: 4491 4492 TEVTE LS
Three-day arrangement as above using Belvedere Hotel (best in Vientiane)
Price: 1 PAX = US$320; 2 PAX = US$230/PAX; 3-5 PAX = US$196/PAX.

They require 25% deposit on booking. This must be sent to A/c No. 5490-1-191 Banque pour le Commerce Exterieur Lao in Vientiane. Full payment is required two weeks before arrival. Your contact is Hoth Phanivong. Cheaper arrangements for Visa authorisation are available using other accommodation. This company will not normally use third class hotels. They are extremely helpful but incredibly slow. (Laos operates at a different pace to the rest of the world!)

Lanexang Travel and Tour Co. Ltd
Head Office, Pangkham Road, PO Box 4452, Vientiane; tel: 856 21 5804/2469; fax: 856 21 5804; telex: 4360 LANTRAV LS VIENTIANE.

Day 1 Transfer from airport or Mekong bridge to hotel Ekarat. Overnight accommodation.
Day 2 Half day tour of the city. Service ends.

	1 PAX	2 PAX	3-6 PAX	7-9 PAX	10-14 PAX	Sup. Sgl.
US$/PAX	240	160	130	110	100	26

Deposit required is 50% of total price. Payment is required by registered mail to Lanexang Travel PO Box 4452, Pangkham Road, Vientiane. Visa authorisation will be sent within three days of receipt. Full payment is required two weeks before arrival.

If you have limited time or don't want the inconvenience of getting your authorisation stamped in your passport in Bangkok, this company will arrange for your visa to be picked up at Vientiane airport for an extra US$32.

Sodetour-Fimoxy Co. Ltd
114 Quai Fa-Ngum, PO Box 70, Vientiane; tel: 856 21 21 6313/21 54 89; fax: 856 21 21 63 14, Telex: 4314 PA CLAO LS.

They can match Diethelm Travel's price for three-day stay with visa authorisation. They can also arrange for visa to be picked up at Vientiane airport for extra cost (add about US$30). Tourists with very limited time may be interested in the tour below, which will, of course, offer visa authorisation.

3 days/2 nights - Sodetour's ref: SVL-02

Day 1	Arrival at Vientiane or via Tha Deua. Flight to Luang Prabang. Upon arrival excursion by boat on the Mekong River to Pak Ou Caves.
Day 2	Sightseeing tour of Luang Prabang. Return flight to Vientiane.
Day 3	Sightseeing tour of Vientiane. Afternoon transfer to airport or bridge over Mekong.

	1 PAX	2 PAX	3 PAX	4-6 PAX	7-9 PAX	10-14 PAX	Sup. Sgl.
US$/PAX	672	396	341	295	267	257	62

Deposit 50% on booking payable at above by registered post. Visa authorisation will follow. Full payment required two weeks before arrival. Highly recommended company with considerable experience. Your contacts in Vientiane are Claude Vincent and Céline.

Raja Tour

Anou Hotel (2nd Floor), 1-3 Hengbourn Street, Vientiane PO Box 3655; tel: 856 21 21 3634; fax: 856 21 21 3635; telex: 4492 TE VTE LS.

This is the only company that I know of that will sell you a visa authorisation permit by itself (no hotel or tour requirement). Your contact in Vientiane is Outsama Souvannasing (Mr).

This currently costs US$40. If you don't want the inconvenience of getting the visa stamped in Bangkok, they will arrange for it to be done at the Friendship Bridge or at Wattay airport. They charge an extra US$30 for this service (around 750 baht). If you want an extension on the standard 15 days, Raja Tours will arrange this for US$3/day (up to another 15 days). They offer very good hotel rates which can be added to the above authorisation as a package. Prices in US$.

Province	Hotel	Standard Room			Meals	
		Single	Twin	ABF	Lunch	Dinner
Vientiane	Anou Hotel	18	24	4	8	9
	Asian Pavillion	44	44	6	9	11
	New Apollo	50	60	Incl.	10	13
	Lanexang	49	64	Incl.	10	10
	The Belvedere	59	80	Incl.	15	17
Luang Prabang	Phousi Hotel	20	20	5	7	7
	New Laungprab.	26	32	5	7	7
	Villa Princess	42	42	6	10	10
	Phou Vao Hotel	58	58	6	10	10
Xieng Khouang	Phou Pha Deng	42	42	6	10	10
	Mitaphab	20	20	6	8	8

A 50% deposit is payable on packages but a 100% payment must be made for authorisation alone.

Through a Nong Khai agency

A traveller entering Laos in March 1994 using the Nong Khai ferry route recommended **Nalumon Tour**, Prasisani Road; tel: 42412565; fax: 42412565. One specialising in business visas but also processing tourist visas is **Udorn Business Travel**, 447/10 Haisok Road; tel: 42411393.

Because of the extra business generated by the building of the Mittaphap Bridge across the Mekong, many guest houses in Nong Khai offer a visa processing service. These include a reliable Australian-owned one called The Meeting Place, Soi Chuenjit; tel: 42412644; fax: 42412644. As well as a tourist visa processing facility they also arrange business visas.

Processing takes five to seven days and costs US$90-120. It includes first night accommodation. Add US$45 for express service (two days).

Through an Ubon Ratchathani agency

The crossing from the west bank to Paksé on the east bank is now open to tourism. The best place to get a visa endorsed for this crossing is Ubon Ratchathani. Currently two tour agencies in this town handle visa processing. The visa must be endorsed with Kaeng Tana (which is the entry point into Laos):

Aranya Tour, 105 Makkaeng Road. Tel: 42247320.

Kannika Tour, 36 Sisattha Road. Tel: 42241378.

If you intend to cross here allow about six days for visa processing. Since there is not much to see in the area it would be better if you requested this border crossing in a Bangkok agency. An express service is available but it involves being parted from your passport for two to three days. Agencies in Udon will allocate you to Sodetour in Paksé. This is quite an expensive agency but can arrange tours to most places in Laos which are open to foreigners. They can also arrange business visas. The clientele here is predominantly Thai; foreigners are very welcome to use their services. This entry route is not recommended. A traveller in October 1994 reported that visa authorisation by Sodetour in Paksé was only being given to Thai clients. Westerners were told that it could only be used as an exit point from Laos. Many westerners have however entered Laos via this route.

Visas for other crossings

Foreigners are allowed to cross the Mekong from:

Mukdahan to Savannakhét

There are currently no agencies in Mukdahan to endorse this crossing on your entry visa. The Bangkok agencies listed should be able to handle it. You will probably be assigned to Inter-Lao Tourisme or Diethelm Travel Laos who have representatives with Savannakhét Tourism in Savannakhét. Book your visa with Diethelm in Bangkok to be certain of getting a Mukdahan/Savannakhét endorsement. It is risky to try to get this endorsement in Udon Ratchathani.

There is a rumour that a bridge may soon be built across the Mekong at this point to allow more direct access to the Lao Bao entry point into Vietnam.

Chiang Khong to Ban Houayxay

This border crossing was opened to foreigners in March 1994. Previously it had only been used as an exit point from Laos. Diethelm Travel in Bangkok can organise a visa endorsed Ban Houayxay because they now have a branch office open in Luang Prabang. They can also arrange for you to travel by fast speedboat from Ban Houayxay to Luang Prabang (over 300km). It is often impossible to use the road between this crossing and Muang Pakbéng because during the rainy season (May to November) it is sometimes just a mud puddle. Slow boats also travel this route and take two days to get to Luang Prabang. From July 1994 Explore Worldwide used the Ban Houayxay crossing to exit from Laos.

Nakhon Phanom to Tha Khaek
This can only be used by westerners as an exit point from Laos.

Crossings which cannot be used by foreigners exiting Thailand
Sang Khom to Ban Pak Ton
Bun Kan to Muang Paksane
Tha Uthen to Muang Hinboun
Khemmarat to Ban Na Muang
Muang Không to Hatxaykhoun

Embassy visas
In Thailand
Laotian visa applications by individuals are not accepted unless they have a letter of authorisation from a Laotian Tour Company or it's for a business visa when the application must be supported by a Laotian sponsor. All tour agencies get tourist visas processed by the Laotian embassy in Bangkok.

In Vietnam
In Ho Chi Minh City
Laotian visas are issued at the Laotian embassy in Ho Chi Minh within a few hours of application. Three application forms are required to be filled in and three passport photographs must be presented. The visa issued will be a transit visa, valid for five days unless you ask for a full visa. Remember that it could prove impossible to extend a transit visa in Vientiane. The transit visa costs US$15 and the full visa US$30 (valid for 15 days).

Laotian Embassy, 181 Hai Ba Trung Street, District 3; tel: 297667. It's open from 08.00 to 11.00 and 14.00 to 16.30 (Mon to Fri).

If you experience difficulty in obtaining a full visa use one of the reputable travel agencies in Ho Chi Minh.

In Hanoi
The Laotian embassy in Hanoi is on the 2nd Floor at 22 Tran Binh Trong Street; tel: 254576. Same opening hours as above. They issue five-day transit visas very quickly but a full visa could require the help of a reputable travel agency and take several days. Prices are similar to the above.

If you want to enter Laos via the Lao Bao entry point, north of Hue, get your visa stamped Lao/Bao entry. This opened in December 1993. You may find that the Laotian consulate will refuse to endorse this on your visa. If they don't you can't try this method of entry. A traveller who tried this in February 1994 in the Hanoi Embassy was forced to fly!

In Cambodia
In Phnom Penh
The Laotian embassy is at 111 214 Street; tel: 25181. Transit visas are issued within hours (valid for five days). They cost US$15. Full visas are generally only issued if you apply for a business visa and you have an official sponsor in Laos. It could take you weeks to sort out.

Worldwide agency visas
In Britain
Regent Holidays (UK) Ltd, 15 John Street, Bristol BS1 2HR; tel: 0117 921 1711 (24 hrs); fax: 0117 925 4866
Regent will obtain visa authorisation on your behalf. You must however be prepared to book a short tour with them. They offer a five day itinerary for US$:

1 PAX	2 PAX	3 PAX	4-6 PAX
815	574	521	471

The visa for this itinerary is charged at £25. It can be picked up on arrival in Vientiane. (A shorter tour is available on request.)

Explore Worldwide, 1 Frederick Street, Aldershot, Hants GU11 1LQ; tel: 01252 319448; fax: 01252 343170; telex: 858954 (EXPLOR G).
Explore Worldwide can be contacted through representative offices on toll free numbers. In USA tel: 800 227 8747. In Australia tel: 008 221 931. In New Zealand toll free fax: 0800 652 954. In Canada tel: 1-800-661-7265.

To obtain a Laotian visa through Explore it is necessary to book a tour.

There are other agencies in the UK which offer visa processing for Laos.

In Australia
Orbitours PTY Ltd, 3rd Floor, 73 Walker Street, North Sydney NSW 2060. PO Box 834 North Sydney NSW 2059 Australia; tel: 612 954 1399; fax: 612 954 1655. American clients can use toll free tel: (800) 235-5895. Australian clients can use the toll free tel: 008-221-796. They can also be contacted at Melbourne, tel: (03) 670 7071.

To obtain the Laotian visa you must book a tour (see tour section for what is available). Their cheapest tour for the 1995-6 season is three days/two nights in Vientiane. Cost for backpackers in a twin share is A$254. With first class accommodation the cost rises to A$399 using Lanexang Hotel and A$459 using the deluxe Belvedere Hotel. In each case you will be provided with a 15 day tourist visa. When applying you will need four passport photographs. Allow them at least one month to process your visa. This company has considerable experience and is very highly recommended.

In the USA
The cheapest way of getting a 15-day Laotian visa is to book a three day/two night Vientiane tour with **Lao Travel (America)**, 338 S Hancock Avenue, South Elgin, 1L 60177; tel: (708) 742 2159; fax: 742 432.

Their cheapest offer for backpackers for the 1995-6 season was US$150. Using the Belvedere Hotel in Vientiane the price doubles to US$310.

Another fairly cheap agency is **Budgetour International**, 8907 Westminster Avenue, Garden Grove, CA 92644; tel: (714) 2216539.

Since the lifting of the American embargo on Vietnam, they have been offering some good deals on complete Indochina tours. They will arrange a Laotian visa as long as they are given at least six weeks' notice. You will be required to book a short tour to secure the visa.

In Hong Kong

Renowned for its budget prices is **Phoenix Services Agency**, Room B, 6/F Milton Mansion, 96 Nathan Road, Kowloon, Hong Kong; tel: 7227378 (5 lines); fax: (852) 3698884; telex: 31671 PHNX HX is very highly recommended.

Contact Becky Bale or the intrepid Lisa Humphries. They can arrange visa authorisation through Christian Piantoni at Fimoxy-Sodetour, Wanchai, who has a contact in the Sodetour office in Vientiane. Becky tells me that if you want to get authorisation on your Laotian visa in Hong Kong you will have to book a two-night package with Phoenix Services. This will cost US$250-290 per person according to accommodation package. It includes transport from the airport into Vientiane.

Phoenix can also arrange a visa for entry via Yunnan through the Botén checkpoint. Clients should however realise that this entry point is difficult in bad weather (June-October) because of mud problems on roads extending through Muang Namo to Luang Prabang. Allow plenty of time for Phoenix to process your requirements.

In Vietnam

The most experienced agency offering Lao visa processing is **Saigon Tourist Travel Service**. They can be contacted at 49 Le Thanh Ton, Ho Chi Minh City; tel: (84-8) 298914-298129-230102; fax: (84-8)-224987-225516; telex: 812745 SGTOUR-VT.

Saigon Tourist Hanoi Branch, Hotel Saigon, 80 Ly Thuong Kiet Street; tel: (84-4) 268501-268502-268503 Ext 339; fax: (84-4) 266631; telex: 411259 SGNHOT-VT.

Their representative in Hamburg can also offer visa processing for Laos, Hamburger Str 132, 2000 Hamburg 76, Postfach 761163 Hamburg, Germany; tel: (49-40) 295345; fax: (49-40) 296705; telex: 213968 HT D.

In the Vietnam branches they require only two days to process a Laotian visa. In Germany you should apply at least three weeks before going. The cheapest option that you can book with them to acquire the 15-day Lao visa is four days/three nights in Vientiane. The 1995-6 price for this is US$714 for two people travelling together. This includes the return flight to Vietnam and a stay at the Ekalath Hotel in Vientiane. Cheaper options are available if continuing into Thailand. If you do take up this offer make sure when you book that they don't issue you a transit visa which will restrict your stay in Laos to five days. You would probably have to cross to Nong Khai to renew this since strictly it is not a visa at all. For other options see tour section.

Other visas

Business visas

Before you can obtain a business visa you must have an official invitation to travel to Laos from a Laotian businessman. Armed with this you can then apply for a 30-day visa at the Laotian embassy in Bangkok or any Laotian embassy worldwide. Embassy visas are nearly always granted to businessmen with letters of introduction.

Embassies worldwide

Australia	1 Dalman Crescent, O'Malley, Canberra, ACT 2606.
Germany	1100 Berlin Esplanade 17, Berlin.
France	74 Av Raymond Poincaré, 75116 Paris.
India	7 West End Clony, New Delhi 110021.
Japan	3-21, 3-Chome, Nishi Azabu, Minato-ku, Tokyo.
Russia	Sis 18, Katchalova, Moscow.
Thailand	193 Sathon Tai Road.
USA	2222 S St NW, Washington DC 20008.

Once you are inside Laos, business visas can be extended indefinitely. They entitle the holder to be granted a maximum stay of 15 days in any one province. After this the permit must be renewed. Embassy-granted business visas cost US$12. One of the most convenient ways of arranging a business visa, which is more expensive than going through an embassy direct, is to contact either: **Aerocontact Asia**, 2/4 Thanon Manthatulat, PO Box 4300, Vientiane; tel: 17 8177; fax: 21 9332 or **Lao Investment Promotion Corporation** (LIPCO), Building 1, Thanon Luang Prabang, PO Box 795; tel: 16 9645; fax: 16 9646/4163.

The usual procedure is to fax your letter of introduction through to their Vientiane office. State briefly your business intention. Both agencies charge US$60 for this service. Visa processing takes only a few days. When you arrive at Wattay Airport, Vientiane, the authorities will already be expecting you and will issue a 30 day business visa on the spot.

Your chosen agency will, at your request, have a representative waiting to meet you at the airport. He will have arranged your first night's accommodation and will be responsible for you throughout your stay. Should you require modern business facilities at your finger tips you will be allocated to stay in the Belvedere Hotel in Vientiane which has a fully equipped business centre, word processor facilities, fax, IDD etc. They will even provide you with a secretary if you wish.

Business visas from Nong Khai

If you are having a brief holiday in northern Thailand you may prefer to arrange your business visa via a reliable agency in Nong Khai. You should, however, be warned that although this service is reliable, it could cost you US$100 for a 30-day visa. A reliable agency for this is: **Udorn Business Travel**, 447/10 Haisok Road, Nong Khai; tel: 411 393.

Journalist and voluntary workers visa

Journalists can apply to the same agencies which deal with business visas in Vientiane. They will need to fax through a brief résumé. A form will be faxed back which requires more details. Once this is sent off one can but wait for a reply. Visas for journalists are issued for 30 days and can be extended quite easily for another 30 days. If the authorities are not satisfied with the purpose of the visit they can of course refuse to issue one. Personally I would advise entry on a normal tourist visa. Journalist visas cost the same as those for visiting expatriates and voluntary aid workers who apply for a non-immigration visa. The cost is US$35.

Extending a journalist and voluntary workers visa

Apply to the Immigration Office, Laotian Ministry of Interior, Thanon Talaat Sao. This is fairly close to the Morning Market in Vientiane. Tourists are advised to get their allocated agency to sort this out for them. If you are travelling on a transit visa don't bother to go to this office. You will need to leave the country and re-apply in Nong Khai. An express service for this exists, any of the listed agencies in Nong Khai can sort it out for you. You will be parted from your passport for two days, and will need three passport photographs. The fee is US$40 on top of what you would pay for a normal package (see Nong Khai entry).

Visitors travelling on a journalist or voluntary workers non-immigrant visa will be granted an extension of 30 days at this office. The fee is US$35. It opens from 08.00-11.00 and 14.00-17.00 (Mon-Fri).

Obtaining a Thai visa in Laos

If you are not travelling on a multiple entry visa when you leave Laos you will of course have to obtain another Thai visa if you intend staying in the kingdom for more than 15 days. The Thai authorities are generally very lenient to foreigners who overstay this period by a few days. You may pick up a small fine at the airport but this will work out cheaper than obtaining a new visa.

Re-entry visas

If you intend returning to Laos after visiting another country you will need a new visa. In Vietnam this can only be obtained in Hanoi and Ho Chi Minh City. In both places, as well as in Phnom Penh, you will probably be given a transit visa. In Ho Chi Minh it is easier to obtain a full 15-day visa, especially if you go through an established agent.

Immigration and customs

Imports

Tourists are authorised to import the following duty free:

Cigarettes 200
Cigars 50
Liquor 1 litre
small gift items not exceeding the value of US$50

Travellers are not allowed to bring more than 100,000 baht into Laos.
The following items are banned completely:

weapons
explosives
inflammable objects
narcotics
pornographic books.

Exports

Goods of a limited commercial value may be exported without a permit. High value goods require an export permit. High value antiques are not allowed to be exported.

GETTING THERE
By air
International flights with transfer connections to Vientiane

Flights to Vientiane via Bangkok are available with Alitalia, British Airways, Eva Airways, Malaysian Airways and Thai Airways from a number of departure points. By using one or other of them you can arrange to land in Vientiane at any day of the week.

All transfer connection flights connect with either Lao Aviation or Thai Airways International.

Ticketing and reservations on Lao Aviation can be made:

In Europe

Berlin	Muller and Partners	(37 (49) 30 282 3262
Paris	Lao Aviation	(1) 4366 7633
Milan	Vivitours	(02) 657 0441

In North America

Toronto	Central Travel	416 531 4467
Calgary	Skyplan	403 250 1605
Fresno	Classic Travel	209 266 6775
Illinois	Lao America	708 742 2159

In Asia

Bangkok	Lao Aviation Branch	236 9822
Phnom Penh	Kampuchea Airlines	25 887
Ho Chi Minh City	Vietnam Airlines	(8) 53 842
		(8) 292 118
		(8) 230 696 8
Singapore	Maple Aviation	538 5515
Kuala Lumpur	GSA Shoppe	441 1913
Hong Kong	CTAS	(852) 853 3488
		(852) 853 3888
		(852) 853 3468
Taipei	Vientiane Corp	(02) 732 1676
Tokyo	Transindo	(3) 3453
	Apex International	(813) 3350

In Australia

Sydney	Orbitours	(02) 221 7322

Direct flights to Vientiane

From	Carrier	Frequency	Depart	Arrive	Cost (US$)
Bangkok (Thailand)	Lao Aviation	Mon, Tue	10.30	11.30	
		Tue	16.00	17.00	125
		Wed	16.00	17.00	
		Thu	16.00	17.00	
		Fri	16.00	17.00	
	Thai Airways International	Tue, Thu, Sat & Sun	10.30	11.35	237
Hanoi (Vietnam)	Lao Aviation	Tue	11.00	12.00	90
	Vietnam Airlines	Sun	11.00	11.55	
		Mon & Thu	11.00	11.55	
Ho Chi Minh (Vietnam)	Vietnam Airlines	Sun	08.00	11.55	190
Kunming (China)	China Southern Airlines	Thu	11.40	12.10	202
Phnom Penh (Cambodia)	Lao Aviation	Fri	11.25	12.55	160

Direct flights from Vientiane

To	Carrier	Frequency	Depart	Arrive	Cost (US$)
Bangkok (Thailand)	Lao Aviation	Mon	08.30	09.30	125
		Tue, Wed, Thu & Fri	14.00	15.00	
	Thai Airways International	Tue, Thu, Sat & Sun	12.35	13.35	237
Hanoi (Vietnam)	Lao Aviation	Tue	09.00	10.00	90
		Mon & Thu	13.00	13.50	
	Vietnam Airlines	Sun	13.00	13.50	110
Ho Chi Minh (Vietnam)	Lao Aviation	Fri	07.00	08.50	170
	Vietnam Airlines	Sun	13.00	17.00	190
Kunming (China)	China Southern Airlines	Thu	13.25	15.55	202
Phnom Penh (Cambodia)	Lao Aviation	Fri	07.00	10.25	160

Airport tax
Airport departure tax is US$6.

By land
Through Thailand
Exciting future trends
The 1995-8 period will be a hectic time for Lao National Tourism. Already the 1,174m Saphan Mittaphap Bridge, which extends from Hat Jommani (near Nong Khai) to Tha Naleng on the Laotian side, is complete. It opened in mid-April 1994. This US$35m project was financed by the Australian government and is managed jointly by Thailand and Laos. Known as the Thai-Lao Friendship Bridge, it will no doubt give a considerable economic boost to developments on both sides of the Mekong. Before very long, when the 624km rail link through Khorat, Khon Kaen and Udon Thani to Nong Khai is extended across the Mekong, visitors will be able to travel by train from Bangkok to Vientiane. Much more is planned for the future. Already underway is a massive project which will link Vientiane with China's Yunnan Province and Vietnam's Quang Tri Province via two separate Trans Laotian Highways. To link with the bridge, road developments to the north of Vientiane have already progressed well beyond Muang Kasi. The massive finance for the project has been provided by the Asian Development Bank, which has made a loan of US$39 million available, and the Swedish government who have also donated millions and had the area surveyed as early as 1992.

By 1997 it is expected that tourists will be able to enjoy non-stop scenic entertainment from Nong Khai via Luang Prabang right through to the Chinese border at Botén and beyond. Here the Trans Laotian Highway running through remote Luang Nam Tha Province will join the Xieng Khouang-Oudomsay Chinese Highway running through Yunnan. There is also a rumour that the road between Phou Khoun (midway between Vang Vieng and Luang Prabang) and Vinh in Vietnam will be surfaced by late 1998-9. This will provide yet another crossing point via the border at Tha Khaek. At the moment this tortuous road through the Xieng Khouang Plateau is nothing but a glorified mud track, especially between Ban Ban and Nong Hét.

Developments in southern Laos are also well underway. The road between Vientiane and Savannakhét has already been improved but still needs massive attention. Another bridge is planned to span the Mekong between Mukdahan and Savannakhét which will give direct route access via Yasothon and Khorat (Nakon Ratchasima) to Bangkok. Long distance buses should eventually be able to cross the Mekong here and drive via Xeno, Muang Phin and Ban Dong to the Vietnamese border at Lao Bao. This route is expected to be completely paved by 1998. Exciting plans are also underway to improve the road which runs from Paksé through the Bolovens Plateau to the Vietnamese border at Plei Can. This road, which links southern Laos with the Central Highlands in Vietnam, will provide another route through to Danang.

What's available during the 1995-6 period?
The Mittaphap Bridge crossing
This is close to Nong Khai where visa processing facilities are available. It opened in mid-April 1994.

Getting there
The 624km journey takes just ten hours from Bangkok's Pahaholyothin Road long distance bus station. It is a four hour journey from Khorat and a 1¼ hour journey from Udon. There are regular train services from Bangkok's Hualamphong Station on Rama IV Road.

Accommodation in Nong Khai
There are many cheap guest houses if you wish to stay in the area while your visa is being processed. These include the **Sukhaphan** on Bamtoengit Road, the **Poonsup** on Meechai Road, the **Prajak** at 1178 Prajak Road and the **Mekong Guest House** (one of the best) on the river front. They are all in the US$10/night bracket.

Crossing into Laos
Remember that your visa must be endorsed 'via Nong Khai'. One of the most convenient ways is to walk; after clearing customs there will be buses and taxis to take you to Vientiane. Both Diethelm Travel and Sodetour can arrange visa authorisation for entry at this point.

The Ubon Ratchathani crossing
You will see in the visa section that this is not recommended. Ubon Ratchathani where Lao visa processing is available is close to Kaeng Tana (Thai/Lao border) where you can take a taxi to the ferry crossing point to Paksé. War buffs may be interested in the fact that during the Vietnam War countless B52 sorties were flown from the US airbase here against the Ho Chi Minh trail.

Getting there
Overnight express buses leave from Pahaholyothin Road in Bangkok taking 11 hours. It takes just 3½ hours by bus from Khorat. There is also a rail link from Hualamphong Railway Station in Bangkok.

Accommodation
Should you wish to stay in the area before crossing to Laos you can sleep at either the Saiwong Hotel on Aduluadet Road, the Queen Hotel at 6-8 Udorn-dutsadi Road or the Saiwong at 39 Adulyadet Road. It should be mentioned again that there is not much in this area to interest tourists. My recommendation would be to get your visa endorsed for this crossing in Bangkok and go straight across.

Crossing
The ferry between the west bank and the east bank runs fairly frequently. Passengers are charged 30 baht. To get to the crossing point from Ubon Ratchathani you will need to take a shared taxi which travels first to Phibun Mangsahan, skirts the Shirintham Reservoir and then heads for the Laos border at Kaeng Tana. There are taxis usually waiting to take you from the Thai/Laos border at Kaeng Tana via Muang Phônthong to the ferry. Expect to pay about 35 baht. If the ferry is not running (they generally take a rest from 11.00 to 14.00) you can hire a boat to take you across for about 60 baht. The ferry does not run on a Sunday.
    Remember that you must have Paksé endorsed on your visa to make this crossing.

Mukdahan to Savannakhét
Getting there and accommodation
There are regular shared taxis from Ubon Ratchathani to Mukdahan. Expect to pay 80 baht. You could hire one yourself for about 700 baht. If you want to stay in the area it is better to overnight in Ubon Ratchathani.

Crossing into Laos
Ferries leave at regular intervals between 08.00-11.00 and 14.00-17.00. During busy periods they will operate without a break. The charge is 35 baht for the crossing and 10 baht departure tax. The Laotian officials on the Salvan side have been known to charge foreigners for their services. Remember that you need a Salvan endorsement.

Chiang Khong to Ban Houayxay
Very few foreigners have used this method of entry into Laos. If there is trouble in Bokeo Province, the authorities will close this point of entry off to foreigners.

Getting there and accommodation
You must first get to Chiang Rai in the extreme north of Thailand. This takes 12 hours on a long distance bus from Pahaholyothin Road Bus Station in Bangkok. It costs 250 baht. A flight from Bangkok costs 2,500 baht and takes one hour twenty minutes. To get to the border at Chiang Không take a *songthaew*. Expect to pay about 70 baht. If you need to stay in the area, good budget hotels (about US$5/night) include: **Lek House** (95 Thanalai Road), **Moon Guest House** (345 Kohloy Road) and **Gerd House** (717/1 Seegard Road). It is far better to stay in one of these than to try to find good accommodation in Chiang Khong. Check with the tourism authority on Singhaklai Road that the border is open before proceeding.

Crossing into Laos
Private boats are available for the short crossing.

From Vietnam
Although the Lao Bao border crossing opened in December 1993, it is very difficult to get this endorsed on your Lao visa. At the Laotian embassy in Hanoi they will tell you to fly and won't give you a visa at all until you show them your flight ticket. Your best bet is to try Saigon Tourist in Ho Chi Minh. If they can't do it, nobody can. If you can't get the endorsement it is pointless to try this entry point.

If you are travelling in Laos before entering Vietnam and want to return via Lao Bao, this can be arranged. When you are in Savannakhét go to the Vietnamese consulate on Thanon Sisavangvong. Tell them what you intend to do. It would probably be better if you entered Vietnam by the Lao Bao route as well. For this, once you have sorted a re-entry visa out with the consulate, go to the Savannakhét Tourism office in the Savanbanhao Hotel. They can arrange your transport to the border and a permit for travelling through Xeno, Phalan, Muang Phin and Ban Dong. They can also arrange for a permit to be issued by the Lao Bao immigrations on your return. Complicated old world isn't it!

THE BORDER AT THA KHAEK (the entry point from Vinh) AND THE BORDER AT PLEI CAN (in the Central Highlands) ARE CLOSED TO FOREIGNERS.

One of the nearest crossing points into Laos from Hanoi for the Vietnamese is at Muong Lat, which is reached via a rough road from Hoa Binh into the town of Sop Hao. It is extremely unlikely that any foreigner would be allowed to enter Laos here. You may be able to travel by 4WD from Phônsavan via Xam Neua (Sam Neua) to Sop Hao, but check first to see if legally permitted. This is likely to become easier when the roads improve in the future.

From China

This entry point into Luang Nam Tha Province can be used by Chinese and westerners providing the mud road is passable. Laotians can obtain the necessary permits to cross into China via Botén.

The Phôngsali entry point into Laos from Mengla in Yunnan is open to Chinese and Laotians with the necessary papers. Currently it is closed to foreigners. Once the northern section of the Trans-Laotian Highway is completed (1996), this could be a common entry point.

Chapter Nine

Transport and Communications within Laos

Travelling inside Laos
More red tape
Lao National Tourism is extremely keen to preserve their country's independence and ancestral way of life. The country's relative inaccessibility to mass tourism to a certain extent safeguards its profoundly religious people from the influence of the west. No strict quota is imposed on the number of tourists allowed to enter as in Bhutan but certain rules help to keep the country blissfully unspoilt. Even when the new network of roads is complete, the system will go a long way to preserving the people's cultural identity. If you make a request that is not granted, then accept it. At all times behave gracefully, dress respectfully and never abuse the privileges that you have been granted.

Rules and regulations
All visitors, when being assigned tour programmes, will be asked to state their preferences. Not all agencies will be able to offer the same option packages. If you have been assigned to an agency that only offers tours to Luang Prabang then this agency will only be able to issue you with a permit to travel there. You will not be able to walk out of the office and just sign on with another agency.

If you want to travel to as many places as possible in Laos, make sure you either:
1. Book a tour with a foreign company offering an extensive itinerary.
2. Go through an agency in Bangkok which will allow you to be assigned to an agency in Laos which has contacts throughout the country. A good one for this in Bangkok is Diethelm Travel, who have their own agency in Vientiane and Luang Prabang. Another good agency to be assigned to in Vientiane is Sodetour, which has offices in Luang Prabang, Paksé, Savannakhét, Bokeo and Xieng Khouane.
3. Get a visa for Laos which doesn't restrict you to any agency, then shop around in Vientiane until you find the one which caters for your needs.
4. Get a business visa. Armed with this you will be free to ask for a programme to almost anywhere in the country.

Lao Aviation domestic flights
The prices quoted are return fares.

From	Destination	Frequency	Depart	Arrive	Cost (US$)
Houayxay	Vientiane	Tue, Thu & Sat	10.15	11.50	180
Luang Nam Tha	Vientiane	Wed & Sat	12.45	13.45	162
Luang Prabang	Vientiane	Wed & Sat	15.55	16.35	
		Sat	14.25	15.05	92
		Mon, Tue, Thu & Fri	13.25	14.05	
Oudomsay	Vientiane	Mon, Wed & Fri	13.00	14.20	145
Paksé	Vientiane	Mon Tue, Thu & Fri	09.10	11.35	190
		Sat	09.10	10.35	
	Savannakhét	Mon & Thu	09.10	09.45	42
Saravane	Vientiane	Sun	10.10	12.35	187
	Savannakhét	Sun	10.10	10.50	38
Savannakhét	Vientiane	Wed	08.45	09.20	
		Mon & Thu	10.30	11.30	122
		Sun	11.35	12.35	
	Paksé	Tue & Fri	08.45	09.20	42
	Saravane	Sun	08.45	09.25	38
Sayaboury	Vientiane	Tue, Thu & Sat	12.25	13.10	71
Thakhek	Vientiane	Fri	08.40	09.40	115
Vientiane	Houayxay	Tue, Thu & Sat	08.00	09.35	180
	Luang Nam Tha	Wed & Sat	11.00	12.00	162
	Luang Prabang	Wed & Sat	14.30	15.10	
		Sun	13.00	13.40	92
		Mon, Tue, Thu & Fri	12.00	12.40	
	Oudomsay	Mon, Wed & Fri	11.00	12.20	145
	Paksé	Mon, Thu & Sat	07.00	08.25	
		Tue & Fri	07.00	09.20	190
	Saravane	Sun	07.00	09.25	187
	Savannakhét	Tue, Wed, Fri & Sun	07.00	08.00	122
	Sayaboury	Tue, Thu & Sat	11.00	11.45	71
	Thakhek	Fri	07.00	8.00	115
	Xieng Khouane	Daily	08.10	09.00	
		Daily	10.40	11.30	
		Daily	13.10	14.00	75
		Tue, Thu & Sun	14.30	15.20	
		Tue, Thu, Fri & Sat	15.30	16.20	
Xieng Khouane	Vientiane	Daily	08.10	09.00	
		Daily	10.40	11.30	
		Daily	13.10	14.00	75
		Tue, Thu & Sun	14.30	15.20	
		Tue, Thu, Fri & Sat	15.30	16.20	

Air travel inside Laos

Foreigners may be charged a higher ticket price than Laotians pay. There is no way around this problem, if you want to travel then you will have to pay the foreigner's rate. The reason for this is that Laotian fares are subsidised by the government. The domestic air departure tax is US$5. The prices charged by the various tour agencies may vary slightly from the prices shown in the table. An example is given below:

Destination (Round Trip)	Lao Aviation New Price 1995/96	Raja Tours 1995/96 Selling Price
Vientiane - Luang Prabang - Vientiane	$92	$96
Vientiane - Xieng Khouane - Vientiane	$75	$79
Vientiane - Savannakhét - Vientiane	$122	$126
Vientiane - Paksé - Vientiane	$190	$195

Lao Aviation Domestic also has irregular flights from:

From	To	Cost (US$)
Vientiane	Attopeu	265
	Khammouane	104
	Muang Không	262
	Phongsali	179
Luang Prabang	Luang Nam Tha	35
	Oudomsay	26
	Phongsali	43
	Houayxay	43
	Xieng Khouane	32
	Xam Neua	44)
Savannakhét	Attopeu	65
	Muang Không	68
	Wat Phou	51

Land travel in Laos

By car or jeep

Your agency will rent you a car. Alternatively you can hire one at the:
  Belvedere Hotel, Thanon Luang Prabang; tel: 856 21 21 3570/4.
  The Lane Xang Hotel, Thanon Fa Ngum; tel: 856 21 21 4101/04/06/07.
  Lao Survey Exploration Service, 66 Thanon Setthathirat; tel: 856 21 17 8704.
  Vientiane International Consultants, Thanon Samsenthai; tel: 856 21 17 3106.
  Burapha, 14 Quaiu Fa Ngum; tel: 856 21 17 5071/2604.
  Types of vehicles available include Toyotas, Peugeots (about US$35 per day), Volvos, Landcruisers and Jeeps (about US$50-55 per day).

From the classy hotels you are more likely to be offered a Mercedes 230E or a luxury Nissan (about US$55-65 per day). Petrol costs 350 kip/litre for super and 280 kip/litre for regular. It is normal practice for the rental agency to provide a driver for long distance travel. The type of vehicle rented will obviously depend on where you want to go. There are restrictions to where you can travel during the rainy season, even with 4WD.

Outside Vientiane, agencies with representatives in other provinces will arrange car or jeep hire.

It should also be pointed out that cars and jeeps are normally hired out to tourists who have paid for travel packages. The package will of course include the cost of the hire, driver and the driver's accommodation and meals. If you can arrange your own unique itinerary, which is very possible if you are travelling on a business visa, then you will be responsible for the expenses incurred by your driver, your agency representative and any extras. Your agency will present you with a breakdown of these expenses on request.

Driving

Take extra care when rounding corners since it is quite common for Laotian drivers to overtake on them. If you are wondering where the speed restriction signs are, there aren't any. Don't copy the locals, who think nothing of going through a red light. If the road is wide enough, Laotian drivers will overtake you even when something is coming, The police in Laos are very unlikely to book you for a minor offence – which in a European country may be considered to be a major offence and carry a hefty penalty.

Roads open to foreigners

Central Laos

Anywhere in **Vientiane Province**.

Paksane in Borikhamsay Province. This 155km journey takes about five hours.

Thakhek in Khammouane Province. This 360km journey takes about ten hours.

Neither Paksane nor Thakhek is a popular tourist destination.

Further south

Savannakhét (Muang Savan) in Savannakhét Province: 490km journey of around 13-14 hours. At Savannakhét there is a tourist office in the Savanbanhao Hotel where you can arrange to visit the surrounding countryside. If you want to travel to Xépôn, which is situated close to the Ho Chi Minh Trail, then you will be crossing the provincial border.

Saravane in Saravane Province. The route which will be chosen by your driver will probably be Highway Number 13, which in recent years has been repaired. This route will take you via Ban Nakala and Ban Xébang-Nouan to Muang Khôngsedon. You will continue to Paksé across the border into Champassak Province. From Paksé your driver will take you via Laongam and Ban Laongam to Saravane. The route taken from Savannakhét will depend on the season of travel and what vehicle you are travelling in. If you have hired a Landcruiser, by far the quickest route is along Highway Number 9 as far as Muang Phin. From here on there is an exciting 4WD route through to Ban Muong and Saravane. This may be impassable in places during the rainy season (worst period July-October). Whether you are allowed to do all this will not only depend on the climate but also on the political situation since you will be passing through several minority strongholds. (Most tourists who travel from Savannakhét to points further south, fly.)

Champassak Province: Practically all visitors who have been allowed to travel overland between Vientiane and Paksé will have registered with Sodetour in the first place. This agency has more contacts in the south than others. The cheapest way to get to Paksé is to use one of the old French buses (with wooden seats) which leave early from the central market in Vientiane. The trip (with overnight stop) takes two days.

Sekong in Sekong Province and **Attopeu** in Attopeu Province: These can be entered overland.

In the north

Luang Prabang in Luang Prabang Province. Between 1991 and 1994, the road has been remarkably improved between Vientiane and Muang Kasi by Swedish road experts. This 320km stretch through Ban Saka, Ban Nog Khay, Muang Vangviang and Ban Phatang can be tackled without 4WD. The remainder of the journey is still however extremely rough and requires sturdy 4WD vehicles such as Toyota Landcruisers. It is also a politically unstable area, so permission to travel this route may be denied if there have been recent local skirmishes or attacks on vehicles. It is hoped that Highway Number 13 will be completely paved by 1996. At the moment there is a checkpoint operating at Muang Kasi. Even during the dry season (November to April) it can take over eight hours to travel this stretch. During the worst period (July-October) it can become impassable. Eventually cars will be able to cover the 420km between Vientiane and Luang Prabang in under ten hours.

Muang Phônsavan in Xieng Khouang Province. Many tourists would like to make this trip overland via Highway Number 13 followed by Highway Number 7. Very few actually make it because of the condition of the roads. First of all there is a rough stretch for 25km beyond Muang Kasi and then another from the Phou Khoun turn off point through Ban Sén Kôm, Muang Souy and Ban Lén. The Department of Commerce don't often allow travel overland to the Plain of Jars, mainly because of the colossal numbers of unexploded bombs found in the area and the risk of being robbed by H'mong bandits.

Tourists by the plane-full fly into Xieng Khouane (Xiang Khouang) and are then taken the 36km to Phônsavan in Toyota Land Cruisers.

Sam Neua in Houaphan Province. From Phônsavan to the provincial border, Highway Number 6 is in reasonable condition. The stretch between Houamuang and Muang Ham is said to be appalling. Only a few Westerners have ever been given permits to travel along this route.

Muang Xay in Oudomsay Province. A small tourist office has recently opened in Muang Xay. It is normally reached by fast boat from Luang Prabang to Muang Pakbéng and then by truck via Muang Bèng. If you have chartered a

4WD vehicle as far as Luang Prabang, there is no reason why you couldn't make this journey. The Lao National Tourist Office next door to the Mittaphap Hotel could help you with this if you didn't already get it arranged in Vientiane. The road to Muang Xay has already been partly improved, since this will be one of the main links through to the Yunnanese border at Botén. If you want to travel in this area, it is well worth contacting SODETOUR. Phoenix Services Agency (Hong Kong) can arrange entry for you into Laos via Botén from Yunnan in China.

Luang Nam Tha in Luang Nam Tha Province. It is very unlikely that you will be able to enter this province from Oudomsay Province during the rainy season (July-October) . The roads are then in a terrible condition. Even during the dry season they are difficult. They will not be improved for at least a year (even though talks between the Chinese and Laotian Governments have been very favourable). Opium is widely produced in this area and it could be dangerous to enter this territory.

Ban Houayxay in Bokeo Province. As long as the political situation is stable then you may enter Bokeo Province from Luang Prabang. The route by road is however a very roundabout one which goes through Ban Khaun and Ban Ta Fa. Tourists wanting to travel there are advised to go by slow boats which cover the 300km journey in two days (cost US$12). The other alternative is to cut the journey in half and go by jeep to Muang Pakbéng (160km) and then by boat to Ban Houayxay. Sodetour, Diethelm Travel and Lanexang Travel & Tour Co Ltd can arrange entry into Laos via this route. They have all recently opened offices in Luang Prabang.

Phôngsali in Phôngsali Province.

Sayaboury in Sayaboury Province. At the time of writing, Sayaboury (Muang Xaignabouri) is off limits due to guerrilla activity, smuggling and ethnic conflicts.

Buses
Buses in Laos are incredibly dilapidated, always full to bursting point, exceptionally cheap and totally unreliable. They use an old French design, with wooden seats. Currently inter-provincial services are few and far between. If you cross a provincial border when travelling by bus remember that it is illegal to do so without a permit (one is required for each provincial border crossed).

Bus routes convenient for budget travel
Central Laos
Buses can be used to get to Paksane in Borikhamsay Province (five hours) - leaves early from Vientiane Bus Station. The onward journey to Thakhet in Khammouane Province is also allowed (12 hours from Vientiane).

Southern Laos
You probably stand a better chance of getting to Savannakhét if you have a journalists' or a business visa. There is one express bus per day, costing US$7, which covers the 490km in about 15 hours. A better bet, if you want to travel by

bus to Savannakhét, is to get your visa endorsed for the Paksé crossing. The intercity bus terminus can be reached by walking to the end of the only straight road in Paksé and then turning right along the road which heads for Champassak. The terminus is about 1km along, just past the market. Buses leave early in the morning and take about seven hours to get to Savannakhét (cost US$0.4 for Laotians and US$3 for foreigners). If you have just arrived via the Mukdahan ferry crossing, to get to Paksé by bus should be easy.

Paksé-Muang Không. From here you can make your own boat arrangements to see the falls. Expect to pay about US$2 for the bus ticket (ferry to Muang Không is included).

Bus services in the north
By 1997 the road should be paved all the way to Luang Prabang. Long distance buses from Bangkok should be able to cover this 1,048km journey in about 22 hours (ten hours to Mekong bridge + two hours for customs + ten hours to final destination). Foreigners are currently not allowed to take the bus from Vientiane, even as far as Muang Kasi, because of ethnic troubles.

Boat travel in Laos
Central Laos
If you just fancy a short trip along the Mekong, hire a river taxi. These elongated craft can be rented for US$4 per hour.

The long distance boat service to the southern provinces is often faster than going by bus (downstream). Paksane in Borikhamsay Province can be reached in only 4½ hours, Thakhet further south in around 9½ hours. There are frequent services between June-November.

The most common type of craft used for this is what the Laotians call a *hua houa leim*. Having a length of around 20m, this floating water bus/lorry combination is capable of transporting a maximum weight of 20 tons. Going downstream, powered by a Datsun car engine, it can reach a maximum speed of 20km/h. (More on the Khemmarat rapids where the water speed can reach 4.8m/sec.)

Southern Laos
Head for the river boat docking point which is on Vientiane's southern outskirts, just past the Australian Club and UNICEF offices. Check when the next boat leaves with the Vientiane Tourist Office on Thanon Prabang. If you have a Lao speaker with you, just ask at the docking site (*Thaa Heua Lak Sii*). Do not attempt to arrange this between November-June, since the service is temporarily suspended. The boat, which generally has a two-tier deck (one used for sleeping), leaves very early (about 05.00). Be there about 04.30 to get a comfortable position. Laotian women travel in the covered section away from the men but this is not expected of Westerners. Bring your own food, plenty of drinking water, mosquito repellent etc. The boat won't get into Savannakhét until around midday the next day so you will have to sleep on the deck. Make sure to absolutely plaster yourself with insect repellent and sun-screen during the day. The return journey takes longer. The cost of the trip is US$7-8. Westerners who are prone to sunstroke are recommended to take along a sunshade. (There may be no room in the covered section of the boat.)

Road routes are used further south, except for the stretch between Sekong and Attopeu. Sodetour offer a very interesting 14-day tour travelling the length of the Mekong in Laos. They also offer a shorter one (four days) from Vientiane to Không Island.

Northern Laos
To Luang Prabang
It is fairly easy to make this 430km journey (contact Inter-Lao Tourisme in Vientiane). The boats leave from the Kao Liaw jetty, to the west of the city. A taxi (*thaek-sii*) or a samlor (*saam-law*) will take you there for about US$1 (7km). The large passenger boats used on this route stop at irregular intervals to drop off passengers and pick up food. It is better to take your own food (enough to last for four days). Don't get off en route because there is very little accommodation available, except at Muang Pak-Lay where there are several small guest houses. You can travel to this half way point and return but you will still need a permit; it costs 5,000 kip. This is the only way for foreigners to get to Sayaboury Province. From Muang Pak-lay it is possible to get a passenger truck to Sayaboury but, because of the ethnic tension in the province, permits are presently not being issued. The remainder of the journey passes through some very spectacular scenery. The boat will not dock again until it gets to Ban Pakneun. Before you arrive at Luang Prabang it will stop once more at Muang Tha Deua.

If you want to take this trip, be at the jetty in Vientiane at about 07.00 (one hour before departure). Don't forget your stocks of water, food, insect repellent etc.

From Luang Prabang
There are some very interesting boat trips which can be taken from Luang Prabang.

To Pak Ou Caves
Diethelm Travel, Sodetour and Lanexang Travel can arrange this trip in Luang Prabang. If you want to keep the cost of the trip down, hire a slow long-tailed river taxi (*héua hâng nyáo*) rather than a fast speedboat (*héua wái*). The latter, which are built in Thailand, skim along the river at breath-taking speed and charge about US$25-30 for a two hour trip. Their fast-living owners will want you to come back as soon as you get there and you will miss the scenic highlights because you will whizz past them. They are also likely to throw up water sprays which wouldn't be very popular with camera owners. If you like speed, then a journey on one of these skiffs should not be missed. You will be required to wear a safety helmet. The slower river taxis, which use much smaller Toyota outboard engines, can be hired for US$25-30 for the whole day. They will stop off wherever you want and they are much safer.

To Ban Houayxay in Bokeo Province
Travel arrangements for this trip are easy to make as long as the political situation is stable. Lao National Tourism may only allow you to travel half way (160km) to Muang Pakbéng if there is ethnic trouble further up the river. By slow river boat the full trip will take two days and cost US$7, the speedboats will cost about US$50 per person as long as there are six fee-paying passengers (US$300 for the whole boat).

To Nam Bak in northern Luang Prabang Province
Boats don't run between mid-February and June.

Muang Xay in Oudomsay Province
Lao National Tourism are allowing tourists to travel on this exciting route since their small tourist office opened in the capital in October 1993. You can only go by boat as far as Muang Pakbéng; from here it's road transport. (See jeep section of this guide.) Sodetour and Lanexang Travel can also easily arrange this.

Interprovincial travel
Whenever possible the Lao National Tourist Office will suggest that you take the boat. If you insist on travelling further north by bus, it is likely that they may ask you to hire a guide to go with you. You will only be allowed to travel to Oudomsay, Bokeo and Luang Nam Tha Provinces if the political situation is stable.

Other transport

Passenger trucks (*sawng-thâew*)
These are used extensively throughout Laos. Because they have only planks for seats they are rarely used by Westerners except on short journeys. They will stop for you on any road if you hold up your hand. They are checked at frequent intervals by the police. On some of the very rough roads in the north they are the only form of transport. Only those with black licence tags can carry passengers.

Jumbo taxis (*jamboh*)
If you are travelling with friends this is a cheap way of getting around. Generally a 4km journey will only cost US$1. They are much safer than the *túk túks* you see in Bangkok because the roads are far less crowded. Watch they don't cheat you.

Car taxi
These do not cruise around, but you will find one outside most of the tourist hotels. They seem to have their own patches so if you hire one outside a particular hotel, the chances are that in a small city like Vientiane you will hire him again at the same place. Some of the drivers are very friendly and will offer you discount rates for full day bookings. Expect to pay US$4 to/from Wattay airport. Bargain hard if you have just arrived since they will probably ask for US$10. Once you know how far it is (6km), you won't be so keen to pay them as much on your return journey. Bargain hard and you can get there for US$2.

Three-wheelers (*saam-lâw*)
These are also called samlors and are slightly cheaper than car taxis. Bargain hard for good fares. They can be rather uncomfortable if used for distances of more than 3km.

Motorbikes
Small motorbikes (100cc) can be rented for US$10-12 per day in some provincial capitals.

Bicycles
These can be rented for about US$2 per day in all the provincial capitals. Hotels and guest houses commonly have them available.

Tour programmes
In addition to the tourist agencies in Laos that can organise your trip for you, there is an ever-increasing number outside the country now dealing in quite comprehensive packages. It's all good news, both for the traveller and for the Laotian economy. Furthermore, in a number of cases prices are being held for 1996 and 1997.

A summary of what's currently available is given at Appendix Four.

COMMUNICATIONS

Currency
The currency is the kip. In March 1995 US$1 = 720 kip. The banks in Vientiane charge a commission fee of US$2/100 changed. Tourists are advised to carry plenty of small denomination dollar notes and plenty of Thai baht. In Vientiane the baht is used almost to the same extent as the kip. US$100 notes are highly sought after by money changers seen in the booths around the Morning Market. Tourist hotels do not generally give a good exchange rate, it is much better to use La Banque pour Commerce Exterior Lao in Vientiane, which will also change travellers cheques (2% commission). All banks are open from 08.00-12.00 and 14.00-15.00 (Mon-Fri). Shops will change US dollars and generally give good rates. If you buy something using fairly large denomination dollar notes they will usually give you the change in kip and/or Thai baht. Remember that once you have changed dollars into kip that you can't change back. Since 1990, the exchange rate has remained fairly stable and there has been no black market operating.

Credit cards
Many of the better class hotels and restaurants in Vientiane accept Visa. The Belvedere and River View Hotel accept American Express as well. The Nam Phu French restaurant in Vientiane accepts American Express and Visa and most of its upper crust competitors will also accept Visa. The only bank at present you can get a cash advance with a Visa card in Vientiane is the Siam Commercial Bank on Thanon Lan Xang. Two of the top tourist agencies, Diethelm Travel Laos and Sodetour will accept payment by American Express and Visa. There is no surcharge if payment is by AMEX but Visa payments incur an extra charge of 4%.

Post
Letters and postcards posted in Laos can take an age to get to their destination. Letters to the UK cost 220 kip and to the USA 260 kip. It is worth collecting a range of Lao stamps to give as presents to children because they are very decorative and feature many local scenes, particularly boats, landscapes and elephants. The postcards available are very basic. If you want your card to get home before you, post it in Thailand when you leave. Post offices are open from 08.00-17.00 (Mon-Sat).

Telephone

Only if you stay at the Belvedere Hotel will you have your own personal International Direct Dialling (IDD). They charge US$20 for three minutes when phoning the USA and US$18 for three minutes when phoning the UK. These rates are about 20% more expensive than using the services of the International Telephone Office, which is on Thanon Setthathirat in Vientiane. The system used is notoriously unreliable especially during the monsoon season.

Fax

You can send an international fax from the business centre at the Belvedere Hotel. I don't know if this is more reliable than using the system available at the post office, but it costs 20% more.

Electricity

Take a two-pin socket adaptor with you since this is the most common fitment. In Vientiane, Luang Prabang, Savannakhét and Paksé, 220 volts, 50 cycles is the voltage. When travelling through rural areas you will have no electricity at all in places (especially in the north). When it is available it sometimes only comes on for a few hours every day; the most common voltage is 110 in the countryside. Never travel anywhere without a torch.

Time

GMT +7 hours.

The media

Newspapers

In every good hotel lobby you will find a copy of the Lao News Bulletin (*Khao San Pathet Lao*), either in French or English. *The Bangkok Post* (usually a few days old) is widely available. Some bookstores have copies of *Pravda,* printed in French and Russian.

Radio

Wherever you are in Laos you can tune into the World Service on 11.955 Mhz shortwave and 3,195 Mhz (76m band). Lao radio is quite entertaining, there are even some programmes in English. Adverts are more common than usual.

TV

A few of the better-off households in Vientiane have satellite television. It is available to those staying at the Belvedere Hotel. Most of the poorer households have a TV set, antennae are however less common than on the other side of the Mekong. There is a thriving video industry throughout the country, especially in Luang Prabang where, as yet, it is impossible to receive Lao National TV broadcasts.

Pak Ou Cave

Part Three
Regional Guide

Chapter Ten

Central Laos and Vientiane

History

During the reign of King Settathirat (1548-71), the seat of the royal capital was moved from Xieng Dong-Xieng Dong (Luang Prabang) much further south to a place which was called Vieng Chan. Vieng Chan (literal translation, City with Walls) became the capital of Lan Xang, the Kingdom of a Million Elephants, which had been established by a Thai prince, Fa Ngum, in 1353. From the fortified city, the king ruled over this domain, which then included the site of the present Thai city of Chieng Mai, most of Thailand's Khorat Plateau and a large slice of present day northern Cambodia.

The first Europeans to arrive in Lan Xang during the reign of Soulinga Vongsa (1633-94) found Vieng Chan to be a prosperous trading centre. When the king died without leaving a son, a high ranking mandarin, Tian Thala, ruled from the Royal Palace. Only six years later he was assassinated by the provincial governor, Nantharat. In the year 1700, a massive army led by Sai Ong Hue (the son of Soulinga Vongsa's brother) attacked Vieng Chan. It fell with very little resistance and Nantharat was put to death. Sai Ong Hue proclaimed himself king. During the period 1707-13 much of the territory of Lan Xang became split into the Kingdom of Luang Prabang in the north and the Kingdom of Champassak in the south. Sai Ong Hue then ruled the central territory, which became known as the Kingdom of Vientiane.

During the reign of successive monarchs, there were many minor forays by the Burmese, Annamese and Siamese. In 1827 the city, which was now ruled by King Anourouth, was sacked by invaders from Siam. The king fled to the Vietnamese city of Hue, where the Emperor Minh Mang came to his aid. In 1828 he attempted to recapture Vientiane with an army of Vietnamese troops but was badly beaten and forced to retreat to the Plain of Jars.

For many decades Vientiane lay in ruin. In July 1889, it was chosen by the French as their administrative centre and rebuilt. Colonial villas and elegant government buildings sprang up amongst the ruins, religious sanctuaries such as Wat Si Saket and That Luang were extensively repaired.

In 1953, the city became the capital and administrative centre of the independent Kingdom of Laos. In 1975 after the abolition of the monarchy, Vientiane grew in stature as the capital of the Lao People's Democratic Republic.

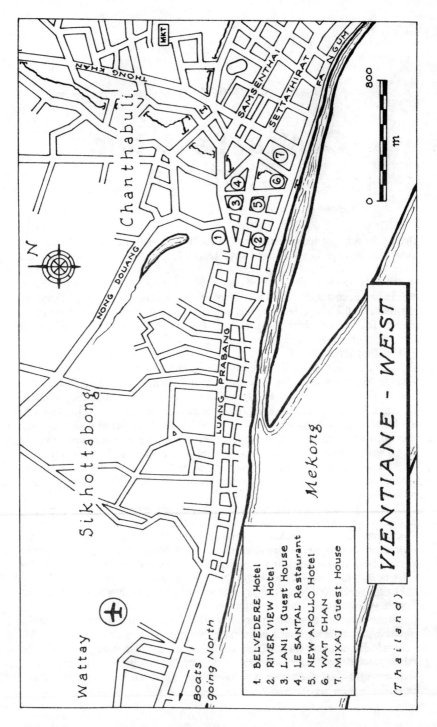

VIENTIANE - WEST

1. BELVEDERE Hotel
2. RIVER VIEW Hotel
3. LANI 1 Guest House
4. LE SANTAL Restaurant
5. NEW APOLLO Hotel
6. WAT CHAN
7. MIXAJ Guest House

(Thailand)

Mekong

Boats going North

Wattay

Sikhottabong

Chanthabuli

Nong Douang

Luang Prabang

Thong Khan

Samsenthai

Settathirat

Fa Ngum

MKT

Getting there

Vientiane can be reached by transfer connection flights via Bangkok or direct international flights from Hanoi, Ho Chi Minh, Kunming and Phnom Penh. Foreign visitors can now get to the city via the Mittaphap Bridge, which was opened in mid-April 1994. This spans the Mekong River between Nong Khai in Thailand and the Lao town of Tha Naleng. Visitors can also travel to the city after crossing the Mekong at four legal entry points.

Arriving by air

Wattay Airport is about 3km west of Vientiane. It takes only 10-15 minutes to get to the centre of the city by taxi from Tha Deua. Expect to pay about US$6 (4440 kip at the April 1995 exchange rate). It is however much cheaper to catch a bus on Thanon Luang Prabang which is about 150m south of the airport terminal. This costs only 250 kip and drops you off near the Morning Market. You can get one back to the airport from here.

Arriving by land

Tourists who were lucky enough to be in the Nong Khai area during mid-April 1994 would have been able to witness the opening of the Friendship Bridge (Mittaphap Bridge) between Thailand and Laos. This, according to the Bangkok Post, was indeed a friendly occasion. Present at the opening were King Bhumipol Adulyadej of Thailand, President Nouhak Phoumsavanh of Laos and the Prime Minister of Australia, Mr Paul Keating. Thousands gathered for the opening ceremony when the £20 million, Australian funded, 1,170m (3,840ft) structure was blessed by Buddhist monks in the presence of 300 guests. Now that the ferry service has been disbanded, visitors will, after checking through customs, be able to walk into Laos. Buses on the other side of the bridge can be caught for the 19km journey into Vientiane (cost 10 baht). Most of these antiquated vehicles are, however, grossly overloaded with people and goods, so tourists would probably prefer to take the taxi option, which costs 100 baht. There are also motorcyclists in the area who offer a ride for 40 baht.

Vientiane today

Vientiane is a quiet city with an unrushed lifestyle. Visitors will be greeted with smiles and good cheer. After the whirlpool traffic chaos of Bangkok, it will come as a pleasant surprise to find oneself somewhere where there are as many pedestrians as bicycles and hardly any traffic pollution. Parts of the city are almost deserted; it's just as if some giant leech has sucked its life blood. As one travels along its quiet avenues one passes old French residences jaundiced by age. Many of the buildings are badly dilapidated, shops are shuttered to protect them from the blistering midday heat. Many children you pass will cry out *'falang, falang'* ('foreigner, foreigner'). Adults may greet you with the characteristic *wài* gesture. With their palms pressed together they will say *'sa bai du'* ('greetings'). You won't find any hard-nosed hagglers here or any of the 'changey dollar mister' brigade because the black market has virtually ceased to exist.

Your memories of Vientiane will undoubtedly be pleasant ones, the *mat-mii* cloth sellers at the Thanon Mahasot Market, the huge bulbous canopies above the stalls of melon sellers and the lofty pinnacles of the That Luang Stupa glistening in the early morning sunshine. To escape from the heat, there's the cool seclusion of the numerous wats and the small outdoor cafes overlooking the Mekong River. It's easy to find your way around even though street signs are in Lao. If you get lost you can always head for the river and retrace your steps. For very little money you can hire a three-wheeler (*saam-law*) or hop onto a jumbo taxi (*jamboh*) to take a tour of the suburbs.

In only two hours you can see its four main districts. Towards the southeast you will find Muang Sisattanak, the site of the Swedish embassy, the headquarters of UNICEF and the Australian Club. Directly west is Muang Saisettha where the Sacred Stupa of That Luang dominates the skyline. On your way back to the city centre you will pass the Pratuxai, a pre-revolutionary 'Monument des morts'. North of here is Muang Chanthabuli where you can visit the Thong Khan Market. Directly east along the river is Muang Sikhottabong where you will find the showrooms of the largest cotton factory in Laos. Here you can purchase garments with distinctive motifs and see cloth dyed bright red with an extract from wood boring insects.

Accommodation in Vientiane

If you manage to get a tourist visa in Bangkok without a tour agency stamp or you have a visa authorisation permit, you will be able to choose your own hotel in Vientiane. Those visitors entering Laos with a visa stamped with a particular agency will be allocated a hotel for the first night by that agency. After that, if they just intend staying in Vientiane they can change to the hotel of their choice. The hotel allocated to you by the agency will depend upon the class of accommodation you paid for when you booked your visa. If you stated that you required superior accommodation you would probably stay in the Belvedere Hotel. The price you paid for your visa would include the cost of the first night's accommodation.

Superior Class

Belvedere Hotel, Unit 9, Bane KM2, Khonta Toong, Samsenthai Road, Sikhotabong District, PO Box 585, S01 Nongno; tel: 856 21 213570/4; fax: 856 21 213572/9; telex: 4363 BWBCLS.

This establishment, managed by Guthrie Hotels International, is the only hotel in this class in the whole of the country. It was built mainly to accommodate upper class international tourist agencies and business magnates. It is fully equipped with a 24-hour business centre, IDD telephones (the only service of this kind in the country) and rooms with their own mini-bars and tea and coffee making facilities. Interpreter and secretarial services are available. Flight connections can be arranged through the hotel's airline reservation desk. They have a complimentary airport transfer service. The hotel, which opened in 1993, is a joint venture undertaken by Singapore and Laotian businessmen. Including the luxury apartment block which is still under construction behind the main hotel, it is estimated that it will have cost over US$12 million to develop. Rooms are naturally very expensive, but reduced rates are available for long stays. The apartment block rooms which are due to become available towards the end of 1995 will be much cheaper but will only be let to clients wishing to stay for a considerable time. A swimming pool and tennis courts are now also available.

It can be booked via the Singapore Sales Office using AMEX, VISA etc at 41 Sixth Avenue, Singapore 1027; tel: 65 4609556/4662555; fax: 65 4682785.

Lanexang Travel Co Ltd offer a very good rate for this hotel when booked with a package. They charge US$75 for a double and US$60 for a single.
Price per room: single – US$90; double – US$130; luxury double – US$145.

First class

The Lanexang Hotel, Thanon Fa Ngum; tel: 856 21 214102/04/06/07; fax: 856 21 214108.
This hotel has been widely used by tour groups ever since Laos opened to tourism in 1986. Well positioned overlooking the Mekong, it has become extremely popular in recent years. If you arrive in Vientiane during the busy tourist season (November to May) it is very difficult to get a room. If you are in Thailand for several weeks before going to Laos, book this hotel early. Since many of the rooms here are held for tourists booking first class accommodation, the easiest way to arrange to stay here is to book your visa with Diethelm Travel in Bangkok who have a branch office in Namphu Square, Thanon Settathirat, Vientiane. Although this hotel is officially designated first class, rooms are nothing special, they are however air-conditioned and have hot and cold running water. The hotel is centrally located, has a nice dining area, a swimming pool, badminton courts and a souvenir shop where you can buy inferior quality postcards, Laotian clothes and handicrafts. Suites have TVs. They accept all major credit cards and give discounts for long stays.
Price per room: single – US$50; double – US$60; luxury suite – US$75; three-room suite – US$90.

The River View Hotel, corner of Fa Ngum and Thanon Sithane Neua; tel: 856 21 9123; fax: 856 21 9127.
In Bangkok, this hotel would be designated second class. It is owned by a Thai company and features an international restaurant specialising in Thai food. It is situated in a quiet area away from central Vientiane and offers superb views of the Mekong. Rooms are all air-conditioned and designed for double occupancy. Luxury suites also have a TV and mini-bar. They accept all major credit cards.
Price per room: double – US$45; luxury suite – US$65.

Vansana Hotel, Phonthan Road, POB 881; tel: 856 21 414189/21 413171; fax: 856 21 413171.
This very classy establishment was completed in 1994. It was designed by its architect owner. It has a car hire service, free transportation to downtown (since it's a little out of the way), telephone in each room and a long-distance call service. They will even lend you a free bicycle. Other facilities include Lao Sauna, swimming pool and satellite cable TV. All 39 rooms are large, immaculately furnished, have air-conditioning and mini-bars. It also has a spacious dining room and a library. You can pay by any international credit card. Lanexang Travel Co Ltd offers doubles for US$46 and singles for US$36.
Price per room: single – US$55; double – US$70.

Tai-Pan Hotel, 2-12 Francoise Nginn Street (near Wat Mixai); tel: 856 21 216223.
This business class hotel was opened in 1993 to cater for the needs of, mainly, Thai businessmen. It has similar facilities to the Vansana Hotel but is a little

cheaper. It can be booked by VISA, AMEX or Master Card on Bangkok tel: 662 260 9888; fax: 662 259 7908.

Second class hotels and guest houses

Samsenthai, 15 Thanon Manthathurath; tel: 856 21 21687/212116; fax: 856 21 212116.
A well kept, very clean establishment with highly polished floors. Situated right in the centre of Vientiane most rooms are air-conditioned but they have a few backpackers' rooms with fans only.
Price per room: single – US$25; double – US$35; backpackers' – US$10.

Ambassador Hotel, Panghkam Road; tel: 856 21 5797; fax: 856 21 2944800.
Centrally located colonial looking establishment owned by the Ministry of Foreign Affairs. At the moment the hotel is incompletely refurbished and noisy due to building alterations. It is still an attractive place to stay. Rooms have air-conditioning, high, decorated ceilings and are extremely spacious. Staff are very accommodating.
Price per room: single – US$35; double – US$45; suite – US$60+.

Hotel Ekalath Metropole, Thanon Samsenthai (near That Dam); tel: 856 21 213420/21; fax: 856 21 215628.
This is owned by a Vietnamese family and mainly features large, luxury, air-conditioned rooms but much cheaper, very basic rooms are available. It has a restaurant which serves Vietnamese and European food. They also have some extremely grim rooms available at a cut-price rate. Better value is the annexe which was opened in late 1994. This has basic accommodation with fans and is excellent for backpackers.
Price per room: single – US$20; double – US$30; basic double – US$15; cut price – US$8; backpackers' US$5–15.

Saysana Hotel, Thanon Chao Anou; tel: 856 21 213580/81; fax: 856 21 212116.
This has a smart exterior and interior which was recently refurbished. All rooms have a bath, telephone, air-conditioning and large beds. Some rooms still only have ceiling fans. Avoid staying on the first floor because you are likely to be disturbed by the disco and live band which plays nightly.
Price per room: single – US$25; double – US$30.

Vientiane Hotel, 72-74 Luang Prabang Road; tel: 856 21 212928; fax - available soon.
Cheap singles with fans are available for US$15. With air-conditioning they cost US$20. Doubles cost US$25 with air-conditioning. Raja Tour use this hotel, which is fairly basic. This hotel is popular with backpackers.
Price per room: single with fan – US$15; single with air-conditioning US$ 20; double with air-conditioning – US$25.

Asian Pavilion Hotel, 379 Thanon Samsenthai; tel: 856 21 21430/1; fax: 856 21 21432.
Popular with businessmen, this is one of the city's long established hotels which has changed its name several times. During 1993 it was extensively renovated

and prices have subsequently risen. The more expensive double rooms have TVs, hot and cold running water and baths. They accept visa card.
Price per room: single with fan – US$30; single with air-conditioning US$ 40; double – US$30/46/55.

Government Guest House, Thanon Tha Deua; tel: 856 21 2888.
If you want a touch of by-gone opulence at a very reasonable price, this is the place for you. Situated about 2½km from the centre of the city, this accommodation was once used by Prince Souvanna Phouma. If you want to stay in his room, ask for room 101; ideal for a family is room 102 where the Princess used to sleep. This has two large double beds, a telephone, refrigerator, air conditioning, hot and cold running water and TV. Cheaper rooms are available in the range of US$25-US$35. They are all extremely spacious, lavishly furnished and have air conditioning but no TVs. The guest house has a small restaurant. If you fancy eating your evening meal here, order it in advance.
Price per room: room 101 – US$65; room 102 – US$50; others US$25-35.

The New Apollo Hotel, 69A Thanon Luang Prabang.
Completely refurbished in 1993 this establishment is one of the nicest second-class hotels in Vientiane. Staff are extremely friendly and all rooms have air-conditioning. Lanexang Travel charge US$46 for a double and US$36 for a single. The Raja Tour price is US$60 double, US$50 single.
Price per room: single – US$25/35; double – US$40/50.

Mùang Lao Hotel, Thanon Tha Deua; tel: 856 21 2278.
Although it is 3½km from central Vientiane, it is a good place to stay. The restaurant is quiet, comfortable and serves excellent western and Lao food. Rooms are air conditioned and cost US$25 for a single and US$35 for a double. Suites are available for US$60+. Prices in this establishment are likely to rise when refurbishment is complete and the swimming pool is finished.
Price per room: single – US$25; double – US$35; suite – US$60+.

Anou Hotel, corner of Thanon Chao Anou and Thanon Heng Buon; tel: 856 21 3324.
If you opt for the lower category of accommodation when booking your visa, there is a good chance that you will stay here. That Luang Tour Co and Raja Tour Co use the hotel because it (no doubt) gives them discount rates. Rooms are plain with no frills. Fans are provided but there is no hot running water. Raja Tours charges US$24 for a double and US$18 for a single. Lanexang Travel Co Ltd charge US$35 for a double and US$25 for a single!
Price per room: single – US$12; double – US$20; family room – US$30.

That Luang Guest House, 307 That Luang Road; tel: 856 21 413370; fax: 856 21 412953.
Very friendly, clean and comfortable but a little out of the way. All rooms air-conditioned. Efficient laundry service.
Price per room: single – US$30; double – US$45.

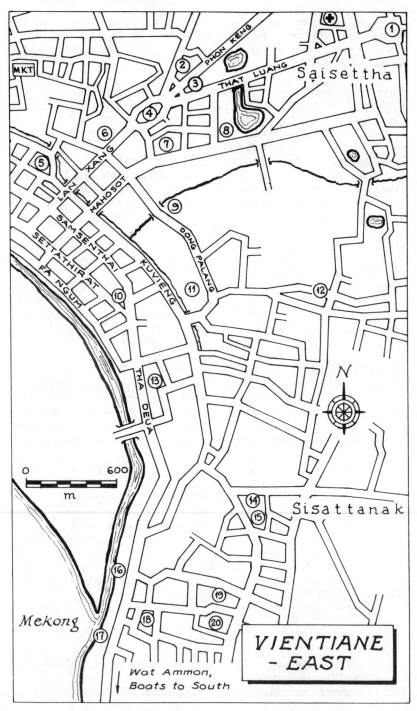

Lani 1 Guesthouse, 281 Thanon Settathirat; tel: 856 21 215639; fax: 856 21 216103.

One of the most popular in Vientiane. A lot of businessmen staying in the city for a long time use this establishment. It is central, has a restaurant where you can order Chinese food as well as more traditional dishes and is very friendly. Businessmen can send faxes from here. All rooms are air-conditioned. A few cheaper rooms are available. This establishment is recommended, book early because it's often full.

Price per room: single – US$30; double – US$35.

Lani 2 Guesthouse, 268 Thanon Saylom; tel: 856 21 2615; fax: 856 21 4175. Similar facilities and prices as Lani I. This establishment was opened in 1991 to accommodate over-spill from Lani I. It is now equally as popular and often full.

Thienthong Guest House, just off Thanon Sok Pa Luang; tel: 856 21 6544. This hotel has a very good Lao restaurant. Rooms are all air-conditioned.

Price per room: single – US$20; double – US$25.

Phornthip Guest House, 72 To Pong Road, Ban Wat Chan (PO Box 3119); tel: 856 21 217239.

Rooms all have air-conditioning and modern amenities.

Price per room: single – US$30; double – US$35.

Senesouk Guest House, Luang Prabang Road; tel: 856 21 215587. Built in traditional Lao style, it also offers traditional Lao hospitality. The Suki-Yaki Restaurant offers superb Lao cuisine. Prices are similar to the Phornthip and discounts are given for long stays.

---

1. THAT LUANG
2. THAI Embassy
3. VIETNAMESE Embassy
4. VICTORY (PATUXAI) Monument
5. Hotel EKALATH METROPOLE
6. LANI 2 Guest House
7. GERMAN Embassy
8. WAT PHONXAI
9. WAT BAN BAI
10. WAT SI MUANG
11. WAT DONG PALAN
12. VANSANA Hotel
13. CHAMPA LAN XANG Restaurant
14. WAT SOK PA LUANG
15. SWEDISH Guest House
16. AUSTRALIAN Club
17. MUANG LAO Hotel
18. RUSSIAN Embassy
19 WAT SI AMPHON
20. SWEDISH Embassy

Syri Guest House, Chao Anou quarter; tel: 856 21 2394; fax: 856 21 3117.
This lovely old house, situated in Vientiane's residential area, is recommended.
There is a balcony where you can sit outside in the evenings and all rooms are
large, air-conditioned and have hot and cold running water. They also hire out
bicycles for US$3/day.
*Price per room: single – US$20; cut-price single – US$12; double – US$25;
family – US$35.*

Lao-Chalerne, Intersection of Thanon Chou Anou and Ka Ngum;
tel: 856 21 2881.
If external appearances put you off, you won't like this establishment. Reception
area also looks a bit grim but rooms are very spacious, have ceiling fans and hot
water. This hotel is often full.
Price per room: US$15-18.

Chaemchanh Guest House, 78 Kuvieng Road, PO Box 1737; tel: 856 21 3002.
Near the above.
Price per room: single – US$25; double – US$30.

Santiphab, 69A Thanon Luang Prabang; tel: 856 21 3305.
Clean, but noisy because of the nightly live band. Rooms are air-conditioned .
Price per room: single – US$20; double – US$30.

The Svenska Gasthuset Guest House; tel: 856 21 2297.
This two-storey Swedish Guest House accommodates a lot of UN workers and
people involved in road building projects throughout the country. Rooms are
expensive. The restaurant serves European food and an English-style breakfast
is included in the cost of a room. This accommodation is recommended but
since there are only seven rooms, it's often full.
Price per room: single – US$30; double – US$40.

Le Parasol Blanc Hotel, Thanon Nahaidio; tel: 856 21 216091;
fax: 856 21 215444; telex: 4343 VICOLS.
Recommended. This modern well maintained establishment is a little beyond
the Patuxai monument. All rooms cost US$35. The restaurant here serves
Italian, Swiss and Lao food, to the accompaniment of piano music. It is one of
the best deals in the city and is thoroughly recommended.
Price per room: US$35.

Wonderland Guest House, Phonesawan Tai, Seesattanak; tel: 856 21 9634.
Recommended by a recent traveller, this small establishment is used by the That
Luang Tour Co. Rooms are air-conditioned. Its only bad point is that it is a little
out of the way, towards the east of the market.
Price per room: single – US$20; double – US$28.

Also worth considering is the **Santisouk Guest House** on the first floor of
Santisouk Restaurant, Thanon Nokeo Khumman; tel: 856 21 3926. Rooms are
available at US$6-10. Some have fans.

Budget hotels and guest houses

There are very few hotels which are very cheap in Vientiane. Recommended to backpackers are:

Mekong Guest House, Tha Deua Road; tel: 856 21 5975.
With a good view of the River Mekong, this clean and noisy establishment is an extremely good deal for backpackers. Head across town from the Mekong Restaurant towards the Tha Deua ferry docking point. The restaurant here serves excellent western, Lao and hot Thai food at very affordable prices. It's a popular meeting point for the city's youth. The management offer very competitive City tour prices and bicycle hire for US$2/day. Don't let the distance from the centre of Vientiane put you off. The owner also accepts payment in kip.
Price per room: US$5.

Vientiane Club Hotel, Thanon Tha Deua Km 3.
This is hard to find unless you hire a *jamboh, saam-law* or *thaek-sii* driver who knows some French or English to take you there. Ask for the **Dok Champa Hotel,** which is its other name. It is one of the few establishments that you can pay in kip. The management here is very helpful and will organise bicycle hire or a cheap tour of Vientiane for you. It's a good place to stay if you manage to get the type of visa in Bangkok which frees you from local agency control. They know students who would like to learn English and French who will accompany you on a trip around town.
Price per room: single – US$8 (5,900 kip); family – 14,000 kip.

Hua Guo Guest House, Thanon Samsenthai; tel: 856 21 8633.
This Chinese-run establishment has basic but clean rooms with fans.
Price per room: US$10.

Lao Chauern Hotel, Thanon Fa Ngum.
Not recommended. Very run down and uncomfortable.
Price per room: US$10.

Manthatourath Road Guest House; tel: 856 21 2313.
Basic but comfortable. Good coffee shop. Can be booked through Ministry of Culture at PO Box 2911, Vientiane.
Price per room: US$10.

Ban Fai Hotel, 31 Dong Palane Road; tel: 856 21 4241.
Excellent dormitory-style accommodation. Would suit backpackers willing to share rooms.
Price per bed: US$5.

The Mixai Guest House, Samsenthai, close to Ekalath Metropole.
Rooms are air-conditioned. A traveller who stayed here in February 1994 recommends it wholeheartedly.
Price per room: single – US$8; double – US$12.

Nong Douang Hotel, Nong Douang Street (opposite the market); tel: 856 21 5334.
Roomy villa style accommodation with air-conditioned rooms. One of the best deals in budget category.
Price per room: US$15.

In wats
A recent traveller to Vientiane says that it is possible, in return for English lessons, to stay at the monks' quarters at Wat Si Saket.

In Vientiane many old buildings are being renovated to open as hotels and guest houses. There are signs all over the place on available land indicating that by 1997 there will probably be many more places for tourists to stay in the city.

Eating in Vientiane
Now the tourist boom has started in Vientiane there are scores of eating places to choose from in everyone's price range.

French food
Le Santal Restaurant. If you are looking for somewhere nice and cool around lunch time this is a good place to go. The grills here are excellent and the chef specialises in some interesting pizza. It is French-run and prices are very competitive. It's opposite Wat Ong Teu.

La Souriya, Thanon Pang Kham (close to the Lao Aviation booking office); tel: 856 21 4411. This is owned by a Meo woman who is said to have royal blood. Prices are high in this classy establishment – expect to pay US$20 for a three course meal with French wine.

Bantavanh, 49 Khoun Boulom. If you want a nice quiet, friendly atmosphere, this is the place for you. Food is excellent but on the expensive side.

Sabaidi Restaurant, near That Luang Stupa; tel: 856 21 5760. This is a little out of the way but excellent value.

Nam Phu, Thanon Pang Kham; tel: 856 21 4723. This is one of the most expensive restaurants in Vientiane. It is popular with diplomats, well-heeled tourists and government officials. It's just off Foundation Square. An Asian menu is also available.

Kaonhot Restaurant, Thanon Sakarin. This one is definitely for the romantically inclined. Low lighting and good wine combined with superb food give it a five-star rating.

La Vendome, Thanon Lupeng. Newly opened in 1994. Offers good pepper steaks and fish grills.

Arawan French Restaurant. If you would like to take the lady in your life to somewhere special, this is the place for you. Expect to pick up a bill of at least US$30. As well as French specialities such as *coq au vin, chicken chasseur* and *escargots* they serve *Wiener schnitzel* and German *bratwurst* and *sauerkraut* can be followed by delicious apple *strüdel* or *kuchen* (cakes). It is located on the Fountain Circle just off Thanon Pang Kham.

If you want really good French food at a reasonable price go to **Le Santisouk**, Thanon Nokeo Khumman. It is advisable to arrive early because this restaurant, probably because of the price, is the most popular in Vientiane. You can have a really slap up meal for around US$6 (4,800 kip). They serve French wine and reasonably priced beer.

Some hotels restaurants also serve French food, such as The Lanexang, Le Parasol Blanc, Muong Lao, Riverview, Tai-Pan and the very expensive Belvedere.

Laotian food

Soukvemarn Restaurant. If you would like to try some of the more exotic Laotian dishes then this is perfect for you. The Laotian culinary tour de force, *pàa dàek* is served here. This is a fermented raw fish dish which will probably not be enjoyed by most westerners. There is also a risk of ingesting the larval stage of a liver fluke which could lead to a serious illness later. One should also be aware of the fact that Laotian salads such as *tam sòm* contain shredded *pàa dàek* together with fermented lettuce, hot chillies, papaya and olives. This looks nothing like a western salad since the ingredients are pounded together in a heavy mortar and served with a small basket containing sticky rice (*khào niaw*) which is eaten using your hands. Another popular dish served at the Soukvemarn is *kaeng paa khai mot* which is a delicious soup made from fish and ant larvae. (You may have seen ant larvae sold alongside fish stalls in the fish market). This restaurant does not have an English or French menu, everything is in Lao. It is very reasonably priced and is just off Thanon That Dam.

Dao Vieng, Thanon Heng Boun, serves a large variety of Laotian dishes and is popular with the locals.

The Pa Phao restaurant just off Nong Bone Road is popular with foreigners.

Nang Kham Bang Lao Food Restaurant, 97/2 Khou Boulom Street (near Russian Cultural Centre); tel: 856 21 217198.

Salongxay Restaurant, Lanexang Hotel. This is another good place to try some exotic foods, such as turtles baked in a vegetable paste and eels grilled on charcoal. Prices are in the 1,500-3,000 kip bracket.

1st May Restaurant. This is well situated on Phag Kham Quay overlooking the Mekong River. Many types of Laotian food are sold, including minced sausages (*naem*) and a dish consisting of minced chicken flavoured with lime and garlic (*làap*). Both can be served with roasted rice (*khào khua*) and a side salad consisting of steamed mango and lettuce leaves flavoured with a sprinkling of mint. This very inexpensive dish is popular with locals who eat it together with a side order of red chillies or a sauce made from pepper and chillies (*jaew*) which will make your eyes run – it's so hot! If you prefer ordinary white rice ask for *khào jâo*. You could have it served with unadulterated pork (*muu*), chicken (*kai*) or fried fish (*jeun paa*). If you would like a side order of vegetables ask for *phák*. Many Laotian dishes which are available here are very similar to Chinese, which may be kinder to the stomach since most Laotian traditional food is very highly spiced. Rice noodle soup (*foe*) almost identical to Vietnamese *pho* is popular for breakfast.

Somchan's Restaurant, Thanon Luang Prabang, serves some very unusual Laotian dishes.

Others
Mekong Restaurant, Tha Deua Road, Km 4 (PO Box 676); tel: 312480.
Namphou Restaurant, 20 Namphou Circle; tel: 216248.
Naxay Restaurant, 188 Nong Bone Road (PO Box 1678); tel: 412782.

Food stalls and noodle shops
There are plenty of these around Vientiane for those on a tight budget. The Night Market (Talàat Thong Khan Kham) off Thanon Mahasot is a good place to buy noodle dishes since there are many noodle shops (*hàan foe*). If you would like them slightly sweetened ask for *khào pûn*, which is a noodle dish served with a coconut sauce (*nâam káti*). Around breakfast time (06.00-08.00) go to the Morning Market (Talàat Sao). As well as *foe* you can buy crusty French bread and even Western-style sandwiches which the Laotians call *khào jii pá-têh*.

For plain western sandwiches go to the **Vinh Loi Bakery,** 111 Thanon Cahu Anou. They also specialise in very sweet cakes.

The Sweet Home Bakery, 109 Thanon Chao Anou, serves Western breakfasts for less than US$2.

Cheap Laotian snacks are sold at the snack bar in the **Lanexang Hotel.** Other good places for cheap breakfasts include the **Venus Cafe,** 94 Thanon Sam Senthai and **Mr Tui's** on Thanon Pang Kham. Freshly made yoghurt can be purchased at the **Yoghurt Shop** on Heng Boun Street.

If you want cheap exotic food go to the That Luang Market on Thanon Talat That Luang. They serve *pàa dàek* in bamboo tubes, roasted crustaceans which look like sand-hoppers (I don't know what they are) and many types of lizards and snakes which are delicious when roasted on charcoal. This market is popular with Vietnamese and Chinese living in Vientiane. I am told that you can even buy bear paws in this market! But I wouldn't bet on it.

Laotian cafes
All over the place in Vientiane you will come across small cafes which cater almost exclusively for the locals. These are very cheap, good value and are recommended. Some of the best Laotian cafes (*hàan kheûang deum*) can be seen along Thanon Samsenthai and Thanon Settathirat. Try the Lao tea (*sáa nóm hâwn*), which is served very sweet, or the coffee (*kaa-féh nóm hâwn*) served with milk and sugar. Many serve Ovaltine (*oh-wantin*), iced coffee (*kaafái nóm yén*) and Chinese tea (*nâam sáa*), which is good for upset stomachs.

If you want a plain breakfast, ask for boiled egg (*khai tôm*), scrambled eggs (*kha khùa*), or fried egg (*khai dao*). Many serve croissants (*kwaa-son*) with butter (*boe*).

For lunch or your evening meal you could try eel (*ian*), grilled prawns (*pîng kûng*), grilled fish (*ping poa*) or roast duck (*óp pét*). If you want fried chicken with no chillies ask for *jeun kai*. If you don't like hot food use the phrase *Baw mak phét*, 'I don't like spicy food'. If you can't use chopsticks (*mâi thuu*) ask for a fork (*sàwn*) and/or a spoon (*buang*). Yoghurt is a good, safe food for travellers, ask for *nóm sòm*. To make sure that the water is fit for drinking ask for *nâam deum*. Avoid taking ice (*nâam sáa*) in your orange juice (*nâam máak kîang*). One of the safest drinks to order is beer (*bia*) in a bottle. Lao whiskey (*lào láo*), which is made from rice, is exceptionally strong.

In Laotian cafes you can easily get a three course meal with beer for around 1400 kip (less than US$2).

Indian food

Taj Indian Restaurant. The service here is excellent. Most northern Indian dishes are served along with many types of Indian bread. Meals tend to be expensive by Laotian standards. The restaurant is on the other side of the road from the Nakhonluaug Bank on Thanon Pang Kham. If you are craving for Indian food and don't want to pay high prices, go to the food stalls along Thanon Saylom. Many serve delicious Indian dishes which cost no more than 500 kip.

Very reasonably priced is the recently opened **Noorjahan Restaurant** at 370 Samsenthai. They specialise in vegetarian curries. Good for takeaways, sandwiches and snacks is the **Deli Café** at 44/2 Settathirat Road; tel: 856 21 215651 (you can telephone and pick up your order later).

There are vendors selling Indian food over the road from the Phonxai Hotel, Thanon Saylom.

Thai restaurants

Thai Food Garden Restaurant, Luang Prabang Road. This is the best place to go for Thai seafood.

Phikun Restaurant, Thanon Samsenthai. This serves delicious hot and sour prawn soup (*tom yam kung*), spicy beef salad (*laab*), which is unlike the Lao equivalent, and lovely pork curries (*kaeng hunglay*). One of the specialities of the house is chicken with garlic and black pepper (*kai tod kratium priktai*).

Saloon Restaurant, just off Samsenthai Road. This is the cheapest in town.

Aahaan Restaurant, Thanon Khun Bulom. This small very cheap place serves most Thai foods. A visitor in March 1994 said that the fish dishes here which are served with a special sauce (*nam pla*) are really good. Another good one is the **Vanh Mixai Restaurant** on Francois Ngin Road.

Chinese restaurants

There are two rather expensive Chinese restaurants which were opened in 1995 to cater for the increasing numbers of international tourists.

Lani's, 281 Settathirat (near Wat Hay Sok). Very reasonably priced food.

Hong Kong Restaurant, 80/4 Samsenthai Road; tel: 856 21 213241, 2 16062; fax: 856 21 21 5995. This serves delicious Cantonese and Sichuan Cuisine. The chef once worked in the King's Palace Hotel, Beijing. It is open daily 11.30-14.00 and 18.00-22.00.

Other options include the **Ban Haysok Restaurant,** 34 Heng Boun Street (opposite Anou Hotel). This expensive establishment specialises in Southern Chinese cuisine. It has VIP banquet rooms and a take away food service. All major credit cards are accepted. At weekends reservations are necessary; tel: 856 21 21 5417/21 5639. There's also the **New Asia Chinese Restaurant,** 278 Samsenthai Road; tel: 856 21 2356. Opened in 1993 this very popular restaurant serves reasonably priced meals. For very cheap Chinese meals go to Vientiane's China Town. It's along Chao Anou Road and Heng Boun.

Japanese restaurants
Sakura Japanese Restaurant, Luang Prabang Road, Km2 (Soi 3, Khountathong); tel: 856 21 212274.

Italian
Girarrosto Ristorante L'Opera, Namphu Square, Sethathirath Road; tel: 856 21 21 5099. This restaurant is similar to the one run by the same company on Sukhumvit Road, Bangkok. They serve home-made pasta, pizza, ice cream, cakes, imported Italian goodies and Italian wines. Expect to pay 5,000 kip for a three course meal.

Vietnamese
Chez Mo, 352 Samsenthai; tel: 856 21 5766. This very basic restaurant serves excellent *pho* (soup), *cha gio* (meat rolls stuffed with green vegetables), *mi xao* (fried noodles) and *banh hoi* (barbecued pork balls).

Stalls along Heng Boun road also serve Vietnamese dishes. The very basic **Vieng Savanh** in this area is very good value.

Recommended to backpackers
The Saloon. This is situated in Pang Kham which is to the north of Hua Guo. It offers almost continuous video entertainment, cheap beer, chips, burgers as well as reasonably priced Laotian and Thai food. If you want to keep in touch with what is going on in the world, they generally have a copy of the *Bangkok Post* available.

Just for Fun. This is situated in Pang Kham, close to the Rain Tree.

The Haan Kin Deum Mixai Restaurant. One of the most popular places in Vientiane because of the cheap beer and view over the Mekong. It's a good place to head for around sunset when you can enjoy a meal or drink while watching the sun go down over Si Chiengmai on the Thai side of the Mekong. If your taste in music is traditional Lao, hard rock, folk, country and western or traditional Thai, the manager here is bound to have it somewhere on his sound system. A few common Lao foods are served together with one or two Thai and English dishes. If you want draught beer ask for *bia sòt*. This brew, made by the Lao Brewery, costs 600 kip for half a litre. Cheaper bottled beer (Bière Larue) costs 400 kip but you don't get as much. The *làa láo* liquor sold here is the Sing Thong brand which costs around 1600 kip a bottle (750ml). A backpacker who visited this establishment in December 1993 said that she didn't find it over friendly and that she hated the cold *laap*. At that time nothing much was available to eat and many of the clientele were the sons and daughters of Australian and British ex-pats. This restaurant/bar is near the intersection of Thanon Nokeo Khumman and Thanon Fa Ngum. If you want a seat for the sunset near to the window, go there at least one hour before. There is a much quieter place with a good view of the sunset along the road to the left of the Mixai.

Another good bar is the one opposite the River View Hotel which is west along Thanon Fa Ngum, close to the Belvedere Hotel. This place, called the **Sala Khounta,** serves cheap Lao meals. If you want peace and quiet go here after the sunset when the place is generally empty.

If you want some plain British food go to the **Aspara Restaurant,** 306 Thanon Samsenthai, which serves beefburgers and chips or the **Sweet Home Bakery,** 109 Thanon Chao Anou, which serves bacon and eggs plus delicious omelettes. Good steaks are served at the **Inter Hotel** overlooking the Mekong River and at the **Ban Tavan,** Khum Borom Street; tel: 856 21 2737. If you can get an invitation there is excellent Western food served in the **Australian Embassy Recreation Club,** Tha Deua Road.

Beer gardens, discos and bars

Beer gardens
Many of these have sprung up in the city in recent years. Popular with aid workers is the **Namphu** opposite the fountain between Thaon Samsenthai and Thanon Settathirat in the city centre. It's also a good place if you want a snack.

Champa Lanexang: a little out of the way this quiet establishment is on Thanon Tha Deua, south of central Vientiane on km 2. As well as a beer garden it also has an inexpensive air-conditioned restaurant which serves good Lao and Thai food.

Discos
Vienlatry Mai: the most popular spot in town particularly on a Saturday night. It's north of the Morning Market along the road to the Patuxai Monument. It features lively bands nightly. The beer here is fairly expensive and the entrance fee exorbitant.

The **Dao Viang** on Thanon Heng Boun has a disco.

Feeling Well: popular with the youth of Vientiane it has live and taped music. It's just beyond the Dong Palan Market.

Another is **Seng Aloune** on Thanon Khou Viang and the rather dingy **Manivan** on Thanon Luang Prabang.

Olympia Disco, Lanexang Hotel, Thanon Fa Ngum. This has a dance on the weekends.

Saysana Club, Saysana Hotel (ground floor), Chao Anou Street; tel: 856 21 213581.

Anou Cabaret, Thanon Heng Buon. Very lively place with loud live bands.

Recently opened are the 'discos' in the Lao Chaleune Hotel and the Saysana Hotel. There are also live bands nightly at the Santiphab Hotel and the Nokkeo Latrymai. It may also be worth considering the **Dok Buoathong Night Club and Restaurant,** Luang Prabang Road; tel: 216821 and **Lanexang Hotel Snack Bar,** Pangkham Street; tel: 214102.

Bars

Nam Phou, intersection of La Fontaine and Mekhala Inthavong. Rather too smart and pricey.

Arawan, 472-480 Samsenthai. Basic and cheap.

An interesting one is the bar attached to the **Sa Loong Xay Asian Restaurant** which features traditional Lao music. This is directly opposite the Lanexang Hotel.

If you are looking for somewhere quiet, go to the **Snake Bar** at the Villa That Luang. They also serve good Thai and western snacks.

A pleasant place for a beer is the **Golden Bamboo** on Thanon Settathirath where you can also have a meal afterwards.

They seem to do more drinking than eating in **Restaurant Vientiane 2** on Thanon Heng Boun.

If you want a seedy nightlife head for **Quai Fa Ngum** where new bars are sprouting like bamboo stalks. This sleazy area where prostitutes ply their trade is perfectly safe (or so I've been told!).

A very rowdy bar is **Les Rendezvous des Amis** which, together with the **Purple Porpoise,** caters admirably for lonely males. Many may be attracted to the **James Bond Bar** on Thanon That Luang only to find that it's completely deserted. They do however serve excellent Lao vodka (*lào láo*).

One of the best for romantics is the **Garden Bar,** known as the Salong Xay, in the plush Lanexang Hotel. Rapidly becoming the most popular amongst the local males are the **White Rose** and the **Kaonhot** on Thanon Sakarin, where many Thai snooker fanatics hang out.

Traditional dance

Natasin Lao School. This is located on Thanon Phoun Hang and is a good place to see *lamvong* performers learning their art. Many of Vientiane's budding theatricals go here to dance to the accompaniment of the *khene*. Arm coordination, balance and graceful gestures are taught by masters. Many of the highly disciplined movements are handed down the generations, some have an

Indian heritage. On special occasions performances of the *mohlam luang*, a form of musical drama, can be seen at this school.

Cultural libraries

The French Club (Le Club France), on Thanon Sethathirat, has a huge stock of books in French. There is also a quiet bar where you can read in peace. It is a good place for French lessons.

The Stockade Library Club, close to the Australian Embassy on Nehru Street (near Independence Monument), has a useful stock of books. You can sit out and read in their garden. It is easy to obtain membership which costs US$10/annum. It only opens on Tuesday and Thursday 15.30-18.30 and on Saturday mornings.

Recreation clubs and saunas

The Australian Club. This belongs to the Australian embassy and is located out of town on Thanon Tha Deua, Km 3. It has table-tennis, squash courts, a swimming pool, snack bar, bar, snooker room and sauna. You must be a member or be invited by one. Tennis equipment can be hired at the Vientiane tennis club and foreigners can also have a swim at the Lanexang Hotel (they charge 900 kip).

Herbal saunas: These are found in wats. The best known are Wat Sri Amphorn Sauna, Thanon Sri Amphorn and Wat Sokpaluang, Thanon Sokpaluang. They are very popular with the Thai visitors and some Lao locals. The new Van Sana Hotel on Phonthan Road has a Lao sauna; tel: 856 21 41 4189 for bookings.

Shopping

Most shops open early (around 06.30) and close around sundown.

Handicrafts

Somsri Handicrafts, Thanon Sethathirat. A good place to buy silk scarves and skirts embroidered in gold thread. Kanchana on Thanon Chantha Kumman is a little cheaper. The *sin* (lao skirts) sold here are magnificent.

Textile Centre, Thanon Luang Prabang. A good place to buy skirts and pottery.

The Handicraft Centre on the same road sells *khene* (bamboo musical pipes).

Union des Entreprises d'Artisanat Lao Export-Import. This establishment on Thanon Phon Kheng has a selection of handicraft articles from many provinces including wood and ivory carvings and pottery.

The House of Dolls on Phon Kheng Road has some attractive articles made from wood.

Kanchana Boutique & Handicrafts, opposite Ekalath Hotel; tel: 856 12 7380.

Lao Pathana Handicrafts, 29/3 Pangkham Street; tel: 856 21 212363.

Phonethip Handicrafts and Ceramics, 55 Saylom Street, Ban Hathsadi; tel: 856 21 216650.

Recommended by a recent traveller is **The Art of Silk** which is located between Pang Kham and Man Tha Hurat. Don't fail to ask to see the silk museum

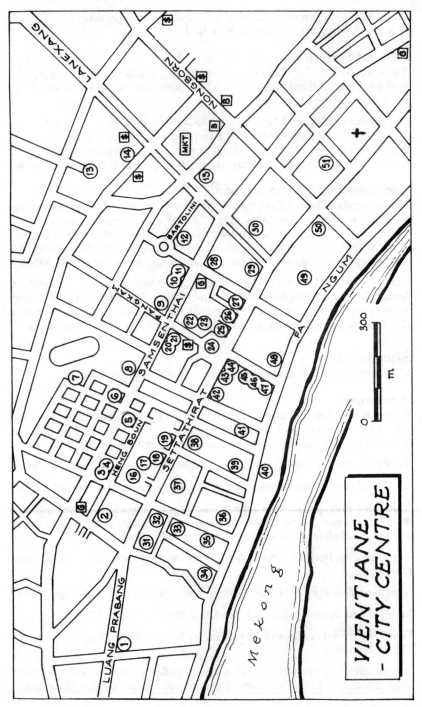

VIENTIANE
- CITY CENTRE

1. NEW APOLLO Hotel
2. THEATRE
3. ANOU Hotel
4. RAJA Tours
5. SHANGHAI Restaurant
6. SANTISOUK Restaurant
7. SYRI Guest House
8. REVOLUTIONARY Museum
9. THAT DAM Hotel
10. ASIAN PAVILION Hotel
11. EKALATH METROPOLE Hotel
12. US Embassy
13. LANI 2 Guest House
14. IMMIGRATION Office
15. POST OFFICE
16. LANI 1 Guest House
17. WAT HAI SOK
18. LE SANTAL Restaurant
19. LANEXANG TRAVEL
20. SETTHA Guest House
21. HONG KONG Restaurant
22. TAJ Restaurant
23. NAM PHU Restaurant
24. NAMPHU FOUNTAIN
25. DIETHELM TRAVEL
26. POLICE
27. TELECOM
28. KUA LAO Restaurant
29. MINISTRY of INFORMATION and CULTURE
30. WAT SI SAKET
31. WAT IN PAENG
32. SAYSANA Hotel
33. La VENDOME Restaurant
34. SODETOUR
35. INTER Hotel
36. WAT CHAN
37. WAT ONG TEU
38. WAT MIXAI
39. MIXAI Guest House
40. MIXAI Restaurant
41. SAMSENTHAI Hotel
42. LAO AVIATION
43. ON TIME Rail Tickets (Thailand)
44. INTER - LAO
45. La SOURIYA Restaurant
46. RAINTREE Bookshop
47. THAI INTERNATIONAL
48. LANEXANG Hotel
49. PRESIDENTIAL PALACE
50. WAT PHRA KEO
51. FRENCH Embassy

upstairs where there is a fabulous selection of intricately woven fabrics. A donation box is near the exit which collects money for the museum's upkeep.

It is also worth visiting the **Inpeng Boutique** close to the Vieng Vilay Hotel.

There are several handicraft shops on Thanon Samsenthai, such as **Nang Xuan** at 385, which sell opium pipes, *mien* embroidery, handsomely carved pirogues and articles in ivory and wood.

Lao Handicrafts, 71/5 Pang Kham Street sell superbly carved wooden sculptures.

Gems and jewellery
M M Bari: One of the few shops in the city where you can buy precious stones mined in the north.

There are a variety of jewellery shops along Thanon Samsenthai which sell silver Lao skirt belts, necklaces and gold pieces.

Antiques
Vanxay Art Handicrafts, Thanon Samsenthai. Remember that if you buy a genuine antique it must be declared at the customs before leaving the country. There are some interesting old tribal antiques sold here and in other shops along the same street and on Thanon Pang Kham.

Nguyen Ti Selto at 350 Thanon Samsenthai sells some particularly nice examples. There is a gallery nearby at 397 Thanon Samsenthai where you can view old sculptures and two art galleries on the same street at 108 and 265.

Nang Xuan Antiques, 385 Samsenthai Road; tel: 856 21 213341.

Clothes shops
Many, such as **La Fantasie** on Thanon Pang Kham, specialise in made to measure garments. A lot of western women find that the wrap around *sin* (Lao skirt) sold in handicraft shops don't contain enough material. They can have one specially made at the **Queen's Beauty Tailor** just off the Fountain Circle.

Lao Textiles by Carol Cassidy, 84 Nokeo Khoumane Street, Ban Mixai; tel: 856 21 212123; fax: 21 216211.

Gallery Lao Antique Textiles, Tha Deua Road, Ban Souanmone (near Souanmone Market opposite the service station); tel: 856 21 212381/312390.

Bookshops
Vientiane is an extremely poor place to buy books. If you are looking for books on Laos, there are very few which can be purchased in Vientiane's **Government Bookshop**. This place, on Thanon Nam Phou, stocks mainly Russian books, a few maps and one of the only coffee table books published in Laos, *Laos* by Roman Ozerski, Serguei Sevrouk and Stanislav Blajenkov (published by Moscou Editions Planeta 1985). It's in French. If you can't get a copy here try the Lanexang Hotel.

Rain Tree Book Shop, 25 Pang Kham; tel: 212031. This is the only place in Vientiane where travellers can swap reading material. It sells new and secondhand books. They have hardly any books on Indochina. The best place to buy books on Laos is in Bangkok.

Art Gallery

Kuanming Art Gallery, 265 Samsenthai Road.

Food shops

One of the best is the 'supermarket' called the **Phimphone Minimarket** opposite the Ekalath Hotel. You can, at a price, buy western goodies here, such as chocolate, imported cheeses, toiletries etc. French luxury food may be purchased at the newly opened **Aranan Charcuterie** at 472 Thanon Samsenthai.

Another is **Foodland,** at 117 Thanon Chao Anou, which sells luxuries imported from Thailand.

A few western luxuries can be obtained at the **Lao Supermarket,** 104 Thanon Khoun Boulom.

The **Department Store** in the Morning Market complex is a good place to buy luxury items imported from Hong Kong, Singapore and Thailand.

A good place to buy alcoholic drinks is the **Friendship Intershop,** 92/3 Thanon Samsenthai.

Chemist shops

These are along Thanon Samsenthai and Thanon Khoun Boulom.

Vientiane directory

Emergencies

Emergency dial **3352.**
Police can also be contacted on:
Chantabouri District; tel: 213907/213908.
Xayasetha District; tel: 412455.
Sikhottabong District; tel: 3958.
Sisathanak District; tel: 412538.

Travel agencies and offices

Aero-Contact Asia, 2/4 Thanon Manthathulat; tel: 856 21 8177; fax: 856 21 9332.
Diethelm Travel Laos, Namphu Square, Settathirat Road; tel: 856 21 178951; fax: 856 21 189044.
Inter-Lao Tourisme, corner of Settathirat and Pangkham; tel/fax: 866 21 3627/3134.
Lanexang Travel and Tour Company, Head Office, Pangkham Road, PO Box 4452; tel/fax: 856 21 215804.
Lao Investment Promotion Corporation, Building 1, Thanon Luang Prabang, PO Box 795; tel/fax: 856 21 9645.
Lao National Tourism, intersection of Thanon Pangkam and Settathirat (near water fountain), PO Box 2912; tel: 856 21 3254/2998; telex: 4348 MICOM LS/4492 TE VTE LS.

Lao Travel Service, 8/3 Lanexang Avenue (PO Box 2553); tel: 856 21 216603/4; fax: 856 21 216150; telex: 4491 TEV LS.

Mixay Travel Services, Fa Ngum Street (PO Box 4661); tel: 856 21 216213; fax: 856 21 215446.

Moradock Tour Company, Nongborn Road, PO Box 4466; tel: 856 21 4837/8233; fax: 856 21 4837/8314.

Nam Ngum Tours, 14 Thanon Heng Boun; tel: 856 21 3467.

Phatana Khet Phoudoi Travel, 118/2 Luang Prabang Road (PO Box 825); tel: 856 21 214673; fax: 856 21 216131.

Phoudoi Travel Company, Sihome Road; tel/fax: 856 21 169236.

Raja Tour, 2nd floor, Anou Hotel, Thanon Heng Buon; tel: 856 21 3660; fax: 856 21 9376.

Sip-sii Mesa Tour Company, 29/4 Pangkam, P.O. Box 2947; tel: 856 21 2979.

Sodetour, 16 Thanon Fa Ngum, PO Box 70; tel: 856 21 4057 fax: 856 21 9022.

That Luang Tour Co, 28 Khamkong Road, Ban Sithane (behind River View Hotel), PO Box 3619; tel: 856 21 21 5809; fax: 856 21 21 5346; telex; 0804 4345 THATOUR VTE LS.

Vieng Champa Tours, Tha Deua Road, Km 3; tel: 856 21 314412; fax: 856 21 14412.

Walter Pfabigan Tours, 14 Fa Ngum Road; tel: 856 21 5236; fax: 856 21 2604.

Vientiane Tourist Office, Sithan Neua Building 11, Thanon Luang Prabang; tel: 856 21 4041; fax: 856 21 5911.

Embassies

Australian, Nehru Street (near Independence Monument); tel: 856 21 2477

Bulgarian, Nong Bone Street; tel: 856 21 3236.

Burmese, Sokpaluang Street; tel: 856 21 2789.

Cambodian, Sophanethong Neua Road; tel: 856 21 4527.

Chinese People's Republic, Sokpaluang Road; tel: 856 21 3494.

Cuban, Sophanethong Neua Road; tel: 856 21 3151.

Czech Republic, Tha Deua Road; tel: 856 21 2705.

French, Settathirat Road; tel: 856 21 2705.

German, Nehru Road; tel: 856 21 2024.

Hungarian, That Luang Road (near Stupa); tel: 856 21 3111

Indian, That Luang Road (close to Ministry of Commerce); tel: 856 21 2255.

Indonesian, Thanon Pong Kheng; tel: 856 21 2370.

Japanese, Si Sung Won Road; tel: 856 21 2584.

Korean, Wat Nak Village; tel: 856 21 3727.

Malaysian, Thanon That Luang; tel: 856 21 2662.

Mongolian, Tha Deua Road; tel: 856 21 3666.

Polish, Nong Bone Road; tel: 856 21 2456

Swedish, Sok Pa Luang; tel: 856 21 5632.

Thai, Phon Kheng Road (near Independence Monument); tel: 856 21 2765.

United States, Thanon That Dam (near Morning Market); tel: 856 21 2384.

USSR, Tha Deua Road; tel: 856 21 5012.

Vietnamese, That Luang Road (near Independence Monument); tel: 856 21 5578.

Airline offices

Flight information available on tel: 212066.
Aeroflot, 409 Samesenthai (close to Lanexang Hotel); tel: 856 21 3501. Also c/o Lao Aviation Booking Office.
Air France, c/o Lao Aviation Booking Office.
China Southern Airlines, c/o Lao Aviation Booking Office.
Lao Aviation, Thanon Pang Kham (near where it crosses Thanon Fa Ngum); tel: 856 21 2093/4; fax: 856 21 9719. These are agents for Air France, Vietnam Airlines, Aeroflot, China Southern Airlines and Thai Airways. Open 08.00-12.00 and 14.00-17.00, Mon-Fri. Sat, open till 11.30.
Lao Aviation Booking Office, 43/1 Thanon Settathirat; tel: 856 21 8710. Head Office, 2 Pangkham Road, PO Box 4169; tel: 856 21 2050; fax: 856 21 21 2056; telex: 4336 LA OAV LS
Thai Airways International, Thanon Pang Kham (opposite Lao Aviation); tel: 856 21 9231. Open 08.00-17.00, Mon-Fri. Sat, open until 12.00.
Vietnam Airlines, c/o Lao Aviation Booking Office.

Car hire

Lanexang Hotel, Thanon Fa Ngum; tel: 3672. US$35/day.
International Consultants, Thanon Samsenthai; tel: 3106. US$30-40/day.
Burapha, 14 Thanon Fa Ngum; tel: 2604. US$25/day (small car), US$45 (Landcruiser), with driver add US$10 per day.

Postal and delivery services

Post Office, Thanon Khou Viang where it intersects with Thanon Fa Ngum.
International Telephone Office, Thanon Settathirat. Open 08.00-22.00. Dial 16 for international operator.
Business Centre, Burapha, 14 Thanon Fa Ngum; tel: 856 21 2604; fax: 856 21 2604.
Lao Freight Forwarder, KM3, Tha Deua Road, PO Box 3145; tel: 856 21 313321/313351/313392; fax: 856 21 314831; telex: 4356 LAOFF VTE LS.
DHL Worldwide Delivery Service, Nongno Street, Sikhottabong District, P.O. Box 2924; tel: 856 21 216830, 212149; fax: 856 21 215414.
TNT Express Worldwide, Lanexang Avenue next to Thai Farmer's Bank (above Lao Travel Service); tel: 856 21 214361.

Hospital services

Australian Clinic, Australian Embassy Compound; tel: 856 21 413603/312343/413610.
Dr Khanh Boulinthong, Sethathirath Street; tel: 856 21 216770/414077/412536.
International Clinic, Mahosat Hospital Compound; tel: 856 21 3113.
Sethathirath Hospital, Phonesaad Road; tel: 856 21 412783/412921.
Swedish Clinic near Swedish Embassy; tel: 856 21 315015/217010/3115018.

Banks and money change

Foreign Trade Bank (La banque pour Commerce Exterior Lao), intersection of Thanon Pang Kham and Thanon Fa Ngum, PO Box 2925; tel: 856 21 21 3200-1; fax: 856 21 21 3202; telex: 4301 & 4315 BCE VTELS. The best place to change travellers cheques and notes. Open Mon-Fri 08.30-16.30. Saturday, open until 11.00.

Joint Development Bank, 33 Thanon Lan Xang (vicinity of Morning Market); tel: 856 21 213530. Same opening times as above.

Nakhorn Luang Bank, 39 Pangkham Street; tel: 856 21 213300-4.

Sethathirath Bank, Sethathirath Street; tel: 856 21 213400/213401.

Thai Military Bank, 69 Khoun Boulom Street; tel: 856 21 217174/216486.

All the above offer money exchange facilities.

There are exchange booths around Morning Market that give extremely good rates of exchange for US$. Many shops offer the service.

Credit cards

You can get up to US$500 advanced to you using a Visa card at the Siam Commercial Bank which is on Thanon Lan Xang just past the southern end of the Morning Market. The superior class and first class hotels listed will take payment with Visa card. Diethelm Travel Laos in Namphu Square will accept payment by American Express cards.

Immigration services

The Immigration Office is near the Morning Market on Thanon Phay Nam. It opens from 07.30-11.30 & 14.00-17.00, Mon, Tue, Thur, Fri, Sat. It opens from 14.00-17.00 on a Wed.

Legal services

DFD (Dirksen Flipse Doran), PO Box 2920, Building 1, Luang Prabang Road; tel: 856 21 21 6927-9; fax: 856 21 21 6919.

Excursions

Around town

Laos is a devout Buddhist nation so, as one would expect, many of the sites of historical interest around Vientiane are religious.

Pha That Luang

This is the most sacred structure in the whole of Laos. It was built on a profoundly religious site which, during the 3rd century AD, was chosen by the Emperor Ashoka as the site of a holy stupa. It has continued to be a place of Buddhist pilgrimage ever since. The original stupa which stood here was believed to have housed a relic of the Lord Buddha. Archaeologists have shown that between the 11th and 13th centuries a Khmer temple stood here. The first structure resembling the present Great Stupa was built during the reign of King Settathirat in 1566. This was damaged during the Siamese raid of 1827, when King Anourouth was force to flee to Hue. When the Ho Chinese invaded in 1875 what was left was flattened. It is thought that the first restoration was carried out under the instructions of King (Chao) Anou at the start of the 19th century. Further work followed at the start of the 20th century when French experts from the l'École Français d'Extreme-Orient slightly altered the original design. This was never accepted by the Laotian Buddhist elite so it was rebuilt yet again between 1931 and 1935. There is a disagreement about who actually carried this

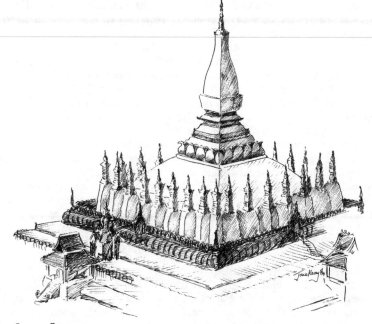

That Luang Stupa

out. The Laotians say that it is a Lao masterpiece. The French say that the structure that you see today was built according to the original architectural drawings of Delaporte, an architect-explorer who spent a lot of time in Vientiane around 1870. They also maintain that it was built by a French team.

Whoever is responsible did a magnificent job. The best time to visit is when the sun is about to set. The central lotus bud spire supported by the third tier and the surrounding 30 smaller stupas all take on a golden glow. The contrast of the tall stylus, topped by a banana flower and parasol against a cerise and mauve sky is totally breathtaking. An aerial view gives one an idea of its almost perfect symmetry. The overall arrangement is that of a three-tiered pyramid, symbolic of Mount Meru. The top platform measures 30m x 30m, the second 48m x 48m and the first 68m x 68m. All are wide enough to allow devout pilgrims to circumambulate the structure. Arched gates (*haw wai*) on each of the four sides allow access to the various tiers which are reached by a series of steps. On the bottom level, offerings are often left at the shrines which resemble small temples. These include numerous silver and gold miniature elongated pyramids, fruit and flowers.

If you walk around the stupa's first level, between it and the outer cloisters, you will see small shrines adorned with white and gold Buddhas, floral pyramids which have been given as offerings and sticky balls of rice which have been stuck on walls. Directly above you is the lotus wall which surrounds the second level. The 30 stupas projecting vertically represent the 30 Buddhist perfections. Originally, these contained small golden stupas (which were carried off by the Ho Chinese). At their centre is the four-sided golden spire which is said to have a brick interior.

Early records indicate that Pha That Luang was originally surrounded by four wats, one in every direction of the compass. Now only two remain – on the south and north sides. Both have classic Vientiane-style architecture, high roofs, rectangular *sims* and prominent doors. Wat Luang Na, on the northern side, features an ornate, three-tiered roof lavishly decorated with sloping dragon spires (*dok sofa*). The steps leading up to the entrance are flanked by dragon parapets, above the doorway is a glorious gilded plaster relief. These sumptuous murals, perfectly proportioned in decorative detail. look at their dazzling best when highlighted by the setting sun. Notice that they are topped by a three-headed elephant, the symbol of old Lan Xang.

The best time to visit Pha That Luang is during the November festival, when you will see members of the *Sanga*, provincial religious leaders (*chao khana khoueng*) and important local dignitaries together with the Supreme Patriarch of Lao Buddhist, the *phra sangharaja*, who leads a procession between Wat Si Muang and the national shrine. It is a time for great festivities and rejoicing.

Pha That Luang is 3km northeast of the city and is reached along Thanon That Luang which starts at the Patuxai Monument. It is open from 08.00-11.30 and 14.00-16.30, Tuesday-Sunday. Admission price is 200 kip.

Unknown Soldier Memorial

This is on Thanon Phon Kheng and can be seen from Pha That Luang. It commemorates many of the Pathet Lao (Revolutionary Soldiers) who died between 1964-73. Built in traditional *thâat*-design, this white obelisk is surrounded by a lotus wall and topped by a metal star.

That Dam

Heading in a southwesterly direction from this monument you cross Thanon Talat Sao and then Thanon Khu. The Black Stupa is down the next turning on the right (Thanon Bartholomie). A local legend says that it houses a fierce seven-headed dragon who is the protector of the Lao people. He is said to have last appeared when Vientiane was besieged by Siamese invaders in 1827, and again in 1875 when the city was attacked by Ho Chinese bandits. This impressive brick stupa is believed to date from the early Lan Xang period.

Wat Mixai

If you continue along Thanon Samsenthai for a short distance and then turn left into Thanon Nokéo Khumman you will come across this wat near the intersection with Thanon Settathirat. This is of minor interest and looks more Thai than Lao. Inside there is a school where foreigners are welcome.

Patuxai

Known also as the Anou Savali or the Victory Gate, this large structure is Vientiane's most prominent landmark. Your first impressions are that it resembles the Arc de Triomphe in Paris. Closer inspection shows that it is a rather drab piece of cement which looks monstrously out of place. It is possible to climb onto the top platform, where there is a good view of the city. This level has four corner towers which surround a central two-tiered one. Running directly underneath it are four paths which meet in the middle. These have access arches which are adorned with cement frescoes. Locals have nick-named

The Patuxai Monument

this commemorative monument, the 'vertical runway' because it was finished with cement originally intended for a new landing strip to be built at Vientiane's Wattay Airport. It was constructed to honour those who died during the 1975 communist takeover. Its old French name was 'Monument aux Morts'. It can be reached from the centre of the city along Thanon Lan Xang. Admission is 50 kip if you want to take in the view of the city.

Revolutionary Museum

If you head towards the Hotel Ekalath Metropole from That Dam and then take the first right turn down Thanon Samsenthai you will soon arrive at this museum. The entrance fee is 200 kip. It has very irregular opening times. Some of the exhibits are labelled in English. Downstairs is a good place to acquaint yourself with important historic sites in Laos. Upstairs you will see many of the triumphs of the Pathet Lao Revolutionary forces which together with the Viet Minh gained outstanding victories against the French. There is a smaller section on the achievements of the Lao Issara ('Free Laos from the French') regime.

Wat Ong Teu Mahawihan

This is further along Thanon Settathirat and is directly opposite Wat Hai Sok. This attractive wat, built by King Settathirat about 1500 AD, houses the largest Buddha in Vientiane. It is well known for its ornate doors which, as with many of its windows, are lavishly decorated with religious motifs depicting scenes from the Indian Panchatantra and Rãmayãna. It is the home of the deputy *phra sangharaja* who is often host to many monks belonging to the *sangha*. They come here together with novices to study canonical works, including Tripitaka manuscripts and other formal disciplinary texts, such as the Vinaya and Paritta.

Wat In Paeng

Further along the road on the left is Wat In Paeng which is worth a visit to see the richly decorated *sim*.

Wat Chan

South of the above, along Thanon Chao Anou, one comes to Wat Chan, which is on the left. Here you will find a magnificent bronze seated Buddha which sits in a small *sim* with attractively decorated wood panels.

Haw Pha Kaew (Wat Phra Kéo)

This is reached by heading down Thanon Fa Ngum, which runs parallel with the river. Near the Mahasot Hospital one turns left into Thanon Mahasot. The wat is on the left near the first intersection. This immensely important wat was originally the home of the Emerald Buddha. It was built by King Settathirat in 1560 as part of a religious building programme when he transferred his capital from Luang Prabang to Vieng Chan. Here he installed the sacred Emerald Buddha in order to protect it from the Burmese who were continually threatening his domain. The hallowed Buddha, made from the finest green jasper, had originally been the symbol of religious sovereignty of the northern Thai Lan Na Kingdom. When transferred to Vieng Chan it became the symbol of Lan Xang. During his lifetime several attempts were made by the Burmese to take Lan Xang, but even the most vicious failed – in 1567. Seven years after his death in 1571 the Siamese, who had fought hand in hand with him against the Burmese, sacked Vieng Chan and carried away the sacred Emerald Buddha, which was never returned. Another Siamese attack in 1827 overcame the forces of King Anourouth and the city of Vieng Chan, including Haw Pha Kaew, was completely sacked. The wat was rebuilt between 1936 and 1942.

The galleries running alongside the *sim*, which are reached by a *naga* guarded staircase, are very impressive. Don't fail to look at the extravagantly carved door which features floral motifs surrounding immaculate Buddha images. The 'rococo' style of ornamentation running along the length of the galleries is more Louis XV than Laotian. Photographers will like the Lao-style sitting and standing Buddhas because some have a very sinister appearance due to their damaged eyes. If the *sim* is open, take the opportunity to see some magnificent Lao sculptures, including a copy of the sacred Phra Bang. Some of the structures here look rather Burmese and others have a district Khmer appearance. There are also plenty of pure Lao figures, including bronze sitting and standing Buddhas. The prize exhibit is a magnificent stone Lao Buddha, said to be the oldest in the country.

Wat Si Saket

This is a little way along Thanon Settathirat on the opposite side of the road to Wat Phra Kéo. It is not far from the Presidential Palace. Built in a distinctive Thai Style by King Anouvong (1804-28), it is the oldest remaining wat in Vientiane which wasn't sacked by the Siamese. It was built in 1818 to house important members of the *Sangha*. One enters the monastic complex through a large courtyard accessed by one gate. The *sim* with its sweeping roof and lotus bud pillar ornamentation is more Thai than Lao. Inside there is one of the most unusual arrangement of Buddha images that you will see in Indochina. Set in numerous recesses are hundreds of small wooden, bronze and terracotta Buddhas, mostly heavily covered in dust. In all, the *sim* is said to contain over 2,000 of these images. Most of the most spectacular and valuable ones have been removed for safe keeping to the *sim* at Wat Phra Kéo. A statue of King Anouvong stands near the main altar. Some of the walls inside the *sim* have faint murals, believed to depict the former lives of Lord Buddha.

It is interesting to come here during the Water Festival (*Boun Pimai*) when the Buddhas are washed in an elongated bath (*hang song nam pha*) which runs alongside the *sim*. To one side of the religious enclosure there is a Burmese-style library which once housed the sacred Tripitaka texts. Admission to the wat is 200 kip. It is open from 08.00-11.30 and 14.00-16.30 on Tuesdays to Sundays. A (free) guide is nearly always available.

Wat Si Muang

If you retrace your steps to Thanon Fa Ngum and head along the river bank in an easterly direction, this wat is in the road which is the second turning on the left. This important religious site contains the city pillar (*lák múang*), the foundation stone of old Vieng Chan. Established by King Settathirat as part of his lavish building programme when he transferred his capital from Luang Prabang to Vieng Chan, it is much venerated by the local population. The stone which was laid here is believed to be an old Khmer boundary stone which once marked the outer limits of Vieng Chan. According to many historians a human sacrifice was made at the time the stone was embedded in the ground.

The original *sim* was destroyed in 1828 and rebuilt around the stone in 1915. Many people with problems come to this wat to pay homage to a stone Buddha who is believed to have the power to grant any wish which is made in his presence. Families with girl children come to ask for a son, businessmen to ask for enlightenment and people with afflictions to ask for a miracle cure.

Short excursions east of Vientiane

Buddha Park

Known locally as Xieng Khouane, this garden sanctuary is the brainchild of Luang Pu, a Laotian holy man who built Hindu and Buddhist statues here in the late 1950s. With financial assistance from the state and donations from devout Buddhists, the park was greatly improved in 1970. One of the finest exhibits is a massive reclining Buddha, which is overlooked by other Buddhist figures and statues of Shiva and Vishnu.

Getting there

Take the Tha Deua bus number 14 from the bus station which stops at many destinations to the east of Vientiane. The 24km journey will take you about 40 minutes and costs 200 kip. There is an entrance fee of 300 kip.

Saam Haa Yai Gardens

Sometimes known as Park 555, this place is a bit of a white elephant (excuse pun). There is not much to see apart from a motley collection of plants, a somewhat unpicturesque lake and a Chinese style pavilion. A lot of people used to come here in the 1980s to see a white elephant which was captured on the border with Vietnam's Central Highlands. The creature was greatly venerated by Laotian Buddhists who saw its presence as a good omen for the future. At festival time it was paraded through the city and decked with flowers.

Getting there

The same bus that goes to the Buddha Park along Route 2 will stop here. The journey takes about 20 minutes (14km) and costs 110 kip.

Tad Leuk Waterfall

Thanks to a new road built by the Swedish Company, Skanska, the Tad Leuk Waterfall on the Nam Leuk River can now be reached in under two hours by car from Vientiane. The new road extends as far as Pakhadine in Borikhamsay Province. This trip is really worth it because the falls is the spectacular equal to the Không Pha Peng on the Mekong near the Cambodian border. In addition there are seven other falls within about 5km of Tad Leuk. The main falls may only drop about 12m but it's a very wild, wide stretch of water. July, during the monsoon season, would be the best time to see it but this unfortunately is the time when it is most difficult to get there. Situated in a dense jungle wilderness, it's a good place to go bird spotting. Species common in the area include brown dipper (*Cinclus pallasii*), Hill blue flycatchers (*Cyornis banyumas*), chestnut-crowned warblers (*Seicercus burkii*) and crested kingfishers (*Ceryle lugubris*).

Getting there

You will need 4WD for the last part of the journey. Take the road out of Vientiane heading south for Paksane. Head for Tha Bok along the newly paved road. This stretch is now so superb that it will only take you about one hour to get there. When you cross the bridge above Houay Hi you will see a green sign with a white arrow on the western outskirts of Tha Bok. It reads Ban Pan Leuk. The road from here is nothing but a dirt track, full of massive pot-holes. If you can't afford the luxury of 4WD, there are many people in Tha Bok who will be able to take you there on their motorbikes. The road leads deep into a forest with an impenetrable bamboo canopy. After about 50 minutes you will hear the roar of water thundering down the falls. The other waterfalls in the area are best reached by foot using a local guide.

Pha Bat Phonsaon

This is an important pilgrimage spot for local people who go there particularly during the Vixakha Bouxa Festival, which is celebrated on the fifteenth day of the sixth lunar month. A shrine was erected here on the site of Buddha's footprint (*pha bàat*). Overlooking the Mekong there is a huge reclining Buddha figure.

Getting there

Leave Vientiane along Auto Route 23 which heads in a southerly direction. Just over 80km from Vientiane, along the Pakxan road, there is a turn-off through coconut plantations to the site. Sodetour in Vientiane will charge US$35 for a day's excursion to the area. If you wish to visit the Forest Reserve (see below), which is fairly close to this area, the price goes up to US$55.

Houei Nhang Forest Reserve

Biologists would find this reserve fascinating. Several days should be spent here if you want to see some of the rarer species. There is a slim chance of seeing the slow loris (*Nysticebus coucang*) and even the pygmy loris (*Nycticebus pygmacus*). Red-bellied squirrels (*Callosciurus erythraeus*) are common and occasionally there is a sighting of a black giant squirrel (*Ratufa bicolor*). A very spectacular looking animal seen here is the brush-tailed porcupine (*Atherurus macrourus*). If you are camping in the area, make sure you carry adequate protection against mosquitoes. Don't leave any food in your tent which is likely to attract hog badgers (*Arctonyx collaris*). Take extra care if you spot a small herd of wild pigs (*Sus Scrofa*) – these have been known to attack humans. Although they are extremely shy and somewhat rare you could see a large spotted civet (*Viverra megaspila*) and a barking deer (*Muntiacus muntjak*). Many bird species inhabit the reserve, the commonest being barbets and warblers. Amongst those reported are the chestnut-winged cuckoo (*Clamator coromandus*), the great-eared nightjar (*Eurostopodus macrotis*), blue magpie (*Urocissa erythrorhyncha*), striated yuhina (*Yuhina castaniceps*) and the little pied flycatcher (*Ficedula westermanni*).

Excursions north of Vientiane

Dau Song

This holy site is greatly venerated by Laotian Buddhists, who come to visit the Buddhist caves. In an idyllic site overlooking the Mekong River there is a cliff, partly obscured by trees. Closer examination reveals a warren of small caves in which there are many Buddha figures. The site is accessed from a local landmark called Dau Song (Flat Stone) near the village of Na Sone.

Getting there

Take Auto Route 13 out of Vientiane. After about 20km the road approaches a bridge near the small village of Ban Hua Khua. The site is about 6km from here, down a narrow track which runs through Na Sone. The road is very bad during the monsoon season. A motorbike taxi is probably the cheapest way of getting here.

Nam Suong Waterfall

It is only worth going here during the rainy season when the rapids are at their highest. The falls are not far from the Animal Project Centre, set up by Australians, about 40km from Vientiane along Auto Route 13.

Lao Pako on Ngum River

Lao Pako is an ecotourism lodge, located on the Nam Ngum River about 50km from the Laos capital. Access is by an interesting drive from Vientiane to the village of Som Sa Mai. From there it is approximately 25 minutes by local boat to the resort. The river trip is fascinating, offering a chance to view natural surroundings and local lifestyle. The resort is constructed almost entirely from native materials, using local techniques combined with European comfort.

A Lao-style longhouse contains three double rooms, each with private facilities and mosquito nets and a seven bed dormitory with a shared bathroom. On the huge veranda, which overlooks the river, there is ample space for just relaxing and taking in the views.

There are separate bungalows for people who like total privacy. Two beds with mosquito nets and en suite facilities are combined with a large, comfortable furnished veranda.

Dormitory accommodation cost US$7 (5,000 kip), a double room US$21 (15,000 kip) and a bungalow US$28 (20,000 kip). They can be booked through Burapha, Walter Pfabigan, 14 Fa Ngum Road or Lao Pako office; tel: 31 22 34. There is a bar where everyone can meet and a restaurant where everyone's needs can be catered for. Community games include volleyball, badminton, boccia, darts, chess and backgammon. Bamboo rafting excursions can be taken on the river. Houses are available for hire. Full moon parties are held every month with barbecue and traditional *Lau Hoi*.

Getting there

By car – Take Route 13 from Vientiane to the south. Turn left at turn 23 (signed) and follow the main road from there (signs at each junction). Cars could, if you prefer, be left at Som Sa Mai, a small village with a sign 'Boat to Lao Pako'. A local boat downstream takes just 25 minutes to get to the resort.

The other possibility is to continue by road after Som Sa Mai for another 12km. There are signs along the way.

By bus – Take bus 19 (Paksane) from the central bus station opposite the Morning Market (*Talaat Sao*). It leaves at 06.30, 11.00 and 15.00 and takes about one hour. Get off at Som Sa Mai and take the boat to Lao Pako. The boat costs 1,500 kip and the bus to Som Sa Mai 300 kip.

Nam Ngum Dam

This very important hydro-electric project is about 90km north of Vientiane. The trip there passes through some interesting areas. The village of Lai, situated along Auto Route 13, is known for its pottery and colourful basket makers. If you are travelling during the monsoon season, get a villager here to direct you to the Nam Khana Waterfall (it's in the general vicinity of the Nam Suong Waterfall, reached via the Animal Project Centre). About 52km from Vientiane the road going north heads past an interesting market just before the town of Phon Hong. It's worth stopping here for a while to see the local minorities which come to trade in the area. It is recommended that you arrive very early since most of the minority people leave before 09.00. Zoologists would be interested in the animal market held daily at Thalat, a little further on. Cages on display hold white-bellied rats (*Niviventer confucianus*) and ordinary house rats (*Rattus flavipectus*) which are considered to be a gastronomic delicacy. Other animals destined for the cooking pot include brush-tailed porcupines (*Atherurus*

Meo couple about to cross the road, Luang Prabang. Note the traditional attire.

Top: Pha That Luang, the most sacred structure in Laos
Bottom: Wat Xieng Thong, the golden city temple

Top: Reflective glass and pearl inlays on the walls of Wat Xieng Thong
Bottom: Hâw tai pha sâi nyàat, the unique reclining Buddha at Wat Xieng Thong

Panning for gold on the banks of the Mekong, near the mouth of the Nam Ou

macrourus), bamboo rats (*Rhizomys sumatrensis*), striped tree squirrels (*Tamiops maclellandi*), pangolins (*Manis pentadactyla*) and lesser gymure (*Hylomys suillus*), which are a relative of the common hedgehog.

The Nam Ngum Dam is now only about 5km away. As far as technological achievements go in Laos, this must be number one. The massive dam holds back water covering an estimated 250km². Photography in the vicinity of the dam wall is not permitted. Below it lies an underwater forest of valuable teak trees which, believe it or not, were not logged before the area was flooded. This however has not put off some enterprising Thai timbermen who continue to salvage what they can. The lake lies in a very picturesque area and is dotted here and there with small islands which have become the home of aquatic birds. It is not uncommon to see the crested serpent eagle (*Spilornis cheela*) which perches on stumps sticking out of the water. There is a chance of seeing the oriental hobby (*Falco severus*) which is more common much further north. Large flocks of little egrets (*Egretta garzetta*) are often disturbed by tourist boats which cruise the length of the lake. The booming sound that can sometimes be heard is the cry of the Cinnamomeus bitterns (*Ixobrychus cinnamomeus*). It is quite common to spot Chinese pond herons (*Ardeola bacchus*) standing motionless on the shore.

The Nam Ngum hydro-electric project first came about because of a feasibility study initiated by the United Nations Economic Commission for Asia and the Far East (ECAFE). In 1957 the Committee for the Coordination of Investigations of the Lower Mekong Basin was born. Its aim was to expand the hydro-electric potential of Laos. The first scheme, the dam on the Se Done River in southern Laos, was a non-starter. Another, built on the Nam Ngum River was the only one to be completed. This massive project was funded by the World Bank, together with monetary aid from France, New Zealand, Canada, Thailand, the Netherlands, Denmark and Australia. By 1968 a transmission line was in place from the 30,000 kilowatt project to the Thai town of Udon in northeastern Thailand. Further money for completion came from the United States Agency for International Development (AID), much of the work was coordinated by Japanese hydro-electric experts. The project is now not only one of the country's highest export earners but also supplies electricity for a large part of central Laos.

Getting there and accommodation

A bus from the central bus station opposite the Morning Market (*Talàat Sao*) costs 300 kip to Thalat. Trucks are available from here for 50 kip to take you the rest of the way. Buses leave Vientiane at 07.00, 09.00, 12.00 and 15.00. If you hire a taxi expect to pay about US$35 for a return trip. If you take the alternative route by taxi you will pass through extremely beautiful scenery. This heads out of Vientiane on Auto Route 10 and passes through Ban Kheun, eventually reaching a ferry which crosses the Nam Ngum Lake. You can expect delays here. Cruises on the lake cost US$3-4. It is a good idea to hire the taxi for two days, then you can stay on the floating hotel on the lake. There is also accommodation near the dam in bungalows which were built by the Japanese. Both can be booked through the Nam Ngum Tourist Office, 14 Heng Boun Street, Vientiane. They cost US$20. In the evening make sure you have plenty of insect repellent if you want to eat at the floating restaurant.

An early start in the morning will take you to the markets at Thalat and the one beyond Phon Hong in plenty of time to see the H'mong people, who are early risers. You can return to Vientiane along Auto Route 13 through the village of Lai, so completing a very enjoyable circular route. Alternatively you can spend an interesting few days in Vang Vieng. which is 71km further north of Phon Hong.

Vang Vieng

For many travellers this small town, 160km to the north of Vientiane, is one of the highlights of their holiday. Its karstic scenery is outstanding, similar in a way to Guilin in China. At the moment there are very few tourists but this could change because a Thai-Chinese resort opened there in January 1994. It's a good idea to stay at the Phu Bane Guest House where the manager will arrange for you to visit the nearby caves. He charges 3,000 kip for one night's accommodation. In the evening you can watch Chinese films in video booths which is rather remarkable since only two years ago Vang Vieng didn't even have electricity. If you want to charter a boat to go up river it costs around 3,000 kip. The caves can only be visited during the June-November period when the water is high enough. There are some interesting H'mong villages in the vicinity. You can get a bus to Vang Vieng for just 300 kip from the bus station. Make sure you make this trip; you will certainly enjoy it. Agencies in Vientiane are charging up to US$80 for a two day trip to Vang Vieng!

Chapter Eleven

Northern Laos

LUANG PRABANG

History

Luang Prabang first became a royal capital under the rule of a 14th century Thai prince called Fa Ngum. He called it Muong Swa (Muong Sua). When he extended his kingdom as far as present day Vientiane in 1353 it became the capital city of Lan Xang (Kingdom of a Million Elephants). When the armies of Annam threatened the city in 1478 they proved to be too powerful for King Say Chakkaphat (1438-79), who was driven into exile. It was recaptured by his son, Crown Prince Thène Kham, who became King Souvanna Ban Lang (1479-86). By then the city had been renamed Xieng Dong-Xieng Dong whose literal translation was 'Copper Tree City'. During the reign of Sai Settathirat (1548-71) it was renamed the City of the Phra Bang (Golden Buddha). When Luang Prabang became a separate kingdom in 1707, the town of the same name became its capital. Its first king was Kitsarat, who had succeeded in ousting his princely cousin, Khamone Noi, in 1707.

In 1887 the city was sacked by the Ho Chinese who carried back to China some of its priceless treasures. By 1893, after the signing of the Franco-Siamese Treaty, Luang Prabang became a French protectorate. By August 21 1941 the French had extended their territory further south to include Vientiane. When independence came in 1953, Luang Prabang remained the royal capital, finally losing its status when the LPDR was formed in 1975.

Getting there

Luang Prabang can be reached by air from Vientiane daily. The current return fare is US$92. Note however that flights to Luang Prabang are fully booked a long time in advance. There are irregular flights to Luang Prabang from Luang Nam Tha (US$35), Oudomsay (US$26), Phôngsali (US$43), Houayxay (US$43), Xieng Khouane (US$32) and Sam Neua (US$44).

Currently the 420km road route from Vientiane is paved just beyond Muang Kasi (320km). Since the remaining 100km takes around eight hours to cover by truck or 4WD, the total journey time is around 15 hours. By 1996, when the highway is complete, it should only take ten hours by bus from Vientiane.

Twenty-ton barges make the journey from Vientiane along the Mekong in four days.

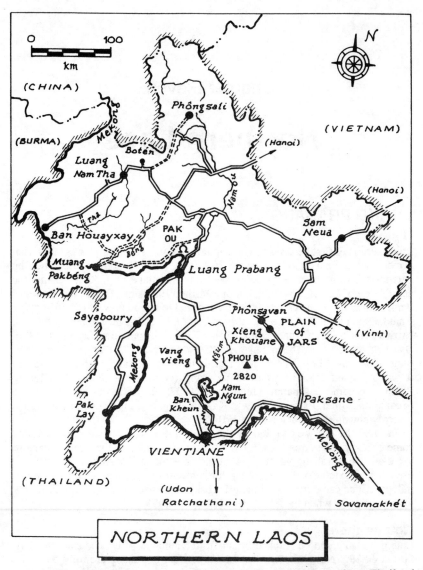

NORTHERN LAOS

Luang Prabang can also be reached by crossing the Mekong from Thailand (Chiang Không to Ban Houayxay) and then taking a fast speedboat (around nine hours to cover the 300km). Slow boats are also available which take two days.

Luang Prabang today

Tourists' first impressions of the City of the Golden Buddha can't help being anything but favourable. From the aircraft the mighty Mekong appears as a mere trickle, the spires of the numerous wats twinkle welcomingly. Even with the current tourist boom which is sweeping the Indochinese peninsula, this 'village city' is never swamped with foreigners. Given the choice of anywhere to go in Asia, this is the place I would choose. People here have a unique, friendly air which is hard to beat. With the peace and slowness of a bygone age it must rate as one of Asia's last Shangri Las.

The physical isolation of the area plus the hard-line Laotian tourist policy of restricting tourism should preserve these friendly people from the evils of the West for at least a few more years. Who knows what will happen when Route Coloniale 13, the old Royal Road, finally gets paved all the way from Vientiane. There's also talk of another threat too, from the north via extensive use of the 300km water highway from Ban Houayxay.

At the moment, however, it still remains a sparsely populated river metropolis which should be renamed the 'City of a Million Welcomes'.

With a pleasant climate at an altitude of only 300m above sea level and with all the attractions within easy walking distance, Luang Prabang will certainly cast a spell of enchantment on all its visitors.

Accommodation
First class
Phu Vao Hotel, PO Box 50, Luang Prabang; tel: 856 71 21 2194.
This has been refurbished during the 1992-3 period by the new owners, who are Swiss. All 52 rooms are comfortably furnished and decorated in a modern style. All have air-conditioning which can be worked by a private generator if the electricity fails. They are also equipped with mini-bars, telephones and private baths, some with tremendous views of the city. The management accept international credit cards. This hotel is usually heavily booked since it is used by many upper class tour agencies. It is the only hotel in Luang Prabang which has a functional swimming pool. In addition it offers bicycle, car and motorcycle rental, Lao and International cuisine, a conference room, a bar and a laundry service. Raja Tours are offering rooms for US$58, Lanexang Travel Co Ltd charge US$68.

It can be booked at the Reservation Office, 10th Floor, Wall Street Tower, 33/45 Surawongse Road, Bangkok 10500; tel: 662 266 7867, 266 7868, 237 0996; fax: 662 238 1294.
Price per room: US$45; room with a view – US$68.

It is rumoured that a Canadian mining company intends to build a new resort opposite the city which will also feature a smart first class hotel.

Second class
Hotel Sisouvannaphoum, Thanon Phothisalat; tel: 856 71 21 2200.
This modern looking establishment, owned by Inter-Lao Tourism, was opened towards the end of 1994. It features 20 rooms with balconies, two grand suites and three junior suites, all fully furnished with modern amenities. It has a garden restaurant featuring classical Lao cuisine and a cosy indoor bar. This efficiently run establishment borders on first class. It can be booked through Inter-Lao Tourism, Vientiane; tel: 856 21 21 4832; fax: 21 6306; telex: 4340 ILT VTE LS. *Price per room: single – US$25; double – US$35; grand suite – US$60; junior suite – US$45.*

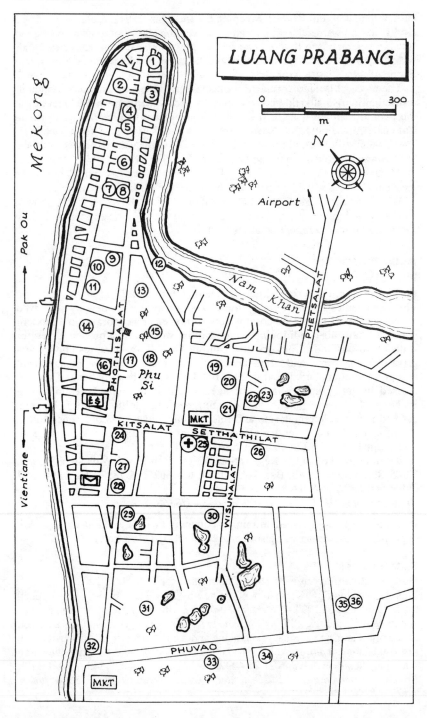

Villa de la Princesse, Thanon Sakkalin; tel: 856 71 7041; fax: available during late 1995.

This classy hotel, with its attractive French-Lao architecture, is owned by Santi Inthavong and his wife Princess Khampha, who is the daughter of the crown prince of Luang Prabang. All rooms have air-conditioning together with hot and cold running water. The hotel is very popular with tour agencies and, since it only has 11 rooms, it is often full. There is a good restaurant but at US$10 for a set menu it's on the expensive side. They hire bicycles for US$4/day.

Available in the not too distant future will be another classy establishment which has been financed by the Bank of Lao. According to Santi Inthavong this will be built on his wife's family land, will feature 14 rooms and be similar to their own hotel.

Price per room: US$45.

---

1. WAT PAK KHAN
2. WAT XIENG THONG
3. WAT KHILI
4. WAT SI BUN HEUANG
5. WAT SI MUANG KHUN
6. WAT SAEN
7. WAT NONG SIKHUNMUANG
8. Hotel VILLA de la PRINCESSE
9. WAT PAA PHAI
10. WAT XIENG MUAN
11. WAT CHUM THONG
12. GARDEN Restaurant
13. WAT PHA PHUTTHABAAT
14. ROYAL PALACE Museum
15. WAT THAM PHU SI
16. WAT MAI
17. WAT PAA HUAK
18. THAT CHOMSI
19. WAT AHAM
20. WAT WISUNALAT
21. RAMA Hotel
22. VISOUN Restaurant
23. YONG KHOUN Guest House and Restaurant
24. PHOUSI Hotel
25. LANEXANG TRAVEL
26. VIENG KEO Hotel
27. WAT HO SIANG
28. WAT THAT
29. VILLA SISOUVANNAPHOUM
30. WAT MANOLOM
31. WAT THAT LUANG
32. WAT PHA BAAT TAI
33. MALY Restaurant
34. Hotel MUANG SWA
35. LAO TOURISM
36. MITTAPHAP Hotel

New Luang Prabang Hotel, Sakkarine Road.
This modern, clean establishment was completed towards the end of 1994. It competes for custom with the Villa de la Princesse. Many would say that the rooms offered here are of a higher standard. They all have air conditioning and hot and cold running water but are slightly cheaper than the Villa de la Princesse. Lanexang Travel Co Ltd charge US$40 for a double/single. Raja Tour has the best price for this establishment, they charge US$26 for a single and US$32 for a double.

Mittaphap Hotel, Thanon Phuvao (PO Box 50); tel: 856 71 7233.
Before the new hotels appeared this was the best accommodation in Luang Prabang. Although it has a superb location on a hillside just on the edge of town, it is a little run down. All rooms have noisy air-conditioning and hot water is frequently not available. It is, however, being refurbished; the derelict swimming pool will soon be in use once again and the restaurant redesigned. By 1996, due to modernisation and other improvements, prices will undoubtedly increase considerably.
Price per room: single – US$25; double – US$35.

Phousi Hotel, intersection of Thanon Phothisalat and Kitsalat Setthathilat; tel: 856 71 7024.
Rooms have air-conditioning and have been completely refurbished during the 1994-5 period. It has a pleasant outdoor restaurant where you can sit out in the evening and watch a menagerie of local fauna pound around in their cages. The food here, both indoors and outdoors, is not up to much. This hotel is popular with tour agencies. Raja Tours can sell you a room here for US$20(!) if booked with a tour.
Price per room: single – US$40; double – US$45; suite – US$55.

Souvanna Phoumma Hotel, just off southern end of Thanon Phothisalat; tel: 856 71 212200.
Rooms here have been recently refurbished. They are large and comfortable. All have air-conditioning and hot and cold running water.
Price per room: single – US$30; double – US$40.

Mùang Swa Hotel, Phouvao Road; tel: 856 71 7056.
New and comfortable. Opened in 1995. All 17 rooms have air conditioning and hot and cold running water.
Price per room: single – US$18; double – US$20.

Third class
Backpackers usually head for the **Hotel Rama,** Thanon Wisunalat, directly opposite the Visoun Restaurant. This can be very noisy because of the disco which is held nightly. Some rooms have a balcony. All are very basic and occasionally have hot water. It is possible to pay in kip. There is no air-conditioning.
Price per room: US$12.

Shoe-string budget

Vieng Kaeo Hotel, Thanon Kitsalat Setthathilat.
Washing facilities here are rather unhygienic. Rooms are poorly cleaned. A backpacker staying here in December 1993 said she suspected that her room was rat invested.
Price per room: US$6.

Wieng Keo Hotel, near Yong Khoune Restaurant.
Another real hovel.
Price per room: US$3.

Sengmany Guest House, Thanon Phothisalat.
Rooms are available above restaurant. Extremely basic.
Price per room: US$2-3.

Eating

Breakfast

For a hearty breakfast the backpacker is recommended to head for the Taláat That Luang Market, situated not far from the Mekong River at the intersection of Thanon Phuvao and Thanon Phothisalat. Here, at the crack of dawn, minority people, mostly H'mong and Khamu, arrive to sell their home grown produce. It's a good place to buy fresh fruit and sample what the locals eat. Small stalls are set up, complete with basic wooden tables and benches. There's no gilt and elegance here but the food is fresh and delicious. I would even go as far as to say it's Luang Prabang's premier dining experience. You can sit opposite one of the H'mong traders and enjoy *áw lám*, a spicy mushroom soup made from different varieties of hill fungus. Some people like it with egg plant. Typically, a trader may beam across the table at you and show off his solid silver teeth as he tucks into his noodles. One of the most unusual dishes here is the stew *kaeng awm*, which is probably too bitter for the Westerner's taste, but is certainly very filling. You can purchase the usual fermented fish, *pàa dàek*, which is said to be safer to consume in the north. If you are prepared to wait for them to kill a chicken you can order *kai ping*, which in the north is grilled on skewers and served with sticky rice. Also popular with the minorities, mainly because it's cheap, is *keng kalami*, a soup which is served with bits of raw fish, cooked meat and cabbage. Whatever you eat you will enjoy the food and the company. Expect to pay only 300 kip for a full meal.

If you want to pay ten times as much for something not nearly as good, go to the Villa de la Princesse Restaurant. Here you can get a Western-style breakfast. Most hotels in Luang Prabang serve pineapple jam (*mak nat kuan*) with the morning toast. Eggs tend to be very hard boiled, guava (*màak sii daa*) or papaya (*màak hung*) is the usual starter. If you are a fussy eater then this place will suit you admirably.

Lunch

If you want something light, go to the Yong Khourn Restaurant or the Visoun next door. Both these are on Thanon Wisunalat, opposite the Rama Hotel. They serve excellent Chinese noodle soup. If you want something more substantial you can order various Chinese dishes including barbecued pork, *dim sum*

(Chinese dumplings), roast duck and frogs' legs in hot chilli sauce. They also serve good light lunches at the Khem Karn Food Garden overlooking Nam Khan River near Wat Pha Phuttabaat.

Dinner

If you want a quiet candle-lit dinner for two go to the **Villa de la Princesse**. They have a standard set menu for US$8-10

The best traditional Laotian food is served at the **Maly Restaurant** on Thanon Phu Wao. Here aromatic herbal ingredients are used liberally. Many of the meat dishes contain turkey since it is readily available locally. One of the nicest meals is chunks of turkey which have been soaked in local wine and spices such as chillies, tamarind and lemon grass added. This is barbecued on skewers and served on a bed of fried rice (*khàa phát*). There are many different versions of it, depending on what meat is used. The Lao name for the dish is *pîng nâam tók*. If you go on a boat trip to Pak Ou you will no doubt stop at a local village. Look out for gauze covered frames which are used to dry green river moss, a local delicacy. In Luang Prabang it is called *khái pâen*. It is stir-fried with various ingredients, the most popular of which is ground up sesame seeds. You can try water buffalo at this restaurant.

Entertainment

There are bars at most of the hotels and a disco every night at the Rama. On the weekend there is one at the Muangsua Hotel. You may be lucky enough to be invited to a Basi ceremony, where you will entertained by *lamvong* folk dancers. If you are not travelling with a tour group, enquire at one of the three local tourist offices. They may be able to arrange for you to join others and enjoy what is the number one attraction in any part of the country.

Short directory

Medical emergencies: Provincial Hospital, Thanon Kitsalat Setthathilat. This is in the city centre.

Airline office: Northeast of Wat Manolom on Thanon Wisunalat.

Bank: 65 Thanon Sisavangvong. The rate for travellers cheques in the north is slightly lower than in Vientiane. They also take a 2% commission. Don't change too much as you can't change it back.

Bicycle hire: Villa de la Princesse charges US$4/day. Rama Hotel charges US$3/day.

Boat hire: There is a docking area to the rear of the Haw Tham (Royal Palace). Bargain hard.

Bus station: Buses leave from the Dala Market area in the middle of the city (Just off Thanon Kitsalat Setthathilat).

Diethelm Travel: 47/2 Sisangrong Road. Tel: 7266

Lanexang Travel: Thanon Soukaseum. Tel: 7225.

Lao National Tourism: next door to Mittaphap Hotel.

Luang Prabang Tourism: Thanon Phothisalat. Tel: 7224.

Post Office: Corner of Kitsalat and Thanon Phothisalat. Open 08.30-17.00 (Mon-Fri).

Sodetour: Close to Luang Prabang Tourism

Taláat Dala Market: Thanon Kitsalat Setthathilat.

Telegraph Office: Directly opposite Wat That. As yet there are no facilities for making international calls from Luang Prabang. This will no doubt change when the highway to the north is extended as far as the city by early 1996.

Excursions
Around the city
A pagoda tour

The ubiquitous temples of Luang Prabang are not only places where devotees go to pray and present their offerings but they are also meeting places for the elderly and a cool sanctuary for everyone. Foreigners are welcome at any time but they should dress respectfully, remove their shoes before entering and possibly leave behind a small donation.

A good way to get around is to hire a bicycle. There is no security problem in Luang Prabang so you can leave it anywhere. If you get one from the Rama Hotel, a good place to start the tour is:

Wat Wisunalat

This wat, also called Wat Visoun, is right next door to the Rama. The structure you see today is not the original which was constructed in 1513. The present building dates from 1898. It contains the largest Buddha in the city, which has pride of place in the *sim*, along with countless other Buddhas donated over the years by local people. Some of the most interesting are the 'Calling for the Rain' Buddhas which are over 400 years old. Nearby are ordination stones of about the same age. From 1507 to 1715, the original wooden wat (which was destroyed by Ho Chinese in 1887) which stood on this sacred site was the most highly revered temple in the north. This is because it contained the sacred golden Phra Bang Buddha. The only part of the original building which remains is the 16th century arch seen on the northwest side of the sim.

The 34.5m (113ft) high semi-spherical stupa standing immediately in front of the *sim* was built by Queen Visounalat, the devoted wife of King Wisun, in 1503. Like the *sim*, this great stupa is not the original, which was badly damaged by the Ho Chinese. During their invasion they committed the sacrilegious atrocity of removing many of the sacred Buddha images which had been enshrined inside the stupa. The ones which weren't carried off to China can still be seen in the Palace Museum. Locals call this stupa That Mak Mo which, translated from Lao, means 'melon stupa'. The one you see today was built in 1895.

Wat Aham

Only a few steps away is this simple sanctuary which houses one of the most frequently visited spirit (*phi*) shrines in Luang Prabang. The people here believe that *phis* control man's destiny as well as being the guardian spirits of places. In order to be successful in anything one must gain the favour of these spirits. A person starting off in a new business or getting married will come to make offerings at this shrine. At one time the head of the Laotian Buddhist *sangha*, the *phra sangharaja* lived at this wat.

Wat That Luang

This is reached by heading in a southerly direction along Thanon Wisunalat, past the Lao Aviation Office, as far as the intersection with Thanon Phu Wao. Near the new Muangsua Hotel one takes a sharp right and peddles along Thanon Phu Wao for about 350m. A road on the right leads to Wat That Luang.

You can see by the number of spires (*dok sofa*) that this was built by a king (there are over ten). The king who built it in 1818, Mangthathourat (1815-36), was well thought of by the people of the area. Even today many devotees will bring offerings to the *sim*. Some will also be left near King Sisavang Vong's golden stupa (also his mausoleum) to one side of the religious compound. He became king of Luang Prabang on March 4 1905 after receiving a formal education at the École Coloniale in Paris. During his reign (1905-59), Sayaboury Province became Thai territory. He is remembered as a stubborn, friendly king who refused to give his backing to the Lao Issara government. This led to his downfall so, rather than lose his kingdom, he relented. He ruled over a united Laos from 1947 until his death in 1959.

This is a good place to come in the early morning to see the promenading of the numerous monks who live here, on their way to collect their daily alms.

Wat Pha Baat Tai

This is at the end of Thanon Phu Wao. It overlooks the Mekong River. There is nothing much to interest the visitor inside except very new looking, slightly psychedelic Buddhas with fairy-light halos. Remember the location of this wat and return here after the pagoda tour is complete. You will be treated to one of the most magnificent sunsets in Indochina. All the tourist guides in Luang Prabang know of this spot so it's a good idea to come early to make sure of a good position if you want to take photographs. (See the cover picture on this book!)

Wat That

Head in the direction you came from for about 50m and turn left into a street which runs parallel with the Mekong. You will pass the That Luang Market and the Luang Prabang tourist office before you come to Wat That.

Part of the *sim* was rebuilt during 1991-2 but most of the restorations were carried out at the beginning of the century. This lovely wat was originally built in the 1500s. It has a style reminiscent of the northern Thai temples. Special attention has been given to the windows, which are lavishly outlined in gold ornamentation. The doors here have some remarkable sculpted figures which are finished in gold. The pillars are richly decorated with *nāgas*.

Wat Mai Suwannaphumaham

This can be reached by heading further along Thanon Phothisalat past Wat Ho Siang (which is itself of minor importance). Wat Mai is just past the bank on the left hand side, quite near the Phousi Hotel. This is a good place to visit at the hottest time of the year (mid-April) when, during the New Year Festival (Boun Pimai), the most sacred Buddha statue in Laos, the Phra Bang, is exhibited in the *sim*. If you come here early on the first day of the festival you may see the two racing pirogues which are stored here make one of their twice-yearly appearances.

The crowning glory of the wat is its long, sweeping, five-tiered roof and its strikingly ornate golden cameo door panelling which depicts one of the final reincarnation stages of Lord Buddha. When you enter the *sim* take a look at the beams which are decorated with scenes from the Rāmayāna. At one time, between 1894 and 1947, the golden Phra Bang was housed here. When this was the home of the *phra sangharaja*, it was known as Wat Souvanna Phommaram. The date of its inauguration is not known exactly (sometime between 1788-1821). It took the original builders over 70 years to complete and remains one of the finest in the north.

Wat Paa Huak
Further along Thanon Phothisalat on the other side of the road is Wat Paa Huak. This has been badly neglected and shows bad signs of decay. It's worth a visit to see murals in the *sim* which show life on the Mekong River as it was centuries ago. There are also some nice bas-reliefs.

That Chomsi
To get here you have to climb the steps all the way to the top of the hill. An entrance fee of 500 kip is charged. You can see its glistening gold spire from many parts of the city. When you get there you will have a fine view, it's a good place to get an idea of the distribution of Luang Prabang's wats. The main procession for the Boun Pimai Festival start here in April. Near the rectangular base of the stupa are small metal bodi trees. If you follow the path down the hill near the canon you will come to the cave sanctuary of Wat Thammothayaram, where you will see what the Laotians call Pha Kachai, a form of tubby Buddha.

Wat Pha Phuttabaat
Originally a wooden wat was built here in 1395. Now it has been replaced by one built in 1959, that shows a mixture of Chinese and Vietnamese architecture. It can be reached by retracing your steps to the entrance on Phu Si Hill and then walking around to the north-eastern side. The wat is built on a profoundly religious site where Lord Buddha is said to have left a footprint. Its other name, Wat Phra Bath, bears this out because in Pali, *bath* translates as footprint.

On the other side of the Thanon Phothisalat is a group of three minor temples. The nicest of these is probably **Wat Paa Phai,** which has some magnificent Chieng Mai style wall canvases which very graphically illustrate scenes from northern Laos as it was over a century ago. If you go into **Wat Xieng Muan,** which is slightly west of Wat Paa Phai, you will see some outstanding ceiling frescoes featuring golden *nāgas* floating in the sky. In nearby **Wat Chum Không** you will see some finely preserved candle rails (*ráan thién*) which are also decorated with *naga* figures.

Wat Non Sikhunmuang
If you go further along Thanon Phothisalat you will see the Villa de la Princesse Hotel on the left. This wat is directly opposite it towards the river. Simple but elegant, this fine little wat was built in 1729. The structure that you see today, which is typical of the northern Chieng Mai style, was built in 1804 after the original burnt down in 1774.

Wat Saen
This is a little further along the road on the left. This wat was constructed in 1718 and was the first in the area to show the distinctive northern Thai style. Its other delightful name, the 100,000 Temple, is sometimes used because it was built with the donations of the people, who managed to raise 100,000 kip. It is

believed that some of the funds were raised from gold panned out of the Nam Khan River.

From here Thanon Phothisalat continues past old French villas which have become discoloured by age. On the left are two wats of minor significance, **Wat Si Muang Khun** and **Wat Si Bun Heuang**. On the other side of the road are **Wat Khili** and the Dutch Pagoda, **Wat Pak Khan**, which has figures embossed on the front door which are said to be Dutch merchants.

Wat Xieng Thong

Near the end of the road, at a prominent position overlooking the Mekong, is the most dashing of Luang Prabang wats. This grand royal wat was built by King Sai Settathirat in 1560. It certainly lives up to its other name, the 'Golden City Temple'. When struck at certain angles by the rays of the sun, many of the walls glitter. Examined closer up, the opulence is dazzling and testimony to the devoted dedication of the original workforce. If this city was the cradle of the Lao culture then this wat must be its greatest treasure house. One of its finest artistic creations is the small reclining Buddha known to the Laotians as the *hâw tai pha sâi nyàat*. This was exhibited in Paris in 1931 and in Vientiane until 1964. The chapel (*hor song phra*) which contains it has some noteworthy architecture. Predominantly pinky-red in colour, its lacquered walls are covered in highly reflective Japanese glass mosaics which depict Laotian rural life. Added in 1957 to celebrate the Lord Buddha's 2,500th birth anniversary, these thousands of reflective inlays twinkle when struck by the rays of the sun. On each side is a traceried window with shapely wooden balustrades. The roof is a two-tiered structure, the bottom tier being supported by highly sculpted gold triangular protrusions. The main entrance door is gilded in gold and features gold embossed figures. The edges of the eaves are finished in gold patterning of a similar type to that seen on the lintels. Inside the wall behind, the reclining Buddha is tastefully festooned with gold-leaf Buddhas. In front of it are several ancient bronze Buddhas in a variety of mudras.

The main *sim* has an elegantly structured, three-tiered, low sloping roof which is one of the best examples of the northern style in Laos. Topped by numerous dragon-shaped spires (*dok sofa*) it was clearly built by royalty. The whole structure is supported by eight ornately designed wooden pillars. Don't fail to have a look at the rear wall of the *sim* which features a magnificent 'tree of life' mosaic set against an orange-brown background. Inside its elegant interior all the walls are black and faced with gold frescoes featuring many Buddha images. You can clearly see that the building has a cruciform ground plan. Towards the back wall is a small enclosure supported by four pillars covered in gold motifs. At its centre is a tall golden Buddha in seated position (Bhumisparcamudra), either side of which are two smaller Buddhas. The front part of the altar has three bronze Buddhas in seated position, 'calling the earth to witness'. Behind these are four others, the most magnificent being seated just in front of the large golden Buddha. On the ceiling you will see numerous *dharma* wheels.

North of the *sim* are golden stupas and a drum tower. East of these is the Funerary Carriage House (*hóhng kép mîen*), which is sometimes known as the funeral chariot (*hor latsalot*). Its walls are extensively embellished in gold mosaic depicting scenes from the Hindu epic, the Rãmayãna. Inside is the high

Wat Xieng Thong, the Golden City Temple

funeral carriage, which was last used on the death of King Sisavang Vong, who was cremated on October 29 1959 and his ashes put to rest inside an urn in Wat That Luang.

At the south side of the *sim* you will see the wonderfully ornate library which contains sacred Buddhist scriptures. To the west of it is the shelter for the pirogue which makes an appearance during the Lao New Year celebrations in mid-April and once more in October to celebrate the Luang Prabang Water Festival.

Dotted around the southern part of the temple enclosure are numerous stupas, the most impressive of which is the octagonal stupa.

To get to the other wats in this area it is necessary to cross the river. You can get there from the pier at the back of the Royal Palace Museum on Thanon Phothisalat. Expect to pay no more than US$3 return.

Wats on the west side of the Mekong
The boat docks at Xieng Maen District. Directly opposite Wat Xieng Thong is the cave temple of **Wat Tham**. This has been neglected and there is no apparent logic to the motley mix of old Buddhas which have been deposited inside. You will need a torch to explore inside.

Slightly southwest of the cave is **Wat Long Khun**. Before Sisavang Vong became king on March 4 1905 he had to spend a period of three days here in retreat. Besides its idyllic, tranquil setting, there is nothing much to attract tourists to this sanctuary. Any murals still existing are badly faded.

It is worth climbing the hill opposite to **Wat Chom Phet** which is perched on the summit. If photographers come here when the sun is low in the sky they can get a magnificent panoramic picture over the Mekong River. The best time is around 17.00 when the sun has not fallen too low. Close to this wat is **Wat Xieng Maen** which, for a short period in 1867, housed the sacred Phra Bang Buddha. It was founded by the son of Settathirat 1 (1548-71), Chao Naw Kaewkumman, in 1592 during a period when Laos was controlled by Burma.

The Royal Cemetery
You can get to this by walking 1km downstream. You will have to go by yourself since Laotian guides believe that evil spirits haunt this place. The ones here are said to be particularly bad since the royalty buried at this place suffered abnormal deaths. Some died as infants and others from horrible, contagious diseases. A spirit which is released after such a death is called a *phi phetu*. People believe that anyone coming into contact with one will be tormented for life. It's worth going to see the sculptures. From here you can see Phou Nang and Phou Thao, two hills which were named after local lovers who, according to a legend, were immortalised as mounds.

The Royal Palace Museum
You can visit this after you return to the east bank. The last member of the Lao royalty to live here was Sisavang Vong's son, Crown Prince Sisavang Vatthana. One of the best views of the general layout of the palace is from Phu Si Hill. Looking directly downwards you can see that the palace has a cruciform ground plan. Twelve steps, made from Italian marble, lead up to a marble platform. Beyond is a gilded double-door above which the Laotian flag flaps in the wind. Just below the eaves you can see a three-headed elephant, embossed in gold leaf. This is the symbol of Lan Xang or, giving it its full title, 'Lan Xang Hom Khao', (The Kingdom of a Million Elephants). Right in the centre of the palace is a cluster of three-tiered roofs, each bearing a curved pointed spire at its apex. These all converge onto a central five-tiered gold coloured tower which is topped by an elongated spire. This leads the eye to the Mekong River which is just to the rear of the palace. It was constructed here so that visiting monarchs, dignitaries and important foreign visitors wouldn't have far to walk after docking. Despite being built in 1904, the roof is the original and is in remarkably good condition. During the fighting between the LPLA and RLA forces in 1975 it survived unscathed. The next year it was converted into a museum after Sisavang Vatthana had handed it over to the Lao government.

Private Chapel
This is one of the most interesting wings of the palace. Here you will see the priceless gold Phra Bang Buddha in Abhayamudra (dispelling fear). You will probably be disappointed when your guide tells you that it is not the original. (This has been locked away in the most secure vault in Laos.) Despite this, it is made from 90% pure gold and is said to weigh 50kg. The original first-century masterpiece is said to have been introduced into Cambodia by Ceylonese monks in the 11th century. It arrived in the northern city of Xieng Dong-Xieng Dong during the reign of King Visun in the 16th century. (Another source says it was during the reign of Fa Ngum.) After the great Thai king, Taksin of Thonburi, had

gained a resounding victory against the Lao in 1778, it was stolen and taken to Bangkok. In 1781 it was returned by King Rama I. The Thais flattened Vieng Chan once more in 1827 and carried the Phra Bang off to Bangkok. It was returned once more in 1867 by King Mongkut. Numerous smaller Buddhas surround it in the Palace Museum. It is interesting that Luang Prabang (more strictly Nakonrn Luang Prabang) is named after this holy structure. Its other name is the 'City of the Phra Bang' (the Golden Buddha). It is intended that the Phra Bang will be eventually housed in a chest in front of the Royal Palace Museum. In the chapel you will also see four other golden Buddhas which are believed to have originated from Cambodia. To one side of the room is a handsome Lao silk screen, embroidered with Theravada images by King Sisavang Vatthana's wife.

Reception Room of the King
The walls are lavishly adorned with painted frescoes which depict rural life in Laos. They look remarkably like those seen on the side of the chapel (*hor song phra*) at Wat Xieng Thong. Busts of dead Laotian kings are on prominent display together with beautifully crafted silk screens. This room is to the right of the entrance hall.

Reception Room of the Queen
This is reached by walking to the left of the entrance hall, beyond the room that was reserved for the king's secretary. Here you will be stared at by faces of royalty. These paintings are by a Russian artist, Ilya Glazunov. They show the king, Sisavang Vatthana, his beloved wife, Queen Kham Phouy, and the Crown Prince Vong Savang who, after the abdication of his father on December 1 1975, was appointed to the Supreme People's Assembly. The Crown Prince's official duties were however short lived. Together with his father Sisavang Vatthana he was imprisoned in Houaphan Province in 1977 after being accused of aiding the cause of the resistance fighters.

The most unusual exhibit in this room is a piece of moon rock presented to the monarch by Leonid Brezhnev in 1967. There is also an assortment of gifts given to the king by visiting diplomats.

Throne Room
This is behind the entrance hall. It houses the royal crystal which is carefully protected behind glass. The Buddhas which you see here are those that survived the onslaught of the Ho Chinese when they sacked the sacred stupa at Wat Wisunalat. Also in this room are the king's swords and his magnificent elephant chair. The wall decoration, which consists of colourful enamelled mosaics on a pinkish-red base, was originally prepared for Sisavang Vatthana's coronation which never took place.

The Royal Library
This had been used extensively by Crown Prince Sisavang Vatthan's father after he had returned to Luang Prabang from the *École Coloniale* in Paris just before his coronation in 1905. During his reign, Sisavang Vong had added to it considerably so that his son could enjoy the same literary privileges he had enjoyed. When he returned from the *École de Science Politique* in Paris he used to study here quite frequently. The library is next to the coronation room.

Music Room
The music room contains a unique collection of ancient Laotian musical instruments. Exhibited are various types of *khene* (harmonicas), *nangnat* (xylophone), *khuy* (flute), a two-stringed instrument called a *so* and a *không vong*, which is a largish semi-circular instrument with 16 gongs arranged around its periphery.

The royal bedrooms are just as they were left when the royalty were forced into exile.

Further afield

Ban Pha Nom
This village, which is said to have practised the art of weaving for over 300 years, is getting rather commercialised. The inhabitants, mainly Lu Chinese, make sarongs (*pha sin*) with dragon motifs (*lái nàak*), shawls (*pha biang*) which are often dyed an indigo colour using a natural dye extract from the plant *Indigofera tinctoria*. Some of the cloth woven in the village is embroidered with delicate silver and gold thread. Girls are taught from a very young age the skills which have been handed down from their forebears in Xishuangbanna District in China's Yunnan Province. The village is 3km east of Luang Prabang (enquire at the tourist offices which offer excursions there for around US$5). You can visit the tomb of French explorer Henri Mouhot on the way there.

Ban Chan
If you would like to see large earthenware water-storage jars being made, go to this village where the inhabitants are very friendly. Any boatman at the docking site at the back of the Royal Palace knows where it is. Expect to pay no more than 4,000 kip for the return journey (about 4km by boat, there and back).

Kuang Si Falls
You can combine this trip with a visit to the Khamu village of Ban Tha Baen which you will pass on the way to the falls. Here you can see baskets being made and, with permission from the village head, enter one of the stilt houses.

The falls is about 29km from Luang Prabang and is reached via the road which heads in a southwesterly direction past the That Luang Market and Wat Pha Baat Tai. The falls is worth a visit particularly during the October-November period when the water level is high. Water cascades over a series of different levels.

Ban Hat Hien
This is a village which specialises in making agricultural tools, gun shot and knives. Metal castings from old artillery shells and bombs are melted down together with any scrap the villagers can get their hands on. The primitive forges used here are worth seeing. Any *saam-law* driver will know where it is. Expect to pay around 1,500 kip for the return journey.

Pak Ou Holy Caves
Fast or slow boats are available from the jetty behind the Royal Palace to take you there. The caves are about 25km up stream from Luang Prabang near the confluence of the Mekong and Nam Ou. When you arrive at this special sacred spot

you will see a series of white steps which lead to the Tam Ting cave-temple. Before the monastery was abolished, the king used to come here on the 15th day of the sixth lunar month to celebrate the Festival of Vixakha Bouxa (the main Buddhist festival of the year). Inside you will see hundreds of small Buddha images which are said to be over 400 years old. It is believed that they were first brought here for safe-keeping when Luang Prabang was threatened by the Ho Chinese.

To get to the upper cave you will need to take the stairs on your left. The cave called Tham Phum has an unusual fat golden-coloured Buddha with huge ear lobes sitting outside. The cave goes into the side of the mountain for about 100m so you will need a torch to see the numerous Buddha images inside.

Longer boat trips
Lao National Tourism will now issue permits to take longer boat trips to Ban Houayxay in Bokeo Province and soon it may be possible during the high water period (June-November) to arrange permits to travel all the way to the heart of Phôngsali Province.

XIENG KHOUANG PROVINCE
History
The semi-independent Phuan Kingdom was founded here by Chet Chuong VII. Fa Nhum incorporated it into the Kingdom of Lan Xang in 1353. By 1478 it had come under Vietnamese influence, until the 16th century, when it was mostly under control of Lan Xang. When the split occurred, dividing the kingdom into Vieng Chan, Champassak and Luang Prabang, Xieng Khouang fell under the influence of Hanoi. When its ruler Chao Noi committed a misdemeanour in 1830, he was immediately summoned to the court of Hue, where he was executed by Emperor Minh Mang. The main reason for this was that he had sided with the Siamese, who were fast developing control in north-east Laos. By the turn of the century Xieng Khouang had become Siamese territory and many of its inhabitants had been forced to leave the country. The province became part of French Laos under a treaty signed by the French and Siamese in 1893.

Between 1820 and 1850 there had been a mass migration of H'mong tribespeople into the area from southern China. These, together with the Thai tribes in neighbouring Phôngsali Province, hated the official French *présence*. Unfair tax burdens, tight fiscal control and increasing dominance by the colonial administration led to riots and hardship. The French, during 1900-22, faced growing opposition from the minorities and the bandits who had infiltrated the area from southern China. When French troops were busy trying to subdue a minority uprising in Xieng Khouang Province, these bandits saw their chance and took the town of Xam Neua (Sam Neua). The French *commissaire* was killed during the attack which took place in November 1914. Tribal rebellions increased in 1919, during which the H'mong leader, Ba Chay, became a prominent figurehead. Right up to 1940 the French learned the hard way that they would have to abide by existing customs and traditions if they were to gain any respect at all from the minorities. They allowed them to retain their own administrative system, headed by the *chao muong*. Below him was the *tasseng*, who had control over six to ten villages, each ruled by its own headman (*nai ban*).

During the period that Xieng Khouang Province was a French Protectorate little was done to improve the condition of the roads, the French concentrating instead on Route Colonial 13 which extended from Luang Prabang to Vientiane (completed in April 1943).

When France fell to Germany in 1940, French control in Indochina seemed at an end, by August 29 1941, Xieng Khouang came under the sovereignty of the Kingdom of Luang Prabang. On March 9 1945, the French were ousted by the Japanese *coup de main*, but, by September 23 1946, the French tricolour once again had been raised throughout the country. As anti-French resistance became more and more intense in neighbouring Vietnam, it was inevitable that the Viet Minh fight for independence would soon extend onto Laotian soil. The first attack came in early April 1953 when the Viet Minh launched an offensive on Sam Neua. This was followed almost immediately by another in the Plain of Jars region. Their victory against the French at the battle of Dien Bien Phu in 1954 meant that no longer could France restore the status quo in Indochina.

By December 1960, the Lao People's Liberation Army (the Pathet Lao resistance government) who had set up their headquarters in neighbouring Houaphan Province in 1953, established control in Xieng Khouang. They were supported by the Hanoi government, who sent in large numbers of Viet Minh soldiers to help further their cause. Bitter fighting broke out between them and the Neutralists (the political faction led by Souvanna Phouma). During the skirmishes many of the 'H'mong secret army' led by Van Pao and funded by the American CIA were killed.

By mid-1960, the Plain of Jars had become a hot-bed of military activity. Larger losses by the H'mong and Neutralists prompted American air strikes which pounded the Tran Ninh Plateau. By 1970, after long periods of intensive bombing, countless villages and towns throughout the province had been pulverised almost to oblivion. The Pathet Lao march on Vientiane had been temporarily halted but the cost had been beyond belief in terms of the numbers of innocent villagers who had lost their lives. (Loss of life in the area continues even in the nineties because of cluster bombs which had been dropped in their tens of thousands.)

By March 1972 thousands of Viet Minh had swarmed into the area to support the large numbers of Pathet Lao forces which had regrouped. The American bombing effort had been switched to the Ho Chi Minh trail and this had given the Pathet Lao the opportunity of retaking Xieng Khouang Province. By 1973 they were fully in control. About a third of the total H'mong population of 300,000 had either been killed or had been forced to leave the country. When the 'Revolutionary Administration' took control in Vientiane on August 23 1975, many hundreds more left the province. After the abdication of King Savang Vatthana on December 1 1975 and the formation of the Lao People's Democratic Republic (LPDR), a motion was proposed to make Phônsavan in Xieng Khouang Province the new Laotian capital. This failed but, despite this, a new airport was constructed with Vietnamese and Russian aid.

The H'mong, who could never accept the new communist government, continued to attack LPA sources. Heavy fighting broke out between 1976 and 1977. It is rumoured that because of the inability of the LPA to bring them under control dirty tactics in the form of 'yellow rain' was used against them. Right up into the nineties, trouble with the H'mong has continued to threaten the peace in the area.

Getting there

There are regular Lao Aviation domestic flights. Currently there are three flights daily, costing US$75 for westerners (US$32 for Laotians) for returns. Return flights are scheduled on some days. Flights are from Vientiane to Xieng Khouane, the ancient capital. There is occasionally a tourist charter flight from Luang Prabang (cost US$32). The journey can also be made overland by jeep via Route Colonial 13 and Route Colonial 7 via Phou Khoun. Other land travel is also possible, but more difficult.

Xieng Khouang today

From the air, the devastation which was inflicted on this province during the war is still evident. The hundreds of craters which cover the whole area are a legacy of the Americans, created by hundreds of thousands of bombs. Many of these have become fish ponds and there is still a roaring trade in bomb metal castings. All over the province, particularly if you arrive by jeep, you will see water containers fashioned from Cluster Bomb Unit (CBU) castings, fence posts made from bomb metal and even stilts holding up houses which have been made 'courtesy of the Americans', as one local put it. Many of the heavier 'saturation raids' had caused some families to live in caves. If you have arrived by 4WD you can go to visit them in the Tham Phiu area just beyond the small town of Muang Kham (33km to the east of Phônsavan).

The whole area is an ethnologist's paradise. Even in the ancient capital of Xieng Khouane you are likely to see a kaleidoscopic mingling of cultures as diverse as Lao, Chinese, Vietnamese, Tai Dam (Black Tai), Tai Neua (White Tai), Tai Deng (Red Tai) and Phuan. During the colonial regime this town was an attractive French outpost consisting of ochre coloured houses with green shutters, pretty villas and wrought iron balconies. Now it's an uninteresting blend of plain wooden houses and hastily erected cement-slab dwellings. The only things of interest to have survived the bombing are the That Phuan Chedi and a motley mix of Buddhas seen in the ruins of Wat Pia Wat. Phônsavan, the new capital, is slightly better but it, too, bears the scars of indiscriminate bombing. Today it is a town which is widely visited because of its proximity to the Plain of Jars.

Accommodation in Xieng Khouane

There is only one rather wacky wooden hotel which is in the main street. There are no frills here. Expect to pay US$2-3 for a room with occasional running water and occasional electricity.

Eating

There are several noodle shops in a local market where you can buy fruit.

Accommodation in Phônsavan

Most tourists coming to the province stay here rather than Xieng Khouane. Accommodation is of the basic variety.

The **Mittaphap Hotel**, about 3km from the town, charges US$25 for a double and US$15 for a single. Booking through Raja Tour in Vientiane, you can get a double reserved for US$20.

The **Muang Phuane Hotel,** near the central market, costs US$20 for a double and US$15 for a single. You can book it through Lanexang Travel Co Ltd, Vientiane.

Avoid the **Hay Hin Hotel** near the market which is grotty.

A better class establishment opened in 1994 1¹/₂km out of Phônsavan towards the east along Auto Route No 7. Called the **Phou Phadaeng**, this can be booked through Lanexang Travel Co Ltd for US$41 doubles/single.

Cabin accommodation

Auberge de Plaine de Jarres. These cabins are located outside the town overlooking a plain. All rooms cost US$55. Customers staying here are warned not to go wandering into the surrounding countryside, which is heavily laden with unexploded CBUs. During the hottest period in April you won't need a sweater if you stay here but in November temperatures can get quite low at night.

Eating

Try one of the hotels. Those staying in cabin accommodation can buy their own food at the market and cook it at the cabin. It is not uncommon for the hotels in this area to have no food available. There are a few noodle stalls in the market area.

Excursions

Plain of Jars

Around 300 of these objects, thought to be rice storage vessels, receptacles for fermenting wine or religious objects from a megalithic age, are scattered over this limestone plateau. This area is still idyllically beautiful despite its torrid history. Consisting of undulating hills which lead the eye to high mountains beyond, it's very dangerous as well. UNDER NO CIRCUMSTANCES GO WANDERING OFF THE BEATEN TRACK. Peasant farmers and their livestock are still blown up periodically by stepping on live bombs. The variety that you find here are particularly nasty. When they explode they release up to 150 'pineapple bomblets' which can tear you to pieces. There are also loads of B52 bombs in the area, some of which were jettisoned by Stratofortress bombers returning to bases in Thailand after bombing north Vietnam.

The jars, which are reckoned to be over 2,000 years old, are made from stone from outside of the province. Archaeologists can merely speculate as to where they came from and what they are. Some contained clues in the form of fragments of ceramics and bronzes, a few had lids. Although some were, of course, damaged during the horrendous bombing raids and skirmishes between the Neutrals and Pathet Lao, a surprisingly large number remain unscathed.

Revolutionary Museum

This is near the Hotel Plaine de Jarres. Most of the war paraphernalia seen here is badly rusted. There are old flags, weapons, helmets, hats, radios and even CBUs and artillery casements on display.

Market

A good place to see local minorities.

Further afield

It may be possible to arrange to visit the immensely attractive Sam Neua area in Houaphan Province. Highway Number 6 is being repaired but the stretch between Houamuang and Muang Kham is very bad. Truck transport is available on this route but whether the authorities will allow you to use it is another thing.

The area is well worth visiting just for the scenery but the caves which once housed Pathet Lao Revolutionaries are an added attraction. One good reason for hiring a guide here is that there are still irregular outbursts of H'mong tribal skirmishes. Another is that parts of the area are classified as 'sensitive' because they contain old re-education camps where tens of thousands of reactionaries were sent for long periods of re-education. People coming out of these disgusting places were quite naturally 'broken', psychologically speaking, many were just skin and bone. It is hardly surprising that these 'restricted areas' are off-limits to tourism. There are rumours (just rumours) that the last people to be released from these was in late 1991!

Easier option
There are plenty of passenger-trucks going to Nong Hét from Phônsavan; this is well worth doing. Nong Hét is close to the border along the road which eventually leads to Vinh in Vietnam. The scenery near the border crossing is beautiful.

The Plain of Jars

Chapter Twelve

Southern Laos

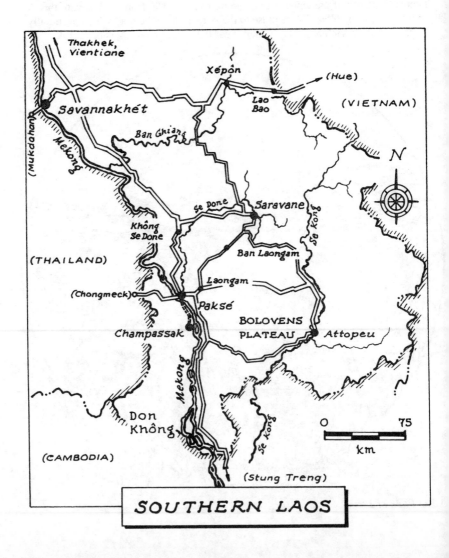

SOUTHERN LAOS

SAVANNAKHET PROVINCE

According to the 1985 census, this province had a total population of 543,611. This makes it the most highly populated province in Laos. In the 1958 census, Savannakhét had a population of 350,000. Few visitors come to this province because there is very little to interest them, the chief attraction being the remains of the Ho Chi Minh Trail around Xépôn. The province is, however, of interest to ethnologists, since there are many different minorities found in the area. These include Bru, Katang, Pako, Suay and Chali who all speak the Mon Khmer dialect. In the capital, Savannakhét, there is a fairly large Chinese community and a scattering of Vietnamese.

Savannakhét

This small city has a population of around 47,000. There is a thriving business community situated around the centre of the city. Chinese goods are common in the shops, particularly ceramics which are mainly sold to Thai visitors. Early in the morning is a good time to go down to the docking site opposite the Santhiphab Hotel, where numerous goods are loaded for transport on the early ferry to Mukdahan in Thailand. Also of interest is the Yai Market (*Taláat Yai*) just off Thanon Udomsin (four blocks into the town from where the boats leave for Vientiane). This is a good place for photographers to visit because of the unusual minorities which come here to trade.

The wats in the town are not nearly as spectacular as those seen in the north. If you arrive on the ferry from Thailand you will see the most important one, Wat Sainyamungkun, in a central position overlooking the river. This contains a seminary where youngsters are taught by venerable old men. Younger monks are taught at Wat Lattanalangsi, which is situated by the Huay Long Kong, not far from the Chinese school and Catholic Church. It's worth going there to see the huge reclining Buddha and the ornate glass-windowed *sim*.

Getting there

There are regular flights from Vientiane on a Tuesday, Wednesday, Friday and Sunday. There is a flight from Paksé on a Monday and Thursday and from Saravane on a Sunday. There are regular ferries from Mukdahan in Thailand. When the river is high enough (between June and November), there is an irregular boat service from Vientiane.

There is one bus a day from Vientiane.

Accommodation in Savannakhét

There are no first class hotels. Several new establishments are under construction but won't be finished till at least 1996.

Tourist class

Nan Hai Hotel, Central.
This new establishment has been recently completed. All rooms are air-conditioned and have hot and cold running water. It can be booked through Sodetour and Lanexang Travel Co Ltd.
Price per room: single – US$45; double – US$60.

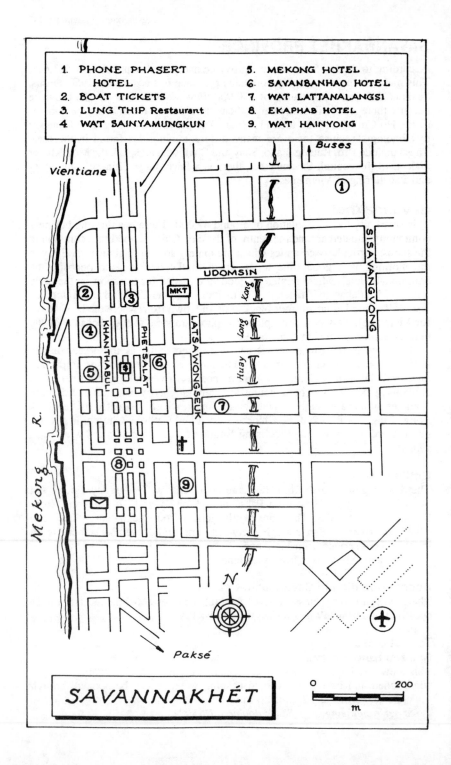

1. PHONE PHASERT HOTEL
2. BOAT TICKETS
3. LUNG THIP Restaurant
4. WAT SAJNYAMUNGKUN
5. MEKONG HOTEL
6. SAVANBANHAO HOTEL
7. WAT LATTANALANGSI
8. EKAPHAB HOTEL
9. WAT HAINYONG

Buses

Vientiane

SISAVANGVONG

UDOMSIN

MKT

Kong

KHANTHABULI

PHETSALAT

LATSAWONGSEUK

Nong

Huay

Mekong R.

N

Paksé

0   200
m

SAVANNAKHÉT

Phone Phasert Hotel, Thanon Sisavangvong; tel: 7620.
This hotel is used by tourist agencies but is not often full because few tourists come to Savannakhét. Rooms are comfortable and have TVs, private baths and refrigerators. Air-conditioning is standard. Rooms are bookable through SODETOUR and Lanexang Travel Co Ltd, Vientiane.
Price per room: single – US$25; double – US$35.

Savanbanhao Hotel, just off Thanon Saenna near the Chinese Temple; tel: 7661.
If you want a single/double/treble/quadruple they will probably have it. Rooms are fairly ordinary, some have air-conditioning, some have fans. Rooms are available with private baths but cost more. If you want to arrange trips into the surrounding countryside then this is a good place to stay because it contains a tourist agency.
Price per room (air-conditioning, no bath): single – US$20; double – US$25.

Budget hotels
Ekaphab Hotel, Thanon Khanthabuli.
Ideal for backpackers who don't mind roughing it.
Price per room: US$4.

Santhiphab Hotel, Thanon Tha Dan.
Basic sort of establishment. Don't let its external appearance put you off. Rooms have fans.
Price per room: US$5.

Mekong Hotel, river front (central).
You can recognise it by its old colonial frontage. Rooms are very basic, catering mainly for Vietnamese traders and businessmen.
Price per room: single – US$10; double – US$15.

There are a few other very dingy looking establishments along the water-front.

Eating
The only decent place to eat is the **Lung Thip Restaurant** off Thanon Phetsalat (near the cinema). Some French food is sold here but the menu is predominantly Lao. They also have a disco.

There are plenty of small Chinese restaurants and noodle shops. The Yai Market is a good place for cheap Chinese and Lao food.

Excursions from Savannakhét
Close to the town
Kengkok village
This traditional style Laotian village is just outside Savannakhét. It is worth going there just to see the lovely countryside which surrounds the town. People are extremely friendly and will probably invite you into their homes. They get very few Western visitors.

That Ingrang
Situated about 14km north of Savannakhét, this four-tier stupa is the best example of this type of architecture in southern Laos. Situated on a 9m base, it

stretches to a height of 25m. Although blackened with age, this superbly symmetrical structure is remarkably well preserved considering it was built in the mid-16th century. Close examination will reveal stucco decorations. Inside the hollow bottom tier you will find a motley collection of small Buddha figures. Women are not allowed to enter. There are more Buddha statues in the small *sim* adjacent to the main structure. One should be prepared to dress respectfully when visiting this site which is the most venerated in the south. A good time to visit is on the 15th day of the sixth lunar month when hundreds of Buddhist pilgrims visit the area to celebrate the Buon Bang-Fay Festival. The wooden buildings near the *thâat* are monks' quarters, tourists are not permitted inside.

Further afield
Huane Hine Khmer Temple
Most tourists would find this site very uninteresting. The temple, which is believed to date from between AD553 and AD700, is a total ruin. Only a few walls remain standing. Locals sometimes call this the Stone Temple (probably because all that is left is a pile of stones).

You will need a 4WD to get to this site which is off the road to Paksong about 75km south of Savannakhét. In Savannakhét it is possible to hire a fast boat which will take you down the Mekong to this site in about three hours. It would cost you about US$30.

That Phon Stupa
Although this is a little out of the way, about 70km south of Savannakhét, you will certainly enjoy the journey there. Don't expect too much when you arrive. The stupa dates from the 16th century and is a dirty white colour. You can visit this area when you travel to the Khmer temple of Huane Hine.

The Ho Chi Minh Trail
People visit this for nostalgic reasons rather than any other. Some of the areas through which the trail passed in this province are still very dangerous because many unexploded bombs have not been cleared. Savannakhét Tourism, in the Savanbanhao Hotel, take foreigners to Xépôn, which is the town closest to the trail. This can take about five hours for the 180km journey. It's an interesting trip which will take you along Route Nationale 9, nearly as far as the Lao Bao border crossing point into Vietnam. (Tourists wanting to visit Vietnam can exit Laos at this point with the correct border endorsement stamp on their visas.)

The trail is about 20km from Xépôn through lush green countryside heavily poxed with bomb craters. You will see quite a few remains of old tanks, bits of rusting aircraft, shell cases and large pieces of scrap metal too heavy for the metal traders to carry off. Many American planes went missing in this area and the search for MIAs still goes on.

The trail, aptly known as 'Hanoi's road to victory', was the idea of the North Vietnam Politburo. Even in 1959 existing pathways extended down from North Vietnam through Laos into Cambodia. Gangs of young men and women known as 'the Youth Shock Brigade' and many units of the Vietnam Peoples' Army were involved in its construction. They were given the code name Army Corps 559. Some of them walked and ran thousands of kilometres. Nguyen Viet Linh, who is remembered as one of the most famous, travelled on foot a total of 41,025km and carried on his back loads totalling 54,192 kilograms. After liberation he became a Vietnamese national hero. The route served as a supply line for ammunition, food, medicine and arms. Czechoslovakian bicycles were the most popular means of transportation, carrying record weights and injured soldiers.

At the start of the construction, teams of men were sent out to survey suitable routes. Before a route was put to use, nylon sheets would be laid along the route so as to leave no trace of footsteps. Relay stations would be set up which would be obscured with trees and rocks. Thanks to the support of the local populations and strict secrecy, the new system of roads were very difficult for the Americans to detect.

Planes were continually sent out from the Dong Ha air-base over the border in Vietnam. Using sophisticated infra-red photography, they pin-pointed many campfires which at night showed up as white dots on this type of film. At first everything was carried along the trail by individuals or on chainless bicycles, their handlebars supported by long extension poles. In 1965 the first Soviet and Chinese built trucks appeared on the trail. The total length of the system was estimated at 16,000km and comprised five main roads, 21 branch roads and thousands of kilometres of detours. There were also 3,140km of camouflaged roads. The defoliation mission of the C123 planes which dropped Agent Orange Blue and White on the trails didn't succeed in showing up the arteries. The North Vietnamese army were not even discouraged by the massive B52 bombing raids in 1971. They just went on rebuilding any section which was damaged. The invasion of Laos by the South Vietnamese army slowed down supplies to the South but due to the tenacity, resourcefulness and courage of the transporters, an estimated 10,000 tons was getting through in late 1971.

The Americans had realised just how effective the trail was very early on but had little success in destroying it. During the 1973-4 period, specially equipped B57 bombers sporting laser guiding systems scored direct hits which disrupted movement along the trail.

Tourists should ask for permission before visiting this area. The roads can become impassable during the rainy season (June-November).

Warning
DO NOT WANDER OFF THE BEATEN TRACK. There are thousands of unexploded bombs in the area. Do not try to get through thick undergrowth. As well as bombs you may come across a yellow krait which often reaches 1.5m (5ft) in length. Green bamboo vipers are common and also deadly.

SARAVANE PROVINCE
Saravane
The town of Saravane is said to have had some fine examples of French architecture, before being obliterated by bombs during the war,. The only building standing which is remotely French is the ochre-coloured post office. Visitors here in the 1960s would have marvelled at the majesty of the Chom Keoh Temple, which was blown to pieces in 1968 by bombs jettisoned by

American B52s returning from sorties over the Ho Chi Minh Trail. The photographs which have survived show that the wat was one of the most magnificent in the south. Devout Buddhists still come here despite the temple now being little more than a pile of bricks. Only a few uprights remain together with a sorrowful looking, headless Buddha.

The market in the town centre is still somewhat of an attraction. Animal lovers should be warned that the sad sights seen here of cages bulging with bluebirds, barely able to move, mynah birds that have lost the zest to sing, and piglets strung up in conical wire baskets, could be distressing. It is painful to see cages full of beautiful birds such as laughing thrushes, rare pale-capped pigeons, wrynecks, nuthatches, firebacks, hornbills, barbets, babblers and even baby eagles, all struggling to survive. Literally anything that moves is bought here, such as lizards, snakes, amphibians and even tortoises; all will end up on plates, many in Bangkok where exotic species are considered a delicacy. If you are an adventurous eater, you can sample snake soup here, followed by roasted cicadas served on skewers. On most days there are snake races which are popular with the locals.

Getting there
There is a plane to Saravane from Vientiane on Sundays, it returns after dropping you off. The return fare is US$187. By road, you can get here from Paksé in about five hours by passenger truck. Expect to be charged around 4,000 kip.

Excursions from Saravane
Near the town
Ba Nom Buah Lake
If you like bird watching, this is a good place to visit. Kingfishers are fairly common including the common kingfisher (*Alcedo atthis*), the black-cropped kingfisher (*Halycon pileata*) and the crested kingfisher (*Ceryle lugubris*). You may be lucky enough to see a brown dipper (*Cinclus pallasii*). There are many varieties of laughing thrush including the black-throated laughing thrush (*Garrulax chinensis*) and the more common white-throated laughing thrush (*Garrulax albogularis*). Babblers, as in most parts of Indochina, are very common. One of the most striking seen here is the golden babbler (*tachyris nigriceps*). Other varieties recorded include buff-throated warblers (*Phylloscopus davisoni*), long-tailed shrikes (*Lanius schach*), velvet-fronted nuthatch (*Sitta frontalis*), scarlet minivet (*Pericrocotus flammeus*) and forked-tail swift (*Apus pacificus*).

Getting there
The easiest method is to hire a jeep with driver. Many locals in Saravane will take you for a small fee. The lake is about 17km to the east of Saravane.

Further afield
Bolovens Plateau
The 'Boloven Revolt' took place in this area in 1901. It involved a chief called Bac My who had a large following in the Bolovens of Lao Theung and Lao Lum. He became so popular that the local people placed portraits of him in many temples. This greatly angered the French authorities who saw him as a threat. When they put up their taxes, he was the first to rebel and gathered together

hundreds of anti-French supporters. In April 1902, they engulfed the French military post at Savannakhét. The French soldiers were frightened by the revolt and fired on them. Over 150 people were killed and countless wounded. Bac My fled to the more mountainous parts of the plateau and hid with his followers for over two years. Being an Alak, he was well used to living in the mountains where he continued to be venerated as a 'holy man'. He was finally captured on the plateau in October 1907 and bayoneted to death under the orders of the French Résident. His principal lieutenant, Kommadam, escaped into the mountains where he continued in Bac My's footsteps. He rallied together a large band of rebels from all over the Bolovens territory and created havoc for many years.

Finally, in 1936, the French were given information about his hide-out on the Bolovens Plateau by a deserter. On September 23 1936 he was caught. The Boloven revolt was finally over.

Today, the area is mostly fertile hill country where there are large areas of grasslands. The plateau's elevation is about 1,200m (3,500ft). The main population living here are Lao Theung which include the Alak, the Ta Oi, Cotu, Yai, Kayon. Suay, Tahoy, Kakang and Chieng.

The best way to organise an excursion is to book with Sodetour. They will take you to some interesting minority villages as well as Lao.

Tha Teng village

A very scenic drive south of Saravane will bring you to the Lao village of Tha Teng. Here you can see numerous beehives and visit the local factory where high quality honey is processed before being exported to many countries. The best time to visit is between June and November when the *dok jampaa* (plumeria) trees blossom. These attract thousands of wild bees which are trapped and put into home-made hives which are kept in the shade. In a good season, it is not uncommon for some families to collect 300 litres of pure honey. The village is also famous for being the homebase of Jean Dauplay, the French Botanist, who was the first to grow coffee on the Bolovens and introduce it into Laos.

Minority villages

Tha Teng is a good base for visiting the minority villages of Tad Soung and Ban Khian. If you intend going, make sure you take plenty of salt and sugar which the Alak people find difficult to afford. Both villages are extremely friendly. You will certainly be invited into their thatched houses. Don't be surprised if you see a rat being roasted because to the Alak it's a delicacy. They will be greatly offended if you refuse one that has been prepared for you! In fact, mortality, premature death and epidemics are scourges in the life of the Alak, who are known for their strange burial rituals. After death, corpses are carried aloft through the village in a carved wooden coffin which has very often been made by the deceased person's family.

Also fairly close to Tha Teng is the Ta Oi village of Ban Paleng. The Ta Oi belong to the Mon-Khmer ethnic group which migrated here from Binh Tri Thien Province in Vietnam during the American War. The village is fascinating and consists of stilt houses, decorated inside with bird feathers and animal horns. During their annual festival in March, buffalo are sacrificed and gongs, *khenes*, wind and string instruments, are played far into the night. They are skilful hunters, many of the young men still go on elephant hunts. Unlike many minorities, they do not make their own clothes. They grow limited amounts of sweet potatoes, manioc, beans, tobacco and maize.

Further along the road to Paksé is the weaving village of Ban Housei Houne where Cotu women make *pha sin* cloth. Photographers would find the water-wheels here of particular interest. The Cotu use these to power their rice pounders which can reduce grains of rice to powder.

Waterfall country

If you are travelling with Sodetour you will no doubt be taken to the Tad Phan waterfall, just outside the village of Paksong. This is certainly no Angel Falls but it does drop for well over 100 feet. It is at its best between May and September.

Tad Lo Lodge

Tour groups will overnight at Tad Lo Lodge (US$35 for a room). It can also be booked through Lanexang Travel Co Ltd in Vientiane.

Run by Claude Vincent, director of Sodetour, this extremely attractive place is set in a pristine condition close to the border with northeastern Cambodia. The management offers elephant rides into the jungle, manned of course by expert Suay minority handlers. Khamphao Bounnhong, one of the country's well known tourist PR experts, is trying to get more foreigners to come here. It is well worth the effort if you have the time since the area is tremendously scenic and contains a large variety of wildlife.

In the forest, you are likely to see striped tree squirrels (*Tamiops maclellandi*), flying squirrels (*Hylopetes alboniger*), brush-tailed porcupines (*Atherurus macrourus*), spotted civet (*viverra megaspila*), wild pigs (*Sus scrofa*) and barking deer (*Muntiacus muntjak*). There are many interesting birds such as silver pheasants (*Lophura nycthemera*), great-eared nightjar (*Eurostopodus macrotis*), brown hornbills (*Buceros bicornis*), blue-winged leaf birds (*Chloropsis cochinchinensis*) and countless varieties of bulbuls and warblers. There are many minority villages which you can visit in the near vicinity.

From here you can travel on to Paksé and visit the classic minority market at Laongam on the way.

Sekong and Attopeu

Sodetour can arrange for you to visit these small towns which as yet see very few foreign tourists. The route from Saravane will take you through remote parts of the Bolovens where you can see coffee, cardamom and tea being grown. It can prove to be quite expensive to get there because you will certainly need 4WD to travel to the southeastern neck of the woods.

Sekong is a strong minority area where you will find tribes that you have probably never heard of, such as the Yai Kayon, Tahoy, Kakang and Lavene. Ethnologists would find the region extremely fascinating. Although hard treks would have to be undertaken to visit some of the more interesting villages, this can be arranged by Sodetour. You would need a lot of time and be prepared for very uncomfortable nights in minority villages. Adventurous travellers who are prepared to rough it would find the area totally captivating. If you do make such a trek, always show great respect for the tribes you visit, dress down, take presents of salt, sugar etc, always ask before you take photographs and never enter a house unless you are asked in. Parts of their houses, such as the room containing the family altar, are sacred to them. Don't touch any of their possessions if you are invited in.

Attopeu (Mùang Samakhi Xai) can be reached by an exciting boat ride down the Se Kong River from Ban Phou. The main problem with visiting the area at present is that there isn't any accommodation suitable for Westerners. This town, which is set in a lush tropical area at the confluence of the Se Khaman and Se Kong Rivers, is best visited during the rainy season when the rivers are high enough to allow you to travel on them. The road route via Paksong from Saravane is then unpassable. During the dry season, it is possible to get to Attopeu from Paksé with 4WD via an extremely rough road which runs through Ban Thongbeng. This is just a mud track in July. If you don't mind roughing it, the area is well worth the trouble to visit. Make sure that you use adequate protection against mosquitoes if you stay in one of the hovels in the town which can be loosely described as a hotel.

CHAMPASSAK PROVINCE

There is historical evidence that this area was inhabited by people who had migrated from the Indian subcontinent between the 5th and 6th centuries AD. During Jayavarman I's reign it was part of the Kingdom of Chenla and was inhabited by the Khmer. It is thought that it didn't come under the jurisdiction of Lan Xang (The Kingdom of a Million Elephants) until the 16th century. The first Lao king of the Champassak Kingdom was Soi Sisamouth Phythanekum (1713-37) who was Soulinga Vongsa's nephew. The kingdom became a vassal state of Siam after being overthrown by King Taksin of Siam in 1778. The kingdom's last king was Youtti Thammathone II (1863-1900) and its last prince was Boun Oum. The French called the province Bassac. In 1970 the area included in today's Champassak Province contained the provinces of Sedone and Sithandone.

The 1985 census showed that it was the second most highly populated province in Laos with 403,041 people.

Paksé

Situated 300m above sea level at the confluence of the Se Dong and Mekong River, this bustling market town is the largest in the south. Today it is an important administrative centre where the colonial style offices with their ochre walls and green shutters remind the visitor that this was once the centre of the French colonial government. Paksé cannot be said to be a pretty town or one with a great deal of character, but the numerous stilt houses and wacky looking Boun Oum Palace are certainly intriguing. The palace was once the dream home of the Prince of Champassak; it was never finished. It is rumoured that this six-story gigantic eyesore could soon become the largest and most luxurious hotel in Laos! Paksé is particularly well situated for tourism. It is the gateway to the Bolovens Plateau and its interesting tribal groups, Champassak and the pre-Angkorian ruin of Wat Phou are only a short boat ride away and the surrounding countryside provides many scenic spectacles. Only a short drive from the town, luxuriantly green rice fields lead the eye towards minority country where the peaks of Batiang, Sa Laou, Ma Long and Nang On give further interest to the skyline.

Airport

Se Done

N

0   300
m

Market,
Buses,
Champassak

1. PHÔNSAVAN Hotel
2. SUKSAMLAN Hotel
3. CHAMPA Guest Ho.
4. BOUN OM
5. WAT THAM FAI
6. WAT LUANG
7. PAKSÉ Hotel
8. MARKET
9. TAXIS
10. SODETOUR

Mekong

Chongmeck

PAKSÉ

Getting there

There is a Lao Aviation domestic flight to Paksé from Vientiane every day
except Wednesday and Sunday. There is a flight from Savannakhét on Tuesday
and Friday. There are occasional unscheduled flights to Paksé from Attopeu,
Muang Không and Wat Phou. Return flights to Vientiane are daily except
Sundays and Wednesdays. The Savannakhét flights are on Mondays and
Thursdays. There is a long distance bus from Vientiane to Savannakhét and
another from here to Paksé. Boats are also available in season from Vientiane.

Accommodation

Tourist class

Salachampa Guest House, town centre; tel: 856 51 8254.
This is an elegant style French villa which has been converted and much
improved to accommodate tourists. Rooms have fans and private baths. Prices
have gone up considerably since the renovations were carried out. They are
bookable through Sodetour and Lanexang Travel Co Ltd in Vientiane.
Price per room: US$43.

Souk Samlane Hotel, town centre; tel: 856 51 8226.
This new medium priced establishment opened in 1994. Rooms are adequate for anyone's needs but are far from luxurious. Some rooms have air-conditioning, some fans. Rooms are bookable through Sodetour.
Price per room: single – US$18; double – US$20.

Budget hotels
Sonksamlane Hotel
Probably the best budget establishment, this is next door to the Salachampa Guesthouse. All rooms are basic with poor amenities and cost US$15.
Price per room: US$15.

Champa Vilay Hotel, town centre.
Basic.
Price per room: US$8.

Phônsavan Hotel, near the market.
Noisy, very basic. Double rooms are large.
Price per room: single – US$5; double – US$10.

Suksamlan Hotel, near the market. Tel: 856 51 8002.
This would be my choice in Paksé. Rooms are clean with air-conditioning and a bath. The price depends on your bargaining power.
Price per room: approximately US$12.

Paksé Hotel, near market
Poor standard, very basic amenities.
Price per room: US$5.

Eating
There are many small cafes serving Chinese food. Around the market area there are a few Vietnamese restaurants. A good one is the **Balian,** near the Souk Samlane Hotel. The premier eating spot is the **Salachampa Guest House** where the decor is elegant and the French food superb.

Tourist attractions in Paksé
There are around 15-20 small wats scattered around the town, the only one likely to appeal to tourists is Wat Luang.
This highly decorative wat has recently been restored at an estimated cost of 30 million kip. The small stupa near the entrance contains the ashes of Katay Don Sasorith, who was Prime Minister from 27 November 1954 to 13 February 1956. They were interned here in the presence of the new premier, Prince Souvanna Phouma, who took office on 20 March 1956. The wat here is very different from anything else you will see in Laos. The gaudy decorations, lavish use of ochre-yellow and shocking pink are more reminiscent of southern Taiwanese sanctuaries. The lavishly carved wooden doors made by a local carpenter are very impressive. Nearby is a monastic school, the biggest in the south, where families send their children to be ordained as monks.

The Boun Oum Palace
Because of its bizarre appearance, this monstrosity is worth a quick look. Many say that the architect who designed it must have been delirious at the time. Some authors have described it as having the appearance of a multi-storey wedding cake without the icing. Personally, I think it makes a great photo and when fully completed by the Thai company which intends to convert it into a hotel, it will be a splendid asset to the area. When originally built, it must have cost a small fortune, since there are well over 100 rooms. The keeper, for a few kip, will show you around. The palace is on the edge of the town on the road to the Bolovens Plateau.

Further afield
Wat Saphay
Situated north of Paksé in the village of Ban Saphay on the road to Tad Lo Lodge, this wat has some fine stone sculptures. You will find the favourite wife of Shiva the Destroyer, who is known to Hindus as Pārvati, the daughter of the mountain. In a prominent position is Indra, the God of the Sky, together with Ganésa, the God of Wisdom, son of Shiva and Pārvati. The wat is about 10km from Paksé.

The village is famous for its *ikat* style silk weaving which has similarities to designs produced over the border in Cambodia. It is produced by the technique of wefting, commonly used in Bali, Thailand and Sulawesi to produce this fine finish. Selective tie-dying produces a distinctive pattern which becomes more complex on repeated tie-dying. Although the cloth is firmly tied with fibre, a certain amount of leakage occurs resulting in a blurring of the pattern which, in experienced hands, can produce a highly attractive finish.

Getting there
A short tour can be booked at the Lao National Tourist office near the ferry jetty, Sodetour, nearby tel: 856 51 8056 or in the Lanexang Travel Office in Thahim Road; tel: 856 51 8226. They will charge you US$15 for a half day tour which will take you to the temple and the weaving village. A cheaper alternative is to catch a passenger truck heading for Paksong on the Bolovens Plateau. They start their journey from the central market area and leave when full. The fare will be no more than 300 kip. If you decide to use one of the three-wheeler taxis which cruise around the market area, it will cost you around 3,000 kip.

Trips to the Bolovens Plateau, Sekong and Attopeu
These are described in the Saravane section of the book. Any of the tourist companies above will arrange these trips. See also the tour section ref: SLS 01 Sodetour. A typical itinerary from Paksé is:

 Minority market at Lao Ngam
 Tad Lo Lodge elephant trek and overnight
 Tad Phan waterfall and minority villages
 Paksong
 Alak, Cotu and Ta Oi minority villages
 Tha Teng
 Saravane

Tours can be arranged to Sekong and Attopeu via rough road which runs through Ban Thongbeng. This is impassable during the rainy season.

Champassak town

This shambles of a town on the west bank of the Mekong is a good stopping-off point for visiting pre-Angkorian ruins of Wat Phou. The town itself has nothing to interest the Western traveller. It consists of run down colonial style residences, a market selling agricultural produce, red coloured dirt tracks and yet another monstrosity left behind by Prince Boum Oum. This one is in a far worse state of repair than the palace at Paksé.

Wat Phou

Established during the Chenla period (5th to 8th century) on the sacred hill of Phou Pasak, this Khmer temple is the most important of its type in southern Laos. Lying towards the base of the hill which Hindus say resembles a male organ (a lingam), it features a nave which dates from the tenth century (early Angkorian period). It also has architectural features which are considered 12th-13th century (late Angkorian period). Although badly crumbled by the force of a thousand storms, it is still regarded by many to be a mini-masterpiece, showing more than a few features of classical Khmer aesthetics. Its setting, backed by the hill the Hindus call Linga Parvata, is especially attractive. Before very long, much of its former glory could be brought to life through elaborate restoration funded by UNDP and UNESCO. Supervised by assistants from the *Musée Guimet* in Paris, the work has already begun.

Wat Phou is located in an immensely important historical area, eight kilometres from the once royal capital of Champassak and only a few kilometres from what was thought to be the site of the old Chenla capital at Cesthapoura. A Royal Road once connected the site with Angkor. Some of the stonework is thought to have been built during the reign of Jayavarman IV who dedicated it to Lord Shiva. Archaeologists have pointed out that the edifice shows features characteristic of the Koh Ker style (921-44). Others think that many of the buildings have a sculptural form which resembles Angkor Wat and conforms to the building style of Suryavarman II (1131-50), the most respected and famous of all the Khmer rulers.

Today, Laotian Buddhists worship here, particularly during the annual pilgrimage to the Wat Phou Festival held on the site during the February full moon. In the past these celebrations have been attended by Laotian royalty including Sisavang Vong (1946-59) and Savang Vatthana (1959-75), the last King of Laos. Savang Vatthana had a small palace renovated on a site overlooking the barray reservoirs near the western entrance.

A good time to visit is when the *dok jampaa* (plumeria) trees are in blossom on either side of the processional causeway. They are just beyond the reservoirs which Hindu visitors arriving during the rainy season can use for their ritual ablutions. The long promenade which leads to the second stage was one flanked by statues of mythical beasts. Beyond the causeway, the first buildings one comes across are the temple pavilions which, although badly crumbled, are still very photogenic. On the left is the Female Temple where women would have worshipped and on the right the Male Temple where men would have worshipped. Built predominantly out of sandstone, these attractive (possibly 12th century) structures have been added to the laterite complex at a later stage.

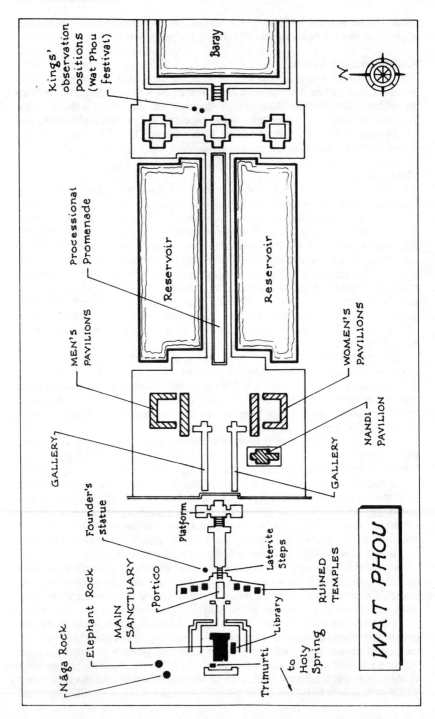

WAT PHOU

The Male Temple, which is the better preserved, is worth looking at more closely. Reliefs, although considerably worn, can be seen on the crossbeams which testify that the temple was originally Hindu. Close scrutiny will reveal Lord Shiva, the Destroyer, mounted on his sacred bull, Nandi, together with his wife Pārvati, the daughter of the mountain. Other reliefs also depict Pārvati. It is also worth looking at the porticoes and sandstone window frames which attest to the skill of the original Khmer craftsmen. If you expect to see intact buildings on this site, you will be disappointed, both pavilions are now mere shells without roofs. Around the back of the Female Temple, on the left, is a crumbled brick structure which is believe to have been the quarters of the queen.

Situated on the next level is the Nandi Pavilion dedicated to Shiva's bull which overlooks the Female Temple. Archaeologists believe that the three chambers it contains would have originally housed important statues. Directly opposite are ruined galleries. If you ascent the laterite steps, heading directly east beyond the next platform, you will come across six ruined brick temples, three on each side of the main pathway. Because of their condition, no-one can be certain of what they are. Heading in their direction you would have passed a statue of Pranga Khommatha who was the original founder of this edifice. Archaeologists believe that the laterite steps may have come from another Khmer ruin, Um Tomo. On the highest level is the holy sanctuary which once housed the lingam (lingaparvata). This was kept in the small brick building at the back of the main sanctuary and was regularly washed with holy water which percolated down Linga Parvati (the sacred hill) from a spring near its summit. The monks who still live on the complex believe that this water has the power to purify the soul. Both King Sisavang Vong and his successor, King Savang Vatthana, have washed in it. Bricks from the building which once housed the lingam have been dated 6th century indicating perhaps that the spring was even an important pilgrimage site to the people of the Kingdom of Chenla. A Buddha statue in front reminds the visitor that the complex later became dedicated to Lord Buddha and is now an important Buddha pilgrimage site. While walking through Wat Phou, you are quite likely to see Buddhist monks who live in a small modern monastery close by.

Look in detail at the main sanctuary particularly the building in front which has an east-west orientation. A crossbeam on the south entrance facing the library has lively reliefs which depict the murder of Kamsa by his nephew Krishna. There is an equally violent carving on a mainbeam above the left entrance which shows Shiva ripping a person in two. On the front of the main sanctuary you will find *apsāras* dancing for the delight of the gods. A perfectly proportioned Vishnu joins in. Indra, the God of the Sky who, according to Hindu belief, resides in a golden palace at the top of Mount Meru, looks down on you from his three-headed elephant mount; (the symbol of the 'Kingdom of a Million Elephants').

To the northeast of the main sanctuary, a little further on, is the Trimurti, statues of Brāhma (left) who, according to Hindu religion, was conceived from the Vishnu's naval while he enjoyed a cosmic sleep, Shiva the Destroyer beside him and Vishnu the Preserver on the right. In a northerly direction just past the quarters used by monks, are rocks carved with figures of a crocodile, *nāga* and elephant. It is widely believed that these were once human sacrificial sites.

Getting there
During the Wat Phou Festival, passenger trucks (*thaek-sii*) run from the ferry crossing to Champassak (8km). On normal days it is possible to hire a *tùk túk* after crossing which will cost around 5,000 kip. It is possible to go by boat from Champassak to Ban Nakham Noi for 9,500 kip and then to walk to the ruins.

Restoration fund
Your entrance fee of 200 kip and your camera fee of 700 kip will go towards the temple's restoration. It is open every day from 08.00-16.30.

Other Khmer ruins in the area

Um Tomo
The temple is in a very bad state of decay and in many ways is a miniature of Wat Phou, which is up river from here. Although partly hidden by the jungle, it is still worth a visit. Who knows what lies undiscovered under the jungle web. All that is visible are numerous slabs of laterite, a multi-headed naga and a few fairly well preserved reliefs.

Getting there
This small pre-Angkor ruin is about 2km from the village of Ban Phia Phay (about 47km south of Paksé). By road the nearest village is Ban Thang Beng. You will need a guide to find it. The easiest way to get there is by boat from Champassak (9,000 kip).

Dong Không and Don Khone Islands
Where the Mekong River comes to the end of its 1,600km journey in Laos, it splits up into many channels beyond the large island of Không. This is about 130km south of Paksé. Không, which is covered by thousands of flame trees and palms, stretches for about 15km. Below it the river splits into a labyrinthine maze creating a mass of small islands. Because there are so many of them they are known to the locals as 'The 4,000 Islands'. The largest falls in the area, 'Khone Falls', also known as 'Li Phi', is very spectacular. There is another amazing one below the town of Khinnak known as the 'Pha Pheng Falls'. Both are at their most awesome during the monsoon season. If you visit the area during the January/February period there is a good chance of seeing freshwater dolphins, known to the locals as *pakha*. Once you have seen this stretch of wild water, you can well imagine how poor Francis Garnier felt when his 1860s Mekong Expedition could go no further. During the French occupation of Laos, a 5km railway (the only line in Laos) was built from the southern end of the Khone island to the north. All that now remains is a ruined railway bridge and a rusting old locomotive.

Getting there
From Paksé a jeep or a local bus can be taken to Hatxaykhoun followed by another to Ban Thakho. The latter passes through Khinnak, the nearest Laotian town of any size to the Cambodian border. This is a good base for visiting the 'Pha Pheng Falls'. The 'Khone Falls' is on the other side of the island. The most exciting way of getting there is to hire a boatman at Ban Nakasong. He will take you as far as Ban Khone, which is close to the falls. Expect to pay 6,000 kip.

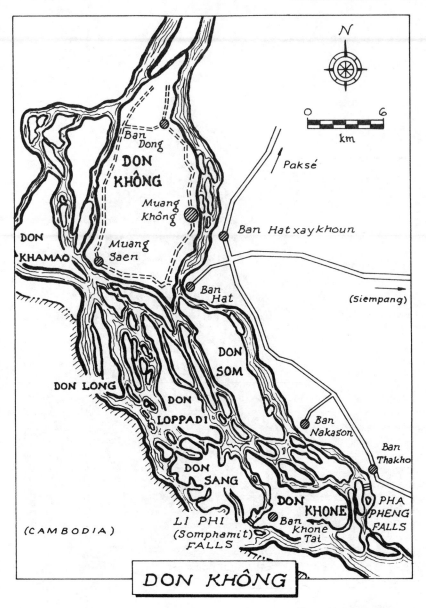

DON KHÔNG

Another route is via Muang Không, where there is a small tourist hotel (cost 15,000 kip/room). It is rumoured that the Dusit group from Thailand will soon build a new tourist resort in the area.

Central Tower, Angkor Wat

Section Three
Cambodia

A stone effigy of Boddhisattva, Angkor Thom

Part Four
The Country and its People

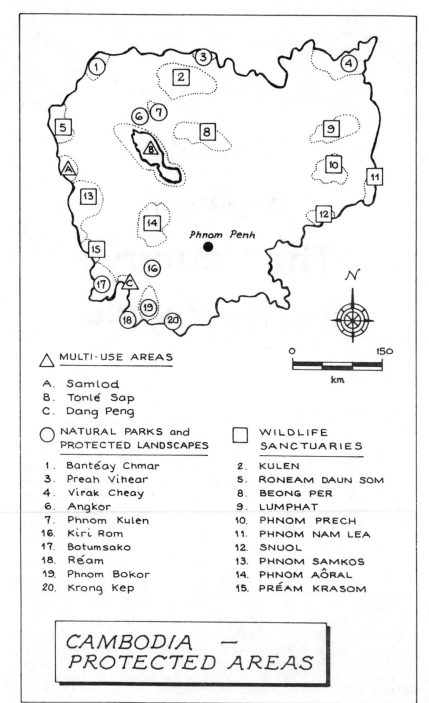

△ MULTI-USE AREAS

A. Samlod
B. Tonlé Sap
C. Dang Peng

◯ NATURAL PARKS and
PROTECTED LANDSCAPES

▢ WILDLIFE
SANCTUARIES

1. Bantéay Chmar
3. Preah Vihear
4. Virak Cheay
6. Angkor
7. Phnom Kulen
16. Kiri Rom
17. Botumsako
18. Réam
19. Phnom Bokor
20. Krong Kep

2. KULEN
5. RONEAM DAUN SOM
8. BEONG PER
9. LUMPHAT
10. PHNOM PRECH
11. PHNOM NAM LEA
12. SNUOL
13. PHNOM SAMKOS
14. PHNOM AÔRAL
15. PRÉAM KRASOM

*CAMBODIA –
PROTECTED AREAS*

Chapter Thirteen

Geography

With an area of around 181,000km² (approximately 69,900 square miles), Cambodia is the smallest country in Indochina. It is bordered to the north and west by Thailand, to the southwest by the Gulf of Thailand, to the northeast by Laos and on the southeast and east by Vietnam.

It has two distinctive geographical areas.

The mountains

These pre-Cambrian formations, the Dangrek Mountains towards the north, the Cardamom Range along the northwest-southeast axis of the southwest border and the Elephant Range towards the south of the Cardamoms all are of less than 2,000m. Predominantly, they are composed of metamorphic rocks, gneiss and granite with some basalt and sedimentary strata.

The plains

Covering two-thirds of the country, these lie within the great semi-circle created by the mountains. It's in this fertile region that most of the population has settled. Fringing the Tonlé Sap swampland is Cambodia's 'rice bowl' which due to decades of war has considerably shrivelled in extent. Irrigation schemes ruined by the Khmer Rouge and American bombing have been largely unrepaired. Due to lack of resources, manpower, political instability and hampered research, major hydrological projects proposed many years ago for the Sambor and Stung Treng areas have yet to materialise. Minor irrigation schemes, such as those begun in the Prek Thnot region, are still a long way off completion.

During the rainy season (June-November), the Mekong River turns the Tonlé Sap Basin into a vast lake. After thundering down the Khone Falls in Laos and navigating the Sambor Falls between Stung Treng and Kratie, it settles down to a more leisurely pace between Kompong Chhnang and the capital. During the dry season the Tonlé Sap River, which flows into the Mekong at the Quatre Bras confluence (opposite Phnom Penh), is a mere tributary. At the height of the rainy season it changes direction, causing the Tonlé Sap Basin to absorb the flood waters. This turns into a great lake which covers around 6,000km² (2,320 square miles), over twice its normal area. Its depth increases from 1-2m (October-June period) to 7-12m. Many of the stilt houses in the region, which for a large part of the year are on dry land, can then be reached only by boat. Massively long fish traps made from plaited bamboo screens are used by the fishermen. Some are several kilometres long and act as long corridors in which complete shoals of fish are trapped. Important commercial species include giant catfish and Siamese carp. Catches can average 100,000-150,000 tons annually.

Climate

The climate in Cambodia is mainly influenced by the southwest monsoons. Since these blow between May and September, this is the rainy season. During this period the annual average for the amount of rainfall is 2,300mm (90in). In Phnom Penh the annual average is 1,470mm (58in). The wettest place in Cambodia is in the Cardamom Mountains, where it is possible to get 6,350mm (250in) of rain in one year.

The hottest months in Cambodia are April and May, when the temperature is generally around 36°F (97°F). The coolest months are January and December, when the temperature is rarely more than 20°C (68°F).

CAMBODIA – GEOGRAPHY

Chapter Fourteen

A Brief History

A captivating mix of legend and history tells the story of the origin of the great empire of the Khmer. Sometime around the dawn of the first century AD an Indian youth called Kaundinya had a dream that the next day he would find a magic weapon that would give him the power to conquer any land he wished. Sure enough, when he awoke he found a bow and some arrows and set off on a voyage of discovery which took him via the Bay of Bengal, around the coast of present day Malaysia as far as the coast of Indochina via the South China Sea. Here his vessel was attacked by war pirogues of a queen named Willowleaf. He was astonished to see that she and her warriors were completely naked. When they approached, he noticed that although she had the body of an angel, she also possessed the fighting spirit of a devil. Rather apprehensively he let fly a magic arrow. This went straight through the side of her pirogue, which immediately sank. Seeing what he had done with just one arrow, her warriors, who had gone to her rescue, laid down their arms. She bowed to his superiority and over the next few weeks became so captivated by him that she later became his wife. As king and queen they ruled over their domain, which became known as Funan.

Funan
Early Khmer history has many dark and misty periods, but there is firm historical evidence that the pioneers who founded Funan did in fact come from India. Its capital city, Vyadhapura, lay on the lower reaches of the Mekong River and the country occupied an area which included most of present day Cambodia and Cochin-China. By the third century, Funan also controlled the affairs of the Malay Peninsula, together with territory which stretched as far as the Bay of Bengal. One of its vassal states was Chenla, towards the north (part of present day northern Cambodia and southern Laos). After the death of the Funan King Rudravarman (514-544), it fell into decline. Earlier, Prince Bhavavarman of Funan had married a Chenla princess and when his father died, Funan became a vassal state of Chenla.

Chenla
Bhavavarman's successor, King Mahendravarman, founded a new capital, Shampura, near present day Sambor. During his reign, Chenla's authority

became more widespread. His son, King Isanavarman (616-27), built a new capital, Isanapura, which became the home of his new bride, a Champa princess. He soon showed himself to be a strong, resourceful leader and established complete hegemony over the remaining vassal states that his father had been unable to subdue. Chenla therefore gradually took control over all the territory previously held by Funan. Due to his marriage, the kingdom of Chenla also included the Champa lands to the west as far as the border of the Mon Kingdom of Dvaravati. Chenla became more and more powerful and during the reign of Jayavarman I in the second half of the seventh century; it absorbed central and upper Laos, its northern border then extending as far as the Thai empire of Nanchao.

Towards the end of his reign his considerable conquests became overshadowed by the division of his kingdoms into two, Land Chenla towards the north and Water Chenla towards the south.

At this time the neighbouring kingdoms of Annam and Champa had been taken by Saliendra, the King of the Mountain, who ruled over Srivijaya (present day Sumatra, Java and part of Malaysia). Having heard that Jayavarman's successor wanted his head on a plate, Saliendra sent a great army and over-ran the kingdom of Chenla; its monarch was beheaded and some of the royal family were taken back to Java. This period of Khmer history is rather nebulous but it is thought that the next ruler of the great Khmer Empire, Jayavarman II (802-50) returned from Java to repair the fractured Chenla.

The Great Angkorian Period

Jayavarman II is remembered as the true founder of the Khmer Kingdom. During his reign the country became known as Kambuja and for many years remained subservient to Saliendra's Empire. Also during this period the site of the capital was moved several times. The first site, known as Indrapura, was close to modern day Phnom Penh. The second, known as Mahendraparvata, was built further north on a mountain top near Phnom Kulen. Here his subservience to Saliendra was terminated. He built a three-tiered temple-mountain and proclaimed himself to be a Chakravartin, a god-king who would acknowledge no earthly overlord. With this came the establishment of the deva-rãja (god-king) cult. He was worshipped as a divine ruler whose every action was transmitted to him by the God Shiva himself. The symbol of the authority of the god-king was the royal lingam which he and future kings of Angkor installed in sacred sanctuaries in their temple mountains. Thus in Kambuja, the worship of the Shivalingam became the religion of the state. Towards the end of his life, Jayavarman II no longer required the extra security that a mountain fortress offered so he moved the site of his capital for a third time, to a point near the great Tonlé Sap Lake. He called this Hariharalaya. After his death, Jayavarman III, his son, became the ruler for 27 years. Hardly anything is known about his reign except that his favourite sport, wild elephant hunting, led to his death in 877. His cousin, Indravarman 1 (877-89) succeeded him and began a pre-classical phase of building construction which was followed by other phases lasting for more than three centuries. During this period many architectural masterpieces sprung up at Angkor.

The overall power of the Khmer expanded quite considerably during the reign of Suryavarman I (1002-5). He was a brilliant military tactician and succeeded in subjugating to the Khmer Empire most of present day Thailand and Laos, the Kingdom of the Mon (Dvaravati) and a large part of the northern Malay Peninsula. During the reigns of Udayadityavarman II (1050-66), Harshavarman III (1066-80), Jayavarman VI (1080-1107) and Dharanindravarman I (Paramanishkalapada) (1107-13) there were many periods of unrest. Extending the territory of Kambuja to the west became impossible by the rise in the military might of Burma's Kingdom of Pagan. During the reign of Suryavarman II (1131-50), the fortunes of the Khmer took a turn for the better. Architectural achievement reached a new zenith with the completion of Angkor Wat and militarily he was successful in subduing the Thai and the Mon. In 1145 he conquered Champa, but lost it again in 1149 after failing in his attempt to conquer Annam two years earlier. Another of his downfalls resulted from his over-zealous building projects and his ruthless exploitation of the peasantry. Minor revolts broke out two years before his death, but it was Yasóvarman II (1160-65), who was to bear the full brunt of his extravagances. The country was brought to a chaotic state by severe peasant revolts but he was not to experience their wrath for long because he was murdered by his successor, Tribhuvanadityavarman (1165-77). During his rule the Cham struck at the heart of the Khmer Empire and in 1177, their king, Jaya Indravarman, sacked Angkor. Jayavarman VII (1181-1219), the great Khmer king who followed the usurper, became sovereign after defeating the Cham during a vicious naval battle in 1181. Champa fell to the Khmer again in 1190 and, except for a short period of rebellion, they held it until 1220. It was during Jayavarman VII's reign that Buddhism spread rapidly throughout Cambodia. The deva-rāja cult became replaced by the Buddha-rāja cult. The Vishnulingam installed for the first time by Suryavarman II became replaced by statues of Buddha. During the reign of Jayavarman VII, countless Buddha statues appeared at Angkor Wat and temples built during the period, such as the Bayon, featured sweet Buddha faces.

The downfall of Angkor

Architectural accomplishments had been immense during the Great Angkorian Period but the lavish building programmes had considerably weakened the coffers of the Khmer. When the menacing armies of the Thai were beginning to appear on the not too distant horizon, it couldn't have happened at a worse time. Already they had ravished parts of the Menam Valley, having captured Sukhotai in 1238. Another threat emerged in the form of the Mongols, who took Nanchao in 1253. Towards the end of the 13th century the cult of the god-king was finally overthrown by the increasing prominence of Buddhist rituals and doctrines. The overall effect of this was to weaken the authority of the king. After the formation of the Thai Kingdom of Ayutthaya in 1350, the Khmer fought battle after battle against them until eventually, in 1431, Angkor was lost. Later the Khmer regained control but were then constantly hounded by the Cham who raided from the west. As their empire dwindled, Angkor, the capital of Kambuja, became too close for comfort to the lands of their worst enemies, the Thai. In 1432 the capital was moved further westwards to Basan and then in 1434 to the site of present day Phnom Penh. Angkor had been abandoned to the jungle but King Ponha Yat felt more secure in his capital. Although the Thais never succeeded in conquering Kambuja, the abandonment of Angkor signalled the end of the period of Khmer grandeur.

Kings of Cambodia

Name	Reign	Architectural Achievement
Jayavarman II	802-850	Kulen
Jayavarman III	850-877	
Indravarman I	877-889	Bakong, Prah Kô
Yasovarman I	889-902	Kravan, Lolei, Bakeng
Harshavarman I	902-?	
Jayavarman IV	921-941	
Harshavarman II	941-944	
Rājendravarman II	944-968	East Mébon, Pre Rup
Jayavarman V	968-1001	
Udayadityavarman I	1001-1002	
Jayaviravarman	1002-1011	
Suryavarman I	1011-1050	Phimeanakas, Ta Kéo
Udayadityarvarman II	1050-1066	West Mébon, Baphuon
Harshavarman III	1066-1080	
Jayavarman VI	1080-1107	
Dharanindravarman I	1107-1113	
Suryavarman II	1113-1150	Angkor Wat, Thommanon, Chau Say Tevoda, Bantéay Samre
Dharanindravarman II	1150-1160	
Yasovarman II	1160-1165	
Tribhuvanadityavarman	1165-1177	
Jayavarman VII	1181-1219	Srah Srang, Angor Thom, Preah Khan, Bayon, Neak Pean, Ta Prohm, Ta Som, Prah Palilay, Leper King Terrace.
Indravarman II	1220-1243	
Jayavarman VIII	1243-1295	
Srindravarman	1300-1307	
Srindrjayavarman	1308-1327	
Paramathakemaraja	1330-1353	
Houeulna	1353-1373	
Thommo Soccarach	1373-1393	
Samtac	1404-1405	
Nippean	1405-1409	
Thommo-Soccorach	1429-1432	
Trailokanart	1448-1488	
Dhammaraja	1494-?	
Neai Kan	1498-1526	
Maha Chakrapat	1548-1569	
Borom Reachea	1569-1576	
Bayinnaung	1576-1581	
Maha Dhammaraja	1581-1590	
Nareseun	1590-1605	
Soryopor (Tributary King)	1603	
	1613-1618	
Chey Chettha	1618-1628	
Thommo Reachea	1738-1748	
Ang Tong	1748-?	
Ang Eng	1779-1796	
Ang Chan	1796-1834	
Any Mey (Queen)	1835-1841	
Ang Duong	1847-1859	
Norodom	1860-1904	
Sisowath	1904-1927	
Monivong	1927-1941	
Sihanouk (Abdicated)	1941-1955	
Norodom Suramarit	1955-1960	

The pre-colonial period

Despite another temple-mountain being built at the centre of the new capital, it was not followed by an extravagant orgy of construction. The Thais invaded again in 1473, badly damaging the capital. When An Chang was crowned king in 1516 he was determined to give his enemies a taste of their own medicine. In 1564 he finally marched on Ayutthaya, the Thai capital, but he was too late because it had already been taken by the Burmese. In 1570 King Settathirat of Lan Xang (Laos) sent a 130,000 strong army against Cambodia, but the attack was unsuccessful. He tried again in 1571 but this time lost his own life and most of his army.

After the death of the Cambodian king, Borom Reachea, in 1576, his son Prince Sattha formed a temporary alliance with Prince Nareseun of Thailand. After just one victorious battle against the Burmese, the alliance was broken. In 1587 Cambodia turned its forces once more against Thailand at the same time that their capital, Ayutthaya, was under attack by the Burmese; it failed. Prince Nareseun of Thailand became king after his father, King Mah Dhammaraja, died in 1590. Three years later he led an attack on Cambodia. In the fierce fighting that raged throughout the country, Babaur, Sattha's brother was killed. He retreated to his capital, which had by now been moved to Lovek on the lower reaches of the Mekong. After a long and bitter struggle, King Naresuen's forces entered Lovek despite considerable bombardment by Sattha's gunners, who had been trained by Spanish and Portuguese settlers. For the final attack he used many war elephants which had been specially trained and kitted out in thick protective metal plates.

King Sattha and his two sons escaped and fled to Laos. He died in Vientiane in 1594 along with his eldest son. His youngest son went on to become King Borom Reachea with the help of a Portuguese rogue called Belloso who was a dear friend of his father. He was however only a nominal ruler and when unrest spread throughout Cambodia in 1603, King Narusuen put the Thai Prince Soryopor in charge as a tributary king. Soon afterwards, Lovek was taken in a surprise attack by the Cambodian Prince Chung-Prey. A new capital was established at Srei Santhor.

Following a rapid succession of weak Cambodian kings, the son of Prince Soryopor, Chey Chettha, became the new monarch and moved the capital once more to Oudong. He married a beautiful Vietnamese princess, which led to parts of Cochin-China being colonised by her countrymen. A period of Cambodian history followed during which there were many disputes about who had the right to sit on the throne. In 1709 during the reign of Thommo Reachea, his son-in-law, Ang Em, seized the throne when he was away in Thailand. Although he returned supported by a Thai army, he was unable to re-establish himself as sovereign. When Ang Em abdicated, his son, Sotha II, became the new king. He was however soon overthrown by court officials who turned against him and Thommo Reachea (1738-47) again became the Cambodian monarch. He was followed by Ang Tong who after years of disputes finally became king in 1755. He was overthrown by his own son, Outey II, who in turn was ousted by Ang Non in 1767 (the grandson of Thommo Reachea). In 1779 Ang Eng (Outey's son) became king at the age of six but the country was governed by Mou, the Regent. In 1782 Ang Eng was forced to flee to Bangkok when Tay Son troops entered Cambodia.

The Vietnamese threat

In 1812, during the reign of Gia Long in Vietnam, a garrison of 20,000 Vietnamese troops was stationed at Phnom Penh to provide protection for Cambodia. The country was ruled by Ang Chan (1796-1834) who had succeeded his father, Ang Eng, who had returned to Cambodia in 1794 after many years in exile. The Vietnamese grip on the country tightened during the reign of Ang Chan. When he suddenly died of dysentery in 1834, Ang Mey, his daughter, became queen (1835-41). She was ruthlessly exploited by the Vietnamese who named her Ba-cong-chua. During her reign the Cambodian capital was renamed Nam-Vieng and court officials were given Vietnamese titles and forced to wear attire characteristic of the court of Hue. Any potential claimant to the throne of Cambodia was imprisoned in Vietnam, Ang Bene (Ang Chan's eldest daughter) was drowned. Waves of protest spread throughout the country followed by a fierce uprising which was supported by the Thai army. By the time the Vietnamese Emperor Thieu Tri (1841-47) mounted the throne most of his army had been ousted from the country. With the threat of Vietnamese annexation temporarily removed, the Cambodian people chose Prince Ang Duong as their new monarch. Meanwhile the fiercely ambitious Prince Ang Em, another potential candidate, had been released from jail at Hue together with three Cambodian princesses. Before he could pose any serious threat he was killed during the civil war in 1843. Phnom Penh fell to the Vietnamese in 1845 and Prince Ang Duong, supported by a Thai army, was forced to withdraw to Oudong. Here he was held under siege until an army of 40,000 Thai sent by King Rama III came to his rescue. The Vietnamese were again forced out of the country. When Emperor Tu Duc (1848-83) came to power, Vietnam faced new adversaries in the form of France and Spain. Rather than commit more troops to the Cambodian problem he was forced to draw up a truce which became official in December 1845. Under the terms of the agreement, all Vietnamese troops were withdrawn from Cambodia and a peace pact was also made with Thailand. Ang Duong became the new sovereign in 1847. He never felt particularly secure in his wooden palace at Oudong because he knew that at any time his country could be overrun by either Thailand or Vietnam. To be completely independent, what he really needed was the protection of a superpower such as France. In 1854 he sent a letter to Napoleon III via the French consul in Singapore. It was the first step which was to ultimately lead to Cambodia becoming a French Protectorate in 1863.

The French Colonial Period (1863-1954)

The French intervention began in 1858 when Napoleon's navy, under the command of Admiral Rigault de Genouilly, started its conquest of Indochina. In October 1860, the same month that Ang Duong died in Cambodia, the French fleet, having just gained a great victory in China, moved in on Saigon. By June 5 1862, a peace treaty had been signed by the Vietnamese. Just over one year later, Admiral de la Grandiere, the new Governor General of the French colony of Cochin-China, presented King Norodom I (1860-1904) with a copy of a treaty which made Cambodia a French Protectorate. This was signed by Norodom I at Oudong on August 11 1863. The Thais refused to accept this situation until France agreed to recognise their claim to the provinces of Siem Reap and Battambang in 1867. By 1884, the country's administration was in the hands of the French Résident Supérieur, a fact which became bitterly resented by January 1885. A revolt, led by Si Vattha, lasted for roughly 18 months, during which the French were severely harassed. In October 1887, Cambodia became part of the Indochinese Federation, which consisted of the protectorates of Annam and Tonkin and the colony of Cochin-China. Laos was added to the French Union in 1893. The governor-general administered the Union and was assisted by economic and financial advisors. Although some of these were Asian, laws governing the affairs of the Union were passed by the French parliament. When a disagreement arose, the Résident Supérieur always had the last say. The French did not interfere with Khmer traditions but in no way did they prepare them for eventual independence. During the 1920s they began to exploit Cambodian resources using Chinese and Vietnamese trade intermediaries. This led to ethnic tension which, no doubt, affected their assimilation policy. This had further been retarded by the small numbers of Cambodians who had accepted Christianity. After Japan and Thailand had signed a treaty of alliance in June 1941, the Vichy French government, which was being bullied by Germany, gave the Japanese further concessions. Japan persuaded Thailand to take back the provinces of Siem Reap and Battambang, which had been returned to Cambodia in 1893. When the Japanese took control in Indochina in March 1945, Norodom Sihanouk, who had been crowned king in 1941, declared his country to be independent. By August 19 1945, just after the horrific Hiroshima and Nagasaki incidents, Japan withdrew its troops. When France, through open warfare, attempted to reassert its authority over Indochina, fierce fighting broke out all over Tonkin, Annam and Cochin-China. Meanwhile in Cambodia, the Khmer Issarak had grown into a formidable anti-French guerrilla force who had never accepted the absorption of their country as an Associated State of the French Union. In 1947, King Norodom Sihanouk, through skilful rallying of nationalist forces, succeeded in establishing a Cambodian constitution with its own national assembly. French interference was hard and fast and as a protest Sihanouk went into voluntary exile in Thailand. He finally got his wish on July 21 1954 when all French troops were evacuated from Cambodia.

Kingdom of Cambodia (1954-70)

Although the Geneva Treaty of 1954 strengthened Sihanouk's position, he abdicated in favour of his father, Norodom Suramarit in 1955. As Prime Minister he formed the Sangkum, a national movement which developed considerable control over the country's affairs. Cambodia rapidly became a one-party state, the Socialist People's Community Party (Sangkum) easily beating its nearest rivals in the polls held in September 1955. The same month, Sihanouk led his country out of the French Union and because of his neutral policy attracted economic assistance from the USA, USSR, China and France. When his father died on April 3 1960, Sihanouk refused to accept the throne and instead became head of state. A new prime minister, Prince Norodom Kantol, took office in October 1962.

Diplomatic relations with Thailand had already been broken off in 1961 and in 1963 Cambodia renounced aid from the USA. Two years later it announced that it was breaking its diplomatic relations with the USA. This led to considerable hardship throughout the kingdom. At first, it affected the living standards of the Cambodian elite but later, after Lon Nol and Sirik Matak rose to power, it sparked peasant riots, which became widespread in 1967 and 1968. One year later diplomatic relations with the USA were re-established. Sihanouk continued with his neutrality policy despite the fact that the war between the USA and Vietnam was hotting up. He was overthrown by a coup on March 18 1970 which was led by Lon Nol. This resulted in the abolition of the Kingdom of Cambodia and the establishment of the Khmer Republic.

The Khmer Republic (1970-75)

Sihanouk's policy of isolating Cambodia from the war which raged in Vietnam could no longer be implemented. In April 1970 over 20,000 American and South Vietnamese troops entered the southeastern part of the country. A long period of military action followed, during which an estimated 600,000 nationals died. Massive carpet bombing of agriculturally important areas led to starvation and chaos. Refugees poured into Phnom Penh, swelling its population from just over half a million to two million. During the war years, agricultural production and foreign trade dropped drastically, corruption became rampant and the Khmer Rouge guerrilla movement, which opposed the Lon Nol government, rapidly increased. By 1973 their number had reached an estimated 70,000 and the morale of the Lon Nol army had ebbed to an all time low. By now, over two million people had become homeless. On April 17 1975, Khmer Rouge troops took Phnom Penh overthrowing the Lon Nol government.

Democratic Kampuchea (1975-78)

A reign of terror followed; 'Year Zero' had begun. To the Khmer people the Khmer Rouge were known as *Angkar*, a force with neither compassion nor conscience who split up families, executed adversaries and committed atrocities the like of which had never before been seen in Kampuchea. Within a few days of entering the city they had marched the entire population into the countryside, even the sick and infirm were forced to leave the security of hospitals. Anyone who was educated or had sympathies with the Lon Nol government or the Vietnamese faced summary execution. Their collectivisation policy meant that the whole of the countryside was turned into a massive labour camp. Everyone was excessively exploited, made to work unearthly hours and put to death if disobedient. Their radical revolutionary policies had begun to materialise in May 1973 when the country was ravaged by civil war and was also experiencing the worst of the American bombing raids. After the end of the Second Indochina War the lives of the people were becoming intolerable as their collectivisation programmes intensified. All private land was confiscated, machinery was wrecked, pagodas and churches burnt, schools and colleges destroyed, monks either killed or defrocked and even Western medicine was forbidden. Books were burned and further persecutions led to attempted coups, which were ruthlessly dealt with. Atrocities increased during 1977, and by April 1978 an estimated two million people had either starved to death, died from the terrible epidemics which spread throughout the country or been exterminated by the barbaric Pol Pot clique. Border clashes had also escalated between Vietnam and Thailand.

The People's Republic of Kampuchea

After the full scale invasion of the country by Vietnamese on December 25 1978, the KNUFNS, Kampuchean National United Front of National Salvation rose to power. Their leader, Heng Samrin, who had been the President of Kampuchea, had been forced to leave the country in 1977. Now he was reinstated as the President of the KNUFNS. Right from its formation in early December 1978 its purpose had been to rid the country of the murderous Khmer Rouge, increase friendship with its neighbouring Vietnam and make Kampuchea into a peaceful, independent nation. By October 1979 most of the Khmer Rouge had fled and the country was policed by some 150,000 Vietnamese and 20,000 Khmer soldiers.

The Heng Samrin government faced problems of enormous magnitude – the infrastructure of the country had been completely crippled; roads were practically unusable; there was no rail, telephone or postal communication; there was no currency in circulation, no financial institutions; and there was very little industry or electricity. People who had been separated from their families and friends during the mass exodus of Phnom Penh had no idea whether they were still alive. Between 1975 and 1981, 630,000 refugees had fled into Thailand, 150,000 into Vietnam and 20,000 into Laos.

A massive aid package was organised from the US$100 million which had been donated by caring people from many nations. However, considering the magnitude of the problem, this was totally inadequate. Over 180,000 tons of food and rice seeds arrived in 1980 but this was followed by a massive famine in 1981. Multilateral donations poured in to help UN agencies which, together with the Humanitarian Aid Agencies, were stretched to their limit, helping to alleviate the crisis.

By the end of 1982, 1.7 million hectares of paddy had been brought under cultivation by providing a few vitally needed irrigation pumps, extra draught animals, tractors, fertilisers and insecticides. This was however only a small fraction of what was needed to be done and the provisions supplied were only a small but vital drop in the ocean. In order to help the recovery no tax burdens were levied for two years. By 1983 it was officially declared by the UN that the immediate emergency was over. During the 1984-5 period the Vietnamese offensive against the Khmer Rouge resistance bases along the Thai border increased. As a result more and more Cambodian refugees were forced further into Thailand. In September 1985, Pol Pot was reported to have resigned as military commander but his troops continued to raid villages deep into Cambodia. They left behind mined roads, broken bridges and scores of dead civilians.

During the 1980s the Heng Samrin Hun Sen government, which was supported by the Vietnamese, faced opposition from the Armée Nationale Sihanoukiste (ANS) led by Prince Sihanouk, the Son Sann, Khmer People's National Liberation Front (KPNLF) and the Khmer Rouge, all factions of the Coalition Government of Democratic Kampuchea (CGDK). Towards the end of the 1980s, the Association of Southeast Asian Nations (ASEAN) failed in their attempts to produce a peace pact between the warring factions. Trouble escalated as Russian aid to the Vietnamese dwindled. In September 1989 most of the Vietnamese troops were withdrawn from the country, now renamed the State of Cambodia.

The State of Cambodia

The CGDK rebels, particularly the Khmer Rouge, stepped up their actions against the weakened regime of Hun Sen, who retaliated with measures to reduce their popularity with the common country folk. Increased tax incentives were given to the peasants, together with other benefits which helped to improve their agricultural yields. Meanwhile corruption in the city reached epidemic proportions, fuelling discontentment with the Phnom Penh regime. Like a disease it spread through the countryside. The Khmer Rouge continued in its efforts to cripple the government's already beleaguered economy. Roads and bridges were blown up and hundreds of people died during the countless minor battles which raged during 1990. Table-talk politics did little to bring about an amicable agreement between the representatives of the four warring factions who had been brought together in the name of the Supreme National Council (SNC) towards the end of 1990. By June 1991, a temporary cease-fire had been agreed which, on the signing of the Paris Peace Accord on October 23 1991, brought an end to Cambodia's 13-year long civil war.

Prince Sihanouk returned to his royal palace in Phnom Penh on November 14 1991, having lived in exile for more than two decades. The tranquil period suffered a temporary hiccup when the Khmer Rouge representative, Kieu Samphan, returned to the city on November 28 1991. Mob violence broke out and he was forced to leave the country. In order to administer the terms of the Peace Accord, a UN peace-keeping mission arrived in March 1992, funded by a US$2 million grant donated by the USA Congress. Officially called UNTAC (The United National Transitional Authority in Cambodia), its function was not only to keep the peace but also to supervise free elections due to take place in May 1993 and to help resettle the thousands of Cambodian refugees who had been forced to live in camps along the Thai border. The strong international team, comprising well over 20,000 military and administrative personnel from 31 countries, was given the powers necessary to perform its unenviable task by the Supreme National Council of Cambodia. With the election pending there were great fears that the Khmer Rouge would create severe problems for the UN military despite the fact that they were rumoured to have no more than 1,500 combat troops. The UN had ten times this number (15,700) but in order to keep the peace throughout the country they were scattered far and wide. Indonesian troops, the largest contingency (1,700), policed Kompong Thom Province where they were attacked repeatedly by Khmer Rouge forces. Pakistani troops (around 1,200) were sent into Khmer Rouge strongholds in Siem Reap and Oddar Mean Chey. The Dutch and Malaysian military regularly patrolled the provinces of Battambang and Pursat. To the east of Phnom Penh, extending along the length of the Mekong and the border with Vietnam, nearly 1,400 Indian troops kept the peace, helped by Bulgarian and Ghanaian soldiers further south. Uruguayans patrolled the Laotian border areas and a small contingency from France were dispatched to areas along the Gulf of Thailand. In addition, there were smaller contingencies from Australia (around 500), UK (around 120), US (around 50), Canada (230) and New Zealand (around 100). A 3,000 strong force of civilian police completed the task force.

It was quite obvious right from the start when the first UN troops arrived in November 1991 that the Khmer Rouge were not prepared to give them an easy ride. To the Angkar or the DKP (Democratic Kampuchean Party), as they were sometimes known, the Paris Peace Accord meant nothing: UN forces came under repeated attack, especially when trying to gain access to Khmer Rouge controlled areas. The worse fighting in 1992 broke out in Kompong Thom Province where the UN Indonesian military had to be reinforced with international firepower. Guerrilla attacks became more frequent towards the end of 1992, a period when the Western press was full of reports about UN hostages being held by the DKP. It was clear that when the DKP failed to register for the election before the expiry date laid down by the UN that the trouble would escalate. The Angkar, who had great hatred for the ethnic Vietnamese, began vicious attacks on them in an attempt to severely daunt the Cambodian people. In one attack over 30 Vietnamese men, women and children were slaughtered. Thousands began fleeing across the Vietnamese border. Word of the atrocity quickly spread and UN Commanders, knowing full well that the whole population was becoming more and more uneasy, feared that worse was still to come. Rumours of arms flooding in from Thailand fuelled their anguish. As the election approached in May 1993, there were almost daily reports of UN personnel being ambushed, election volunteers being killed and villages being ransacked. On 18 May 1993, one week before the election UNTAC launched a massive security operation throughout the whole of the country. Heavily armed units protected by flak jackets were flow in to protect ballot boxes. Despite Khmer Rouge propaganda, intimidating threats and promises of reprisals, 90% of the population turned out to vote on 25 May 1993.

The result was that Sihanouk's party, FUNCINPEC (Front Uni National pour un Cambodge Independent Neutre, Pacific et Cooperatif) gained 58 seats compared to their nearest rival, SOC [State of Cambodia Government; formerly the CPP (Cambodian People's Party)] led by Hun Sen who obtained 51 seats. Next came the Buddhist-Liberal Democrats (BLDP) headed by veteran Son Sann with 10 seats. Of the remaining 17 parties only the Liberal Democratic Party (LDP) obtained a single seat. With 45% of the vote, Prince Norodom Sihanouk became the State President on 14 June 1993. On 1 July 1993 a new government was officially formed, with Hun Sen and Prince Norodom Ranariddh sharing the post of prime minister. Ratification of the new constitution meant that Sihanouk, who had relinquished the throne in 1955 somewhat reluctantly, became King of a constitutional monarchy.

When UNTAC was withdrawn in October 1993, Cambodia was finally left in the shaky hands of the new coalition. With the government in a far from stable condition and Khmer Rouge attacks continuing across the country, Cambodia faces a bleak future. The sad news of westerner tourists being killed in 1994 and headlines in the western press such as 'Khmer Rouge turn Cambodia into a holiday in hell' threaten business investment, acquisition of increased revenue through tourism and general recovery.

Living with mines

Living in a country which has been called 'the biggest minefield in the world' can be a never-ending struggle. The lethal legacy left behind by the Americans, Vietnamese and Cambodians themselves disrupts everyday life, poses a daily death threat and undermines economic recovery. Today there are an estimated 4-8 million mines in Cambodia, and there are between 25,000 to 35,000 amputees per month. There are few Cambodian families indeed who don't have their own horror story.

Mine-laying began with a vengeance even before the Civil War started. Teams of special forces, courtesy of the American military , would infiltrate Cambodian territory from South Vietnam. In 1967, the US airforce dropped thousands of tons of mine garbage along the eastern border of the country, adding to the thousands of others deposited there by the North Vietnamese. The Khmer Rouge practised extensive mine-laying – to prevent infiltration by the Vietnamese along the eastern border and to guard new interests along the western border with Thailand. When driven by the Vietnamese across the Thai border in late 1984, they laid 2-3 million antipersonnel devices as they left. People living in this zone (the 'K5 belt'), even today face unimaginable suffering in their everyday lives. Many refugees, tempted back into the area by a US$50 handout, find that their old farm land has been turned into little more than an explosives dump. Ploughing can be a risky business and hunting can be more deadly for the hunter than the prey. A fisherman beaching his craft at an unknown docking point can be risking his life. A woman venturing into a forest to gather bamboo shoots to sell in the market can become maimed for life.

An average Cambodian family consisting of a husband, a wife, two children and a grandmother needs around 60,000 a month to live. The husband may be a soldier who used to earn 12,000 riels/month but is now lucky to get paid this sum in three months. The children if old enough will be forced to find work with neighbours. During the rice growing season they may be lucky to earn as much as 1,000 riels a day. At other times, they may be reduced to woodgathering, bringing in only 500 riels/day. Their mother is forced to weave straw mats, being paid, perhaps, 3,000 riels for three days' work by a middleman who makes huge profits at no risk to himself. Working very hard, they barely manage to survive. One day, the wife takes a short cut into the forest and is blown up by a mine. If she survives at all she will probably face an amputation. Her family will then be stretched to the limit to find the funds required for the operation. Drugs will be in short supply and the woman may be forced to discharge herself prematurely because of financial pressure. If it happens to the man, he could find himself on the streets of Phnom Penh begging for enough money to buy food for his family. In this situation he will be treated incredibly badly by most shop keepers who will look upon him as the lowest of the low. Probably, though, with the increase in tourism he may earn as much as 2,000 riels per day begging. Few tourists walking into their posh hotels or plush cafe-bars will even notice him!

Chapter Fifteen

Economy

Following the attempt by the Khmer Rouge to restart history by returning the country to 'Year Zero', Cambodia has remained a nation in tatters. Even after the end of this brutal era the population's resilience was further tested by the US-led embargo which was to continue for 12 unrelenting years. In order that the wind of recovery could start blowing, vital developmental assistance had to be sought from humanitarian aid groups such as Oxfam (UK), HEKS (Switzerland), CCDP (Cambodia Canada Development Program) with the backing of world-wide Christian Aid campaigns. Organisations such as Church World Services (USA), Catholic Commission for Justice, Peace and Development (NZ) and Action Cambodia (UK) risked life and limb to help alleviate the immense suffering. Others, such as the Swedish Red Cross, Lutheran World Service, Mennonite Central Committee (Canada), World Council of Churches (Switzerland) and Redd Barna (Norway), showed their support and solidarity. They continue to do so.

Recovery has been an extremely hard uphill struggle; many learned authorities think that things will never return to how they were in the Sihanouk era (1960s), when over 60,000 tourists a year visited Cambodia.

Following the *Angkar's* reign of terror, over 360,000 people remained in Thai Refugee Camps, nearly 200,000 in the country itself had been displaced. Most country dwellers had lost their homes and were living in makeshift accommodation. Every single person had his or her own tale of terror. Some families had only a few surviving members, many carried mutilation scars. The adult population was 64% female, 50% were under 15 years of age. The crippled economy could give little support to the thousands of orphans badly in need of loving care.

Agricultural recovery was severely hampered by 'eternal sentinels', antipersonnel mines which maimed but did not kill. Further economic strains were put on country folk by lack of money to buy fertilisers, pesticides, irrigation pumps, seeds, ox-carts and mechanical aids. Those who managed to obtain rice seeds worked from dawn to dusk, often relying on primitive hand-made irrigation wheels called *rohat*. Friends and relatives massed together to support workers in the fields.

During the 1980s, despite all the hardships, rebel activity and constraints imposed by the civil war, rice production increased nearly fivefold. Towards the end of the decade, when the withdrawal of Vietnamese troops saw the economy fall to an all time low, rice production was badly hit by inclement climatic conditions and guerrilla sabotage. The collapse of the Soviet Union lost another source of subsidies and the escalation of the civil war further drained the Phnom Penh Government's coffers. The hyper-inflation which followed the 50% devaluation of the riel in 1992 put many foodstuffs beyond the reach of peasants. Pork, for example, which in February 1992 had cost 750 riel/kg had soared to 4,250 riel/kg by October. Fish prices had also rocketed and rice was only barely affordable.

As the ordinary Cambodian suffered misery and starvation, the Khmer Rouge grew fat on the proceeds of their logging activities. In the Palin area alone they were minting over one million dollars per month from timber sold to Thai traders. With inflation rising to well over 250% the State of Cambodia Government (SCG) had joined in, in an attempt to raise vital revenue from timber companies from Japan, Indonesia, Malaysia, Thailand and Singapore. Over one million hectares of forests were cropped in 1992. This suicidal deforestation rate was reduced slightly at the end of 1992 by a logging moratorium. Unscrupulous merchants, using portable sawbenches, continued, despite the new legislation. Many were soldiers fed up with their meagre US$10 a month, some were fishermen who, because of the deforestation, had greatly reduced catches in the Tonlé Sap River which in places had silted up badly. Many saw their incomes rise to a massive US$850/month while ordinary peasants and city workers were lucky if they could equal the Gross Domestic Product (GDP) of around US$150 per capita per year. Even highly educated medical workers and doctors were taking home no more than US$5-8/month, some weren't being paid at all. During 1993, with inflation running at a staggering 350%, many country girls sought employment in Battambang and Phnom Penh. Many worked for 16 hours a day in the new restaurants and hotels which catered for UNTAC (UN Transitional Authority in Cambodia) workers, humanitarian groups and an ever increasing number of tourists. Some took quick profits from prostituting their bodies. Many had no choice since relatives back home relied heavily on them.

Ever since the signing of the Paris Peace Accord on 3 October 1991, the Khmer Rouge, deprived of funding from the Beijing government, had sought out new ways of obtaining cash to fund their cause. Their deforestation exploits had badly affected the economy of fisherfolk, mechanical gem mining had increased the siltation problem and prospecting for oil was contaminating waterways. Their refusal to comply with the terms of the Accord no doubt blighted the tourist industry. Terrorist activity continued despite the presence of a 20,000+ strong UNTAC international team. Their presence was no doubt responsible for the sudden increased business boom which hit Phnom Penh at the beginning of 1992. New hotels and restaurants began to sprout like bamboo stalks. Businessmen from Thailand, Singapore, Hong Kong, Malaysia and Taiwan began to invest a great deal of money in service industries. Many had already started to reap quick profits in neighbouring Vietnam due to an extraordinary influx of tourists. They were 80% convinced that the same would happen in Cambodia. Although there has been no meteoric rise, the signs are all there. Streets buzz with motorised traffic, tiger beer flows freely, international flights arrive daily from Bangkok, Ho Chi Minh, Hong Kong, Singapore and Vientiane. Flights to Angkor have increased from two a day in 1992 to five a day in 1995. Reports in the national press that the Khmer Rouge are turning Cambodia into a tourist no-go area are no doubt putting off the more squeamish travellers. Sad reports of Westerners being taken hostage and killed by the guerrillas during 1994 for a short time deterred even the most adventurous of travellers but since then, tourist traffic has improved. During 1995 the building boom has continued and although the economy is rife with corruption and extremely badly managed, there are still signs of light at the end of a very long, dark tunnel.

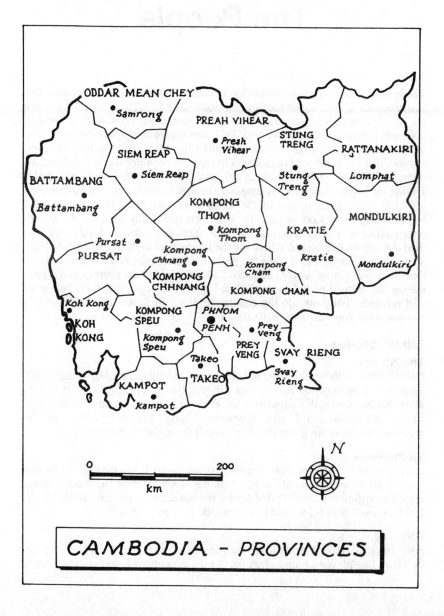

CAMBODIA - PROVINCES

Chapter Sixteen

The People

There have been very few population censuses carried out in Cambodia. The major census in 1962 stated that the population was 5,748,842. In peaceful times the UN estimated that the average increase in population size was approximately 2.8% per annum (between 1965-70). This would have meant that the population would have reached nine million by 1981. The May 1981 census, however, showed that the number of inhabitants living in the country was 6.7 million. An estimated 600,000 fell because of military action between 1970 and 1975. During the reign of the Pol Pot-Ieng Sary clique, an estimated two million died (1975-8). The figures quoted by the world's press regarding the number killed by summary execution is said by some eminent authorities to be greatly exaggerated. Realistically journalists now agree that between 80,000-150,000 died directly by this means, others say the figure is far higher. Indirectly through war-induced famine and disease the projected figure may be far more realistic. One must also remember the estimated 850,000 who left the country as refugees during the 1975-81 period. According to UNHCR sources, 350,000 people were still refugees living outside the country in 1982. In September 1995 the UN estimated the population to be 10,400,000.

Ethnic groups
The Khmer
Colonisation of the area by the Khmer began around the second century AD. They now constitute the majority of the population, about 85%. Ethnologists think that the present day population has evolved from an admixture of Negritos, Malay, Mongols and Indian Brahmans. Those presently living in the mountainous areas are given the tribal names Brao, Saoch, Kuy and Pear.

Vietnamese
According to UNHCR sources, these constitute about 3% of the population and are mainly concentrated along the Mekong River. During the mass exodus period an estimated 250,000 fled across the border into Vietnam. After March 1979 around 130,000 returned to Cambodia.

Chinese
An estimated 210,000 died during the genocidal Pol Pot-Ieng Sary era. Before this they had played an important part in the economy of the country in their

roles as traders, businessmen and co-ordinators. Large numbers settled throughout the country during the 18th and 19th centuries. Between 1975 and 1978 it is reported that China sent nearly 10,000 advisors to the country. There are very few ethnic Chinese still living in the country.

Cham-Malay
Emigration of Cham Muslims into the country began in the 15th century and continued until 1822 when large numbers, under the leadership of Prince Po Chon, arrived via Chau Doc and Tay Ninh. Today there are an estimated 100,000 still in the country. A large number can be seen in Khet Chraing Chamres District in Phnom Penh, where they built the Nur ul-Ihsan Mosque in 1813. In the countryside they are mainly found along the lower Mekong where they fish, breed cattle and silk worms and grow traditional Khmer crops. An estimated 250,000 Cham lived in the country in 1975; 90,000 were killed during the Pol Pot era.

Burmese
Very few now live in the Palin area where they once mined gems.

RELIGION
Brahminism and Hinduism
One of the most ancient religions of the Khmer is Brahminism, which teaches belief in Brahmā, the Creator. It is believed that this originated in northwest India (Punjab) around 4,000 years ago. Its fusion with Hinduism in Cambodia over many centuries produced deities which are still seen vividly portrayed on the walls of temples at Angkor and throughout the country. Bas-reliefs show Brahmā with four faces, his neck adorned with a necklace and his two pairs of hands clutching vases. He is sometimes mounted on a sacred goose (*hamsa*). Vishnu, who is another member of the trinity, is known as the Protector of the World, Krishna is one of his incarnations; Rama is another. In sculpture he is usually depicted riding on a mythical bird (*Garuda*) wearing a cylindrical crown; his four hands hold ritual objects. He is particularly represented in the bas-relief seen at Angkor Wat which was originally dedicated to him.

Earlier temples are decorated with another member of the trinity, Siva. He is the Destroyer and Creator. Usually he has five faces, a central third eye, his hair is in a knot, snakes coil around his neck and he rides the sacred bull (*Nandi*). In some sculptures, Siva and Vishnu are merged together in the form of the God Hari-Hara.

After the trinity comes Indra, chief of all the gods who reside on Mount Meru. You will see him seated on a three-headed elephant on the walls of some of Angkor's temples.

Lesser gods such as Kāma, Ganeśa, Skanda and Kubera are also depicted on Khmer temples.

Buddhism
There is evidence that original inhabitants of the country were firm adherents to 'Greater Vehicle', Hīnayāna Buddhism. This evolved independently from Hinduism but during their early development they certainly fought for

supremacy. On many wall frescoes you will see both religions illustrated. Later conquering monarchs constructed Buddhist temples. Suryavarman I (1002-49) left behind Ta Kéo and the West Baray, Jayavarman VII (1181-1200) constructed the fabulous Bayon Temple. Here you will see the smiling faces of the Lokesvara sect which is believed to have over thirty reincarnations. In other temples you may come across some of them, such as Maheshvara and Ishvara. The other Hīnayăna sect, Avalokitesvara is not so widely represented in Cambodia.

At the beginning of the 15th century, the 'Lesser Vehicle' Buddhism known also as Theravăda Buddhism was introduced from Ceylon. Today 90% of the population practise this religion. Since 1979 there has been a merger of its two orders, Mohanikay (common) and Thommayuth (aristocratic). Originally sacred sutras were written in Sanskrit, most of these were destroyed during the Pol Pot era. Under his brutal regime an estimated 25,000 Buddhist monks were executed. Those that survived received inhuman treatment. Before 'Year Zero' began there were 3,054 wats in the country. Since 1979 many have been revived and there are an estimated 2,397 which have been largely rebuilt and reinhabited. Before 1975, there were 65,000 Buddhist monks, many who survived had to leave the country as refugees. Since 1979, over 7,000 new monks have been ordained. Religion in the country is now administered by the National Front for Construction and Defence, previously it was the responsibility of the Ministry of Cults. Strict rules have been introduced governing the ordination of monks; only men over 50 years of age are accepted.

Islam
The Cham Muslim community was treated very harshly by the Pol Pot clique. Many of those that survived can be seen in 'Muslim Village', very close to the Tuol Tom Pong market in Phnom Penh. They worship at the An-Nur an-Na'im and Nur ul-Ihsan Mosques on the outskirts of the city.

Other religions
The Chinese community are all Taoists. There are about 55,000 Catholics in the country and around 20,000 Protestants.

Chapter Seventeen

Culture

FESTIVALS

Bonn Chroat Preah Nongkoal

This is the Royal Ploughing Ceremony, the first agrarian festival of the year, held in April/May. When it was first performed, the opening of the Sacred Furrow, which still marks the beginning of the ploughing season, was inaugurated by the king. It was carried out in a sacred rice field within the confines of the capital. Today's ritual is enacted by a man, known as King of Meakh, whose plough is followed by a woman sowing seeds (Queen Me Hour). The sacred plough, drawn by sacred oxen, is led around the rice field three times and finally comes to a halt at a religious sanctuary where a prayer is said to ask for the protection of the Gods. The oxen are then led off for their reward, greens, rice and corn, served to them on three silver trays. Alongside these are four other trays containing water, alcohol, herbs and other edibles. According to their choice, predictions are made about the new year. If they drink the alcohol, this spells disaster in the form of severe droughts, unrest and general hardship. If they eat the cereal, this is a good omen and indicates a bumper harvest. Eating the herbs indicates that the cattle of the Kingdom will be plagued with diseases. Drinking the water indicates that rainfall will be abundant.

Today's ceremony is colourful and attracts crowds from all over the country. In the audience you may see His Majesty Preah Bat Samdech Preah Norodom Sihanouk Varman, King of Cambodia, and his Queen Norodom Monineath Sihanouk. Alongside them on the Royal Platform will be the First Prime Minister, HRH Samdech Krom Preah Norodom Ranariddh and the Second Prime Minister, Samdech Hun Sen. Since the promulgation of the new constitution in September 1993, the Minister of Tourism, Veng Sereyvuth, has promised foreign visitors that the festival will never be forgotten once seen.

Bonn Chaul Chham

This new year festival occurs in April. Children all over the country build sand mountains, which are representations of Mount Meru in Indian cosmology. They are always given five or nine towers which, according to the tradition of Angkor's god-kings, are the sacred numbers. In some agricultural communities along rivers, masked women race against each other in canoes.

At this time children play Khmer games such as *Leak Kansaneg, Chaol Chhoung, Angkunh* and tug-of-war. Their parents visit temples, taking with them offerings to honour the Devoda of the coming new year. Houses are bedecked with flowers, cleaned and family altars are lavishly decorated.

Bonn Dak Ben and Bonn Phchoum Ben
This festival, known to the Khmer as the 'Spirit Commemoration Festival', occurs in September. It commemorates the spirits of the dead. During the 15 days of Bonn Dak Ben, food offerings are given to monks. The 15th day of the ceremony is the most important; it occurs on the full moon and is known as Bonn Phchoum Ben. It is most important at this time that the family of the deceased should visit a temple and make offerings to his/her spirit. If this is not done, not only will the spirit of the dead person be cursed, but the family will also be plagued throughout the coming year.

Bonn Kathen Festival
This also occurs in October, immediately following Bonn Phchoum Ben. Monks are offered new robes and simple gifts by devout worshippers. This important festival lasts for 29 days. People throughout the country flock to temples where monks will be given new saffron robes. This not only brings spiritual merit but also enhances friendships.

Bon Om Touk Festival
This is also known as the 'Turning of the Water Festival'. The date for this festival is fixed by the lunar month of *Kadoeuk*, (late October or early November). This three-day festival celebrates the change in direction of the Tonlé Sap River. During the first day of the festival over 100 boats each with 40 oarsmen assemble on the Mekong. These racing pirogues have been stored in pagodas until the great day arrives. Before launching, eyes are painted on the prows of the boats. Sitting in the prow of the boat the skipper will beat out the correct paddling rhythm using a lacquered ceremonial paddle. The helmsman will steer the pirogue using a free oar. Each boat also carries one or two clowns dressed in comical outfits who entertain the onlookers by singing satirical songs. The canoes race against each other in pairs until a final winner is recognised. As the sun drops towards the horizon on the final day, there is a grand finale. All the boats that have competed gather en masse in front of the spectators. One of the most highly decorated crafts heads out into the Mekong to perform the 'cutting of the imaginary string' ceremony. The festival has performed its duties in honouring the mighty Mekong and celebrating the ending of the floods.

Important dates in the Khmer calendar
January 7   National Day. This corresponds to the day that Pol Pot's troops were expelled from Cambodia in 1979.

February 1   Friendship Day. This celebrates the signing of the Friendship Treaty between Vietnam and Cambodia in 1979.

March 8   Women's Day. Many colourful processions with streaming banners march through towns.

April 13-15 Cambodian New Year.

April 17	Victory Day. This commemorates the collapse of the Lon Nol government in 1975.
May 1	International Workers Day. There are parades in the city.
May 2	Day of Remembrance for the victims of Pol Pot's brutal regime.
May 9	Remembrance Day. A day to remember those who lost their lives because of the atrocities committed by the Pol Pot-Ieng Sary clique. Also known as Genocide Day.
June 19	Revolutionary Armed Forces Day. The Revolutionary Armed Forces of Kampuchea were founded in 1951.
July to September	Buddhist Lent.
October 31	Birthday of His Majesty Preah Bat Samdech Preah Norodom Sihanouk Varman, King of Cambodia. Everyone throughout the country celebrates in regal fashion. He was born on October 31 1922. There is a spectacular firework display on the banks of the river in the capital after sundown.
November 9	Independence Day (from the French) which occurred in 1953. There are grand parades in front of the Royal Palace featuring spectacular floats, gala celebrations which include marching bands and spectacles which highlight the nation's achievements.
December 2	National Reconstruction Day. The National Front for Reconstruction was founded in 1978.

THE ARTS

Art and architecture

There is almost nothing which compares with the splendour of Angkorian architecture and art. Visitors to Cambodia with plenty of time on their hands will be able to visit no fewer than 72 temples and monuments in the Angkor area alone. The vagaries of nature, the rampant growth of the jungle, root penetration, erosion, water percolation, heat deterioration, bio-chemical degradation and senseless destruction have, over the centuries, all taken their toll. What remains is still a priceless seductive treasure-house of six centuries of Khmer art.

Music and dance

Music

Two types of orchestras are seen in Cambodia, the all male *pip-hat* and the all female *mohori*. Both contain 11 musical instruments but in the mohori most of them are stringed. All are elaborately decorated with carvings, some have inlaid ivory panels. The leader plays the *roneat-ek* which has 21 bamboo keys. Its sound box, which is made from wood, is shaped like a boat, which makes this xylophone instantly recognisable. Another xylophone, the *roneat-thoum,* has 17 keys and a flat sound box. Chimes which give the distinctive tingling sound to Cambodian music sometimes consist of 21 bronze plates. This instrument is known as the *roneat-dec.* Other performers strike gong-chimes with leather padded hammers. These instruments are arranged in the form of a semi-circle, the performer sits in the middle. They either have 16 or 17 gongs. Stringed instruments include the *chapey-toch*, a form of guitar, the *chapey-thom*, a long lute and the *takhe*, a three-stringed guitar. Trill sounds are made by the *kloie*, a flute and the *sralay*, a form of oboe.

At important festivals, a traditional Khmer orchestra, known as the *Phleng Pinpeat*, will perform court music, known as *Phleng Mohori*, if the king is in attendance. The Khmer guitar, the *chapei*, features prominently during chanted performances of *Chrieng Chapei*, which is a story in song. Ballads sung by women and men are often improvised, a tradition known as *Chrieng Tar*. During an *Ayai* performance these improvisations can last for several hours. At a Khmer wedding ceremony, a type of orchestra called *Phleng Khmer* will perform; this also accompanies magic rituals.

Cambodian music has similarities to Thai music – there is virtually no harmony and performers have their own improvised variations. There appears to be no system of musical notation.

Dance
It is evident from the stone panoramas at Angkor depicting the early court life of the kings that temple dancers were an important part of the monarch's harem. Today Khmer classical dance (*lamthon*) is performed at the Fine Arts Theatre in Phnom Penh. Dressed in colourful elaborate costumes which bear a distinct resemblance to those of their Thai neighbours, members of the Royal Ballet, some of whom survived the Pol Pot era, still dance for tourists. Many young girls from the Phnom Penh orphanages are selected for their beauty and grace to undergo a strict training which can take many years. Performances are governed by a precise rhythmical language which has been handed down through the generations. On their head they will wear the traditional mitre crown, the *mokot* which is smothered in gold ornamentation. Like their earrings, it is made from finely wrought gold. Above their left ear is a delicate rose and hanging over their right cheek is a floral wreath. Dancers are dressed in gold and velvet costumes, occasionally brown, blues and reds are used to enhance their appeal. Every inch of their regal attire is embroidered with intricate designs made from the finest silk. Around their ankles they wear silver clasps, their feet remain bare.

Theatre
Royal theatre performances are often based on the Reamker (the Cambodian version of the Rāmāyana epic). It describes in 48,000 lines the life and adventures of Prince Rāma, a Vishnu incarnate. Trials and tribulations of the hero's life are immaculately depicted; artists perform in colourful masks, King Ravana looking the most evil and Sita, Rāma's wife, looking the most beautiful. Hanuman, the Monkey God, features prominently, and, together with the God of the Wind, successfully rescues Sita, who has been abducted by Ravana. The story is more than 2,000 years old. Khmer theatre dates from pre-Angkor times (6th century). Various forms of folk theatre exist today. These include the *Lakhon Khaul*, *Lakhon Bassac* and *yoke*. Classical dances are often performed depicting the life of Lord Buddha (Jataka). Masked theatre, known as *khaul*, is also popular.

Nang Sbaek Thom (shadow plays)
This very expressive form of shadow puppet theatre depicts kings, queens, everyday folk, gods, goddesses and clowns. Their shadows come alive during important festivals, weddings and even funerals. They are narrated by actors

positioned below the puppet screen. Intriguing performances are given, depicting religious scenes, comedy, historical battles and everyday life by master puppeteers. Puppet-making skills, which involve cutting outlines and chiselling details, have been handed down by masters of the art who were originally centred around the Siem Reap area. Because of their intricate designs, many take over three weeks to construct. Cow skins, which cover part of the final puppet, have to be cured in the sun before use. The final design has moveable arms and is brightly coloured with lines accentuated with black ink.

Contemporary drama

Performances are often given in the capital which tell the story of the life of Cambodia. Contemporary history charts the French era, the Sihanouk regime, Lon Nol, war and the barbarism of the Pol Pot era. Recently popular performances depict the United Nations effort and the crowning of King Sihanouk.

Stilt House, Tonlé Sap

LANGUAGE

Before 1975, French was widely spoken throughout Cambodia. Most of the country's educated elite were killed by the Khmer Rouge and the language has never regained its former popularity. Today, English is taught in many Cambodian schools and there are numerous classes held throughout the city. A lot of the cyclo drivers attend, because to them it makes economic sense to be able to communicate with foreigners. Most visitors will not need to know any Khmer words at all but this section is included for those who would like to know a few.

The Khmer language is very difficult for Westerners to use because some of the sounds do not have English equivalents. The large number of vowels and 33 consonants used add to the problem. Those who want to attempt to master Khmer pronunciation should obtain a copy of *Courtesy and Survival in Cambodia* by Tran Kien and David Smyth, School of Oriental and African Studies.

Khmer words

Numbers

1	moo-ay	9	bprum boo-un
2	bpee	10	dop
3	bay	11	dop moo-ay
4	boo-un	20	m'oay
5	bprum	50	hah seup
6	bprum moo-ay	100	moo-ay roy
7	bprum bpee	1,000	moo-ay bpohn
8	bprum bay		

Useful words

No	te	Yes	jas (used by women),
Please	suom		bat (used by men)
Pagoda	wat	Police	police
Doctor	krou peit	Fish	trei
Dentist	peit thamenh	Market	psar
Soup	somlor	Eggs	poung sat
Chicken	maan	meat	saach
Toilet	borng-goo-un	Bank	ta-nee-a-gee-a

A few useful phrases

Hello	suor sdei
Excuse me	suom tous
How are you?	tau neak sok sapbaity jea te?
Thank you	or-goon
I don't understand	mun yoo-ul dtay
It's an emergency	nees jea pheap ason

Days of the week

Monday	tha-ngai chan	Tuesday	tha-ngai angkea
Wednesday	tha-ngai puot	Thursday	tha-ngai preuo-haou
Friday	tha-ngai sok	Saturday	tha-ngai sav
Sunday	tha-ngai atit		

See also Appendix One for a glossary for use in Cambodia.

Part Five
Practical Information

Chapter Eighteen

Getting to Cambodia

VISAS

Visas for air entry

Entry visas when coming in by air are issued free of charge at Pochentong Airport, Phnom Penh.

Visas for land entry
In the United Kingdom

Regent Holidays (UK) Ltd, 15 John Street, Bristol BS1 2HR; tel: (0117) 921 1711 (24 hrs); fax: (0117) 925 4866.

This company normally requires you to book a short tour or accommodation. Recommended, if you live in the UK. Cambodian visas for land entry from Vietnam can be issued in advance for US$100. Visas for air passengers are issued on arrival in Phnom Penh. Their US$100 visa requires three passport photographs and a photocopy of the information pages in your passport. It can be picked up in Bangkok or sent direct to them in the UK. It takes a long time to get a land entry Cambodian visa sent to the UK, so if you use Regent's service, make sure you give them plenty of time.

Through a Bangkok travel agent

Most of the travel agents listed in Appendix Three will process a tourist visa for land entry through Vietnam. One of the most reliable is the Saigon Tourist representative in Bangkok: **Air People Tour and Travel,** 307 Sa La Daeng Road; tel: 2352668; fax: (662) 2436005. They have considerable experience having run tours into Cambodia since 1985. **Diethelm Travel,** Kian Gwan Building 11, 140/1 Wireless Road are another good bet.

This service is very expensive; currently a Cambodian visa issued for land arrival from Vietnam costs a minimum of US$80. You will need to present the travel agent with three passport photographs and a photocopy of the personal details in your passport. It will take a week to issue.

In Singapore

If you intend travelling on the direct Silk Air flight from Singapore to Phnom Penh you can arrange a visa through the booking agents: **Airtrust Pty Ltd,** 3 New Industrial Road, Singapore 1953; tel: 65 280 7133. This takes about a week and requires three passport photographs. Since visas are now issued on arrival, there is little point in doing this unless you need a business extension for a long period.

In Hong Kong
Since there is now a direct flight by Dragon Airlines to Phnom Penh, they can handle visa processing on the same basis as above. **Hong Kong Dragon Airline Ltd,** 22nd Floor, Devon House, Talkoo Place, 979 Kings Road, Quarry Bay, Hong Kong; tel: 590 1328; fax: 1333; telex: 45936 DRAGH HX. Only use this service if you need a business extension.

Phoenix Services Agency, Room B, 6th Floor, Milton Mansions, 986 Nathan Road, Kowloon; tel: 7227378 (5 lines); fax: 852 3698884. These have a similar service. Contact Becky Bale. Phoenix will also arrange a land entry visa from Vietnam in advance.

Airtrust, Room 902, Wing Yue Building, 60-64 Des Voeux Road West, Central; tel: 852 549 4484. Similar service to their office in Singapore.

Australia
Orbitours, GPO Box 2209, Sydney 2000; tel: 02 221 7322; fax: 02 221 7425. This agency will arrange a visa for land entry through Vietnam for around US$100. Visas are normally issued in conjunction with a short tour.

In Vietnam
One of the cheapest and hassle-free ways of obtaining a visa to enter Cambodia is to go along to the **Cambodian Consulate** in Ho Chi Minh City. This is at 41 Phung Khac Khoan Street; tel: 92751. As long as you have three passport photographs and US$25 cash they will issue you with a two-week visa on the spot. If you intend to travel into Cambodia overland via the Moc Bai/Bavet border crossing, this should be stipulated when purchasing the visa. Check that you have this stamped on your visa before you leave the office. You can also get a visa in Hanoi: **Cambodian Consulate,** 71 Tran Hung Dac Street; tel: 53788

In Laos
A visa may be obtained at the **Cambodian Consulate** in Vientiane: Thanon Saphan Thong Neua; tel: 2750. Three passport photographs are required, a two-week visa will be issued on the spot for US$25 for land entry if you intend to fly to Ho Chi Minh first. Remember to stipulate that it's for land entry.

In India
If you are heading for Bangkok with a stop-over in New Delhi, get your Cambodian visa there. The **consulate** is at C4/4 Paschimi Marg, Vasant Vihar; tel: 11 608595. Three passport photographs are required; it takes a minimum of four days to issue a land entry visa from Vietnam. Make sure that they don't give you an air entry visa because you can get this when you arrive in Phnom Penh. Expect to pay US$120+ for a land entry visa.

Visa extensions

Visa extensions, when granted, are handled by the Foreign Ministry, intersection of 240 St and Quai Karl Marx. It could take up to three days. If your visa has expired, you will be charged US$3/day on leaving the country. If you only want a few days' extension this fine could work out much cheaper than an extension, which costs US$20 for two weeks.

Immigration and customs
Imports

Tourists are authorised to import the following duty free:

Cigarettes 200
Cigars 50
Liquor 1 litre
small gift items valued at no more than US$50.

There is no limit to the amount of cash which can be brought into the country. Luggage, if of unreasonable quantity, will be detained with levied storage fee.

Tourists are advised not to bring into Cambodia weapons, explosives, inflammable objects or narcotics such as marijuana, heroin and morphine.

Exports

Goods of a commercial nature and articles of high value require export permits issued by the Customs Service.

GETTING THERE AND AWAY
By air
Fares to Phnom Penh

It is very difficult to obtain a cheap bucket fare return to Phnom Penh. The best offered in February 1995 was £540, from Student Travel Association, 86 Old Brompton Road, South Kensington, London SW7 3LQ; tel: 071 581 4132; fax: 071 581 3351.

The cheapest way to get to Phnom Penh safely is to take one of the bucket flights to Bangkok. Then buy a return by Kampuchean Airways, Thai International or Bangkok Airways to Phnom Penh.

The Friday flight to Phnom Penh from Vientiane will cost you just US$170 by Lao Aviation. Cambodian International Airlines have one on Wednesday for US$150.

Another very good way of doing it is to get a cheap bucket return to Bangkok and then go overland to Laos via the Nong Khai crossing.

THE LAND CROSSING INTO CAMBODIA FROM THAILAND IS EXTREMELY DANGEROUS AND NOT RECOMMENDED.

Direct international flights to Phnom Penh

From	Carrier	Frequency	Depart	Arrive	Cost (US$)
Bangkok	Bangkok Airways	Daily	13.30	14.30	167
	Thai Airways International	Daily Mon, Wed, Fri Sat	10.50 14.40	12.00 15.50	242
	Kampuchea Airways	Daily Sat & Sun	10.50 11.50	12.00 12.40	167
Ho Chi Minh	Vietnam Airways	Daily (exc Wed)	07.00 14.25	07.45 15.10	121
	Kampuchea Airways	Mon, Thu, Sat Tue Sat	18.00 08.00 15.00	18.45 08.30 15.30	121
Hong Kong	Dragonair	Tue Thu	08.20 15.00	09.55 16.30	440
	Cambodia International Airlines	Sun Mon Thu	08.30 16.55 17.25	09.50 18.15 18.45	349
Kuala Lumpur	Malaysian Airways	Daily			
Singapore	Silk Air	Tue, Thu Sat Fri	08.40 13.30 10.10	09.40 14.30 11.10	552
	Cambodia International Airlines	Mon, Tue, Sun	18.30	19.30	442
Vientiane	Lao Aviation	Fri	07.00	10.25	170

There are also irregular scheduled flights from Moscow by Aeroflot. These cost US$1188 (one way).

In addition, look out for the new carrier, Royal Air Cambodia. This is a joint venture with Singapore Airlines, and promises to provide further international links.

Airport tax
Airport departure tax is US$10.

Bucket shops in the UK
Great care should be taken when buying cheap airfares through London 'bucket shops'. The best way to avoid being cheated is to choose one which has been in existence for a long time.

Direct international flights from Phnom Penh

To	Carrier	Frequency	Depart	Arrive	Cost (US$)
Bangkok	Bangkok Airways	Daily	10.00	11.30	178
	Thai Airways International	Daily Mon, Wed, Fri, Sat	13.15 17.05	14.25 18.15	242
	Kampuchea Airways	Daily Sat & Sun	09.00 10.20	09.50 11.10	167
Ho Chi Minh	Vietnam Airways	Daily Mon, Tue, Thu, Fri, Sun	08.30 15.55	09.15 16.25	121
	Kampuchea Airways	Mon Sat	19.00 13.40	19.30 14.10	121
Hong Kong	Dragonair	Tue Thu	10.55 17.30	14.30 21.05	440
	Cambodia International Airlines	Mon Thu Sat	12.35 13.10 16.20	15.55 14.30 19.40	349
Moscow	Aeroflot	Irregular			1188
Singapore	Silk Air	Tue, Thu Mon, Fri Sat	10.30 12.10 15.30	13.30 15.10 18.30	552
	Cambodia International Airlines	Tue, Fri, Sat & Sun	13.30	17.40	442
Vientiane	Lao Aviation	Fri	11.25	12.55	170
	Cambodia International Airlines	Wed	16.30	17.50	150

One of the best bets in London is **Trailfinders,** 194 Kensington High Street, London W8 7RG; tel: 0171 938 3939 or 42-50 Earls Court Road, London W8 6EJ; tel: 0171-938-3366. They can also be contacted at 58 Deansgate, Manchester M3 2FF; tel: 0161-839-6969 or at 48 Corn Street, Bristol BS1 1HQ; tel: 0117 929 9000. They also have a new office in Glasgow at 254-284 Sauchiehall Street, Glasgow C2 3EH; tel: 0141 353 2224. Their best Bangkok return in February 1995 was £340, £198 one way. Their best around-the-world ticket was London-San Francisco-Honolulu-Bangkok-London for £740.

The cheapest Bangkok return in February 1995 was £320 from **ITC Travel Ltd**; tel: 0171 493 4343.

Indirect international flights with transfer connections to Phnom Penh

Airline	Coming From	Frequency	Plane Change
Cathay Pacific	London, Paris, Frankfurt, Los Angeles Osaka, Seoul, Taipei Melbourne	Tue, Sun Mon, Wed	Hong Kong Hong Kong
Malaysian Airways	Los Angeles, London, Amsterdam Frankfurt	Mon Sat	Kuala Lumpur Kuala Lumpur
Singapore Airways	London Paris New York	Thu Thu, Fri Tue, Wed, Thu, Sun	Singapore Singapore Singapore
Thai Airway International	Seoul, Taipei, Jakarta, Singapore, Hong Kong, Paris Kathmandu London, Sydney, Kunming Los Angeles, Hanoi, Melbourne, Delhi Calcutta Guangzhou, Beijing Auckland	Daily Daily exc Mon Mon, Tue, Thu, Sun Mon, Wed, Sat Mon, Thu, Fri, Sat Tue, Thu, Sun Wed, Sun	Bangkok Bangkok Bangkok Bangkok Bangkok Bangkok Bangkok

Students may wish to book at the **Student Travel Association,** 86 Old Brompton Road, South Kensington, London SW7 3LQ; tel: 0171 581 4132; fax: 071-581-3351. Contact Andy Horwood. Their best Bangkok return from London in February 1995 was £380. They also had a London-Phnom Penh for £540.

Other good Bangkok returns in February 1995 were offered by:
   Nelson Travel (tel: 0181 951 5566) - £339
   Benz (tel: 0171 439 4181) - £325
   Travelbag (tel: 01420 80828) - £325
   Airline Network (tel: 017 72 72 72 72) - £342
   Oceans Apart (tel: 01628 799700) - £335

Slightly more expensive were:
   Bridge The World (tel: 0171 911 0900) - £398
   Rockfords (tel: 0171 436 2644) - £415
   Wexas International (tel: 0171 589 3315) - £375
   Heck-In Travel (tel: 0171 637 3104) - £380

It may also be worth trying **Flights Plus** (tel: 0161 343 2134) who claim that nobody will beat their price.

Bucket shops in the USA

Now the American embargo has been lifted, Transworld Airways, American Airlines and Continental Airlines have transfer connection flights to Ho Chi Minh City. Some good bucket fares were offered by **Mekong Travel** in New York; tel: 212 420 1586. New York-Ho Chi Minh return for US$920 – you can then get to Phnom Penh by bus very cheaply. **Budgetour International** were offering LA-Bangkok return for US$960. **Tour East**, tel: 213 290 6500, had some good frequent flyer deals.

Bucket shops in Canada

Try **Club Voyages Berri** who are particularly strong on destinations in the Far-East (tel: Montreal 982 6168/6169). I have heard that there are some good student fares from Canada but don't have details.

Bucket shops in Australia and New Zealand

Although the cheap flight bonanza has not yet reached these countries, some reasonable APEX fares are available. Try **Orbit** in Sydney (tel: 612 2217 322) and the **Flight Centre** (tel: 612 2332 296). The lowest possible return to Bangkok you are likely to get is around A$950 from Sydney. You are more likely to have to pay as much as A$1,600 return. In New Zealand the current fares to Bangkok (February 1995) are in the NZ$1,700 to NZ$1,900 bracket using APEX tickets. In New Zealand try Tony O'Callaghan's company, **Destinations**, based in Auckland (tel: (09) 390 464).

By land

The road route from Vietnam

Cars can be hired from 155 Nguyen Hue Boulevard, Ho Chi Minh (close to the Rex Hotel), for US$150 to take you to Phnom Penh.

Limousines from the Cambodian Consulate, 41 Phung Khac Khoan Street, cost an incredible US$300 for the Saigon to Phnom Penh trip.

One of the cheapest ways of doing it is to get together a group of five people and hire a taxi from outside the Sinh Cafe in Ho Chi Minh. Drivers in January 1995 were charging US$10 per head to take passengers to the border crossing at Moc Bai. When they arrived they could, after clearing customs, walk across to the Cambodian side. It isn't absolutely certain that taxis will be available to go on to Phnom Penh at a similar rate but, if there isn't, one can always get the bus which is subjected to a four-hour delay at this border. If you start off at around the same time as the bus, ie 05.30, you couldn't possibly fail (unless the bus is full!).

The bus which leaves from 155 Nguyen Hue Boulevard, Ho Chi Minh, should be booked at least one day in advance. There is an air-conditioned service on a Thursday, Friday and Saturday which costs US$8. Both will have a four-hour delay at the border if there are many Vietnamese or Cambodians travelling to Phnom Penh. At the border cash dollars can be exchanged but the rate (US$1=2,000 riels) is 500 riels lower than the bank rate. It is debatable whether you need to change any at all since the riel and dollar are parallel currencies in Cambodia.

In the opposite direction, air-conditioned buses leave on Thursday, Friday and Saturday from the booking office opposite 180/182 Street, Phnom Penh, at 05.30. Non air-conditioned buses leave at the same time on Monday, Tuesday and Wednesday.

If you attempt this journey, make sure your visa is stamped with MOC BAI/BAVET BORDER.

The road route from Thailand

THIS IS CLOSED TO FOREIGNERS. It is, in any case, extremely dangerous.

The road route from Laos

THIS IS CLOSED TO FOREIGNERS.

Chapter Nineteen

Transport and Communications within Cambodia

Air travel inside Cambodia

The safest way to get about within Cambodia is by air. It's also the most reliable.

Seats can be confirmed to/from Siem Reap only on an 'in principle' basis. Tickets for return flights are sold only one day before actual travel.

Flights to Siem Reap are sometimes cancelled at short notice. Stand-by seats are sometimes available if you turn up at the airport. Expect to pay more; US$125 for Siem Reap flight is the normal asking price.

There are also occasional flights for Cambodian nationals to Samrong, Lomphat, Kompong Cham and Mimot. At the time of writing, flights to Sihanoukville could be arranged for foreigners through Apsara Tours, No 8, Street R V Senie Vinnavaut Oum, Norodom Boulevard, Sangkat Chaktomuk, Khan Daun Penh, Phnom Penh; tel: 855 15 911 634 / 914 199; fax: 855 23 26 705.

Airport transfer

Pochentong Airport can be reached by travelling out of Phnom Penh along USSR Boulevard. Backpackers can get a motorbike ride there for US$2. For a car expect to pay US$15-20 for the 7km ride. Cars are available at all major hotels.

Airport tax

The international airport tax is US$10.

Domestic flights to Phnom Penh

From	Carrier	Frequency	Depart	Arrive	Cost (US$)
Battambang	Trans Air Cambodia	Mon, Fri	10.05	11.10	40
	Kampuchea Airways	Mon, Tue, Thu & Sat	12.30	13.15	60
Koh Kong	Kampuchea Airways	Mon, Tue, Thu & Sat	12.30	13.15	60
Stung Treng	Kampuchea Airways	Tue, Thu, Sat	09.25	10.10	60
Siem Reap	Kampuchea Airways	Daily	09.00	09.45	95
		Daily	09.15	10.00	
		Daily	14.00	14.45	
		Daily	16.30	17.15	
		Daily	17.00	17.45	
	Royal Air Cambodge				

Domestic flights from Phnom Penh

To	Carrier	Frequency	Depart	Arrive	Cost (US$)
Battambang	Trans Air Cambodia	Mon, Fri	08.00	09.05	40
	Kampuchea Airways	Mon, Wed, Fri, Sun	11.10	11.50	45
Koh Kong	Kampuchea Airways	Mon, Tue, Thu & Sat	11.00	11.40	60
Stung Treng	Kampuchea Airways	Tue, Thu, Sat	07.50	08.35	60
Siem Reap	Kampuchea Airways	Daily	07.45	08.30	95
		Daily	08.00	08.45	
		Daily	10.30	11.15	
		Daily	13.30	14.15	
		Daily	15.30	16.15	
	Royal Air Cambodge				

Land travel in Cambodia

Travelling by bus out of Phnom Penh is illegal, except if you are heading for the Moc Bai border crossing into Vietnam. Roads in Cambodia are in extremely bad shape, bridges without exception are guarded by the military. Driving standards are appalling; Cambodia has the highest road accident rate in Southeast Asia.

The road to Siem Reap

To get to Angkor you will need to get to Siem Reap. The most reliable, and by far the safest, way is to travel by plane. Taxi drivers in Phnom Penh, particularly those that hang out around the Capitol Hotel, will tell you that it is perfectly safe to travel to Siem Reap by taxi. For five sharing they will charge around US$15/head. This journey is ILLEGAL, DANGEROUS and is NOT RECOMMENDED. There have been reports from travellers staying at this hotel that taxi drivers have been stopped by the police/military and money demanded from them at gun point. Backpackers travelling with them have been robbed or fined. By doing this you could lose everything. There have also been reports of soldiers firing at the taxi's tyres if it won't stop. Remember also that this road is filled with potholes, is very dusty and vehicles using it have tyres which would have failed a Western MOT test about five years ago. The chances of a breakdown are high because of the condition of the vehicles. Radiators often boil over, tyres frequently burst. The mini-buses which sometimes travel this route are no better equipped. Between Sisaphon and Battambang the roads are in a horrendous condition. If you are foolish enough to try this and get stranded in Battambang, the safest way out is to take the Phnom Penh flight (two/day on Mondays and Fridays). Having said all this, it is also only fair to add that, according to travellers staying in the Capitol in Phnom Penh, many people have successfully completed this journey without incident. It takes a minimum of ten hours to travel the 370km (allow another two hours for breakdowns).

This information was provided by Pat Yale (February 1994).

Continuing into Thailand

When you are at Angkor you are about 160km from the Thai border. The Thai Embassy in Bangkok confirmed that in February 1995 the border was still closed to everyone. Thais and Cambodians who take this route are doing so illegally. A traveller in February 1994 met a Frenchman who cycled to the border from Phnom Penh. He was not allowed through although two French boys who had taxied to the border from Phnom Penh managed it. Apparently, the Thai guards had gone home around 16.30. The Cambodians had been very reluctant to stamp them through but relented when offered a US$2 bribe. When they got through they had gone straight to the Thai Immigration in Bangkok to make things legal. They were just told 'don't do it again'. It is also worth pointing out that a month and a half earlier there had been a border incident at Surin (December 1993). Khmer Rouge had attacked the area killing hundreds of villagers. The Cambodian border point is at Poipet, which leads to the Thai border crossing at Aranyaprathet. YOU WOULD HAVE TO HAVE A DEATH WISH TO ATTEMPT IT.

Boat travel to/in Cambodia

Independent travel by boat in Cambodia is illegal for foreigners. More and more backpackers are, however, ignoring this and using this method to get to Angkor. Fishermen in Trat in Thailand have been offering to take Westerners to Koh Kong Island in Cambodia where entry visas are available. A few foreigners have taken the boat from Tan Chau on the Mekong Delta in Vietnam to Phnom Penh.

The boat to Angkor

Fast and slow boats leave for the Siem Reap area from the docking bay north of the Chruoy Bridge. Any cyclo driver will know where it is. Boats leave early in the morning on a daily basis. They are extremely crowded, with no safety measure whatsoever – if the boat sinks you will have no alternative but to swim for it. If a boat does break down, they don't even have oars to get you to dry land. It should also be pointed out that there are many sob stories in circulation about these boats. They frequently break down and they have no navigation aid on board to help in the very wide parts of the Tonlé Sap Lake. According to the notice board at the Capitol Hotel one of those boats which broke down near the shore was fired upon. None of the westerners aboard were injured.

The slow service to Angkor takes four days and costs US$10. The fast boat should get you there in 24 hours but, because of breakdowns, this is frequently 24 hours late. This costs US$12. Should an emergency arise, no boat is equipped with a radio. If you break down it is quite likely that you will be transferred onto another boat which is already crowded. This can be very hazardous and it is likely that you will be separated from your travelling companion. You may be asked for more money by the owner of this boat. When you arrive you will be tired out. Since there is no shade you could easily be suffering from heat exhaustion. If you are foolish enough to attempt this journey take along plenty of water, food and an umbrella to shade yourself from the sun. The docking site near Angkor is just a mud-bank. A lift on a motorbike from here to Siem Reap costs about US$1.

I am indebted to independent traveller Pat Yale for this information. Pat made this trip in early February 1994. She, however, agrees that the most sensible way to get to Angkor is to fly.

The soft option

If you fancy a boat trip on the Tonlé Sap, book with Phnom Penh Tourism for their half day cruise to Oknhatey Island. Here you can visit a handicraft centre. In 1995 foreigners attempting to board the train or buy tickets have been reported to the authorities. This clamp-down follows the kidnapping of three foreigners by Khmer Rouge after a train attack in 1994. Very sadly all three were later found murdered.

Train

There have been many incidents recorded regarding train travel in Cambodia. When a train does run, it is heavily guarded. The first two carriages on the front of the train are left empty. Locals frequently travel on them because no fare is charged. They will be the first to be blown up should the train hit a mine field. Not only is it dangerous and illegal for foreigners to travel by train, but it is also very uncomfortable and unreliable.

Other transport inside Cambodia

Taxis and car hire

No taxis cruise the streets in Phnom Penh. Service taxis can be hired at Psar Chbam Pao, which is a taxi station very close to the Chbam Market. As long as you have a valid visa stamped with the Moc Bai border stamp, you can get into Vietnam by taking a taxi, costing US$20 from here.

Cars can be hired from most of the first class hotels for around US$50 a day with driver. Phnom Penh Tourism charges US$40 a day with driver.

Motorbikes

Many students and other people supplement their income by transporting tourists. It's a good cheap way of getting to the 'Killing Fields of Choueung Ek', to Oudong and Tonlé Bati. Expect to pay US$5-7 a day. You will also be required to pay for the fuel, which in February 1995 cost 680 riels/litre. Many people sell bottles of fuel on the roadside in Phnom Penh. Petrol Stations generally close around 15.30.

Cyclos

Everywhere you go in Phnom Penh you will be pestered by cyclo drivers. Very rarely will they accept payment in anything except dollars. When you have found one you can trust, stick with him. Towards the end of the day when a tourist group is about to pack up and head for its respective hotel, masses of them will often appear. You shouldn't pay them more than US$1 to go anywhere throughout the city. If you hire one for the whole morning, about US$3 would be a fair price to pay but remember most Cambodians don't earn more than US$5 in one month! These days hoards of them hang out around the Capitol Hotel. In the evenings you will find lots outside the No Problem Cafe, especially around closing time.

Bicycles

Riding bicycles in Phnom Penh can be extremely hazardous as motorised traffic has increased phenomenally over the past three or four years. They have absolutely no mercy on cyclists, especially foreign ones. Bicycle hire shops don't exist but if you insist on buying one, go to the bicycle shop on 182 Street, it's between 163 and 141 Street. If you purchase a Vietnamese bicycle, give it a good check over because they are very unreliable. Wherever you park it, there is a good chance that it will be stolen because of lack of bicycle parking lots. A heavy chain and lock will provide some protection.

Permits

Permits are required to visit Angkor and the Silver Pagoda in Phnom Penh.

Tour programmes

As in Laos, there is a growing number of agencies who can organise fairly comprehensive packages. This opens up certain areas of the country that are often impossible for the lone traveller.

A summary of what's currently available is given at Appendix Four.

COMMUNICATIONS

Currency
The currency is the riel. In September 1995, US$1=2,500 riel. Banks charge a commission fee of US$2/100. Most things in Cambodia can be paid for in dollars cash. Take plenty of small denomination dollars. Large hotels, such as the Cambodiana, have exchange facilities but only offer about US$1=1,900 riels.

Travellers cheques can be changed into riels at the Foreign Trade Bank of Cambodia, 24 Tousamuth Road. This opens from 07.30-15.30. They charge a 2% commission. Don't change too much because it can't be changed back. Credit cards are not accepted apart from as payment for accommodation at the Cambodiana Hotel.

Money can be cabled into Cambodia. In the United Kingdom contact: Moscow Narodny Bank Ltd, 24-32 King William Street, London. In the USA contact Banque Nationale de Paris, 499 Park Avenue, New York, NY 10022. The Commonwealth Bank of Australia will do this for you in Sydney.

Post
Letters posted to Cambodia can take up to six weeks to arrive. Postcards sent home can take well over a month because they are sent via Moscow. The flight service from Phnom Penh to Moscow is very irregular (sometimes only two flights a month).

Telephone
The international telephone service is expensive but efficient. Calls are routed via Moscow on a satellite link. Expect to pay US$20 for a three-minute call to the UK or USA.

Fax
You can fax information from the Cambodiana Hotel Business Centre to anywhere in the world.

Electricity
220 volts 50Hz (alternating current).

Many parts of the country are without electricity. Major hotels have their own generators. If you are staying in budget accommodation only expect the electricity to be on for a few hours every day.

Time
GMT + 7 hours.

Newspapers
The Bangkok Post is available in Phnom Penh. Any foreign magazines which are available in the larger hotels are very outdated.

Part Six
Regional Guide

Chapter Twenty

Phnom Penh

This sprawling city, with a population of 633,500, was founded in the 14th century by a lady named Penh. It was after her that one of the city's main landmarks, the sacred hill, or Phnom, was named. The city lies on the Mekong River close to where it joins the Tonlé Sap at a place called 'Four Arms' (Quatre Bras). Phnom Penh's 'golden age of tourism' was before 1970 – it was nothing for 100,000 visitors a year to land in this tourist paradise. Early brochures had advertised luscious parks teeming with exotic plants, a plethora of magnificent architecture including quaint French villas and a Shangri-La type atmosphere. Now this city of intrigue still welcomes them wholeheartedly but much of its flamboyant past has been lost for ever. Many of the buildings look drab, scarred by war and neglect; two-thirds of them were destroyed soon after the start of 'Year Zero'. Today its gentle people, torn apart by sorrow and turmoil, try to forget the carnage and face every day challenges and difficulties with considerable dignity as they strive for a better life. Many welcome tourists as if they were long-lost friends.

Many of its inhabitants still have nightmares about the return of the 'radical revolution' of the Red Khmer. There are very few inhabitants who didn't lose somebody between 1975 and 1979. Some have life stories which read like an extract from *Cambodge Anneé Zero*, written by a French priest and published in Paris in 1977. All are still desperately poor; many are lucky to have a job at all. Even the highest paid are unlikely to earn more than US$20 per month, the average is more like US$5-10. The cyclo-pouses which peddle around tourists in their tricycle-rickshaws probably do better than most. Since the collapse of the riel between 1991 and 1992 everyone wants to be paid in dollars. Street crime has worsened as more and more people find themselves unemployed. With the country's infrastructure in ruins, the city's beleaguered resources fail to attract many business ventures.

But since the signing of the Paris Peace Accord in 1991, the citizens have begun to fight back. Private enterprise, although on a small scale, is increasing. The tourist industry has begun to boom but savage inflation (currently running at around 200%) continues to be an obstacle which suffocates the economy.

If the number of vehicles seen on Phnom Penh's boulevards can be used as an economic indicator then things must be getting better. Roads are still filled with potholes and a whirlpool chaos is sometimes created by the lack of traffic lights. Services that we in the West take for granted are still crippled beyond belief. Electricity is a luxury and few properties have adequate water supplies. Alcoves are piled high with garbage and fetid smells from broken sewers percolate nostrils.

Accommodation in Phnom Penh

The city is experiencing a wave of building activity to cope with the large numbers of tourists expected to visit the country in the future. Accommodation is being updated, so the days when Phnom Penh was a haven for budget travellers will soon be numbered. Booking months in advance is strongly recommended. Over 20 million dollars have been spent on the Hotel Cambodiana and consequently prices have rocketed. During the 1988-9 period you could stay in the best hotels in the city for around US$25-30, now the price has more than doubled. Brand new hotels include the Paradise, Ambassador, Pacific, Orchides, Mittaphap and the Neakpoan.

Superior Class

Hotel Sofitel Cambodiana, 313 Karl Marx Avenue; tel: 2326139 (IDD), 26288 (local dialling); fax: 855 23 26390; telex: 583 1715426 C8DA-X.

Work began on this well situated riverside hotel in 1967. Construction has been repeatedly halted because of the political situation right up to 1987. A consortium of businessmen from Singapore and Hong Kong then invested massively in the project. The result in 1995 is the best superior class hotel in Phnom Penh.

This establishment has 184 deluxe rooms, 16 junior suites and 8 executive suites.

Complete with a well equipped, modern business centre, swimming pool, gymnasium, boutique, travel office, tennis courts, well appointed Lobby and Cyclo Bar, Art and Crafts shop together with facilities for holding banquets; it has attracted world-wide custom. Rooms have superb air-conditioning and international facilities such as IDD telephones, satellite TV, video, safe deposit boxes and mini-bars.

International cuisine is served in the Royal Pavilion, La Terrasse and the ultra luxurious Mekong Restaurant. The establishment also offers a limousine tour service, laundry and valet facilities.

Rooms should be booked well in advance. International bookings are taken by Orbitours Pty Ltd, Sydney; tel: 612 954 1399; fax: 612 954 1655; telex: AA127081. American clients can use Orbit's free phone on tel:800 235 5895 (direct from the USA.) and tel: 008 221 796 free phone is available to Australian clients. Germans can book through Saigon Tourist, Hamburg on tel: 4940 295345; fax: 4940 296705; telex: 213968 HT.D. UK clients should get in touch with Regent's Holidays on tel: 0117 921 1711; fax: 0117 925 4866. In Singapore it can be booked directly with any international credit card through Cambodian Investment; tel: 2980733; fax: 2987022. Phoenix Services Agency; tel: 7227378; fax: 852 3698884 handles bookings in Hong Kong. Two companies are presently offering the best deals on this hotel. They are Diethelm Travel Cambodia Ltd; tel: 855 23 26 648; fax: 855 23 26 676. They offer singles at US$168 and doubles at US$179.20 (until 31/10/96). Also competitive are Aroon Tour Co Ltd; tel/fax: 855 23 26300 or 855 23 64397. Until January 1997 they are holding their prices to US$181 for a single and US$194 for a double. Apsara

Tours, a member of The American Society of Travel Agents, are charging US$198 for a single and US$234 for a double (they can be contacted on tel: 855 23 26 705/914 199) up to the end of 1996.
Price per room: single – US$170-195; double – US$200-220.

Phnom Penh Floating Hotel, moored on Karl Marx Quay; tel: 23-25231, 23-26585.
This hotel has the usual international facilities associated with accommodation in this price bracket. Every room has satellite TV, mini-bar and ultra efficient air conditioning. The two restaurants serving European and Asian dishes are very expensive. The pool bar serves more reasonable snacks. The Thai company which runs this establishment has spared no expense providing ultra luxury furnishings throughout. Businessmen on long stays can book discount rates with Cathay Pacific Holidays; tel: Bangkok 23361059, Hong Kong 7471888, Ho Chi Minh 223203, Paris 40689899, Sydney 131747 and Tokyo 033504 1531. Saigon Tourist in Ho Chi Minh take international bookings on tel: 84 8 295534/296000/225887.
Price per room: single – US$190; double – US$225; business suite – US$250.

Royal Phnom Penh Hotel, Lenin Boulevard; tel/fax: 855 18 810221.
Another newly opened ultra luxurious establishment aimed at businessmen. Small (40 twin deluxe rooms) by comparison with the Cambodiana, this Thai hotel was finished in 1994 and offers friendly service, rooms with IDD telephones, minibar, satellite television, and inhouse movies/BBC/CNN. Expect to pay US$10+ for a meal in the well run Bassac restaurant which serves excellent Chinese, Cambodian and Thai cuisine. They also have a small nightclub. Clients staying here can take advantage of the limousine tour service (US$60/day). Discount prices are available through Diethelm Travel, Bangkok; tel: 255 9150/60/70; fax: 256 0248/9 or Phnom Penh; tel: 26648; fax: 26676. Until 31/10/96 they are charging US$134.40 for singles and doubles.
   International tour operators have reported that the service in this hotel is better than in the Cambodiana.
Price per room: approx US$150 (some US$120-135).

Olympic Hotel & Tower, 158-166 Preah Sihanouk Boulevard, Phnom Penh; tel: 855 18 811579.
This will probably be opened by late 1995. Situated next to the Olympic Stadium, ten minutes from Pochentong airport, this is the country's first mixed development featuring hotel and service apartments, shops and office space. All 200 hotel rooms have facilities equal to the Sofitel Cambodiana. 40 service apartments are available (enquire with Olympic Development Pte Ltd, 10 Anson Road, 24-03A, International Plaza, Singapore 0207; tel: 65 225 3962; fax: 65 222 9987). The hotel features IDD telephones for business clients, an ultra-modern fully equipped business centre, fitness centre, swimming pool and sauna. The adjacent tower has 10 office floors, a night club and two shopping floors. A 24-hour security system is in operation. Prices for hotel rooms have still to be announced but will be in the same expensive bracket as the Sofitel Cambodiana. Rooms can be booked through the Singapore number given above or direct using international credit cards.

First class hotels
Ambassador Hotel, Corner USSR, Keo Mony Street; tel: 26029.
This new well appointed establishment has a restaurant, bar, swimming pool and air-conditioned rooms.
Price per room: single – US$90; double – US$120.

Diamond Hotel, 172-184 Monivong Boulevard; tel: 23 26635/23 27221; fax: 26636/7.
This classy establishment has seven single rooms, 55 twin rooms and 13 deluxe rooms. It is ideal for businessmen looking for friendly, reasonably priced accommodation. It is equipped with a modern business centre, IDD telephones, a money exchange facility, satellite TVs in all rooms and an in-house video system. Its coffee shop has a homely atmosphere. It also has a hi-tech shop, laundry and valet service. Rooms are all air-conditioned. Until 31/12/96 Diethelm Travel will be offering them for US$70 singles and US$94 doubles. Until 31/10/96 Aroon Tours' price for the same period is US$75 singles and US$96 doubles. Apsara Tours' price is US$130 for a double and US$120 for a single.
Price per room: single – US$90; double – US$120.

Holiday International Hotel, 84 Street, Monivong; tel: 23 25085.
This is a fairly small luxury hotel with 10 single and 31 twin rooms, all air-conditioned. It was opened recently to compete for business clientele. It has a modern, well equipped business centre, IDD telephones, money exchange facility and laundry and valet service. Reasonably priced meals (US$6-lunch, US$7 dinner) are served in the cosy Palms Cafe. Coffee and drinks can be ordered in the Orchid Lounge. Diethelm's price until 31/10/96 is US$67.20 for all rooms, Aroon Tours is charging US$70 for all rooms over the same period.
Price per room: single – US$75; double – US$100.

Wat Phnom Hotel, opposite Wat Phnom Pagoda near the intersection of 51 and 96 Street; tel: 23 26065.
This newly opened hotel has similar facilities to the Diamond. It can be booked directly through International Travel and Tours; tel: 23 27248 and Preferred Indochina Travel; tel: 23 25350; fax: 23 26625.
Price per room: single – US$80; double – US$110.

Cambodiana Inn, 313 Karl Marx Quay; tel: 25059.
This very pleasant bungalow accommodation has been largely refurbished during the 1991-3 period. Like the Cambodiana adjacent to it, there is a wonderful view out over the confluence of the Mekong, Tonlé Sap and Bassac Rivers. All rooms here are now air-conditioned and there is a pleasant bar and restaurant.
Price per room: single – US$50; double – US$70-90.

Phnom Penh Novotel
This large establishment will be open in 1996. It is very central on Achar Mean Boulevard.

Le Royal Hotel, No 1 Daun Penh District; tel: 23051/24151.
This hotel has been considerably up-rated and consequently prices have increased. Journalists staying in Phnom Penh may remember it as the Hotel Samaki. It is owned by the Ministry of Commerce, which plans further renovations. It featured in the film, *The Killing Fields.* Every room is air-conditioned and has its own refrigerator. It has a very popular nightly discotheque. The hotel, although put into the first class category, is slightly down market.
Price per room: single – US$35; double – US$45; bungalow – US$70.

Monorom, 89 Achar Mean Boulevard; tel: 26149 (international dialling), 24951/24549 (local dialling).
This hotel can be booked directly through Phnom Penh Tourism; tel: 25349/24059; fax: 855 23 26043.
Many tourist groups use this well established hotel. It is heavily booked because it is also popular with journalists and aid workers. The restaurant on the sixth floor has a marvellous look-out terrace where you can view the city. A dance is generally held here on the weekends.
Price per room: single – US$35; double – US$45-60.

Hotel Pacific, directly opposite the Pailin Hotel; tel: 23547.
This new establishment has elegant traditional Khmer architecture. Accommodation is all on the ground floor but security is said to be no problem. Rooms are all air-conditioned. There is a nightclub situated on the first floor which is open nightly (8-11pm). Overspills from this hotel end up in The Paris Hotel across the road which is much cheaper but has poorer facilities.
Price per room: single – US$45; double – US$60.

Hotel Orchidee, 262 Achar Mean Boulevard; tel: 22659.
The Orchidee was opened in December 1991. Featuring classy accommodation with air-conditioning and TVs, this is regularly used by Phnom Penh Tourism for tourist groups. It is one of the most modern hotels in the city.
Price per room: single – US$55; double – US$75.

La Paillote Hotel, 234 Street; tel: 22151; fax: 26513.
Fast becoming very popular with tourists seeking a medium priced, good value establishment. Quite a few Thai businessmen stay here. Facilities include satellite TV, mini-bar and IDD telephones in every room. The restaurant features mainly French cuisine. It is well situated for sightseeing near the Central Market. Bookable on their number, tel: 26739 or direct with the hotel. Reservations are recommended.
Price per room: single – US$50; double – US$65; de luxe double – US$100.

Allson Star Hotel, PO Box 533, corner of Monivong Boulevard and Kampuchea Krom Boulevard; tel: 23 62008; fax: 855 23 62018.
This new establishment has 17 standard rooms, 40 superior rooms and 10 executive rooms. Services include fax, postal, taxi/limousine, laundry and valet. It has a small coffee shop. All rooms are air-conditioned.
Diethelm Travel offers them for US$67.20 (until 31/10/96).

Aroon Tour Co Ltd offer single standard rooms at US$72, twins at US$84. For superior rooms their price is US$90 for a single and US$102 for a double. The 10 executive rooms which would suit businessmen sell for US$104 (singles) and US$116 (doubles). These prices are valid until the end of 1996. Apsara Tours' price is US$130 double, US$120 single.

Reservations can now also be made in Singapore tel: 65 336 2526, fax: 65 334 0631; Hong Kong tel: 852 375 0130, fax: 852 375 0167; Kuala Lumpur tel: 60 3 201 0019, fax: 60 3 201 0018; Bangkok tel: 66 2 651 8010-15, fax: 66 2 255 7903; Frankfurt tel: 49 69 285566, fax: 49 69 283661; Milan tel: 39 2 33105838; fax: 39 2 33105827 and on toll free number Malaysia tel: 800 3789. *Price per room: US$70.*

1. FINE ARTS SCHOOL
2. BANGKOK AIRWAYS Office
3. KONG KEA Restaurant
4. HOLIDAY INTERNATIONAL Hotel
5. CALMETTE Restaurant
6. WAT PHNOM
7. TONLÉ SAP 2 Restaurant
8. FERRY : Ministry of Transport
9. TONLÉ SAP 1 Restaurant
10. FERRY : Psar Cha (Municipal)
11. MONOROM Hotel
12. ASIA Hotel
13. SANTE PHEAP Restaurant
14. CHAMPA Restaurant
15. SOBHAMONGKOL Restaurant
16. MILITARY Museum
17. WAT OUNALOM
18. NO PROBLEM Cafe
19. PHNOM PENH TOURISM
20. KAMPUCHEA AIRLINES
21. NATIONAL MUSEUM of ART
22. RENAKSE Hotel
23. ROYAL PALACE
24. SILVER PAGODA
25. DEJA VU Restaurant
26. CONFERENCE Hall
27. CAMBODIANA Inn
28. CAMBODIANA Hotel
29. AUSTRALIAN Embassy
30. CZECH Embassy
31. VICTORY Monument
32. CIRCUS Training School
33. NEW ART Gallery
34. BUDDHA Factory
35. BASSAC Theatre
36. RUSSIAN Embassy

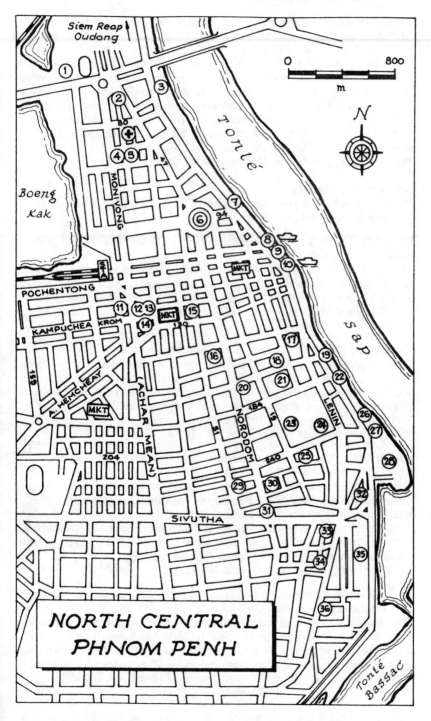

NORTH CENTRAL PHNOM PENH

Juliana Hotel, 16 Juliana, 152 Street, Sangkat Veal Weng, Khand 7 Makara; tel: 855 23 66070; fax: 855 23 66072.
This establishment was opened in 1994. It is aimed at businessmen. It has 43 single rooms and eight twins, all air-conditioned. Facilities include business centre, conference room, hairdresser, fitness centre, sauna, Thai massage, money exchange, office rental, air bus service, laundry and valet service. International cuisine is served in the Vanda Restaurant where lunch costs around US$7 and dinner around US$10. Coffee and drinks can be ordered in the Juliana Lounge.
　　The hotel can be booked directly through Khemara Travel; tel/fax: 23 27434, who charge from US$65 for singles and doubles.
Price per room: single – US$120; double – US$140.

Second class hotels
These are much better value since most have been refurbished but the prices, as yet, have not rocketed.

Hawaii Hotel, 18 St 130, Quarter Phsar Thmey Market, Khand Daun Penh; tel/fax: 855 23 26652.
This newly opened establishment has 28 single rooms, 35 twins and five suites, all air-conditioned. Facilities include fax and postal service, laundry and car rental. There is a small coffee shop. Diethelm Travel are selling rooms for US$33.50 until 31/12/96. It costs US$8 for lunch and US$11 for dinner.
Price per room: US$40.

La Paillote, 234 St 130-53, in front of Phsar Thmey Market.
This newly opened hotel has 24 rooms which are air-conditioned. It has fax and IDD facilities and a laundry service. You can eat in La Paillote Restaurant, which is on the expensive side at US$13.50 for lunch and US$16.80 for dinner.
　　East West Travel, Phnom Penh are selling them for US$23 (single) and US$34 (double). Tel: 855 23 26189 for reservations.
Price per room: single – US$25; double – US$37.

Regent Hotel, 7 St 109, Group 41, Boeung Rang, Khand Daun Penh; tel: 855 23 27649; fax: 855 23 27649.
This is another new hotel which has 17 single and 18 twin air-conditioned rooms. Facilities include fax and postal service, laundry and car hire. There is a small coffee shop where meals are not available.
　　Diethelm Travel sell rooms here for US$42.60 (single) and US$48 (double). If you are taking one of their tours, Angkor Voyages, tel: 855 23 27268, will let out rooms here at only US$35 as part of the tour package.
Price per room: single – US$45; double – US$53.

Renakse Hotel, opposite the Royal Palace; tel: 2326036 (international dialling), 22457 (local dialling); fax: 2326036.
This colonial style establishment is becoming a firm favourite with aid workers and journalists. Although the building is fairly old it has been extensively renovated. It first opened as a hotel in September 1991. It has a bar, small restaurant and travel service counter. Rooms are all air-conditioned and can be booked through Naga Tours Company (situated in hotel), tel: 26288.
Price per room: single – US$25; double – US$35.

Pailin Hotel, 219 BC Monivong Boulevard; tel: 855 23 26697/8;
fax: 855 23 26376
This is very close to the International Restaurant. Journalists who haven't been
to Phnom Penh recently will remember it as the White Hotel. Rooms have been
extensively renovated in 1992 and are all air-conditioned. In the medium price
bracket this is the most popular in the city. Staff are very friendly. The bar serves
the cheapest drinks in Phnom Penh.
Price per room: single – US$30; double – US$50-65.

Dosit Pitou Hotel, 103 A 108 Street; tel: 26386.
Recently renovated and recommended by Phnom Penh Tourism. This can be
booked directly by fax: 855 23 26043. Rooms are air-conditioned and well
appointed.
Price per room: single – US$25; double – US$35-50.

Royal Hotel, 92 Street junction with Achar Mean Boulevard; tel: 24151/23051.
During Cambodia's 'golden age of tourism', this colonial style establishment,
built around 1911 was called the Hotel le Phnom. It is still popular with war
journalists who once stayed here, although it has altered appreciably due to
refurbishments. It is recommended that you book well in advance, particularly if
you require one of the few bungalows available. Reservations can be made
through Transair, tel: 26298 and through Phnom Penh Tourism, tel: 25349/23949.
The bar here is very reasonably priced and generally full of aid workers and
journalists.
Price per room: single – US$35; double – US$50.

Champs-Elysees, 185 63 Street; tel: 27268.
Popular with French tourists, this hotel has very friendly staff. It is slightly
cheaper than the Royal Hotel.
*Price per room: single – US$25; double – US$30; studio single – US$36;
studio double – US$42.*

Mittaphap Hotel, 262 Achar Mean Boulevard; tel: 22778.
In the same price range as the Champs-Elysees, this rather down-market looking
place is rather better than its exterior suggests. A few travellers have said that
the restaurant here is cheap but serves very mediocre food.

Hotel Sukhalay, intersection of 126 Street and Achar Mean Street.
Prices here depend on what floor you want to stay on – cheaper on higher floors
(a better rate can be negotiated with bargaining). The hotel is rather run down.
There is a restaurant on the ground floor. Renovations have started so expect to
pay more when they are complete.
Price per room: US$15-20.

China Nanjin Hotel, Corner Street, Kampuchea Krom/Khan 7 makara;
tel: 855 233 27101.
This newly opened establishment has nine large air-conditioned double rooms
and 28 singles. The manager, Chhin Ky, is very accommodating.
Price per room: single – US$25; double – US$30.

China Town Hotel and Restaurant, 49 Street, 214 Boeung Rang, Daun Penh; tel: 855 23 27821.
Clean and comfortable with friendly staff. The manager, Mr Tong Seng, speaks some English and will arrange conducted tours of the city.
Price per room: single – US$30; double – US$35.

Green Hotel, 145 Street, Preah Norodom Boeung Keng Kong, Chomneas; tel: 855 23 26055.
Newly opened in the vicinity of the Victoria Monument, this comfortable small hotel has 23 single rooms and 10 doubles, all with air-conditioning. Because of its family atmosphere this establishment is ideal for people looking for friendly and hospitable accommodation. Mr Sim Lang Hor, the manager, is a real knowledge-box on Cambodia.
Price per room: single – US$40; double – US$60.

Le President Hotel and Restaurant, 68 East Street 125, Phsar Depo 11 Toul Kok; tel: 855 23 27055.
Managed by Mr Leheng, this new hotel has similar facilities to La Paillote. Although fairly large by Phnom Penh standards, it retains a friendly atmosphere. There are 44 singles available and all 64 doubles are extremely spacious.
Price per room: single – US$20; double – US$30.

Lido Hotel and Restaurant, 96 Street/217 Orussey IV, 7 Makara; tel: 855 23 27419.
Newly opened, this establishment has 48 rooms available with air-conditioning.
Price per room: US$25.

Lucky Inn Hotel and Restaurant, 11 Street/254 Chak Tomok, Saun Penh; tel: 855 23 27044.
This cosy, small establishment has seven single rooms and 13 doubles available.
Price per room: single – US$20; double – US$25-30.

Oriental Garden Hotel, 23 Street/80, Daun Penh; tel: 855 23 24245.
Managed by Mr Van Michel, this new establishment has 27 single rooms and 25 doubles available. It can be reserved by faxing Intra Travel on 855 23 27153.
Price per room: single – US$25; double – US$30.

Phnom Penh Garden Hotel, 66 Boeung Keng Kong, Khan Cham Carmon; tel: 855 23 27264.
Extremely fairly priced singles are attracting many customers. There are 16 available. There are six doubles which are very large and would suit families. Early booking is recommended through Hanuman Tours, tel/fax: 855 23 26194.
Price per room: single – US$20; double – US$45.

Rama Inn East, 17 Street/9, Sang Kat Tonle Basac; tel: 855 23 27048.
Newly opened classy establishment.
Price per room: single – US$35; double – US$42.

Rama Inn West, 8-10 Samdeach Luvir Em Road, Beung Keng Kang; tel: 855 23 25667.
Similar to the above this new establishment is owned by the same company.
Price per room: single – US$35; double – US$42.

Hotel Sakal 1, junction of 240 and 51 Street; tel: 25744.
This small friendly establishment opened in 1995. The air-conditioning is very primitive and water supply irregular. The area in which the hotel is situated, Khand Don Penh, looks fairly seedy but is said to be safe. Once it was one of the most attractive suburban areas of the city, situated just over 1km from the river. Ask a cyclo driver to take you there since it is difficult to find because it is partly obscured by a blackened wall.
Price per room: single – US$30; double – US$38.

Hotel Sakal 2, 51 Street; tel: 22404.
About half the size of the Sakal 1, this hotel is close by but has a much better outlook. Air-conditioning is standard, baths are antiquated and water supply irregular. You will be lucky to get any hot water but with the average temperatures in Phnom Penh, this will hardly be a problem for hardened travellers. Your room rate will depend on how hard you are prepared to bargain.
Price per room: US$20-30.

Asia Hotel, 136 Achar Mean Boulevard; tel: 22751.
This has standard and superior rooms which have been modernised after a complete refit. Aroon Tour Co Ltd are selling standard rooms at US$27 (single), US$42 twin and superior rooms at US$48 twin. Apsara Tours price is US$46 double, US$33 single.
Price per room: single – US$30; double – US$45; superior double – US$50.

Recommended highly
Hotel Paradise, intersection of Achar Hemcheay Boulevard and Achar Mean Boulevard.
Opened in 1993 this establishment is far too classy to be put into the Phnom Penh Tourist second class category. Rooms, which are all air-conditioned, cost US$40 for a single and US$55 for a double. Currently it is used as an overspill to accommodate visitors who have booked first class accommodation. By 1997 this will probably be charged at a higher rate.
Aroon Tour Co Ltd are offering singles for US$33 and doubles for US$44 until the end of 1996.
Apsara Tours price is US$46 double, US$33 single.

Third class hotels
Santepheap Hotel, Achar Mean Boulevard intersection with 136 Street; tel: 23227.
This is very basic accommodation. They have a cheap restaurant.
Price per room: US$15.

Blue Hotel, directly opposite above.
Similar.

ι, 10-12 Street 144, Sk Veal Vong, Kh Makara; tel: 855 23 27422.
, ιriendly establishment, owned by Mr You Sang, has five doubles
ـ،ie.
ιιce per room: US$15.

Bopha Tep Hotel and Restaurant, 463 Street 1; tel: 855 23 27480.
Newly opened, this fairly basic establishment has 22 singles and 22 doubles
available.
Price per room: single – US$15; double – US$20.

Borey Thmei Hotel and Restaurant, Street 127, Veal Vong, 7 Makara; tel: 855
23 27476.
Friendly and clean, this new hotel, owned by Mr Kong Chun, has 15 singles and
30 doubles available.
Price per room: single – US$10; double – US$20.

Chathay Hotel, 123 Street, 110 Wat Phon; tel: 855 23 27188.
Newly opened and run by friendly manager Mr Chhun Sokheng, this place has
23 doubles and several singles available.
Price per room: single – US$16; double – US$20.

Dusit Hotel and Restaurant, 2 Street, 120 Phsar Thmei; tel: 855 23 22188.
Another new one which has 10 singles and 16 doubles, all with fans.
Price per room: single – US$10; double – US$20.

Gold Hotel, 12 Street, 282 Boeung Keng, Kang Chamcar Mon;
tel: 855 23 27558.
Good budget accommodation. A new hotel with charm and friendly service. It
has four singles and 31 doubles available. Mr Meas Sary, the owner, will help
tourists who need student interpreters to show them around.
Price per room: single – US$20; double – US$25.

Golden Gate Hotel, 6AB Street, 278 Boeung Keng Kang 1, Chamcarmon;
tel: 855 23 27618.
20 rooms are available in this new establishment.
Price per room: US$15.

Hong Kong Hotel and Restaurant, 419 Street, Monivong Boulevard,
Boeung Pralit, 7 Makara; tel: 855 23 27108.
Clean and comfortable but a little out of the way, this hotel has 10 singles with
fans and 27 similar doubles.
Price per room: single – US$15; double – US$20.

Indochina Hotel, 251 Street, 1 Phsar, Phasar Kandal, 1 Daun Penh;
tel: 855 23 27492.
Newly opened, this hotel has seven singles and three doubles.
Price per room: single – US$10; double – US$12.

Phkar Chhouk Hotel, 258 Monivong Boulevard; tel: 2 6696.
Situated close to the Capitol II Guesthouse, this newly renovated property is owned by an enterprising Cambodian family. Rooms are very clean and aimed at the budget traveller who doesn't want to pay more than US$20. Air-conditioning is adequate and all rooms have bathrooms attached. It represents very good value and if you can afford it it is far superior and has much better security than the Capitol Guesthouses.
Price per room: no more than US$20.

Phkar Chhouk Tep Hotel, Intersection of 336 Street and Montreth Boulevard; tel: 2 7446.
Good budget establishment. Air-conditioned rooms.
Price per room: US$20.

Beauty Inn, 215 Monivong Boulevard; tel: 855 23 64505.
If the above are full, this establishment which is just down the road, offers similar facilities at a budget price.
Price per room: US$17-28.

Amara Hotel, just off Preah Sihanouk Boulevard near the Lucky Market which is at 160A.
Owned by a very friendly Cambodian family, this small newly decorated establishment will suit travellers looking for a homely atmosphere. Rooms are air-conditioned and most have adjoining washing facilities. Recommended.
Price per room: US$20.

International House Hotel, 35 Street, 178 Phsar Thmei, 111 Daun Penh; tel/fax: 855 23 26246.
Small and friendly, this new place run by Mr May Narat has five singles with fans available and five similar doubles
Price per room: single – US$10; double – US$15.

JB Hotel, 5 Street, 242 Chak Tomouk, Daun Penh; tel: 855 23 26630.
This accommodation is good value with 13 singles and two doubles available. Mr Robert King, who owns it, will escort foreigners around the city, arrange bicycle and car hire.
Price per room: single – US$10; double – US$15.

Kim Sea Kim Kok Hotel, 79R, 63 Beunt Ring, Daun Penh; tel: 855 23 62471.
Newly opened and run by Mr Bon Song, this hotel is clean and has good amenities for the price. There are four singles and several doubles, which are much larger.
Price per room: single – US$15; double – US$17.

Kimhoa Hotel and Restaurant, 379 Street/Sisowat Boulevard; tel: 855 23 25816.
Named after its owner, Mr Kimhoa, this small new establishment is friendly and clean. It has four singles and 13 doubles.
Price per room: single – US$10; double – US$15.

22E Street, 217 Phsar Thmei, 11 Daun Penh; tel: 855 23 25778.
establishment has three singles and nine doubles.
room: single – US$10; double – US$15.

Makara Hotel, 33 Chak Tomok, Duan Penh; tel: 855 23 25540.
All rooms have hot and cold running water (when available). 48 rooms.
Price per room: US$20.

Monaco Hotel, 137 Street, 162 Phsar Depo 11, Toul Kork; tel: 855 23 26629.
Opened in February 1995 and owned by Mr Yan Buntha, this has 49 singles available, all with fans. There are five spacious doubles.
Price per room: single – US$13; double – US$15.

Morakat Hotel, 33 Street, 107 Sk Monorom, Kh7 Makara; tel: 017 201 424.
Very inconveniently situated, a long way out, this establishment has 20 rooms available. Contact Mr Chea Rithy.
Price per room: US$20.

Neak Poan Hotel, 331 Monivong Boulevard, 7 Makara; tel: 855 23 27361.
This fairly small new building has five singles and 17 doubles available.
Price per room: single – US$10; double – US$15.

New World Hotel, 88 Street, 214 Boeung Pralit, 7 Makara; tel: 855 23 81277.
15 double rooms are available.
Price per room: double – US$15.

Oriental Hotel, Street Salde Gold Orussey 1, 7 Makara; tel: 855 23 64988.
Run by a very friendly manager, Mr Kung Triv, it has four singles and 47 doubles. Good value, second class amenities.
Price per room: single – US$15; double – US$20.

Pacific Hotel, 234 Street, Monivong; tel: 018 810 064.
Rather out of the way in a quiet part of the city, this new place, owned by Mr Steven Lay, has two singles and 14 doubles.
Price per room: single – US$10; double – US$15.

Penchet Hotel, 87 Street, 136 Sang Kat Phsar Kandal 1; tel: 855 23 24448.
Run by a friendly Cambodian family, this hotel accepts payment in riels. Amenities are fairly basic.
Price per room: single – 12,000 riels; double – 15,000 riels.

Pich Nil Hotel, 27 Street, 184 Sang Kat Phsar, Thmei 111;
tel: 017 200 380/017 200 489.
A long way from central Phnom Penh, this newly opened establishment, owned by Mr Sath Boon Hua, has 10 singles and 22 doubles available.
Price per room: single – US$10; double – US$15.

Ponleur Pich Hotel, 160 Street, Mao Se Tong Boulevard; tel: 855 23 26027.
Very good value. 16 rooms are available. It can be booked direct by contacting the manager, Mr Heng Sok.
Price per room: US$20.

Heng Heng Hotel, 110A, Okhna In Road (136), Phsar Kandal 11; tel: 017200972. Recently opened in the outer suburbs of the city, this well appointed establishment would suit those wanting to escape the city madness. Mr Song Sam Raing, who owns it, is extremely friendly. You can count on VIP treatment because of its small size. Five singles are available and five doubles.
Price per room: single – US$10; double – US$12.

Ripole Hotel, Street 126-118, Sangkat Phsar Thmei 11, Daun Penh; tel: 855 23 22713.
Seven singles and 20 doubles are available. Basic but clean.
Price per room: US$15.

Sakur Hotel, 30 242 Road, Sangkat Chark Tomuk, Daun Penh; tel: 855 23 27362.
Small and comfortable, this newly opened small establishment has four singles and six doubles.
Price per room: single – US$10; double – US$15.

Singapore Hotel, 62E, Monivong Boulevard, Phsar Thmei, Daun Penh; tel: 855 23 25552.
Run by Mr Ngor, this smallish establishment has 10 singles and 15 doubles available.
Price per room: single – US$10; double – US$15.

Sonex Hotel, 29 Street, 310 Boeung Keng Kong; tel: 855 23 23148.
All rooms in this newly opened hotel are large and have fans. 36 are available. It is named after the owner, Mr Sonex, who will accept letter bookings.
Price per room: US$15.

South East Hotel, Street Trorsark Pheam Chamkamon; tel: 844 23 62443.
Run by Mr Lim Koung, this hotel has 10 singles and five doubles available.
Price per room: single – US$10; double – US$15.

Sovan Borei Thmei Hotel, 25 Street 211, Sk Veal Vong Kh 7 Makara; tel: 855 23 27830.
All its 36 rooms are designated doubles.
Price per room: double – US$15.

Sydney International, 37 Street, 360 Beung Keng Kang 1, Charmcar Mon; tel: 855 23 27907.
Newly opened and owned by Mr So Song, who will accept letter bookings. All 27 rooms are large and have air-conditioning.
Price per room: US$15-20.

Tai Seng Hotel, 56 Monivong Boulevard; tel: 855 23 27220.
Run by Mr Ly Hong Sinh, this establishment is good value. Most rooms (45) have air-conditioning, but there are four with fans only which are cheaper.
Price per room: with fan – US$15; with air-conditioning – US$20.

TS Hotel, Corner of Kampuchea Krom & Moa Setung Phsar, Depo 11, Toul Kok; tel: 855 23 66468.
This has 12 small rooms. All have air-conditioning. Some have TVs.
Price per room: single – US$10-15.

Wat Phnom Hotel, Oknha Santhomuk, Sk Wat Phnom, Daun Penh; tel: 855 23 25320.
Newly opened and run by Mr Nheim So Pall, it has nine single rooms and 40 doubles, all air-conditioned.
Price per room: single – US$15; double – US$20.

Yang Chouv Hotel, 28R, Street 252, Sk Charkto Muk, Kh Daun Penh; tel: 855 23 27423.
This small hotel, owned by Mr Khau Ngorn, opened in April 1995. It has three singles and 16 doubles, all air-conditioned. Clean and modern, this establishment is bound to become very popular with budget travellers.
Price per room: single – US$15; double – US$20.

Shoe string category
Every backpacker heads for the **Capitol Hotel,** which is a real hovel situated on the corner of 107 Street and 182 Street. The staff here are very friendly and some English is spoken. The notice board, which is upstairs, is a good place to get constantly updated information about things like street theft and police extortion, which are both rife in Cambodia. It's a good place to make friends to accompany you on trips. Splitting the cost of vehicle hire makes good sense and there is always more safety in numbers. You may meet some Cambodian students here eager to improve their English. Take them along with you, police are far less likely to try to extort money out of foreigners travelling with Cambodians.
   If you have any major hassle while staying in Phnom Penh, don't forget to pin up a note before you leave so that others can at least learn from your misfortunes.
Price per room: US$10 (some available at US$5).

Capitol Hotel 2. This opened in 1994 around the corner from Capitol Hotel 1, it's on 111 Street.
Price per room: US$4.

Happy Guest House, 107 Street. This is another similar sort of place down 107 Street.

Pasteur Hotel situated in a narrow road off Achar Mean Boulevard. Run by a Cambodian family, it is very friendly.

Number 20 and 22, 111 Street and another called **Inn House.** These recently opened private guesthouses are run by kind families and charge no more than US$5 for a room.

City Lotus Guest House, 59 53 Street which is close to the Central Market. They also have a good Indian Restaurant.
Price per room: single – US$4; air-conditioned single US$5; double – US$6; air-conditioned double US$7.

Timorda Inn, 128 Street.
No air-conditioning but family run.

Amara Hotel, 176 Street, 63 Boeung Keng Kang 1; tel: 855 23 27240.
Run by Mr Ted Ngon, this basic, clean establishment offers good value. It has four singles and 10 doubles.
Price per room: single – US$8; double – US$10.

Angkor International Hotel, Street 148, Phsar Kandal 1, Daun Penh; tel: 855 23 26675.
Don't confuse this with the Angkor Hotel owned by Mr You Sang which is listed in the third class category. This is a newly opened backpacker establishment with 20 singles and 16 doubles.
Price per room: single – US$9; double – US$11.

Khemara Guest House, 199E 1 Street, Sok Hok, Orussey 7 Makara; tel: 855 23 64214.
One of the cheapest in the city and owned by Mr Ly Sareth, this place is ideal for someone wanting to spend as little as possible for good accommodation. It has 16 singles and seven doubles, all with basic amenities.
Price per room: single – US$3; double – US$4.

Kim Heng Hotel, 681 Street, Kampuchea Boulevard, VN, Toul Kork; tel: 855 23 27960.
This hotel has 13 singles, all with very basic amenities and no air-conditioning. Two doubles with fans are also available.
Price per room: single – US$5; double – US$6.

Phnom Pich Guest House, 100 Street, 315 Boeung Kok 11, Toul Kork; tel: 855 23 62016.
Owned by Mr Sok Visa, this cheapie is good value. It has 12 singles and three doubles.
Price per room: single – US$4; double – US$5.

Phnom Penh Thmei Hotel, 88 Corner Street 350, Toul Svay Preyu; tel: 855 23 26219.
Owned by friendly Mr Chhorn Seang, this reasonably priced hotel has 16 rooms with fan.
Price per room: US$10.

Preap Sar Hotel, 77 Street, 240 Sang Kat Chak Tomok, Daun Penh; tel: 855 23 27218.
This hotel has three singles and 14 doubles, all with air-conditioning.
Price per room: US$10.

Vimean Khmer, 538 Street, Kampuchea Krom, Sk Phsar Depo 11;
tel: 855 23 27375.
Seven singles and 10 doubles are available. All have fans and very basic
amenities.
Price per room: single – US$5; double – US$10.

Backpacker establishments opened in 1995

To cater for the increasing tourist boom, several new family-run guesthouses
have opened recently. These are government approved and, although very basic,
they are extremely friendly, clean and incredibly cheap. Expect to pay no more
than US$3. Owners of these establishments will put you in touch with places
you can hire bicycles and motorbikes at a fraction of what you would normally
pay. The **Seng Sokhom Guest House** on 111 Street is nearly always full since
the owner treats foreign travellers as if they were his adopted sons and
daughters. He has recently gone into the bicycle and motorbike hiring trade and
will undercut prices charged by the Capitol Hotel.

If he's full, ask a cyclo to take you to **Sok Sin's** which is down an alleyway
near the Holiday International Hotel on 84 Street. Look out for Monivong
Boulevard near an old colonial style building which used to be the French
Embassy. The owner takes backpackers on escorted tours and has many contacts
all over the city. If you fancy a trip outside Phnom Penh and you are a little
nervous about where to go, ask him to accompany you.

Also opened recently is the **Vimeansvor Hotel,** 217 Street, which is fairly
easy to find because it's near the sports stadium. With hard bargaining, expect
to pay no more than US$5.

The newly built **Mekong Thmey,** opposite the old market offers some rooms
at backpacker prices during the low season. This is a good deal since they
normally charge US$25+.

The management of the **Sukhalay Hotel,** near the more expensive **Hotel
Asia** on 136 Street, have been known to drop their prices for backpackers rather
than lose trade. Their top price for backpackers is around US$20 and their
bottom price around US$5-7. (Expect to be put on the 7th floor for this price).
Recommended.

It's also worth trying the **Vimean Ekameach Hotel,** 188 51 Street, whose top
price is around US$15. Run by a pleasant Cambodian family it is clean, secure
and very friendly. Although situated a little out of the way in Khand,
Chamcarmon, it is very good value, has air-conditioning and is my choice in
Phnom Penh.

Eating

Food in Phnom Penh is fairly cheap if you are prepared to eat at the numerous
foodstalls scattered around the city. They generally have a very quick turnover
so you can be certain that the ingredients are fresh. At all times it is best to be
on the safe side and ask for your meal to be well cooked. Stir-fried ingredients
are ideal, killing organisms likely to cause debilitating diarrhoea and hepatitis.
Always refuse *thnot* (sugar cane juice) with your meal because unpurified water
is often used to top it up.

Because it contains very little fat, Cambodian food, like Vietnamese, is
generally very healthy. The emphasis is on rice rather than meat or eggs. Dried,

salty fish is readily available, as is fresh. Both are served with *prahoc*, a delicious fish sauce. A spicy variety called *tuk trey* made with ground peanuts should be ordered if you like your food hot. Those with a taste for Indian food will certainly like the Cambodian culinary 'tour de force', *an sam chruk*, made from soyabeans and pork which has been marinated in a hot sauce made from ginger, pepper and chilli. It is usually served wrapped up in sticky rice on a palm leaf. If you have a taste for the exotic, why not try *pong tea kon* (a duck egg with an embryo inside) or cicadas roasted on charcoal. If you order the latter, (*chong roet*) try them with *kepi* (a paste made from crab meat), add a dash of lime juice. Many of the kiosks seen around the six main markets in the city specialise in *khao phonne*, a very inexpensive dish made from noodles.

Whatever your choice, expect to pay no more than US$1 (3,350 riels) at these stalls. They can be found around the railway station, scattered around the Central Market's western side (junction of Achar Hemcheay Boulevard and 118 Street), all over the Tuol Tom Pong Market (junction of 163 and 450 Streets), the O Russei Market on 182 Street, the Olympic Market on 286 Street, along the riverside near the Royal Palace, close to the backpackers' hotel, the Capitol, and in the centre of the Old Market on 106 Street. Masses have recently opened along USSR Boulevard.

If you prefer Vietnamese food, head for the stalls along 117 Street, which serve mouth watering *pho* (a wheat noodle soup made with a meat stock which has been seasoned with chillies, mint, coriander and other herbs). Some of the ones along Kampuchea Vietnam Road serve a very spicy variety called *hu tieu*, which is commonly sold in Saigon. Because fish are readily available from Tonlé Sap Lake, many serve *canh chua dau ca* (a sour fish soup) and *mien luon* (an eel dish served with slivers of chicken, fungi and shallots). There are also numerous Vietnamese foodstalls on 242 Street and along Achar Mean Boulevard.

Budget restaurants

To cater for the ever increasing backpacker trade, numerous small cafeterias and snack bars have opened between 1992 and 1995 along Kampuchea Vietnam Boulevard. Two course meals are available for about US$2 (6,700 riels). Typical menus include *maan* (chicken), *puong sat* (eggs), *mee* (noodles), *saach* (meat dishes) and *suop* (soup). Some, such as the **Leem Tear Hae Restaurant** at Number 8, serve Chinese dishes – bean curd with pepper sauce, barbecued ribs of pork, braised meat balls, chicken with salt and pepper, steamed fish and fish in spicy bean sauce. In the **Cafe Khanara** at Number 50 you can watch Western video films while tucking into *khao phonne* (a Cambodian noodle dish). Especially recommended is the **Samapheap Restaurant** at Number 39 which is one of the most popular eating spots in the city. Another recently renovated establishment is the **Thmor Da Restaurant** at Number 90 AB, which is immediately recognised by its brightly lit exterior. Tourists arriving in March, April and May, when temperatures reach 36°C in the city, will certainly not mind paying a little extra to eat in the air-conditioned lounge here. They offer both Khmer and Vietnamese cuisine. University students favour the pleasant open-air **Faculty of Medicine Restaurant** on Achar Mean Boulevard, which also serves European food, and a rather trendy cafe near the Achar Hencheay roundabout where loud rock music blares out till

SOUTH CENTRAL
PHNOM PENH

11pm. Many of the city's youth head for the **Chbouk Rak Disco** near the junction of the Keo Mony Boulevard and Pokamber. Delicious snacks can be purchased here at very reasonable prices. The nearby **Chenla Restaurant** also fills up very quickly. Other trendy ones include the new **Heart of Darkness Restaurant** on 51 Street and the **California** on Surutha Road. Another good place for breakfast is the **Chef's Deli** at 52 Charles de Gaulle Boulevard. They also serve pastries in their tea room.

If you are looking for a friendly homely atmosphere head for the **Oasis Restaurant** at 139 Pokambor Boulevard where you can even get bacon and eggs for breakfast.

French dishes at a very economical price can be purchased at the **Bassac Restaurant** in the Phnom Penh Hotel, the **Chez Lipp** on Achar Mean Boulevard, the nearby **Apsara Restaurant** (at 208), the **Bayon** (at 174) and **La Mousson Restaurant**, upstairs in the **No Problem Cafe** at the junction of 55 Street and 178 Street (close to the National Museum). This now opens daily from 11am to 12pm.

Others in the US$2-5 bracket which also serve European dishes include the **Capital** on 182 Street, **Dejavu** on 240 Street, the **Thai Coca Restaurant,** very close to the Phnom Penh Tourist office, the **Golden Eagle** on 144 Street and the slightly more expensive **BK Bistro** at 22 240 Street. The **Foreign Correspondents Club of Cambodia** at 363 Sisowath Quay serves good Western dishes including French meals.

1. PAILIN Hotel
2. OLYMPIC Hotel
3. MUNICIPAL Theatre
4. WAT MOHA MONTREI
5. AUSTRALIAN Embassy
6. LUCKY MARKET (Shop)
7. WAT LANG KA
8. VICTORY Monument
9. TUOL SLENG Prison Museum
10. WAT TUOL TOM PONG
11. LAOTIAN Embassy
12. Former US Embassy
13. HUNGARIAN Embassy
14. VIETNAMESE Embassy
15. POLISH Embassy
16. INDIAN Embassy
17. MONIVONG BRIDGE
18. FERRIES

Pizzas can be purchased at the **PP Pizza** at 293 USSR Boulevard, at **Happy Herb's Pizza** at 295 Pochentong Boulevard and at the **Lotus,** 121 Karl Marx Boulevard.

The least expensive seafood restaurant is probably the **Raksmay Boeng,** which is situated on the side of Boeng Kak Lake in the northern district of Phnom Penh. This together with the noisier **Boeng Kak Thamet Restaurant,** which is close by, also serves Chinese and Western dishes. For a romantic atmosphere try one of the floating restaurants, either the **Kong Kea** or the **Chaktomuk** moored at the Karl Marx Quay or the very new Thai floating restaurant which has been moored on the east bank of the Tonlé Sap River. Boats are available to take you there opposite the Royal Palace.

More expensive restaurants

If you have money to burn why not treat the lady in your life to a sumptuous meal at **La Paillotte** (234 Street) where a candle-lit French dinner with wine will set you back around US$34 for two.

Equally pricey are the **Royal Pavilion** and **Mekong** Restaurants at the Hotel Cambodiana. The former is said to serve the best Chinese food in town but a recent tourist said she preferred the Chinese cuisine at the **Ly-Ly Restaurant** at 117 Achar Mean Boulevard which is about one tenth the price!

Recommended very highly is the expensive **Crackers Restaurant,** 13 90 Street and the **Gecko Club** at the junction of 114 and 61 Street. The Gecko features jazz and blues music nightly.

A little cheaper but exceptionally good value is the **International Restaurant** in the Pailin Hotel. The Chinese food here is excellent and it fills up very quickly in the evening. A reservation is recommended (tel: 25485).

A good place to be at sunset is the restaurant on the 6th floor of the **Monorom Hotel** at 89 Achar Mean Boulevard. Expect to pay US$20 for two, including drinks.

If you like northern Indian style cooking then the place for you is the **Taj Mahal Restaurant** which is situated in Tou Samouth district near the Independence Monument.

Japanese food is available at **Midori,** 145 Norodom Boulevard.

Expensive Thai food is available at the **Coca** at the junction of Achar Mean and 240 Street and the **Ban Tai** at 1, 306 Street. These specialise in Thai curry (*kaeng kari*), beef in oyster sauce (*nua phat nummunn hoy*), fried fish with ginger (*pla pad ging*) and spicy lemon soup (*tom yam*) to start. The **Chao Pra Ya** at 62 Tou Samouth is the most expensive and specialises in Thai buffets.

Author's choice: the medium priced **Kong Kea** floating restaurant which has a nightly live band, superb seafood and reasonably priced tiger beer.

Evening entertainment

Bars, discos and nightclubs

If you are looking for a pleasant relaxing atmosphere head for either the Lobby Bar or Cyclo Bar at the Hotel Cambodiana or the luxury lounge at the Novotel. Both have live music until 23.00 nightly.

Drinks available include Angkor, Tiger and Saigon Export beer together with hard liquors imported from the former Eastern Bloc countries. Schnapps and vodka are popular. The main soft drink sold in these establishments is *soda kroch chhmar* (soda water with a dash of lemon). If you order Heineken expect to pay three times the price of the local brews.

A nice place with a superb river view is the Foreign Correspondent Club at 363 Karl Marx (Sisowath Quay).

One of the most popular places in the city is the Rock Hard Cafe which due to ever increasing demand is now open every night until 23.00. Students go here to play chess and backgammon. Another favourite student haunt is the trendy Heart of Darkness Bar on 51 Street, where loud western pop music blares out until 22.00. If you liked Apocalypse Now in Saigon you will certainly like this place which was set up by the same owner. A big attraction here (for some) are pool tables and delectable young ladies who hang around waiting for custom. When full the place is unbearable due to lack of air-conditioning.

A good place for lonesome males looking for young ladies with *laissez-faire* morals is the Kong Kea Floating Restaurant, which has live music nightly and the nightly dance at the Royal Hotel on 92 Street. An area which is fast becoming a sleazy hotbed of titillating temptation is Boeng Kak, especially the northern side where many Cambodian prostitutes ply their trade until around 23.00. Bars in this area tend to be very small – sometimes no more than one or two tables set up in the open.

To find out what the current political situation is go to the Gecko Club on 110 Street where journalists (and people pretending to be journalists) hang out.

If you have just flown in from Bangkok or Manila don't expect to find discos or clubs which rival those in Patpong or Ermita. The best you can hope for is live entertainment of the rather tame variety. Bands can be enjoyed at San Miguel's on 178 Street, sixth floor of the Monorom Hotel, Hotel Le Royal at 1 Daun Penh Street, Chbouk Kak Restaurant on Keo Mony Boulevard, Hotel Neak Poan on Anchar Mean Boulevard (1st Floor), Martini Bar on Sarak Boulevard, Holiday Restaurant on USSR Boulevard and Rock Hard Cafe at 315 Karl Marx Boulevard (Thursday, Friday, Saturday and sometimes Sunday afternoon). There is also a nightclub at the Cambodiana Hotel. Another recommended is the Dancing Restaurant on 128 Street.

Karaoke clubs
China Town Karaoke, No 46-49 Street 214; tel: 855 23 27973.
Pacific Nite Club-KTV, Karaoke, No 234-238 Monivong; tel: 855 18 810289.

Cambodian ballet
The finest evening entertainment is at the Municipal Theatre, where students from the Fine Arts School perform classical Cambodian ballet. Enquire at the Ministry of Information and Culture, tel: 24769.

The choreography, costumes, music and decor are outstanding. Every girl wears elaborate headgear, rich silks and lavish decorations around her neck and limbs. One of the most interesting dances is the classical Dance of the *Apsaras* which is performed with pronounced, deliberate movements which are dignified and intricately graceful. Many of the movements are related to Thai traditional dance. When Angkor was overrun by the Thais in the 15th century, many musicians and dancers were kidnapped and forced to live in Thailand. The Royal Ballet was revived in Cambodia in 1847 and since then it has been patronised by many members of the royal family, some of whom have sold jewellery to keep it going. In the past many of the prima ballerinas have been princesses. During the dance every gesture of hand and foot has a particular significance. The most famous of all the repertoires is a theme which is elaborately depicted in Angkor's bas-relief and on the lintels at the Bantéay Srei Temple. This is the kidnapping of the beautiful Sitō, the wife of Rāma, by the Demon of the Underworld, Rāvana. The ballet ends with a combat between the two kings.

Due to popular demand by tour groups, the Hotel Cambodiana now features classical Khmer dancing on Saturday nights.

Cinemas
There are two cinemas in Phnom Penh, the Mouscou and the Prachea Chun, both on Achar Mean Street. Western films can be seen at the Foreign Correspondents Club at 363 Karl Marx Boulevard on Saturday nights.

Satellite TV
Available at Cathouse Bar, 51 Street.

Shopping
Phnom Penh is no shoppers' paradise. Handicrafts sold include rubbings of bas reliefs on rice paper, models of *pteah* (Cambodian stilt houses), reproduction Buddha images, Khmer statues and *papier mache* masks, paintings of Angkor and jewellery made from silver and precious stones such as onyx, rubies and sapphires mined at Pailin. A good inexpensive buy are the *kramas* (Cambodian scarves), usually made from cotton. These are about one yard in length and are available in chequered colours, red on white or blue on white. Very handsome ones made from silk can be bought if you take an excursion to Oknhatey Island situated in the Mekong just north of Phnom Penh. Many ladies would like the *sampots* (ankle-length skirts) manufactured here, particularly the ceremonial ones made from brightly coloured silk. *Sarongs* (shorter skirts) made for men are also available. You may also like the variegated silk shirts, known as *hols*.

Handicraft centres
Many of the more expensive hotels sell handicrafts, the best selection is at the Cambodiana. If you want well-made Khmer reproductions go to the shop at the back of the National Museum of Arts, junction of 19 and 184 Street. Khmer pottery is available from Kheng Song Souvenirs at 99 Achar Mean Boulevard. Other more general handicraft shops are located near the Central Market, junction of 118 Street and Achar Mean Boulevard. Recommended are Vicheth Sal, 121 Achar Mean, Souvenir Khmer Rachakna at 139 Achar Mean, Bantéay Srei at 108 Achar Mean, Kheng Song Souvenirs at 99 Achar Mean and Ratana Souvenirs on 118 Street. Local paintings can be viewed at the New Art Gallery, 9 20 Street.

Recently opened is La Boutique, 36 Sihanouk Boulevard; tel: 855 23 60053. Here you can buy sophisticated, intricately produced dyed silk known as *Kha Bang Neang Sok Kra Ob*. Featuring strong patterns, floral designs, animal and historical motifs in green, violet, red, ochre and blue hues, the silk can be customised into *hohls* and *phamuong*. These are the formal equivalents of *sarongs* and *sampots*. Westerners are often tempted by beautiful scarves made from patterned silk using the same technique. This involves wrapping silk stands in their raw state on to a wooden frame. Using threads made from banana leaves they are tied into distinctive patterns. The silk is then dyed, removed, remounted and re-tied, adding new coloured dye to produce a sophisticated product.

Jewellery and silverware

If you don't want to pay over the odds for these items some of the local markets offer the best deals. Old coins, antique silver and old original Khmer statues can be purchased at the Old Market (*Psar Cha*) situated between 13, 106 Street and 110 Street. Some antique stalls have been set up at the O Russei Market on 182 Street, the large covered Central Market just off Achar Mean Boulevard and the Tuol Tum Pong Market near the Tuol Tum Pong Pagoda in the southern part of the city. Don't forget to bargain hard.

More expensive buys may be obtained at the State Jewellery Shop, Bijouterie d'Etat at the junction of 13 and 106 Street. Very nice silver belts, boxes and bangles may be obtained at the Silver Shop, 1 Achar Mean Boulevard.

Proving very popular with Western tourists are tiny ankle chains known as *chang kraang chheung* made out of silver (70-92% purity) for babies.

At the newly opened Tan Sotho Fine Antiques Shop, No 188 Street 13; tel: 855 23 26194, you can buy delicate filigree work made in traditional Islamic style.

Kramas and traditional Khmer clothing

Most of the city's markets have a cheap selection. Many Western women buy cheap *sampots* to wear as a mark of respect when visiting pagodas. If you don't have a hat it's a good idea to buy a krama to wrap around your head when visiting Angkor as even on cloudy days the ultra violet light penetration can lead to severe problems. If you want to see what the elegant Cambodian man around town wears go to the House of High Style at 263 Achar Mean Boulevard or Nobel Trailleur at 169.

Duty free

Bayon Duty Free, No 34 Street 214; tel: 855 23 27756.
TAT Duty Free, No 105 Pochentong Boulevard; tel: 855 15 912974.

Supermarkets

Don't expect these to be like the ones in Thailand. Recommended is the International Supermarket at 35, 178 Street. Here you can even buy some luxury Western goods (at a price). There is less choice available in the smaller one at 131 Street and McSam's at 21, 13 Street.

You could also try Bayon Market, No 133-5 Monivong Boulevard; tel 855 23 29962, Le Shop, No 129-131 Street 118; tel: 855 23 26644, Lucky Market, No 160 Sihanouk Boulevard, or International House, No 35 Street 178; tel: 855 2326246.

Beauty shops

Bantéay Srey, No 108 Street 136; tel: 855 15 912371.
Chenda Salon, No 64 Street 63; tel: 855 18 811249.
Kampuchea, No 227 Monivong Boulevard.

Lhoor Torn Cheth, No 115 Street 130.
Sak May Thmey, No 30 Street 128.
Madame Beauty House, No 73 Street 115; tel: 855 23 23116 or 855 15 911899.

Photographic shops
There are two photographic shops on Kampuchea-Vietnam Boulevard, Photo Selpak at 56 and Le Photo at 105. On Achar Mean Boulevard there is City Colour Photo at 123 and Diamond Film and Processing at 209.

Money change
Travellers cheques and dollars cash can be changed at banks and kiosks. All of these are in the Phnom Penh directory. The only visa card outlet at present is at the Banque du Commerce Exterior du Camodge at the junction of Soeung Ngoc Mong Street and Achar Mean Boulevard.

Post office
Corner of 126 Street and Achar Mean Boulevard; tel: 23324. IDD telephones are available here with payment preferred in dollars. It is open from 07.00-19.00. There is another at the junction of 13 and 98 Street.

Medical supplies
The best advice I could give anyone is to bring your own. Medicines are not readily available. General pharmaceutical goods can be purchased at Pharmacy Monorom, 103 Achar Mean Boulevard, Pharmacy Santepheap close to the Hotel Dosit Pitou on 118 Street and Pharmacy Chok Chey at 41 Kampuchea-Vietnam Boulevard.

Medical emergencies
Only limited facilities are available in Phnom Penh. Westerners are advised to contact the SOS International Medical Clinic at 83 Issarak Boulevard; tel: 912765. The other alternatives are to contact the Khmer Soviet Hospital (Calmette Hospital) on Monivong Road or report directly to the lobby at the Cambodiana Hotel where reliable help will be given. US citizens can contact the US Mission, 16, 228 Street; tel: 26438, which is geared up to assisting its citizens.

Other facilities include
Access Medical, No 203 Street 63 @ 818.
Doctor: Gavin Scott, tel: 855 15 912100,
Nurse: Suzanne Smith, tel: 855 19 913358
Polyclinique Aurore, No 58-60 Street 113; tel: 855 18 810339.

Worth repeating here is that because of the standard of medical treatment in Cambodia being far inferior to that in the West, it is better to take out special insurance before you leave. SOS Assistance Far East Ltd, PO Box 1080, Robinson Road, Singapore 9021, tel: 65 226 3937, will arrange for you to be flown out of the country immediately. Their nearest office to Phnom Penh is at Interlink Resources Pte Ltd, 135 Nam Nghi Street, District 1, Ho Chi Minh City; tel: 230 499; fax: 290 583.

SOS International Assistance membership is also available from Eurasie Phnom Penh Travel.

Phnom Penh directory
Travel bureaux

Acacia Tourism, No 44, Street Sothearosh, Sk Chey Chum Neash, Doun Penh; tel: 22457; fax: 26100

Angkor Tourist, No 178C, Street Tro Sork Pheim, Sangkat Beung Keng Kang I, Doun Penh; tel/fax: 62169

Angkor Voyages, Champs Elysees Hotel, 185, 63 Street; tel: 27268

Apex Cambodia Travel Service Co Ltd, No 53B, Street Trodork Phar Em, Beung Ring, Doun Penh; tel: 27787; fax: 26595

Apsara Tours, 29, 150 Street; tel: 25408 and at No 8, Street 254, Chaktomuk, Doun Penh; tel: 26705.

Aroon Tours, 201 Achar Mean Boulevard; tel: 26300 and at No 2, Street 120, Phsar Thmei II, Doun Penh; tel/fax: 64397

Asia Booming Travel, No 25 ED0, Street 282, Sk Beung Keng Kang I, Chamcarmon; tel: 15 91427G

Asian Lines Travel, No 79E Street 134, SK Mittaphap, 7 Mkara; tel/fax: 66150

Bophar Angkor Tour, No 797, Street Prah Monivong, Sk Beung Trobek, Chamcarmon; tel/fax: 27933/27406.

Cambodia Voyage, No 81, Street Lyoklay, Sk Chey Chum Neash, Doun Penh

Cambodian-Australian Travel, 6, 222 Street; tel: 26225

Cams-Air Travel, 187 Keo Mony Boulevard; tel: 26739

Chinta Travel, No 46 Street 241, Sk Beung Ring, Doun Penh; tel/fax: 26097

CK International Travel, No 177E0, Street 130, Sk Phsar Thmei I, Doun Penh; tel: 22584; fax: 26312

Da Xing Travel, No 311 Street Tep Phorn, Sk Tuk La Ork, Toul Kok; tel: 18 812160

Diethelm Travel, No 8, Street Samdach Sothie Ros, SK, Chey Chom Neas Khan, Doun Penh; tel: 26648; fax: 26678

Diethelm Travel Cambodia Ltd, 8 Lenin Boulevard; tel: 26648; fax: 26676

Direction Generale du Tourisme, junction of 232 Street and Achar Mean; tel: 22107

East West Group Co Ltd, No 17E0+E1, Street 144, Sk Phsar Thmei I, Doun Penh; tel: 27118; fax: 26189

East-West Travel, 170, 114 Street; tel/fax: 26189

Eurasie Phnom Penh Travel, 86 Pasteur Khan Daun Penh; tel: 27144/27374; fax: 27374.

Eurasie Travel, 97 Achar Mean Boulevard; tel: 23620; fax 26268

Explotra Travel, 361 Karl Marx Boulevard; tel/fax: 27177 and at No 43 Street 105; tel/fax: 27973

Fsun Tourist, No 15, Street 228 Sk Beung Ring, Doun Penh; tel: 15 314 386; fax: 27425

Hanuman Tours, No 188, Street 13 Sangkat Chey Chum Narsh, Doun Penh; tel/fax: 26194

International Travel & Tours, 339 Achar Mean Boulevard; tel/fax: 27248

JHC Angkor Tour, No 313, Vithei Sisovath, Sk Chakto Muk, Doun Penh; tel/fax: 26860

Khemara Travel Company, 134 Sivutha Boulevard; tel/fax: 27434

Kim Kok PC Travel Services, No 79 Street 63, Sk Beung Ring, Doun Penh; tel/fax: 60321

MS Tourist Co Ltd, No 86 E0, Street 126, Phsar Thmei II, Doun Penh;
   tel: 15 914331; fax: 62119
Naga Tours, Renakse Hotel, Lenin Boulevard; tel: 26288
National Tourism Office, junction of 232 Street and Achar Mean Boulevard;
   tel: 25607
Orient Express Tour Company, 19,106 Street; tel: 26248; fax: 26313
Peace Penh Tourism, junction of Karl Marx and Lenin Boulevard; tel: 23949;
   fax: 26043
Peninsula Travel Agency, No 117 E0, Street 136, Sk Phsar Kandalm,
   Doun Penh; tel: 15 912008
Pich Tourist, No 228, Street Preah Monivong, Sk Phsar Thmei II, Doun Penh;
   tel/fax: 26586
Prasat Tourism, No 81 Norodom Boulevard; tel/fax: 26880
Preferred Indochina Travel, Monorom Hotel, Achar Mean Boulevard;
   tel: 25350
Seng On Travel Service, No 473E0, Street Preah Monivong, Sk Beung Prolit,
   Khan 7 Makara; tel: 27499
Skylink Travel, 124 Tou Samouth Boulevard; tel: 27010
Star Travel, No 587 Eo, Street Monivong, Sk Beungkengkong II,
   Chamkamon; tel: 26648; fax: 26676
Sunrise Travel, directly opposite Cambodiana Hotel; tel/fax: 26762
Suraya Voyages Travel Services, 27, 134 Street; tel: 21619; fax: 26189
   and at No 117 E0, Street 294, Sk Beung Keng Kang, Doun Penh;
   tel: 15 9116; fax: 60105
Trans Air Cambodia Travel, No 16, Street Preah Monivong, Srash Chork,
   Doun Penh; tel: 18 811173; fax: 23 27977
Transindo Travel Service, 16 Achar Mean Boulevard; tel: 26298
Transpeed Travel, No 19 Street 10; tel/fax: 27633
TSC International, No 7 Eo, Street 19 SK Chey Chum Neash; tel/fax:
   26137

Embassies

Australian, 11, 254 Street; tel: 26254
Bulgarian, 227 Tou Samouth Boulevard; tel: 23181
Cuban, 30, 214 Street; tel: 24281
Czechoslovak, Tou Samouth Boulevard; tel: 25881
French, 22, 242 Street; tel: 26278
German, 76, 214 Street; tel: 26381
Hungarian, 773 Achar Mean Boulevard; tel: 22781
Indian, 777 Achar Mean Boulevard; tel: 22981
Indonesian, 179, 51 Street; tel: 26148
Japanese, 75 Tou Samouth Boulevard; tel: 27161
Laotian, 111, 214 Street; tel: 25181
Polish, 767 Achar Mean Boulevard; tel: 23581
Russian, Lenin Boulevard; tel: 22081
Thai, 43 Tou Samouth Boulevard; tel: 26182
United Kingdom, 75 Street; tel: 50400
Vietnam, junction of Achar Mean Boulevard and 436 Street; tel: 25681

Air travel

Aeroflot Airlines, 8 Tou Samouth Boulevard; tel: 25787
Air France, No 313 Sisowath Boulevard at Sofitel; tel/fax: 26426
Air Kampuchea, 62 Tou Samouth Boulevard; tel: 25887
Air Vietnam, 16 Achar Mean Boulevard; tel: 5629
Bangkok Airways, Hotel Dosit Pitou, 118 Achar Mean Boulevard; tel: 26298
Cambodian International Airlines, 19 106 Street; tel: 26248
Dragonair, No 19 Street 106; tel: 27652
Helicopter Service to Koh Kong and Sihanoukville; tel: 25105
Kampuchea Airlines, No 152 Norodom Boulevard; tel: 18 810274
Lao Aviation, No 58 Sihanouk Boulevard; tel: 26563
Malaysian Airlines, Diamond Hotel, ground floor, No 207 Monivong
  Boulevard; tel: 26688; fax: 26665
Silk Air, 19,106 Street; tel: 22236
SK Airlines, No 17 Pochentong Boulevard; 18 810047
Thai Airways, No 19 Street 106; tel: 22335; fax: 27211
Tranair, 16 Achar Mean Boulevard; tel: 26298
Vietnam Airlines, No 527 Monivong Boulevard; tel: 27426

Car hire

Taxi Service, World Trade Cambodia, No 33 Street 208; tel: 27072/27073

Postal, delivery and information services

Business International, Foreign Correspondents Club, 363 Karl Marx Boulevard
DHL Worldwide Express, No 17 Street 90 @ 75; tel: 18 810838
National Library, 92 Street
Oversea Courier Service, No 313 Sisowath Boulevard @ Sofitel Office;
  tel: 18 810227
Press Office of Foreign Ministry, junction of 240 Street and Karl Marx;
  tel: 22241
Shipping Services, 19 Street (see Transpeed Cargo); tel: 26248; fax: 26313

Banks and money change

Bangkok Bank, 26 Tou Samouth Boulevard; tel/fax: 26593
Bank of Commerce of Kampuchea, 26 Achar Mean Boulevard
Bank of Foreign Trade, corner Achar Mean and Soeung Ngoe Ming;
  tel: 24863
Banque du Commerce Exterior du Cambodge, junction of Soeung
  Ngoc/Achar Mean
Banque Indosnez, 70 Tou Samouth Boulevard
Banque Municipal de Phnom Penh, 102 Street, junction with 13 Street
Cambodian Commercial Bank, junction of 118 Street and Achar Mean
  Boulevard
National Bank, junction of Tou Samouth and 118 Street

Government offices

Bureau d'Immigration, Pokambor Boulevard; tel: 24794
Ministry of the Interior, junction of Tou Samouth Boulevard and 214 Street.
Ministry of Information and Culture, junction of Achar Mean and 180
  Street; tel: 24869

PHNOM PENH - CITY CENTRE

0 500

metres

1. WAT PHNOM
2. TONLÉ SAP 1 Restaurant
3. FACULTY of MEDECINE Restaurant
4. STUPA
5. HAPPY HERB'S PIZZA Restaurant
6. GECKO BISTRO
7. MONOROM Hotel
8. SUKHALAY Hotel
   ASIA Hotel
9. SANTE PHEAP Restaurant
10. BREAKFAST Bars
11. HAWAII Hotel
12. SOBHAMONGKOL Restaurant
13. THMOR DA Restaurant
14. BLUE Hotel
15. SANTEPHEAP Hotel
16. CHAMPA Restaurant
17. Hotel PARADISE
18. PACIFIC Hotel
19. PAILIN Hotel
20. JULIANA Hotel
21. REGENT Hotel
22. ORCHIDEE Hotel
23. MILITARY Museum
24. KAMPUCHEAN AIRLINES
25. CHAO PRA YA Thai Restaurant
26. NO PROBLEM Cafe
27. NATIONAL FINE ART Museum
28. ROYAL PALACE Grounds
29. BICYCLE HIRE
30. WAT MEAS
31. CAPITOL Hotels 1 and 2
32. HAPPY Guest House
33. SPORTS COMPLEX
34. WAT MOHA MONTREI
35. TOURIST Office
36. AUSTRALIAN Embassy
37. CZECH Embassy
38. VICTORY Monument
39. WAT LANG KA
40. BAN TAI Restaurant

EXCURSIONS

The Royal Palace complex

Red tape

Foreign visitors are allowed to enter the Royal Palace complex after paying a fee of US$4. For every camera carried they will be charged an extra US$2. Since Prince Norodom Sihanouk returned to live in the palace in November 1991, a permit has been required before anyone is allowed to enter the Silver Pagoda. The Throne Hall is currently out of bounds to foreigners. You can obtain a permit from Phnom Penh Tourism. Before entering the Silver Pagoda you will be asked to leave your camera outside. Photography is allowed in the rest of the complex but obviously you will not be permitted entrance to the Prince's residential quarters. Dress respectfully when you visit the complex, which is open 08.00-11.00 and 14.00-17.00.

Chan Chay pavilion

This marks the entrance to the complex which is situated opposite the Tonlé Sap River between 240 and 184 Streets. To find it walk along Lenin Boulevard in a northerly direction. About 50m after its junction with 214 Street you will see the entrance on your left. Directly ahead is a walled compound which prevents access to Prince Sihanouk's residence. This, together with the rest of the palace grounds, was a present to King Norodom (Prince Sihanouk's great grandfather) from the French in 1866, three years after Phnom Penh became the capital of a French Protectorate. Originally it had been made out of wood and possessed design features which were similar to those used in the construction of the old palace at Oudong.

The Throne Hall

This highly attractive building, built in 1917, has three-tiered steep-pitched roofs edged with sun-faded blue and green tiles. The roof's largest expanse is covered in golden orange tiles and towards its western end is topped with a six-tiered tower culminating in a pointed spire which protrudes out of the heads of a four-faced Buddha image. These are effigies of the Buddhist deity, Lokésvara. The roof eaves are extravagantly extended into long curves. Rows of plain pillars support the bottom tier which appear to be held in place by *apsara* figures. Another golden spire projects out of the top of the southern entrance porch. The main entrance is on the eastern side and is reached via a flight of steps flanked by many headed *naga* parapets.

Once, the kings of Cambodia were crowned inside this hall. During the ceremony they would be seated on a tiered pedestal representing the earth. Over their heads would be a representation of the heavens in the form of a nine-tiered umbrella made out of the finest silk. Four holy *Garudas*, with their wings spread, would look down on them from above. The audience, who consisted of royal dignitaries, members of the royal family and friends, would be seated on plush chairs. These yellow chairs with their Louis Quinze legs are still there, along with conch shells which would have been used to summon the audience. The frescoes which adorn the roof, painted in lavish pink and vieux rose, are still in a remarkable state of preservation. They depict scenes from the Hindu epic, the *Rāmayāna*. The king's ceremonial throne is still there, too, along with

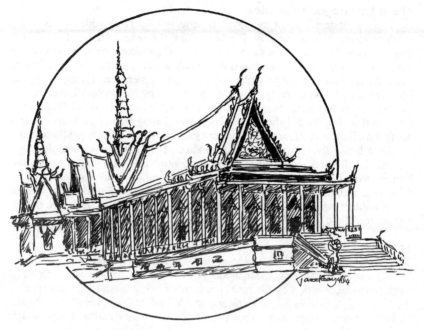

The Throne Hall, Royal Palace, Phnom Penh

the queen's more lowly one. Towards the back of the hall are the king and queen's chambers where they would have slept apart before the grand coronation.

Elephant Dock building
This is slightly towards the north of the Throne Hall. Here the king could comfortably mount his elephant. On ceremonial occasions he would wear a crown, encrusted with zircons, rubies and other precious stones, which was designed specifically for riding on the back of an elephant. One can imagine an elephant, bedecked in state regalia, jewelled saddle and gold bands wrapped around its tusks, backing into this structure.

The Napoleon III villa
Further south past the royal treasury is the Napoleon III villa, which is situated directly in front of the royal offices. This present from the French Emperor to King Norodom commemorated the signing of the 1863 treaty which made Cambodia a French Protectorate. Typically French, with shuttered windows and a balcony surrounded by iron lacework, this two-tiered structure was originally presented to the Empress Eugenie. It had been used as her residence when she attended the ceremonies concerned with the completion of the Suez Canal. Piece by piece, it was later shipped out to Cambodia, together with a statue of her husband sitting on a magnificent horse.

The Silver Pagoda complex

Beyond the eastern side of the pavilion there is a doorway which leads into a corridor running in a westerly direction along the outer gallery of the Silver Pagoda complex. This leads to the north gate, the visitors' entry point into the complex. To the left, as you enter, is the library which once housed sacred texts. In the far northeastern corner is the stupa which commemorates King Norodom. South of it is the mounted horse presented to him by Napoleon III. Notice that the rider now has King Norodom's head (which replaced that of Napoleon). Beyond it is the stupa dedicated to King Ang Duong (father of Norodom and Sisowath). Beyond that, near the southern gallery, is a small holy pavilion which is said to house the footprint of Lord Buddha. Moving in a clockwise direction around the Silver Pagoda (ie towards the centre) one first comes across the Phnom Mondap, a holy stupa, followed by another which is dedicated to Sihanouk's daughter. In the southern corner is the Pavilion for Royal Celebrations, which is alongside the stupa dedicated to King Norodom Suramarit. There is a bell tower in the western corner of the complex.

The Silver Pagoda

This pagoda, sometimes referred to as the Emerald Buddha Pagoda (Wat Preah Kaeo), was built by Prince Sihanouk in 1962 to replace the one originally constructed from wood by his great grandfather, King Norodom. He imported the best Italian marble for its steps and inside laid 5,000 silver tiles. Even the barbaric Khmer Rouge didn't dare disturb the precious Buddha figures which are its crowning glory.

A priceless statue of the Emerald Buddha, sculpted from baccarat crystal and believed to be more than three centuries old, stands in the centre. Behind it there is a magnificent heavy golden Buddha lavishly decorated with 9,584 diamonds. Many of the diamonds embedded in this structure were believed to have been taken from King Norodom's diamond-studded hat and other jewellery in 1906. To either side of it are silver and bronze Buddhas. Protected by a glass case is a holy stupa made from silver and gold which is believed to contain a relic of Lord Buddha which originated in Ceylon. Directly behind this dais is a Burmese marble Buddha. A litter stands nearby which was used on ceremonial occasions. Along the walls are presents given to the monarchy by visiting dignitaries from many countries, Khmer masks, vessels, sequinned robes, bracelets and Khmer ornaments.

Museums

The National Museum of Art

This ornate, red building, also known by its French name, Musée des Beaux Arts, is typically Khmer in design, its tiered roofs have generous extended eaves and porches are crowned with elongated pointed spires. It can be visited after exiting from the Royal Palace because it is just north of it on 13 Street. Walk along the river front on Quay Karl Marx nearly as far as the Phnom Penh Tourism office. Turn left down 184 Street and take the first right into 13 Street. Admission costs US$2 and the museum is open from 07.00-11.30 and 14.00-17.30 Tuesday-Sunday. Guides are available who speak good French and English. Photography inside is prohibited.

The building has recently undergone some reconstruction in an attempt to remove the numerous bats which once nested under the roof. During the Khmer Rouge rule of terror many of the precious sculptures held at the National Museum were destroyed or severely damaged. The museum's director was killed and its staff joined the terrified thousands who fled from the city. It wasn't re-opened for another four year.
Exhibits include pre-Angkor and Angkor sculptures.

Pre-Angkor period

Relatively few sculptures have survived from the earliest part of the Kingdom of Funan, a period ruled by King Rudravarman. 6th century figures found at Phnom Da were exclusively male and include Vishnu, the Preserver, depicted with a pointed head-dress, Adonis type features and sometimes wearing a distinctive *sampot* and belt. Statues of the god Shiva, the Destroyer, can be recognised by their weird third eye in the middle of their forehead and towering hair style arranged in masses of small curls. Most have four arms and in the earliest the torso is left bare. Buddha statues are depicted with the facial characteristics of Hindu gods, their rounded features giving them a happy appearance and close slanting eyebrows suggesting strength of character. Both standing and later seating styles are exhibited. Less impressive are rather rougher statues of King Bhavavarman I.

Female statues appeared during the period of the Tchen-la Kingdom at the Sambor Prei Kuk complex about 150km to the southeast of Angkor. Dated between 600-50 these included depictions of the female Hindu goddess Umã, also known as the gracious one. One of the most voluptuous statues came from Isanapura (named after the ruler Isanavarman who reigned from 616-35). After marrying a Chenla princess he set up a new capital here and called it Sambor. Many more female figures of beautiful goddess were carved but few have survived. One of the most magnificent, depicting Laksmi, the Goddess of Beauty, came from Koh Kuk temple close to the riverine town of Kratie. A rather unusual male statue is that of Hari-Hara which combines features of Shiva (Hara) and Vishnu (Hari) with a very muscular torso. Notice the pointed head-dress of Vishnu and the masses of hair curls of Shiva.

Later female statues are slimmer, such as the dainty statue of Laksmi removed from the Prasat Thleang. Similar slender sculptures of Hari-Hara, Shiva and Vishnu, typical of the more delicate Prei Kmeng Style (635-700), have survived together with the four-faced Brahmã, the Creator. Bodhisattvas (beings who have not yet reached the state of nirvana) and Buddhas from the period tend to be small and made from bronze. The style can be easily recognised by their distinctive eyebrows.

Statues made during the rule of Jayarvarman I (657-81) came from Prasat Andat which is believed to have been quite close to Angkor. Males from the period had mitre crowns, exposed ears, slender faces and thin moustaches. Females were more voluptuous than the Prei Kmeng Style and had tiny waists which tended to be emphasised by their full skirts. Particularly impressive is the sculpture of Hari-Hara (after whom the city of Hariharalaya was named) which was unearthed close to Kompong Thom. Perfectly proportioned and immaculately finished, this masterpiece of Khmer art is regarded by many archaeologists to represent the apogee of early Cambodian craftmanship.

During the period which followed, depicted by the Style of Kompong Preah (706-800), many of the statues made were inferior to their predecessors. As this was a time of great turmoil during which the country was split into 'Land Chenla' and 'Water Chenla' many of the temples, such as the one at Phum Prasat, were equally unimpressive. Another era of imaginative, figurative design wasn't to dawn until the reign of Jayadevi (Jayavarman's widow) came to an end; a period which also marked the fall of Funan.

Angkorian period (802-1201)

During the reign of Jayavarman II (802-50), the first *devarāja* (god-king) statues were built to adorn the Mount Meru-type temple constructed at Rong Chen near Kulen. These all male, macho-looking sculptures with stern expressions had mitre crowns, moustaches, longer hair and shorter *sampots* (loincloths). They were very similar to those unearthed at Prasat Ak Yom on the Angkor plain.

The style which followed, Prah Kô (875-95), represents a golden period of Khmer art during which Indravarman I (877-89) erected the ornate temple-palaces at Rolous, south of Angkor. Male statues became more compressed with short, dumpy legs, moustaches became thicker and side whiskers appeared on the face. Women wore more lavish dresses with more complicated adornments. They were full bodied and had decorative crowns on their heads. For the first time group sculptures appeared. Many unearthed from the site of Hariharalaya, the first Khmer capital (where you find the temple complexes of Prah Kô and Bakong), were very similar to the Koh Ker Style unearthed at the Prasat Thom temple complex, which dated between 921 and 944. In the interlude another Khmer city, known as Yasodharapura had been built by Yasovarman I (Paramasivaloka) (889-900). In the vicinity of its temple-mountain, the formidable Phnom Bakheng sculptures discovered were thinly built with narrower faces. Women were depicted with large breasts, pleated skirts and two-tiered crowns. When Isanavarman II (922-8) became king he ordered the construction of huge human and animal figures among the brick temples of his capital at Koh Ker. Massive semi-divine beings called *yaksas*, some evil some good, competed for attention with other demi-gods; scaly-bodied serpents called *nāgas*, with fan-shaped multiple heads, appeared alongside *Garudas*, their dreaded enemy, on motifs. Hindu gods are depicted in the basic Prah Ko Style but sampots have double pleats and women's dresses are heavily adorned with jewellery.

As Khmer architecture developed a more classic style during the reign of Rajendravarman II (944-68), sculptural evolution did not follow suit. Rather unique were the sandstone lion-parapets scattered along the level of the first terrace of the laterite temple of Pré Rup.

Figures from the Bantéay Srei complex, which date between 965 and 1000, are small compared to any others seen on the Angkor plain but exhibit similarities with earlier styles. Some of the female figures here are divine expressions of the best in Khmer art. Classically carved in red sandstone these masterpieces, produced under the orders of Yajnavaraha (who was the grandson of King Harshavarman), exhibit a luxuriance which far surpasses any at Prasat Thom Temple at Koh Ker, after which the complex is modelled. The female sculptures have exquisitely fine features and are some of the most graceful and sensual ever produced. As well as beautiful *apsaras* the temple is watched over by gruesome looking demons, Vishnu's mount, the Brahmani kite *Garuda* and smiling *dvarapalas* (guardians or protectors).

Figures carved during the reign of Jayavarmán V (968-1001) also exhibit a degree of classicism repeated in the style of the Northern and Southern Khleng. Women are radiantly beautiful with low hanging skirts which show off their navel. Males have finely chiselled features and wear simple loincloths.

There is evidence that sculptural expression became highly ambitious during the reign of Suryavarman I (1002-50) and his son Udayadityavarman II (1050-80). The only piece which survives at the National Museum is the badly damaged bust of Vishnu which was originally part of a massive bronze statue. It depicts the god reclining in a relaxed pose with one of his arms extended and the other close to his head. His left arm is missing. It was found in the Western Mébon temple, 4km to the west of Angkor Thom. Other sculptures in the Baphuon Style are elegant and slim bodied. Females wear knotted belts and males pleated *sampots*.

The Khmer carvers who lived during the reign of Suryavarman II (1113-50) produced masterpieces in sandstone which are unrivalled on any other part of the Indochinese peninsular. The figurative ornamentation seen all over Angkor Wat seems more likely to have been sculpted by the gods themselves rather than by mere mortals. The number of statues which have survived is extremely small. Reproductions of what they were like are sold in the museum shop. The Angkor Wat Style (1100-75) can be recognised by looking at the hair. This was either tied in a *mukata* (single knot) or a *jata-mukata* (double knot). The workmanship involved rivalled that seen in the temple itself. Figures were more distinctly Khmer, showing very little resemblance to the Indian Gupta style seen in much earlier ones. Dress is simpler, head-dresses less lavish, outlines are much softer and garments have slightly serrated edges.

The monarch who followed Udayadityavarman, Jayavarman VII (Mahaparamasaugata) (1181-1219), is remembered as a great Khmer king who was responsible for the introduction of a very flamboyant style of sculpture. The great fortified city of Angkor Thom was built under his instructions. At its centre was the Bayon, where 216 smiling Buddha heads, each resembling its creator, looked out to every point of the compass. Weathered by ten thousand storms these giant faces, effigies of the Buddhist deity Lokésvara, are now partly crumbled. Perfectly intact, however, and seen in a state of blissful meditation, is the sculpted head of Jayavarman VII (Mahaparamasaugata) which was recovered from the Preah Khan temple. Also extremely noteworthy is the remarkable Buddha figure discovered in the Bayon's central sanctuary which shows the Buddha in a state of meditation, perched on a giant *nāga* serpent with many heads. This early 13th century statue was one of the last to be built at the end of the Angkorian period.

Tuol Sleng Prison Museum

From the National Museum of Art this can be reached by heading west along 184 Street until it intersects with Achar Mean Boulevard. Turn left and walk down as far as its intersection with 350 Street. Turn right along this street and cross 105 Street. The next right turning you will find 113 Street where there is an entrance to the museum on the western side. It opens from 07.00-11.30 and from 14.00-17.30. Photography is allowed in the grounds of the prison and in all the rooms.

WARNING: Some of the pictures here are highly explicit, it may well rate as one of the nastiest places you have ever been. Because of this there is a rumour that the Ministry of Tourism may well soon close it down and also prohibit visits to the Killing Fields of Choeung Ek.

On entry a typical commentary given to visitors would sound something like this. 'In March 1970 King Norodom Sihanouk was overthrown by a coup d'état headed by General Lon Nol. By December the NUFK, the National United Front of Kampuchea, held around 75% of the country. A period of civil war followed and by April 17 1975, Phnom Penh had fallen to the army of the Khmer Rouge led by Saloth Sar, a former teacher known better as Pol Pot. It was his clique who converted this high school, formerly known as Tuol Svay Prety, into a prison called S21. It was here that he imprisoned 20,000 innocent victims – engineers, doctors, monks, ministers, peasants, teachers, students and foreigners. In all, during the three years, eight months and 20 days of his barbaric rule, he was responsible for genocide on a scale 'without historical precedent'.

In the quadrangle of the prison visitors are shown the area where, using ropes, soldiers had broken the bones of Lon Nol's supporters and then ducked them in huge earthenware jars until they nearly drowned.

Many of the cruel inner secrets of this place may well be too much for many people to take. They will see small rooms where many inmates were starved to death shackled to iron bedsteads, pictures of agonising torture techniques and a chamber of horrors which will make even the most hardened traveller wince. Once you have been here you will never forget the fear in the eyes of thousands of people photographed awaiting interrogation and almost certain death. The graphic detail of this place produces a reaction of stunned silence. If you are of nervous disposition, give this place a miss.

Wats

Wat Phnom

This impressive temple-tower, built in 1434 during the reign of King Po Nhiazat, was constructed at a site where a lady named Penh found four Buddha statues which had floated down the Tonlé Sap River. Today it is an important landmark which can be seen from all over the city. The hill of Penh, on which it stands, is at the intersection of 96 Street and Tou Samouth Boulevard. The temple can be entered from the eastern side via a sandstone staircase dominated on either side by *nāga* serpents. Every day people from throughout the city arrive to present offerings of fruit, jasmine and magnolia at its central altar inside the main sanctuary (*vihara*). This has been rebuilt many times during the turbulent history of the country, first in 1434, then in 1806 and 1894 and finally in 1926. The large stupa nearby is said to contain the ashes of King Ponhea Yat who ruled from 1405-67. People who come here in droves on a Sunday also bring gifts to lay on the altar of Preah Chau which is around the corner from the main entrance to the temple. Here you will see a statue of the Hindu god Vishnu. A statue of Lady Penh can be seen in a small building between the stupa and the *vihara*.

Wat Ounalom

You probably noticed this important wat when you visited the National Museum of Art. It is situated where Lenin Boulevard crosses 154 Street. Originally in 1443 a monastery stood on this site. During the rule of the Red Khmer considerable damage was inflicted upon this structure which is one of the most important Buddhist sites in the country. They destroyed its irreplaceable treasure of religious books, dumped a statue of Samdech Huot Tat in the river and, worst of all, killed this greatly esteemed Buddhist leader, who was the functional head of 500 monks who lived here. Visitors today can still see his statue, which was later salvaged from the depths. When the national religion, Theravăda Buddhism, was reinstated in 1989, Wat Ounalom again became the official centre of the Khmer Buddhist patriarchate.

The bookcase that you will see on the second floor is all that remains of the massive library of sacred texts. The marble Buddha on the third floor is of Burmese origin. It was massively damaged by the Khmer Rouge but has been carefully reassembled. On the walls you will see religious scenes from the life of the Buddha.

The wat is currently only open during services, which are held every day at 07.00 and 18.00.

Wat Koh

Currently this wat, which is one of the oldest in the city, is being restored. The *vihara* (sanctuary) is being rebuilt. You will find it between 178 Street and 174 Street.

Wat Lang Ka

Before being nearly completely wrecked by Pol Pot's soldiers this temple housed well over 100 monks. Many of these were slaughtered. Stupas built after 1979 now surround the structure, which has been largely rebuilt. Beautiful paintings, depicting the life of the Buddha, adorn the main sanctuary.

This wat is located on Sivutha Boulevard to the west of the Victory Monument.

Wat Moha Montrei

It is worth going here to see the murals, which are painted in traditional Khmer style. The Khmer dancers you see in the murals are angels dressed in ballet costumes which are lavishly decorated with fine jewels. They wear the elaborate headgear characteristic of Royal Ballet performers. The wat (which was built in 1970) is dedicated to Chakrue Ponn, a highly respected member of King Monivong's government. Dotted around the main sanctuary are statues of Lord Buddha which were constructed after 1979 to replace those destroyed by the Khmer Rouge. The wat is situated between 173 Street and 163 Street along Sivutha Boulevard.

Other religious buildings

An-Nur an-Na'im

This incomplete humble brick structure replaces the once imposing building which originally stood on this site. This was completely sacked by the Khmer Rouge. Eventually it is hoped that a minaret can be added together with a small school to educate Phnom Penh's Muslim children. It is situated on the outskirts of the city.

Nur ul-Ihsan

Badly damaged by the Khmer Rouge this sanctuary still lacks its original minaret. Repaired and reconsecrated in 1979, it now serves Phnom Penh's Cham and Malay communities. It is just beyond the outskirts of the city and can be reached along National Route 5.

Excursions outside the city

The Killing Fields of Choeung Ek

Every Cambodian in the country prefers to forget *peal chur chat*, 'the sour bitter time'. About 15km from the city, beyond the southwestern suburbs is an eternal reminder of the countless exterminations which were carried out by the Khmer Rouge. Here you will see the exhumed mass graves, 129 pits in all, which contain the skeletons of nearly 9,000 people. Amongst this sickening sight you will see skulls still blindfolded, some with their sides caved in, broken faces and fragmented limb bones. A memorial stupa contains thousands of skulls which are clumped together behind glass.

Koki Beach

Few westerners go to this riverside resort, which is reached by turning off Auto Route No 1, about 12km from Phnom Penh. With its attractive surroundings and tranquil atmosphere, it is popular with Cambodians, especially on a Sunday. People like to lounge about on the elevated platforms overlooking the river.

Oudong

This attractive site, once the seat of the Cambodian monarchy is 40km north of the capital along Auto Route No 5. Oudong reached its heyday between 1618 and 1866. Today, due to decay and the savagery of the Khmer Rouge, it is a virtual ruin. The scenic trip passes the villages of the Cham minority who fish in the Tonlé Sap. It is possible to break your trip at one of the Cham Muslim villages to visit a mosque and school. During the Khmer Rouge reign of terror over 90,000 Cham were brutally murdered and their Koranic schools and mosques burnt to the ground. Once Oudong was a sumptuous Royal City with highly decorative temples and stupas built during the reign of King An Chan (mid 16th century). It was the site of many regal ceremonies, including the coronation of King Norodom. Massive damage was inflicted upon the site when, due to occupation by Khmer Rouge guerrillas, it was bombed to oblivion by Lon Nol.

It is still well worth visiting because from the top of this mountain sanctuary there are wonderful views over the Tonlé Sap River. At the base of the mountain is a memorial, erected in 1982, to those savagely killed by the Khmer Rouge. Wall drawings and a display of skulls and bones are an eternal reminder of their barbaric deeds. A long flight of steps (240) lead up the mountain to the site of the original temple on the south side. The original Royal City was built on two parallel ridges. The remains of the Ta San Mosque tops the smallest ridge. Reminders of the battle fought here stand in the form of bullet-pocked walls. The Cham Muslims in the area have already begun to restore the mosque which in accordance with their religious beliefs looks out in a westerly direction towards Mecca.

Topping the larger ridge opposite are a row of decayed stupas which are believed to contain the ashes of Cambodian Kings. The one on the left, known as Chet Dey Mak Proum, contains the ashes of King Norodom. It is well worth having a close look at this structure because of the unusual decorative style which features elephants, *Garudas* and sculpted images which appear to be effigies of the Buddhist deity, Lokesvara (Avalokitesvara). A little further on in the centre is King Ang Duong's stupa, known to Cambodians as Tray Troeng. King Norodom has this erected to hold the ashes of his father. The final stupa contains the ashes of King Soriyopor. Cambodians call it Damrei Sam Poan.

Further away from the laterite staircase on the Hill of Royal Fortune (the largest ridge) are the scanty remains of the 'Vihara of the Nine-Metre Buddha'. The original Buddha is barely recognisable after being blown to bits in the 1977 attack. The brick structure to the northwest of this is known as Vihara Preah Kó because it contains a statue of the sacred bull, Preah Kô. Nearby is another vihara containing a Buddha in seated posture (Preah Keo) and close to this is another containing the Prak Neak Buddha.

Restoration of the complex is underway from money pledged by the Phnom Penh government in 1992.

Tonlé Bati

This profoundly religious site, built out of laterite by Jayavarman VII (1181-1200), is in Takeo Province, 33km south of Phnom Penh. It is reached via Auto Route No 2, the main road to the town of Takeo. Well before Jayavarman's time in the 6th century it is believed that a religious shrine stood on this site. Beside the main temple of Ta Prohm there is the smaller temple of Yeay Peau, which is named after a fisherman's daughter. A statue of her stands inside the main sanctuary alongside one of Lord Buddha. There is a lovely old Khmer legend which tells the story of how the complex was originally named. One day the king of Angkor came to the site and fell instantly in love with the fisherman's daughter. She later bore him a son who was delivered to the Royal Court, where he became known as Prohm. Once he had been highly educated in his father's palace he was sent back to Takeo as governor. Inspired by the architectural delights he was so familiar with at Angkor he decided to have a laterite masterpiece constructed in his new home territory. Resembling temples which stood on the Angkor plains which had been built by his father, King Preah Ket Mealea, the new edifice bore his name: Prohm. The smaller temple he had built nearby was dedicated to his mother, it bore her name: Yeay Peau.

The main sanctuary of Ta Prohm at Tonlé Bati was badly damaged by the Khmer Rouge who inflicted their savagery not only on its five chambers but also the linga statues they housed. Like most of the temples on the Angkor plain, it is best entered through its impressive eastern gate. After walking in a westerly direction for about 15m one comes across an impressive bas relief on the northern side of the central chamber (on the right). This depicts a woman with a box on her head. According to an old Khmer legend this is supposed to contain the afterbirth of a child. The woman looking down at the small man is a midwife who was upset by the way she had been treated by the mother. Because of the disrespectful behaviour she has condemned the woman to carry the afterbirth on her head forever. The husband is begging her to forgive and forget.

If you then head directly north, facing you will be a fearsome statue of Lord Vishnu with six arms. On the left-hand side before proceeding to the Vishnu figure is a bas relief depicting a regal scene. High on the wall, a king sits on a

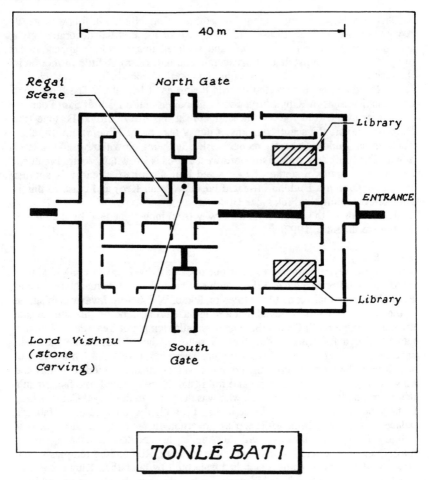

TONLÉ BATI

throne accompanied by his faithful wife. Below this scene, she is shown being trampled to death by a horse for her evil doings.

Continuing further north, one comes across the Hindu God of Childless Couples, Preah Noreay. People sometimes come to pray to him to give them a child. Here the surrounding laterite is in very poor condition.

By the Yeay Peau Temple you may have noticed a badly crumbled cement structure. This is what remains of Wat Tonlé Bati.

It is worth continuing northwest from the north exit point to the Bati River where stalls selling refreshments have been set up. The best day to visit is Sunday when many pilgrims come to worship here and later picnic by the river.

Phnom Chisor

An Angkorian design brick and laterite temple stands on the top of this hillock. You can enter it through the eastern gate on which there are wooden carvings of humans standing on the backs of pigs. If you stand in the entrance and look directly east you will see the small Khmer temples of Sen Ravang and Sen Thmol. If you climb up on the gallery you will get an even better view of the picturesque plain. The temple itself is badly decayed and consists of crumbled walls. Some of the lintels still retain some of their former carved splendour. Nearby are the very humble homes of monks who live on the site.

Getting there

The temple is 21km south of Tonlé Bati (about 60km from Phnom Penh). It can be reached by turning off Auto Route No 2, 55km south of the capital near Prasat Neang Khamau.

Some tour companies visiting the area stay in the Vimean Suor Hotel in Takeo for the night before continuing to Angkor Borei and Phnom Da in the morning. These sites are about 19km to the east of the town.

Phnom Dar

This is well worth going to see as it is one of the few cave sanctuaries that you will come across in Cambodia. A statue removed from this site stands in the National Museum in Phnom Penh. On the top of Phnom Dar is a tower made from laterite.

Angkor Borei

This was a very important site during the Water Chenla period (8th century). Today the village of Angkor Borei stands on the spot which was once occupied by the Vyadhapura capital.

Sihanoukville

Formerly called Kompong Som, this port, which was built during the early 1960s, is being developed for tourism. Situated 230km from the capital, it can be reached by air from Phnom Penh. By 1996, the road link will be greatly improved, due to a US $24 million project, which will undoubtedly enhance tourist related traffic. The upgrading and renovation of Highway 4 means that tourists visiting Cambodia will be treated to miles of dazzling white sand, lapped by the warm clear waters of the Gulf of Thailand. It is hoped that the nearby islands (kohs) which include Koh Ta Keo and Koh Puos will prove to be real tourist paradises. It is expected that even during the monsoon season (June-October) the resort, which does not suffer undue rainfall, will be popular. It will be an ideal escape location during the hot season when sea breezes counteract the excessive humidity experienced in the capital. The coast is a haven for snorkelling, the crystal clear water teeming with iridescent fish and phosphorescent coral reefs.

A 2.3 billion dollar project (casinos, golf courses, etc) has already been started. Kim Gjemmestad of Eurasie Phnom Penh Travel informed me that tourists visiting the area in 1996 will have facilities such as jet skiing, water skiing, skeet shooting, archery and a new beach club. Eurasie Travel is involved and will be offering snorkelling, bathem diving, fishing and wild-life watching. They will be running a five-day scuba-diving certificate course, deep-water fishing and boat rental.

Tourists will be able to visit the upland pepper plantations, durian farms and experience the charm of the local people.

It is also hoped that Kep, east of Sihanoukville and once a fashionable resort at the turn of the century, will also be developed. It is 90km from Sihanoukville and 165km from the capital. An area of outstanding natural beauty, it boasts sheltered, sweeping bays, miles of golden sand and a scenic backdrop of tropical woodland. From here, by mid-1996, fishermen will be taking tourists on magical trips to tropical islands such as Koh Tonsay and Koh Po.

Getting there
Flights can be booked through Apsara Tours. At the time of writing, the timetable was irregular.

Hotels
Presently there are eight hotels suitable for tourists with adequate facilities. The price range is from US$20-40, bookable through any tourist agency in Phnom Penh.
Chey Chumneas Hotel, Sopheakmaingkol Street. 30 rooms.
Hawaii Hotel, Ekareach Street. 28 rooms.
Kolap Hotel, 7-1 Street. 30rooms.
Kolap II, Ekareach Street. 20 rooms.
Koh Rong, Sopheakmaingkol Street. 32 rooms.
Luon Heng Hotel, Ekareach Street. 22 rooms.
Okinawa Hotel, Sopheakmaingkol Street. 19 rooms.
Sorya Hotel, Ekareach Street. 34 rooms.

Off limits
At the time of writing, AREAS NORTH OF PHNOM PENH, KOMPONG CHAM, KRATIE AND STUNG TRENG WERE OFF LIMITS. CAMBODIA'S SECOND CITY, BATTAMBANG, TOWARDS THE THAI BORDER, WAS ALSO CLOSED TO TOURISM.

Chapter Twenty One

Angkor

History

Archaeologists divide the Angkorian period into two phases. The first phase (9th-11th century) has five distinctive styles. These are seen in Kulen, Preah Kô, Bakheng, Koh Ker and culminate in the classical style of the Bantéay Srei. The second artistic phase (11th-15th century) features the architectural styles seen in the Baphuon, Angkor Wat and the Bayon.

Kulen was built a little to the northeast of present day Angkor by Jayavarman II (802-50). In accordance with the tradition of the Funan, he was worshipped as an incarnation of the Hindu God Shiva and given the title god-king. Now nothing virtually remains of his three-tower edifice. It was during the reign of Indravarman I (Isvaraloka) (877-89) that a pre-classical style of Khmer art emerged at Roluos along with its funerary cult temple complex of Preah Kô. It was this monarch who built the first of the great sandstone temple-mountains that were symbolic of Mount Meru. The Bakong (881AD) represented the basic format which would become the artistic template for future pyramidal edifices. His successor, Yasovarman I (889-900), built the Lolei Temple, which was never completed, to commemorate his father, Indravarman. Like the Bakong, this featured simple bas-reliefs.

At the end of the 9th century Yasovarman founded the city of Yasodharapura, which became a great metropolis, the capital of the Khmer Empire. At its centre he built Phnom Bakheng in 893 which, with its numerous towers, represented the whole cosmos in miniature. In 921, Jayavarman IV (921-41) moved the whole capital to Koh Ker, to the northeast of Angkor. The enormous seven-tier pyramid of Koh Ker is now extensively a ruin, but the Koh Ker style can still be clearly seen by visiting Baksei Chamkrong.

The seat of the great Khmer Empire was moved back to Angkor in 941 where Rājendravarman II (944-68) built the Eastern Mébon Temple (952), Pré Rup (begun in 961), and the miniature red sandstone masterpiece, Bantéay Srei (967).

During the reign of Jayavarman V (968-1001), the three-tiered Phimeanakas was begun which featured new style lofty galleries completed in sandstone by Suryavarman I (1002-50). By the second half of the 11th century, sandstone-vaulted galleries appeared on the two lower stories. The Baphuon, built Udayadityavarman (1050-66), features this style. Suryavarman II (1131-50)

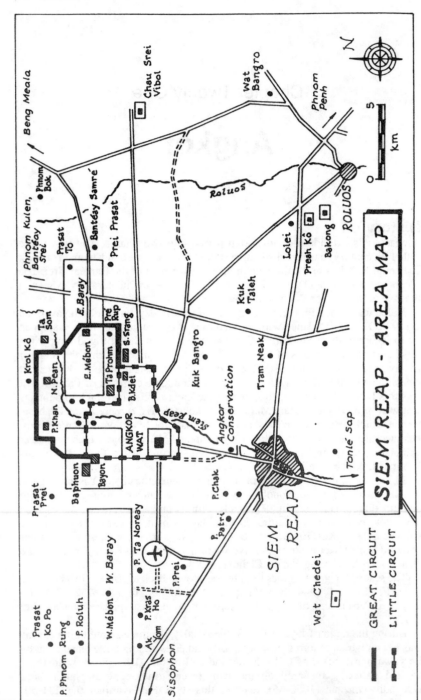

built the greatest and most famous temple of all, Angkor Wat. He dedicated it to Vishnu (rather than Shiva). Many 12th century minor temples such as the Beng Meala, Bantéay Samre, the Thommanon and Chau Say Tevoda had allied styles.

A period of decline set in after Angkor had been greatly damaged by the Cham in 1177. Jayavarman VII (1181-1200) partially subdued the Cham and built the monuments of Angkor Thom with its cult temple, the Bayon. On the central edifice, a rugged though beautifully sculpted mountain of masonry, he immortalised countless heads of the Boddhisattva, Lokesvara. During his reign, the great Buddhist monasteries of Ta Prohm (begun in 1186) and Prah Khan (begun in 1191) began to take shape.

At the end of his reign, a succession of wars against the Thais saw artistic achievement fall into decline. The destruction of Angkor followed in the mid-15th century but the glory of the Angkorian period still remains.

ANGKOR FROM THE HEAVENS

As the space shuttle *Endeavour* passed over Angkor, its Earth-imaging radar was switched on. This, with its ability to detect variations in texture and penetrate 5m into open, dry ground, was expected to show details as yet undiscovered.

Expectations were met.

Features never recognised before include linear tracks (probably paths or roads) and what is thought to be a dam. This latter may suggest that the irrigation system at Angkor was more complex than archaeologists have ever suspected.

Angkor gives up its secrets but slowly, and it is to be hoped that NASA may be persuaded to use this powerful tool again to speed up the process.

Getting there

The only safe way is to fly although land and river routes are possible. There are five direct flights daily from Phnom Penh to Siem Reap. These are very heavily booked because they are used extensively by international tour companies. One of the most reliable ways of being certain of a seat is to book a short tour with Phnom Penh Tourism or by booking the flight directly with them on their fax number: 855 23 26043. Any of the international tourist companies listed in the tourist programme section will book a flight for you but it will be more expensive than booking direct. Book your return Siem Reap flight several months in advance. The early morning flight is always full.

By the time you read this it is quite likely that there will be direct flights from Bangkok to Siem Reap. There are occasional special charter flights from Ho Chi Minh to Siem Reap. These cater exclusively for tour groups and are run by Saigon Tourist and Vietnam Tourism. It should also be pointed out that flights from Phnom Penh to Siem Reap can be cancelled without prior notice. This has happened to the writer on two occasions. Both times the reason for the cancellation was not given, but, at the time, the political situation was very unstable.

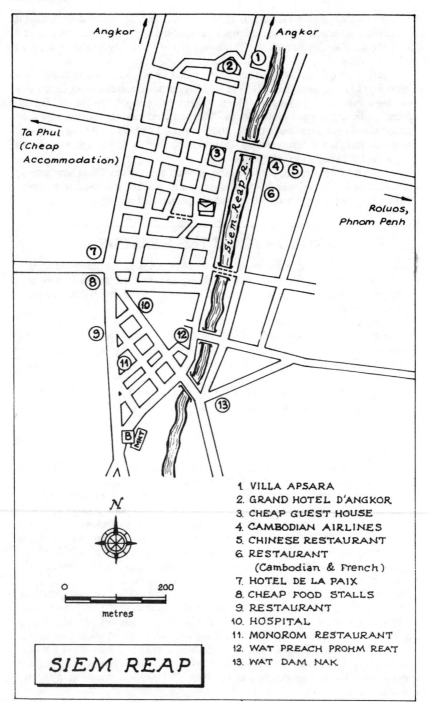

1. VILLA APSARA
2. GRAND HOTEL D'ANGKOR
3. CHEAP GUEST HOUSE
4. CAMBODIAN AIRLINES
5. CHINESE RESTAURANT
6. RESTAURANT
   (Cambodian & French)
7. HOTEL DE LA PAIX
8. CHEAP FOOD STALLS
9. RESTAURANT
10. HOSPITAL
11. MONOROM RESTAURANT
12. WAT PREACH PROHM REAT
13. WAT DAM NAK

SIEM REAP

Arriving at Siem Reap

When you buy your return ticket to Siem Reap you could be asked to purchase a permit to visit Angkor. This can cost US$120 for the first day's sightseeing which includes the services of a guide plus transport. At Siem Reap airport you will be met by a tourist bus run by Angkor Tourism. This will take you to your hotel or, if you are on a one-day tour, directly to Angkor. If you are travelling independently a taxi to Siem Reap will cost you US$3-5 depending on your bargaining power. Motorbike taxis are far cheaper if you are travelling light. Everyone staying in the Angkor region usually has a hotel reservation. Since well over 90% of the people on your flight will be travelling on an organised tour everything will be arranged for them including confirmation of the return flight. If you are travelling independently remember to confirm your return flight before leaving the airport. If you experience difficulty contact one of the Angkor tour representatives because, at the time of writing, the Kampuchean Airline office in Siem Reap was only open at irregular times. You may have to hand over your return ticket to the representative who will take details of your hotel reservation. If you don't have one, arrange to pick up your return ticket at the Grand Hotel reception. If you want a cheap hotel head for the town of Siem Reap which is 7km away. The Angkor Tourism bus will drop you off .

Accommodation

Cheap accommodation in Siem Reap

To accommodate the large numbers of visitors expected in the future, many small guest houses have been built at Siem Reap. These are located mainly at Ta Phul Village, Quarter 1. To reach this from the road which leads to the Siem Reap River, head along Route No 6 for 300m towards the airport. Recommended are **Mahogany, Mum's** and **Daves**. All are in the US$10 bracket and have been renovated to suit foreigners.

Recommended

Guest House, at 260 Ta Phul Village. They charge US$5 for a double room with a shared bath. Rooms with a private bath are available at extra cost. Meals are available on request. They speak good French at this establishment. They will rent out bikes, motorbikes (US$5/day) and also sell fuel (700 riel/litre) and maps of the Angkor area.

Sun Rise Guesthouse, 592 Kroum 4, Phnom Wat Bou (near market). Good standard rooms for US$10.

Expensive category

Ta Prohm Hotel, southern side of Siem Reap on the road to Phnom Krom; tel: 855 15 913130. A luxury establishment built to cater for well-heeled tourists. It is usually fully booked by Diethelm Travel Cambodia and Phnom Penh Tourism who use it for tour groups. All 58 rooms are very modern, have air-conditioning, satellite TV and mini-bars. It is the best on offer in the Angkor region. Singles sell for US$55 and doubles US$70. Rooms are bookable through Diethelm Travel Cambodia Ltd; tel: 855 23 26 648; fax: 855 23 26 676. Most international operators such as Regent, Orbitours and Phoenix Travel Services (HK) can book this hotel.

Diamond Hotel, Vithei Achasva Road. Another favourite with tour groups, this second class establishment offers modern amenities including air-conditioned rooms, fridge and hot and cold running water. Rooms cost US$40 for singles and US$55 for doubles. They are bookable through Diethelm Travel Cambodia Ltd.

Bantéay Srei Hotel. Another new establishment which has been opened near the Siem Reap River to cater for the increasing number of tour groups. Amenities and prices are similar to those of the Diamond Hotel. Owned by Bopha Angkor Tourism, this is one of the best in Siem Reap. It has 55 tastefully furnished deluxe guest rooms which are spacious and air-conditioned with hot and cold running water. They have mini-bars, refrigerators and multi-channel satellite TV. The restaurant serves Cambodian, Western and Chinese cuisine. There is lively entertainment weekly. It can be booked directly at Bopha Angkor Tourism (BAT), Phnom Penh Head Office, No 797 Bis Monivong Boulevard; tel: 855 23 27933/62069; fax: 855 23 27406/27933/62069.

Bayon Hotel. Fairly central, overlooking the Siem Reap River; tel/fax: 855 15 911769. Rooms are all air-conditioned and clean. Singles cost US$40, doubles US$55.

Hotel de la Paix, Sivatha Street, Sangkat II; tel/fax: 855 15 912322. This is located by walking south along the Siem Reap River from Route No 6. After 400m you will reach a footbridge. The hotel is 300m directly west. Formerly decayed and unattractive, this three-storey establishment underwent complete refurbishment during the 1992-3 period. It is now fairly presentable and offers modern facilities. Rooms cost US$30 for singles and US$40 for doubles. Cheaper rooms are available with bargaining.

Bopha Angkor Hotel. Yet another new one which is worth checking out. It features 22 modern rooms which can be booked on tel: 855 23 26330/24596; fax: 855 23 26330. Prices and facilities are similar to the Diamond Hotel.

Accommodation at Angkor

These are all in the expensive category and, except for the Baray, cater exclusively for well-heeled tourist clientele.

The Grand Hotel d'Angkor; tel: 855 15 911292; fax: 855 15 911291.
This plush establishment has catered for the rich and the famous since it opened in 1928. 62 rooms, all air-conditioned, have satellite TV and have been extensively renovated. Renovations by the new owners who took over in 1992 are still continuing. Eventually, after hundreds of thousands of pounds have been spent, it should be restored to its former glory. Accommodation is getting more expensive all the time. A single costs US$40 and a double US$55. Expect to pay much more towards the end of 1995. The restaurant here is exceptional. Lunch and dinner costs US$10 but is well worth it.

Villa Apsara. This is directly across the road leading to Angkor Wat from the Grand Hotel d'Angkor. It is, in fact, part of it, with the same telephone and fax numbers. These bungalows are classified by tour agencies as Grade A accommodation, which, naturally, means they cost more. They are also used by visiting dignitaries. Expect to pay US$60 for a double room.

Baray Hotel. Situated on the same road as above between the Minefield Bar and Solid Rock Cafe. Rooms are nothing to write home about and cost US$25 (only 12 are available).

Eating

The **Neak Pean Restaurant and Bar.** This is a very friendly establishment offering good Cambodian food and excellent vegetable curries. If you stay there talking in the evening the management will very often send a complimentary fruit basket to your table. Recommended.

Steak and chips is served at the new **Minefield Bar** near the Baray Hotel.

You can get Chinese food at the **Morodom Restaurant,** 300m south of the Hotel de la Paix and at the **Bayon** on Route No 6. The **Sampheap Restaurant,** close to the bridge near the Grand Hotel d'Angkor, serves Chinese food.

There are food stalls opposite the Hotel de la Paix and the Covered Central Market sells an excellent selection of take away food suitable for your Angkor excursions. Plain foods such as peanuts, bread and cheese are readily available. To get to the Covered Market head south along Route No 6 for 1½ km towards the Roluos group of temples.

Recently opened is the **Green House Restaurant** at Ta Phul Village, Quarter 1 near the guest houses. This serves excellent Thai food at reasonable prices. Another Thai restaurant has opened near the Diamond Hotel.

Travel agents in Siem Reap

Angkor Tours, No 282, Phum Vihear Chin, Siem Reap;
tel/fax: 855 233 62169.
Apsara Tours, No 81, Mondol 1, Sk 2, Siem Reap; tel: 913902.
Bophar Angkor Tour, No 089, Phum Salar Kanseing, Street 2,
Siem Reap; tel: 855 15 913839.
Diethelm Travel, No 4, Street 6, Sk 2, Siem Reap; tel: 855 15 12888.
East West Group Co Ltd, No 0147, Street Phum Wat Dam Nak,
Sk Siem Reap 4, Siem Reap; tel: 855 15 913629.
Paradise Angkor Wat Tour, No 126, Phum Slor Kram, Sk 1, Siem Reap;
tel: 855 15 914128/855 23 27106; fax: 855 23 27106.

Angkor Wat

VISITING ANGKOR

Cheaper permits

If you want to book a tour with a guide and transport head for the tourist office near the Villa Apsara. They change US$30 for a car with driver for one day. At the entrance gate you will be met by officials who hand out lists of visiting options. Permits are issued according to which option you choose. You will be asked to tick the temples you want to visit and will then be charged accordingly. The most expensive option costs US$71, for this you can visit all the temples. Needless to say, you will not meet any backpackers around Angkor who have paid this price. For four days you can get away with paying only US$41, which is still expensive, but considering that you will see the greatest architectural wonders of the world, it is very good value. If you are a hard-nosed haggler and are travelling with a friend, you may be able to get a joint ticket for the full tour for US$75, but it will mean that you have to stay together. One day permits cost just US$13. For some reason the Roluos group of temples can be visited free (one backpacker reported that he was charged US$5). If you want to be selective it will cost you US$15 to visit Bayon and surrounding temples, US$13 for Angkor Wat, US$10 for Bantéay Srei. Diethelm Travel charge US$56 for a day out at Bantéay Srei for two.

Getting around

Roads around Angkor are getting better all the time, in expectation of increased tourist traffic, so getting around will become easier.

It is worth following the order given in this guide for a grand tour of Angkor. This has been recommended by Phnom Penh Tourism and takes into account the position of the sun, which is ideal for photographers. Contrary to popular belief, you do not have to hire a guide to go everywhere with you, unless you have booked everything via Phnom Penh Tourism or Angkor Tourism. One will be waiting for you each day in the lobby of the Grand Hotel d'Angkor. If you don't use the services of a guide, a compass and a map are essential. Most of the stalls which have erupted all over the place in recent years will be able to sell you one. Most also have a copy of Henri Parmentier's guide, which is well worth purchasing. The best way of getting around is to hire a motorbike in Siem Reap for US$5/day. Fuel inside the Angkor complex is sold in bottles for 800 riels/litre, 100 riels more than if purchased elsewhere. Once you have negotiated a permit deal at the entrance gate, it is necessary to use this gate everyday. Wherever you go, take care, DO NOT WANDER OFF THE BEATEN TRACK. 'Beware of the mines' signs sometimes appear along the tour circuit. If you see one keep well away from the area, some tourists have been stupid enough to steal them as souvenirs! To get around the full circuit you will need at least four days.

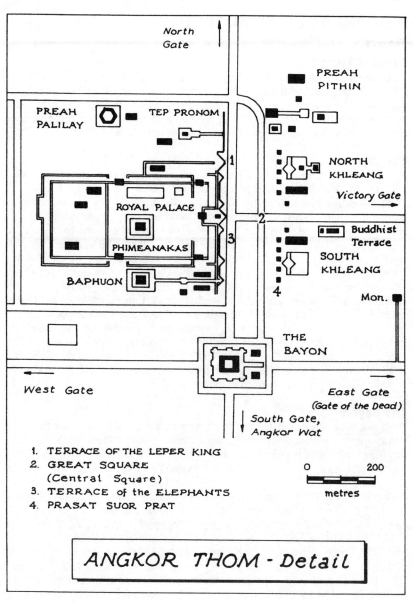

North Gate

PREAH PITHIN

PREAH PALILAY

TEP PRONOM

NORTH KHLEANG

Victory Gate

ROYAL PALACE

PHIMEANAKAS

BAPHUON

Buddhist Terrace

SOUTH KHLEANG

Mon.

THE BAYON

West Gate

East Gate
(Gate of the Dead)

South Gate, Angkor Wat

1. TERRACE OF THE LEPER KING
2. GREAT SQUARE
   (Central Square)
3. TERRACE of the ELEPHANTS
4. PRASAT SUOR PRAT

0   200
metres

ANGKOR THOM - Detail

A GRAND TOUR OF ANGKOR
Day 1
Angkor Thom

To obtain a panoramic view of King Jayavarman VII's great royal city head for Phnom Bakeng and climb to the top. You will see that the whole complex is surrounded by a huge moat which is now overgrown with grass. Directly to the north is the spectacular South Gate, the entrance to one of the most sublime examples of human achievement seen in South East Asia.

The Giant's Causeway

Spanning a 100m moat, this is just one example of the five causeways which lead to Angkor Thom. Directly ahead, the South Gate looks particularly attractive when highlighted by the early morning light. Its central tower is topped by giant faces, effigies of the Buddhist deity, Lokesvara. As you approach you will catch the stare of 54 giants which make up the balustrades of the bridges on both sides. The guardian spirits of the underworld are on your right and the genies of the heavens are on your left. Both are struggling with a giant *nāga* serpent. This theme, known as 'the Churning of the Sea of Milk' you will see immaculately depicted on a massive stone panorama on Angkor Wat's first corridor. Take a careful look at the balustrade figures, each has a different facial expression. The gods (*asuras*) on the left look calm and composed while the demons (*devas*) on the right have intimidating stares. All according to Hindu mythology are involved in the creation of the world. (For a more detailed explanation see bas-relief at Angkor Wat). The eclectic nature of the sculptures is further enhanced by reliefs to either side of the entrance, where the God Indra is depicted riding a three-headed elephant.

The Bayon

Built exactly at the geometric centre of Angkor Thom, this important temple is extravagantly adorned with sculpture ornamentation. Words such as 'awe-inspiring' and 'extraordinary' are totally inadequate when it comes to describing what surely must be one of the finest examples of Cambodian architecture. Every one of its 54 towers is sculpted with four giant faces, effigies of the Buddhist deity, Lokesvara (Avalokitesvara). Many authorities say that the images all bear a resemblance to their builder, Jaravarman VII. In its prime, early in the 13th century, it must have been very magical to have stood anywhere within the complex and glanced up at the numerous intact smiling faces of the god-king. These days a few are still well preserved although, inevitably, because of the soft sandstone used, some of the gopuras have suffered structural damage. During the Thai invasion, the outer corridor was considerably damaged and the roof which fell in has not been replaced. This extends for 1,200m (1,320 yards) and has countless bas-reliefs which materialise in stone – scenes from Khmer history.

As you enter through the south gate, turn to your left along the outer corridor and you will pass reliefs showing temple guardians and dancers. Stretching for a long way along the wall on your right is just one immaculate example of a three-tiered battle scene. As you circumnavigate the complex you will be reminded of the battles against the Cham. Some military frescoes show war

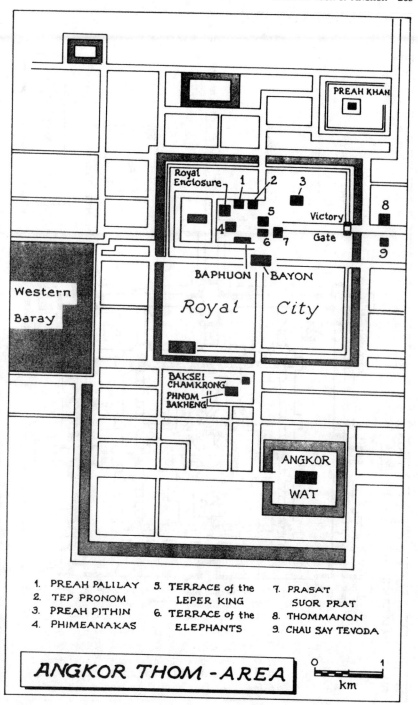

1. PREAH PALILAY
2. TEP PRONOM
3. PREAH PITHIN
4. PHIMEANAKAS
5. TERRACE of the LEPER KING
6. TERRACE of the ELEPHANTS
7. PRASAT SUOR PRAT
8. THOMMANON
9. CHAU SAY TEVODA

ANGKOR THOM -AREA

0   km   1

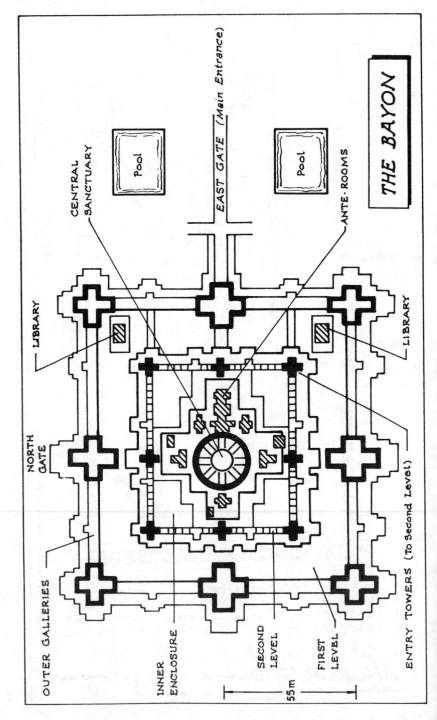

THE BAYON

EAST GATE (Main Entrance)

Pool

Pool

CENTRAL SANCTUARY

ANTE-ROOMS

LIBRARY

LIBRARY

NORTH GATE

OUTER GALLERIES

INNER ENCLOSURE

SECOND LEVEL

FIRST LEVEL

ENTRY TOWERS (To Second Level)

55 m

1. BATTLE SCENE WITH WAR ELEPHANTS
2. ELEPHANT PROCESSION
3. (BADLY DAMAGED)
4. ANIMAL PROCESSIONS & SCENES FROM EVERYDAY LIFE
5. ROYAL PROCESSION
6. BATTLE: KHMER vs. CHAM
7. RIOTING
8. TEMPLE CONSTRUCTION, ELEPHANT PARADES & MAN HUNTED BY TIGER
9. BATTLE SCENES
10. NAVAL BATTLES, FISHING, CRAFTS
11. SOLDIERS MARCHING & SCENES FROM EVERYDAY LIFE
12. ROYAL PROCESSION
13. LEGEND of the LEPER KING
14. SHIVA
15. ROYAL PROCESSIONS

16. SCENES FROM THE MAHABHARATA
17. SHIVA, PÁRVATI & KÁMA
18. SERVANTS PRESENT OFFERINGS TO THE KING
19. CHURNING OF THE SEA OF MILK
20. PALACE SCENE
21. TEMPLE CONSTRUCTION
22. APSÁRAS DANCING FOR THE KING
23. VISHNU ON HIS GARUDA
24. A TIGER DEVOURS A MAN; VISHNU WITH APSÁRAS
25. DANCE OF THE APSÁRAS
26. SOLDIERS & MUSICIANS
27. AN ARMY ON THE MARCH, THE COMMANDER ON AN ELEPHANT
28. CHAM & KHMER SOLDIERS
29. HUNTING & ANIMAL SCENES

OUTER GALLERIES ⎫
INNER GALLERIES ⎬

(VIEWING ROUTE: ANTICLOCKWISE)

THE BAYON – Distribution of Bas-reliefs

pirogues, infantry marches, charging war elephants, wounded soldiers, the clashing of armies and even beheadings – all meticulously portrayed in stone. One of the nicest examples is a low relief showing a Cham naval fleet in the process of attacking Angkor. Another very distinctive relief shows elephants supporting an infantry advance.

If you have plenty of time, take a look at the incredible details seen on every figure. Khmer warriors are depicted grasping javelins, every finger is in the right position, you can even see the embroidery patterns on their tunics. Apart from war scenes, the walls of the outer corridor are also covered in reliefs depicting boar fights, hunters looking for storks, circuses, a river teeming with fish, the birth of a baby and many peaceful customs. There are many more along the walls surrounding the inner sanctuary which predominantly have a legend theme.

One of the most remarkable features of the Bayon is its near-perfect symmetry. All the towers and gopuras have a cruciform ground plan. The third storey has a cross-shaped terrace which supports 20 towers. Right at the centre, the tallest tower extends to a height of 42m, the highest point of the temple-mountain.

Before you leave, see if you can find various scenes from every day Khmer life, the most famous are the argument, cooking, moving goods, the market, tending the sick and blowing a charcoal fire. As you approach the northern exit observe the delicately sculptured *apsarās* (celestial dancers) on every lintel and the upright *dvārapalas* (temple guardians) on either side of the exit door.

The Terrace of the Elephants
Continue in a northerly direction from the north exit of the Bayon. After about 200m you pass the entry to the Baphuon, which is on your left. About 50m further on is the Terrace of the Elephants. This was built towards the end of

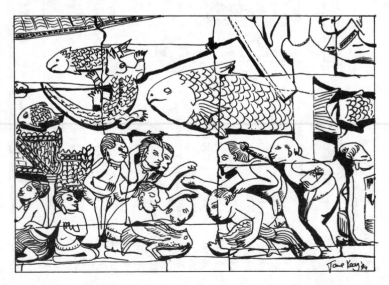

Detail of Bas relief, The Bayon

the 12th century. Notice the herd of elephants, some of which are indented with holes which have been carved on the walls. The terrace stretches for around 250m and has three platforms projecting towards the road. Have a look around the side of each platform to see the elephant trunk supports. On the front of each platform, *garudas* appear to be supporting the upper level which is topped by lions and *nagas*. It was the intention of Suryavarman I, the builder, that the palace reception halls, conference rooms and court houses which once stood on the terrace should appear to float to the heavens, held aloft by the garudas. The terrace runs along the east face of the former Royal Enclosure.

The Baphuon

This is entered just south of the southernmost platform of the Terrace of the Elephants. This is very often neglected by tourist groups because of its bad state of preservation. Built by Udayadityavarman II (1050-66), this is another god-mountain, a pyramidal representation of Mount Meru. It is thought that this five-storey step pyramid once reached a height of over 50m. Sadly, the top tier has not survived. Its sandstone base extends for 120m and is 100m wide. Restoration was attempted by a skilful team led by Bernard-Philippe Groslier but halted immediately the Khmer Rouge began their heart-breaking reign of terror.

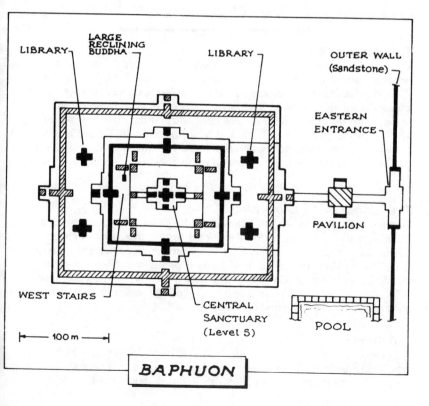

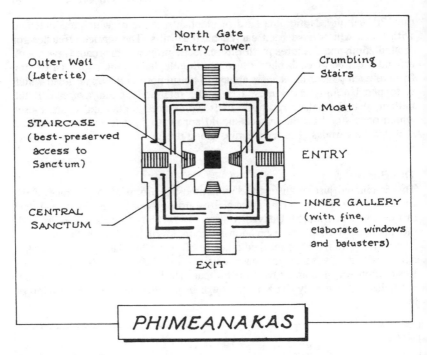

Diagram labels:
- North Gate Entry Tower
- Outer Wall (Laterite)
- Crumbling Stairs
- Moat
- STAIRCASE (best-preserved access to Sanctum)
- ENTRY
- CENTRAL SANCTUM
- INNER GALLERY (with fine, elaborate windows and balusters)
- EXIT

PHIMEANAKAS

The Phimeanakas

Lying at the centre of the Royal Enclosure, this pyramidal temple-mountain is believed to have been started during the reign of Rājendravarman II (Sivolaka) (944-68). The laterite base, which, when complete, extended to three tiers, was added during the reign of Jayavarman V (968-1001). It is known that he favoured the use of laterite from studies of other edifices built during his reign. The sandstone gallery which marked a distinct shift in Khmer architectural design was added later, during the reign of Suryavarman I (1002-50). Compared to a lot of temples at Angkor, this, with its roughly hewn blocks, is rather crude looking.

The Terrace of the Leper King

Situated slightly north of the Terrace of the Elephants, this takes its name from the enigmatic seated figure of King Yasovarman, Angkor's founder, which dominates this structure. Although it is not proven, he is thought to have died from leprosy. On the terrace wall he is depicted alongside his concubines, mandarins and court officials. Masses of seated celestial maidens adorn the front wall. They are arranged in five tiers. The 7m high terrace is believed to have once been used for ceremonial cremation.

Tep Pronom

This cross-shaped terrace lies at the base of a Buddhist pagoda which has now completely decayed. It lies 200m west of the Terrace of the Leper King, close to a large Buddha statue. A private wooden Buddhist monastery is close by.

Preah Palilay Temple

This lies beyond the foundations of the Tep Pronom in a square which is directly north of the Royal Palace. This highly decorative temple, shaded by trees, was built during the second half of the 12th century. Only the central part of this structure remains intact. Seated directly in front of it is a remarkably preserved Buddha encrusted in lichen. To either side of it are two highly ornamental doorways.

ANGKOR WAT

Nothing spells out more clearly the absolute genius of Khmer craftsmanship than this huge temple-mountain. Representing the zenith of human ingenuity, it is unparalleled by anything else in the world. Invariably, Khmer temples face towards the east with their main entrance on the eastern side. Angkor Wat is an exception, it faces west and its main entrance is on the western side. For this reason it is best visited in the afternoon when the sun is in the best position for photography.

A city within a city

Just before your plane comes into land at Siem Reap airport, take the opportunity to get a glimpse of just how colossal Angkor Wat really is. From the air you can see a vast moat which has a perimeter of 16km. It creates a giant rectangle which surrounds parkland covering an estimated one million square metres. At its centre is another rectangular moat which surrounds a distinctive temple-mountain sanctuary. This triple-terraced masterpiece, topped by five dramatic towers and surrounded by rectangular galleries and cruciform courts, is the 'Holy City' of Angkor. This is symmetrically arranged within a walled rectangle measuring 1,500m long and 1,300m wide. Originally the vast area surrounding it contained the 'Royal City'. where court officials, dignitaries and religious leaders resided. Now, nothing remains of their dwellings or palaces and the land on which they once stood has been largely reclaimed by the jungle.

An aerial view of the "Holy City" gives one an idea of its pyramidal geometry, which is symbolic of Mount Meru, the sacred mountain home of the gods. One can also appreciate the three-dimensional grandeur of this enormous monument, a miracle in stone which arose in the heart of the Cambodian jungle. In all, it is estimated that 350,000m^3 of rock was transported over 40km from Kulen to satisfy the ambitions of the god-king Suryavarman II. Tens of thousands of workmen laboured for over 37 years before it was finally finished.

The western entrance

The western entrance to Angkor Wat is just over 7km (4½ miles) from Siem Reap and about 16km (10 miles) from the airport. It is reached via Route 29. This follows the course of the Siem Reap River until it branches directly west and runs parallel with the southern part of the wide moat which surrounds Angkor Wat. It then heads directly north past the main entrance and causeway. Photographers who would like to get a shot of the main temple complex surrounded by tropical jungle should continue north as far as Phnom Bakheng. On a clear, sunny day from its summit you can see for miles. It is even better later in the day when the sunlight is not so harsh.

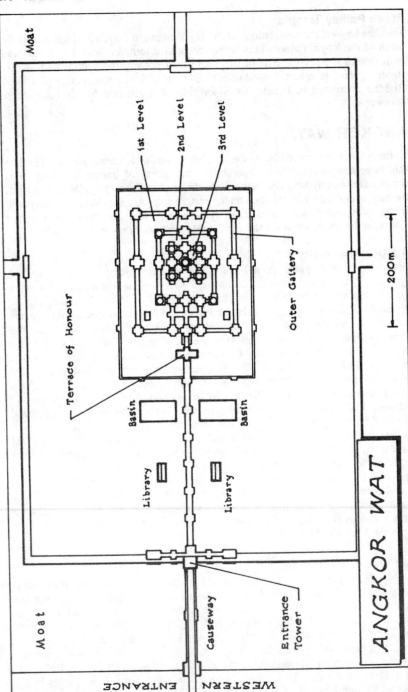

ANGKOR WAT

There is still a stall selling refreshments near the main entrance. It is recommended that you should take along a few bottles of water. It can get extremely hot inside the main temple and with humidity levels as high as they get in Cambodia you will dehydrate very quickly. Many tourists like to pose for their photographs at this point alongside one of the crouching lions. The moat is crossed heading directly east over a 200m long, 11.6m wide sandstone causeway. This is flanked on both sides by an ornate balustrade, crowned in places with *nāga* (serpent) statues. Ahead is the imposing western gateway to either side of which an impressive vaulted gallery extends towards the north and south. Inside the gate tower of the entrance pavilion is a large sandstone statue of Vishnu.

Entering the Holy City

From the western entrance to the Royal City another causeway, 8m wide and 360m long, extends as far as the entry steps to the 'Holy City'. Paved with irregularly shaped sandstone slabs and bordered by sculpted parapets, this terminates at a triple-towered gateway. The buildings to either side of the causeway, about half way down, are the libraries, which are 40m long and have a cruciform layout. These can be entered by four median staircases. Directly to the east of them there are two large, rectangular basins, often filled with water, 65m long and 50m wide, reflecting the gopura on very still days. As you get nearer you can see that the 'Holy City' is built on an elevated platform. The front causeway provides access to the column-supported cruciform terrace. During the early 1960s, when Cambodia was one of the most popular tourist destinations in the far-east, temple dancers would perform the Royal Ballet in front of the entrance to the 'Holy City'.

The Outer Gallery

Vast galleries, their half-vaulted roofs supported on the outside by stone pillars and on the inside by walls, extend for 800m around the perimeter of the Holy City. Along its inner wall you will find vast sandstone canvases which display 2m storied friezes depicting Hindu epics such as the Mahabharata and Ramayana. These fine sandstone 'frescoes' cover in total nearly 1,200m² and are only interrupted at entrances and on corners.

Bas-reliefs

Don't fail to walk around the whole of the Outer Gallery. Start along the southern part of the western gallery (to your right when you are facing the main entrance). On your circumnavigation you will come across eight distinct sculptured panels, most of which are 160m long. The pavilions on the southwest and northwest corners are well worth examining in detail.

South section West Gallery

A right turn from the main entrance will bring you to the south section of the West Gallery. Here the reliefs, which reach to a height of 2.7m, show in detail the Battle of Kurukshetra, an Indian province so vividly described in the Mahabharata. The epic story of the war between Kauravas and Pandavas is immortalised in stone. If you start at the left of the panel, you will see Kauravas and a huge army consisting of foot soldiers, men on horseback and elephants advancing on another which is led by Pandava who wears a pointed headpiece.

In the centre of the panel the battle is in full swing. According to Indian Vishnu mythology, the two armies are attempting to restore the balance between what is good and what is evil. It all stems from the Bhagavad Gita, Hindu religious teachings, which, when chanted in temples, helps to maintain universal homeostasis. If you examine the panel very carefully you will see Bisma, the commander of the Kauravas army (towards the entrance) severely wounded by a Pandavas arrow. His loyal followers surround him and try to give assistance but all is in vain. On the other side of the panel (towards the centre) the leader of the Pandavas, Arjuna, is being urged on by Lord Krishna (Vishnu's reincarnation), who rides on a war chariot beside him. Notice that the relief is arranged in tiers with the infantry troops on the bottom and the wat elephants and officers above. Towards the southwest corner, in places where it's not worn too smooth, you can find various figures of Vishnu to whom the temple is dedicated.

Southwest Corner Pavilion

Before proceeding in an anticlockwise direction around the outer galleries, proceed in a clockwise direction around the corner pavilion.

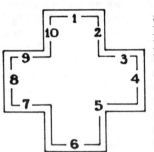

Starting at 1 on the cruciform ground plan, look above the door. Here there is a relief from the Reamker, the Cambodian version of the Ramayana. A golden stag (the demon Marica) is being slaughtered by Rāma after he attempts to abduct his wife Sita.

On panel 2 directly to the right, the guardian of shepherds, Krishna, is sheltering them from a torrential rainstorm created by Indra. He shows off his great power by lifting up Mount Govardhana as an umbrella.

Panel 3 shows a water festival, an event which has considerable importance even now in the Khmer calendar.

Look above the door at position 4 to see an offering ceremony.

Further south at position 5 there is a fierce fight depicted between the monkey king, Sugriva, and Vali his brother (top). Below this, Vali is killed by Rama's arrow.

Also above the door at position 6, a demon is being murdered.

At 7 there is a lovely relief of Shiva sitting beside his loving his wife Pārvati. The mountain depicted is Kailāsa.

At 8 just above the door is an indistinct relief, thought to be Krishna pulling at the roots of a tree.

Directly north at 9 a chameleon or some kind of lizard (representing Rāvana) enters Indra's palace.

Position 10 shows a small version of the Bagavata-Pourana, the epic Indian story of the 'Churning of the Sea of Milk' which is displayed in all its glory along the east gallery.

West section South Gallery

Proceeding from southwest pavilion in an anticlockwise direction, you will enter the south gallery (west section). This panel is of immense historical importance. A masterly creation in stone shows Suryavarman II (also known as King Parama

Vishnouloka), creator of this grand edifice. In one relief he is seated on his throne protected by *nāga* serpents. War tactics are being discussed with troops while his devoted friend, Srivarddha, sits by his side. On a lower level, below the king, there is a regal procession and the army is being reinforced by soldiers coming down the mountainside.

Further on, in an easterly direction along the panel, the king is standing on an elephant, shielded from the sun by 15 umbrellas held by servants. Lord Vishnu is depicted riding a *garuda*. Military commanders mounted on elephants can be seen in the parade heading towards the advancing army. The king urges them on by waving his sword in their direction. The magnificent procession, which consists of scores of standard bearers, musicians and jesters, moves forward in a lively fashion. On the lower part of the panel are more troops, some of which are on horseback.

The final part of this very historical panel shows Brahmans and holy men transporting the holy flame to the battle site. Here it will ensure victory against the Cham. Mercenaries (Thai troops recognised by their plaited hair, thin moustaches and pleated *sampot*) join the march against the Khmer's sworn enemy. Part of the scene is missing due to artillery shell damage.

Eastern section South Gallery

This three-tier masterpiece (66m relief) is a representation of the 37 heavens and 32 hells recorded in the Hindu epic the Ramayana. The panel (C on the plan) begins with an immaculate depiction of the Day of Judgement. People who in life have not followed the right path are being punished while those that have, are being rewarded. Look out for the God of Hell, Yama, who is in the centre. He is riding on a buffalo waving around his many arms. The figures by his side are his trusty servants, Shitragupta and Dharma who stand among the numerous dead (lower tier). Above are numerous *apsarās* and several *Garudas*. The top tier depicts Yama's judgement over who enters hell and who enters heaven. Some of the panel has been badly damaged and crudely filled with cement.

South section East Gallery

This 50m panel (D in plan) is sumptuously decorated with the most significant of all the Angkor bas-reliefs. The corbelled vault has been removed for restoration purposes. It depicts the Hindu creation myth, the 'Churning of the Sea of Milk'. On the far left is the 21-headed figure of the leader of the underworld, Ravana. In the centre is the Hindu God Vishnu and on the far right is the Monkey God, Hanuman. They are grasping a *Vāsuki*, a *nāga* serpent which is being used like a rope to churn the Ocean of Milk, the source of the *amrta*, the elixir of life. Both gods *devas* and demons *asuras* assist in the stirring process. According to the story of the Bagavata-Pourana, an epic from the Hindu Ramayana, the *Vasuki* is forced to vomit poison which, if allowed to mingle with the waves, would undoubtedly kill the *devas* and *asuras*. This is prevented by Shiva who has been ordered by Brahma to drink the lethal potion. Once he does so the *amrta* is free to gush forth. With all this disturbance going on, the sea is in turmoil. Creatures such as huge fish and ugly monsters are forced to rise to the surface. To prevent the *asuras* claiming the elixir for themselves, Lord Vishnu, who has been reincarnated as the beautiful Maya, intervenes. The upper tier depicts the flight of the *apsarās* born from the churning foam which is the ambrosia of life.

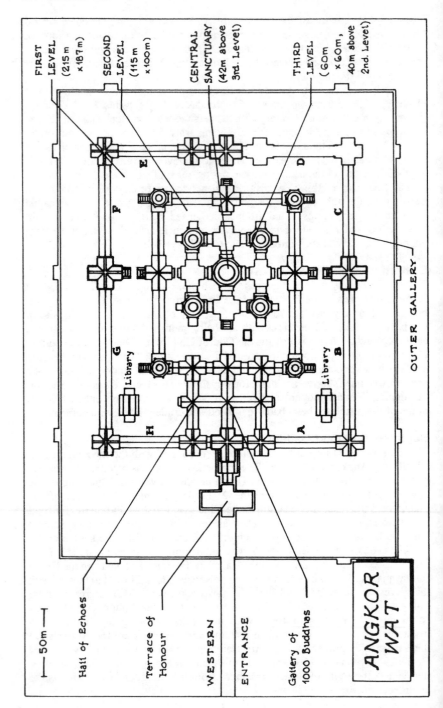

FIRST LEVEL (215m x 187m)

SECOND LEVEL (115m x 100m)

CENTRAL SANCTUARY (42m above 3rd. Level)

THIRD LEVEL (60m x 60m, 40m above 2nd. Level)

OUTER GALLERY

Library

Library

50m

Hall of Echoes

Terrace of Honour

WESTERN ENTRANCE

Gallery of 1000 Buddhas

ANGKOR WAT

You can recognise the *asuras* who are assisting Ravana on the left by their piercing stares and evil looking expression. The *devas* who are assisting Hanuman on the right have appealing expressions and cylindrical hair styles. Look carefully and you will see Indra and his three-headed elephant and Laksmi, the goddess of beauty.

Northern section East Gallery

Continuing in an anticlockwise direction you will enter the northern section of the east gallery. Slightly crude workmanship and a change of style suggest that the bas-reliefs here were added at a later date, perhaps as late as the 15th or 16th century. They depict the Hindu god Vishnu, mounted on a *Garuda*, fighting off demons (*asuras*) who are attempting to possess the ambrosia of immortality. Vishnu is seen killing the demons while his soldiers on horseback – or riding peacocks – charge the demon's chariots, which are pulled by monsters.

Eastern section Northern Gallery

This panel (F on the plan) is not nearly as distinct as those already described. It depicts an attack on a city which Krishna, on the back of a *garuda* leads, followed closely by the God of Fire (Agni) who is on the back of a rhinoceros. A portion of the relief shows the *garuda* putting out a huge fire which has engulfed the city, while the demon, Bana, comes to investigate from another direction.

Western section Northern Gallery

The bas-reliefs on this panel (G on the plan) are again very indistinct. They represent a battle between demons *asuras* and gods *devas*. In all, 21 gods are shown. The person with the bow and arrow is the God of Riches, Kubera, who is riding on the shoulders of a supernatural being, a *yaksa*. The warrior riding a peacock is the multi-headed God of War, Skanda. Other gods which can be recognised include Yama, the God of Death, who is riding in a chariot pulled by bulls, and Vishnu on his mount *Garuda*. The god standing on the five-headed *nāga* is the God of Water and the one riding the sacred goose *hamsa* is Brahmā, the Creator. Shiva is seen with a bow and arrow while the God of the Sun, Surya, speeds past in a chariot pulled by stallions.

The Northwest Corner Pavilion

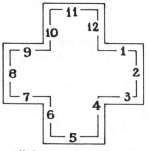

This is well worth examining thoroughly since it has some remarkable reliefs. Start at number 1 on the cruciform ground plan. The reliefs are on three levels. The lower tier shows nine *devas*. Recognisable are Brahma, the Creator, mounted on *hamsa* his sacred goose, Surya the Sun God, with his chariot pulled by stallions and Kubera, the God of Riches, riding on the shoulders of a *yaksa*.

The middle tier consists of a flight of heavenly maidens *apsarās*. The top tier shows Lord Vishnu reclining on Ananta, a serpent.

The eastern side, panel 2, shows Rama and Laksmana his brother on the left and the monkey king, Sugriva, to their right.

This panel (3 on the plan) shows Vishnu himself and as his reincarnation, Krishna. They are at the head of an army which is returning from Mount Maniparvata. Soldiers transport the remains of an *asura*. The archer shown in area 4 on the plan is Rama. His wife Sita is also depicted. You have to look above the door to see the relief in position 5 on the plan. There is a battle scene between Rama and his brother Laksmana who are fighting with a cruel looking monster.

At position 6 on the plan there is a lovely bas-relief of Lord Vishnu who is surrounded by heavenly maidens (*apsarās*).

In position 7, Sita, much beloved in the tales of the Ramayana, is talking to the Monkey God, Hanumăn, in a wooded area. He presents her with a ring to show his great affection for her.

High above the door in position 8 is Rāma once again with his brother Laksmana. They are completely surrounded by a monkey troop.

At position 9 there is a gorgeous relief of a chariot which is being pulled by the geese. Rāma, after a great victory, is returning to Ayodhya, the kingdom over which he is the monarch.

The relief in position 10 is badly damaged.

You will need to look hard above the door at position 11 on the plan. The relief, which is indistinct, shows Sita, Rāma's wife, who is being abducted.

It is not totally clear what is shown in the relief at position 12.

Northern section West Gallery
This should certainly not be missed. It is at its finest just before sunset when it takes on a wonderful golden glow. The panel (H in the gallery plan) shows the battle between the demon king, Rāvana, who is frequently seen in bas-reliefs, trying to abduct Rāma's wife, Sita. The Battle of Lanka depicted is well recorded in the Rāmayāna. Look at the fine detail of the monkey soldiers who are prepared to fight to the death for Rāvana. Equally well-carved are the *rāksasas* and Rāvana himself who is depicted with 10 heads and 20 arms. Further down towards the western entrance there is wonderful bas-relief showing Rāvana's war chariot being drawn along by fierce lions. Suddenly they come to an abrupt standstill when one of them is grabbed by Nala, the monkey.

Once you have completed the circuit, go around once more. The bas-reliefs at Angkor Wat will remain in your memory for ever.

The Cruciform Courtyard
This lies just beyond the central main entrance. Consisting of two finely architectured galleries which cross one another at right angles, the courtyard exhibits a precise symmetry. Each corner has an ablution tank in accordance with Hindu custom. Small library buildings with high plinths face the entrance. Before you take a look at these, observe the exquisite panoply of *apsarās* (heavenly maidens) which decorate the courtyard galleries. Note the variety of head-dresses, drapery and facial expressions. Some smile adoringly, others appear to be more sexually alluring as if to attempt to satisfy the carnal desires of the onlooker. The enchanting beauty of *apsarās* is eulogised in some depth in the Mahabharata Hindu epic, here it is immortalised in stone tapestries by 12th century Khmer carvers.

The central temple is built on three levels, the Cruciform Courtyard is on the first level.

The second stage

Following the same west-east axis one proceeds upwards gradually rising a further 6.4m on an external staircase. You will observe that the gallery encircling this level has been blocked off since it is a sacred area originally intended only for priests. Notice the bare nature of the walls. This extends for 115m and is 100m wide, it supports much of the tremendous weight of the central towers.

The third stage

This 60m^2 structure is accessed via three staircases on each side. Originally only the king and the high priest were allowed to climb the 12 staircases to the sacred sanctum of the gods. Four lotus-bud shaped towers surround the massive central tower, which is firmly buttressed by four strong porches. This soars to a height of 65m (42m higher than the upper level).

Once you have climbed up the 40 steps to the third level you will have a tremendous view of the general architectural layout of this incredible edifice. Observe the cruciform gopuras, cross-gabled roofs and ornamental mouldings of the traceried windows which have stone balusters which look just like they have been carved from wood. Look above you at the detailed carvings on the central prasat, charming *apsarās* will smile down at you from almost every level. Restoration experts have estimated that there are around 1,700 of these heavenly maidens scattered throughout the complex.

The large sanctuary on the third level would have originally contained the great image of Vishnu which was installed around 1131. In the late 12th century, however, this was replaced by four Buddhas because King Jayavarman was converted to Buddhism after Angkor had been sacked by the Cham in 1177; he believed that the Hindu gods had failed as Angkor's protectors.

Day 2
Temples east of Angkor Thom
Chau Say Tevoda

Dedicated to Shiva, this temple was built by Suryavarman II (1113-50). It is very close to the Victory Gate, which is the most southerly of the eastern gates. The north entry tower is very badly crumbled, as is most of the temple. The outer wall has long since disappeared and the whole complex has deteriorated badly. Nevertheless, there are some well-preserved sculptures, notably of Vishnu and Shiva, as well as floral designs on the three false doors in the Central Sancturary and on the walls of the ante-room.

Thommanon Temple

Situated almost next door to the above, it is reached by crossing the road in a northerly direction. It has similar features to the Chau Say Tevoda and is believed to have been built early in the 12th century. Its surrounding walls have largely crumbled and its central tower is nearly completely ruined. Archaeologists say that once both this structure and the badly decayed Chau Say Tevoda would have an elaborate hall which would have been linked to the central part of the temple. It would also appear that there were originally four access gates. Now only those on the east and west sides remain. Like the Chau Say Tevoda, it is dedicated to Shiva.

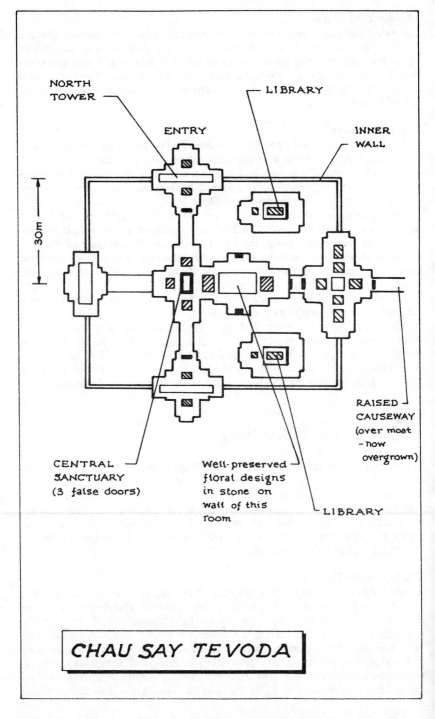

NORTH TOWER

LIBRARY

ENTRY

INNER WALL

30m

RAISED CAUSEWAY (over moat – now overgrown)

CENTRAL SANCTUARY (3 false doors)

Well-preserved floral designs in stone on wall of this room

LIBRARY

CHAU SAY TEVODA

Selling chickens at Tuol Tom Pong market, Phnom Penh

Top: Sunrise over the Tonlé Sap River
Bottom: Photographs of victims of the Khmer Rouge regime face visitors to Tuol Sleng Pris
museum, Phnom Penh

Eastern entrance, Wat Phnom, a prominent Phnom Penh landmark

ANGKOR WAT
Top: Southern entrance
Bottom: Details from bas relief showing 'the churning of the sea milk'
Left: Asuras assisting Ravana
Right: Ravana grasping a Vāsuki to churn the source of the elixir of life

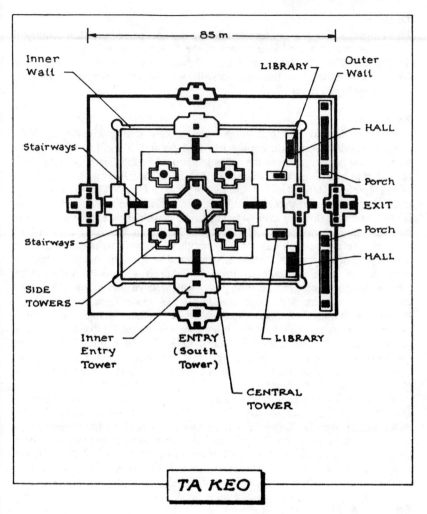

TA KEO

Ta Keo

This lies to the east of the Victory Gate. Started by Jayavarman V between 980 and 1013 this five-towered temple pyramid was never completed. Since it was built during the preclassical period, it lacks elaborate sculpturing. Its base was made out of laterite, like the Phimeanakas, but the upper tiers, which were believed to have been added during the reign of Suryavarman, are made out of sandstone. It was the second temple at Angkor to have been built largely from this material (the first was the Bantéay Srei). Because of its harsh cubical exterior it is not particularly attractive. The central tower rises to a height of 45m, 23m above the fifth tier. This prasat has a cruciform base, four porches protrude in each direction of the compass. Other prasats form a typical quincunx arrangement often seen on Angkor's temple-mountains. When originally discovered this was just an earth mound.

Ta Nei

This temple, which was consecrated during the later part of the 12th century, is located towards the northwest corner of the eastern lake. It is almost directly north of Ta Kéo. The gables here have elaborately sculpted horizontal bands. Although bullet marked, the relief is still beautiful and is typical of the style adopted by Jayavarman VII.

Ta Prohm

This once classical Buddhist temple was erected during Jayavarman VII's frenzied building period during the late 12th century. It was one of many that arose on the Angkor plain in the ashes left behind by the Cham. Although it is dedicated to Lord Buddha it is believed that it was modelled on the magnificent Hindu temple of Beng Meala (40km east of Angkor Thom). The arrangement of three concentric enclosures seen at Ta Prohm is also seen at Beng Meala. This is now extremely difficult to envisage because, as with many of the temples built hurriedly during this period (1181-1219), Ta Prohm has been engulfed by tropical vegetation which has not only smothered most of its masonry but also severely restricts access. Since it was modified many times during its construction it is difficult to imagine what it originally looked like. Archaeologists discovered an inscription which stated that within the temple complex there were 566 stone dwellings, 288 made from bricks and 39 sanctuaries. Within these prasats there were 260 Buddhist statues and a divine image of Jayavarman's mother. The inner complex housed 2,740 priests, 18 high priests and well over 2,000 assistants. Over 66,000 people lived in the surrounding residences. It is believed that the temple had a rich treasury containing more than 11,000 pounds of silver and gold, countless precious stones and over 40,000 pearls.

Ta Prohm was consecrated five years after Jayavarman came to the throne in 1186. When it was rediscovered in the 19th century it was left exactly as the archaeologists found it. Today it is intriguingly attractive. Tendrils compete for the smallest crack, aerial roots of banyan and silk-cotton trees clamber around its base, thick canopies disguise its stone tapestries and an ever increasing web of verdant jungle eats into its masonry. Few would dare to delve deeply into its mantle of greenery which has become the home of emerald green, Hanuman snakes.

Bantéay Kdei

This is very close to the overgrown temple of Ta Prohm which it resembles in many ways. It is entered via the east gate in front of which is the large lake of Srah Srang. This sacred lake, which is about 800m from east to west and 400m from north to south, was once used by high priests. The temple was constructed towards the end of the Bayon period (last part of the 12th century). Many archaeologists have suggested that it was hurriedly constructed because both its architectural layout and statuary are inferior to those of many other temples constructed by Jayavarman VII.

The east gate through which the second enclosure is reached has a plain projecting porch supported by unsculptured cubical blocks of sandstone. Side walls have recesses which house unspectacular Buddhist images. The entrance building has a cruciform ground plan. Lichen-covered *garudas* stand either side of the sandstone steps leading to the fairly plain tower gate. Inside there is a Buddha statue.

Prasat Kravan

This can be reached by following the road which runs between Banteay Kdei and Srah Srang in a southerly direction. After a short distance it branches towards the south west. Prasat Kravan is on the left (south) side of the road.

This, like Bantéay Srei, was not built by a king. It was originally intended to be a temple where Hindus could worship. Built around 921, this comparatively plain, five-towered structure has some extremely fine bas-reliefs on its inner walls. The best are inside the large central tower, where Vishnu is seen mounted on the back of a fierce looking *garuda*. Another shows him with eight arms. Phnom Penh Tourism often call this temple Bantéay Kravan.

Pré Rup

This is about 2km directly east of Bantéay Kdei. It was built by Rajendravarman in 961. This king had very different ideas about temple construction, compared to those of his predecessor Jaravarman IV. The Pré Rup temple-mountain is a three-storied pyramid made of laterite. It has a scorched look, no doubt produced from centuries of exposure to the harsh rays of the sun. The five brick towers which crown the third tier have a quincuncial arrangement and are distinctly paler than the rest of the edifice. The central prasat in particular, with its closely compacted brick summit, is faintly reminiscent of towers built by the Cham in Vietnam. Many archaeologists think that the Pré Rup Sanctuary was built to mark the epicentre of a royal city which Rajendravarman (944-68) constructed east of Yasodharapura.

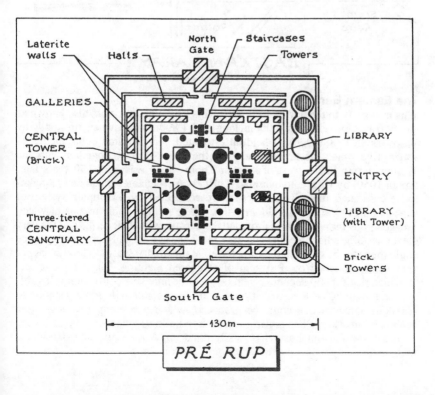

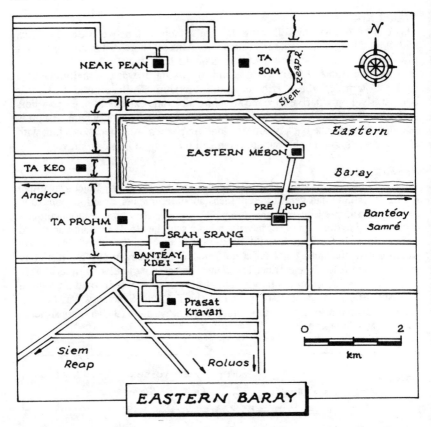

EASTERN BARAY

The Eastern Baray

This is slightly to the north of Pré Rup. This irrigation reservoir, also known as the Barray Oriental, was 7,000m long and 1,800m wide when first built by Yasovarman I (889-900). It held an estimated thirty million cubic metres of water, five times the amount held by the Lolei Barray. Together with the Western Baray to the west of Angkor Thom which was built 150 years later (about 1050) by Udayadityavarman II (1050-66), it enabled the plain of Angkor to be cultivated intensively. These were connected by a complex system of canals and in total could hold an estimated 75 million cubic metres of water. The generous monsoon rains provided the barrays with their refills and the very clever use of gradient feeding channels made the system self-perpetuating. Rice could then still be cultivated during the eight month dry season. Three crops per year were produced by a system of staggered planting. There is historical evidence that 60,000 hectares could be used for intensive cultivation using this unique gravitational feed irrigation system. In exceptionally good years up to 150,000 tonnes of rice could be produced, which partly explains how these ancient Khmer kings had sufficient wealth to build such lavish temples.

Today the Eastern Baray has totally dried up. A road runs across it to the north of Pré Rup which passes the Eastern Mébon Temple.

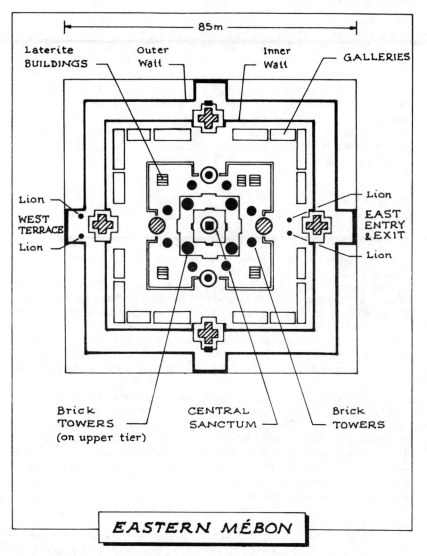

| 85m |

Laterite
BUILDINGS

Outer
Wall

Inner
Wall

GALLERIES

Lion

WEST
TERRACE

Lion

Lion

EAST
ENTRY
& EXIT

Lion

Brick
TOWERS
(on upper tier)

CENTRAL
SANCTUM

Brick
TOWERS

EASTERN MÉBON

The Eastern Mébon Temple

This was built on a small island in the centre of the Eastern Baray by Rajendravarman II (944-68). Although smaller than the Pré Rup, it has an almost identical design with five brick towers arranged in a quincuncial style. The three-tiered pyramid is, again, made of laterite and it also has very similar concentric enclosures.

One of the best features of the Eastern Mébon is the delicacy of its ornate sandstone lintels. Take a look directly above the prasats and you will see that the temple is clearly dedicated to the god Shiva. Notice also the fine sculpted octagonal columns.

Ta Som

If you carry on along the road in a north-westerly direction from the Eastern Mébon Temple you will come across the Ta Som Temple which is on the right hand side, 1km after crossing the Siem Reap River. Like the Ta Prohm this has been left just as it was then it was first discovered. It was built by Jayavarman VII in the late 12th century. The main entrance gate, which is its best feature, is covered in a green furry mantle, roots have eaten into its foundations and seeds have germinated in every crack available. It is still, however, immensely photogenic, varicose lichens, mostly green-blue in colour, contrast vividly with algal encrustations and large varieties of bryophytes in every shade of green. The structure is topped by a huge face of Buddha.

Preah Khan

This is another 2km further on, just north of Angkor Thom. Built by Jayavarman VII, it was consecrated as a Buddhist temple in 1191. It is enclosed by tall walls made from laterite which extend for over 800m from west to east and 650m from north to south. Four gates provide access to the interior sanctuary.

Few tourist groups are brought here because many of the bas-reliefs have been badly damaged. Those that remain tell the story of Hindu epics such as the Mahabharata and Rāmayăna. There is a fairly well-preserved one which tells the story of the Churning of the Sea of Milk. You will see numerous holes which are not bullet wounds. Originally much of the structure was covered in plaster and wooden pegs were used to secure it in place. The holes were left when the pegs rotted. Although covered by climbing plants, the temple is still attractive.

At Preah Khan you will see a pillared structure, the function of which is not understood. It is arranged in two tiers, the top tier being supported by ten plain sandstone pillars on each side. The only ornamentation are the carved bands at the base and around the top of the pillars. No staircase leads to the upper level. The prasats in this temple-monastery do not exhibit the usual design, several-storeyed roofs adorned with sculptured pavilion. Instead the roofs are dome-shaped and poorly structured. The *apsarās* here are not so precisely carved, some are pitted and weather worn.

Neak Pean

The road takes a sharp left to the north of Ta Som and continues in a westerly direction. At around the 2km point one can stop and walk directly south to the ruin of Neak Pean. Preah Neak Pean lies to the east of Preah Khan. It was constructed during the later part of the 12th century on a small island in the centre of a large lake. The central tower which remains is dedicated to Lokeshvara. Notice the two *nāgas* which are encircling the seven-tiered base. On one side there is a peculiar looking figure which looks like a horse with human legs.

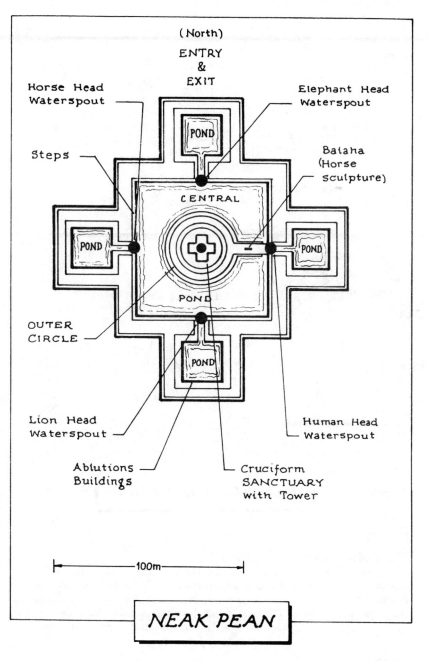

(North)

ENTRY
&
EXIT

Horse Head
Waterspout

Elephant Head
Waterspout

Steps

Baiaha
(Horse
sculpture)

POND

CENTRAL

POND

POND

OUTER
CIRCLE

POND

Lion Head
Waterspout

Human Head
Waterspout

Ablutions
Buildings

Cruciform
SANCTUARY
with Tower

├──────100m──────┤

NEAK PEAN

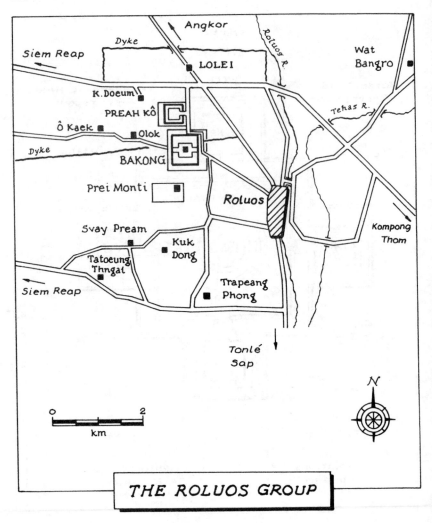

Siem Reap

Angkor

Dyke

LOLEI

Wat
Bangro

Roluos R.

K.Doeum

PREAH KÔ

Tehas R.

Ô Kaek

Olok

Dyke

BAKONG

Prei Monti

Roluos

Svay Pream

Kuk
Dong

Kompong
Thom

Tatoeung
Thngat

Siem Reap

Trapeang
Phong

Tonlé
Sap

N

0   2

km

THE ROLUOS GROUP

Day 3
The Roluos Group of Temples

Jayavarman II (802-50) built his capital, Hariharalaya, towards the southeast of Angkor. His successor King Indravarman I (877-89) built Jayavarman II's funerary temple, Prah Kô, at this site in 879. In the centre of the city of Hariharalaya he erected the Bakong sandstone pyramid in 881. Twelve years later his son, Yasovarman I (889-900), constructed the temple of Lolei on a small islet.

Preah Kô

This temple, together with others included in the Roluos group, can be reached along National Route 6 from Siem Reap. After travelling east for about 12½km

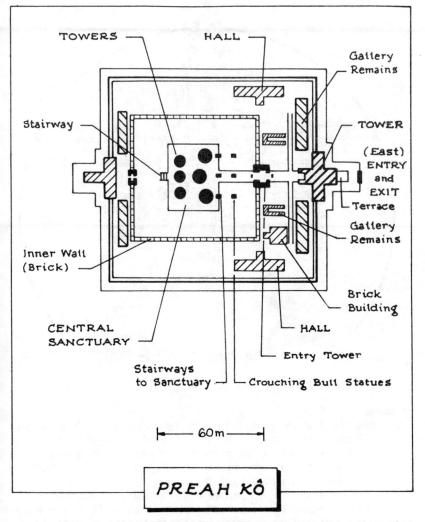

TOWERS

HALL

Gallery Remains

TOWER

(East) ENTRY and EXIT

Terrace

Gallery Remains

Stairway

Inner Wall (Brick)

Brick Building

CENTRAL SANCTUARY

HALL

Entry Tower

Stairways to Sanctuary

Crouching Bull Statues

|← 60m →|

PREAH KÔ

the road passes the ruin of Kandak Doeum which is on the right. About 1km further on there is a turn off to Preah Kô, also on the right.

This large temple complex is dedicated to the God Shiva. It is interesting that the name of the city where it was constructed, Hariharalaya, is derived from the God Hari-Hara whom Hindus worship as Shiva and Vishnu. It is believed that this temple is modelled on others seen at Sambor Prei Kuk. The prasats here are arranged on a single terrace in two rows of three. The central prasats are the tallest and reach 15m in height. The whole structure is made out of sandstone bricks. The lintels above the doorways are beautifully carved. Either side of the doorways, guardians (*dvārapālas*) stand guard. Parapets on either side of the entrance step consist of fierce looking lion figures. The elongated structures are libraries which once housed sacred texts.

Bakong

This five-tiered sandstone pyramid is topped by a great prasat which was built over two hundred years after the base. It is surrounded by eight others, four of which are still in a good state of preservation. Some ornamentation has been lost. The whole complex is surrounded by a moat which extends 360m from east to west and 340m from north to south. It is 60m wide.

The remains of the original prasats which once adorned this edifice were removed when it was restored in the 12th century. Originally 60,000 metric tons of sandstone were used in its construction. The top tier can be reached by four stone staircases, the tops of which are 15m above ground level. The entrance gopuras, which give access to the staircases, are fairly plain structures. Originally lion parapets stood on either side of each staircase on each level of the pyramid. Many have been damaged or lost. This is also the case with the stone elephants which once stood on the corners of each of the lower levels. It is believed that, when first constructed, the temple-mountain in the centre represented the Holy City. The city proper lay beyond the surrounding moat and was surrounded by another moat 22m wide. This formed the perimeter of a rectangle which was 800m long and 700m wide. Nothing remains of the original dwellings which must have surrounded the central temple.

The Bakong is well over a kilometre south of National Route 6.

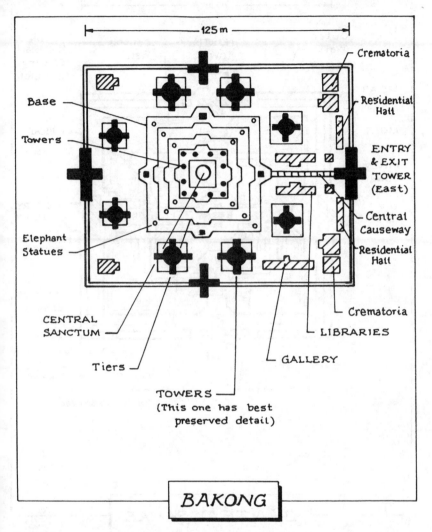

BAKONG

Lolei

Built in 893 on a small island in the middle of a large barray, this four-towered temple is incomplete. Originally, according to historical evidence, Yasovarman, who built it, intended that it should consist of six towers. The reservoir in which it stands is now dry but during the reign of Indravarman it provided vital water for the city of Hariharalaya. It has some fine statuary built into alcoves on the sides of the towers. One shows a full-breasted woman holding a staff. Every detail of her pleated skirt, ornate belt and pointed hat can be seen. The alcove is surrounded by a highly ornamental frieze which has been sculpted in the form of an arch. King Yasovarman dedicated these towers to his ancestors. Sanskrit inscriptions which can be clearly seen on the door supports say that two of them were built to honour his parents.

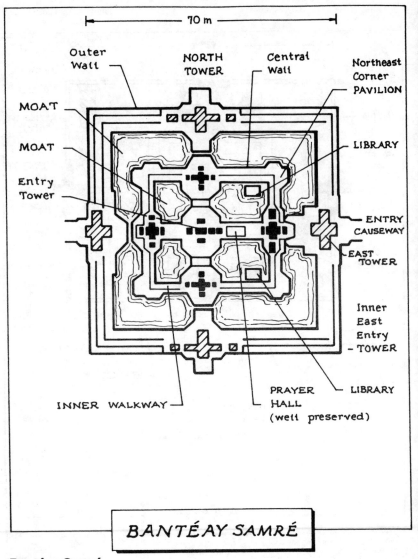

70 m

Outer Wall

NORTH TOWER

Central Wall

Northeast Corner PAVILION

MOAT

MOAT

Entry Tower

LIBRARY

ENTRY CAUSEWAY

EAST TOWER

Inner East Entry - TOWER

INNER WALKWAY

PRAYER HALL (well preserved)

LIBRARY

BANTÉAY SAMRÉ

Bantéay Samré
If you intend to go all the way to this temple by car, think again. The last kilometre or so is extremely rough. The temple is about 450m to the east of the Eastern Baray and is reached via a pleasant Cambodian village. Situated inside a laterite wall (40m x 30m) the main temple has features reminiscent of the style seen at Angkor Wat. It is thought that it was built towards the end of the 12th century. It features stone-vaulted galleries, open arcades and unusual stone spikes which run along the top of the gallery roofs. Similar to Angkor Wat, the main temple has a distinctive cruciform ground plan. In front of the high temple entrance porch which protrudes into a courtyard is a prayer hall. On either side of this are two well preserved libraries.

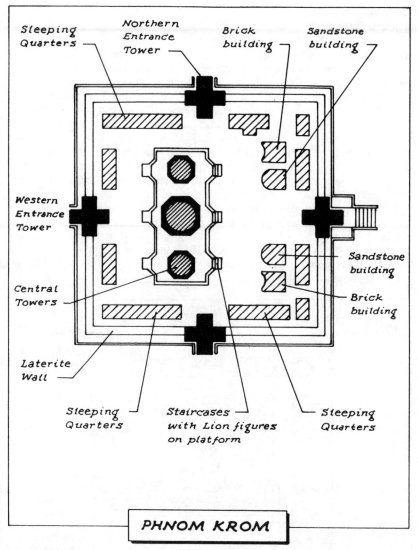

Sleeping Quarters

Northern Entrance Tower

Brick building

Sandstone building

Western Entrance Tower

Sandstone building

Central Towers

Brick building

Laterite Wall

Sleeping Quarters

Staircases with Lion figures on platform

Sleeping Quarters

PHNOM KROM

Phnom Krom

Few tourists visit this three-towered sanctuary which is situated about 11km southeast of Siem Reap. From here you have a wonderful view of the Tonlé Sap Lake which extends for an enormous distance during the rainy season (June-November). Come here during the dry season (November-May) and you will see just a river, which finally flows into the Mekong.

The central tower is dedicated to Shiva, the north one to Vishnu and the south one to Brahmā. Inside the latter there is still a damaged statue of Brahmā. The towers are very weather-worn which is hardly surprising since they date from the 11th century.

Day 4
Phnom Bakheng

This admirable brick replica of Mount Meru was built in the centre of Yasodharapura, a Khmer city founded by King Yasovarman. Archaeological excavations have shown that this city once had a perimeter of 12km. Built on a mound, it enables visitors to get a panoramic view of the surrounding countryside. It is surrounded by a wall which is 650m long from north to south and 440m wide from east to west. It is entered via a median causeway which leads to five flights of steps rising to a height of 60m. The overall beauty of the edifice is enhanced by 12 prasats, made of sandstone, which stand on each of its five lower levels. The characteristic quincuncial arrangement of prasats is seen on the sixth tier. In addition, surrounding this enormous monument, which is 60m square, are another 44 minor prasats, again cleverly constructed from sandstone bricks. The temple-mountain was built in 893 and, considering its age, it is remarkably intact. The smaller prasats along the edge of the terraces have survived far better than the ones at the top. On this terrace the central sanctuary has lost its roof and only the bases of the other four prasats are still intact. In all, the complex has a total of 108 prasats which symbolise an early calendar. If you consider that each lunar cycle takes 27 days, then the number of prasats represent four of these cycles.

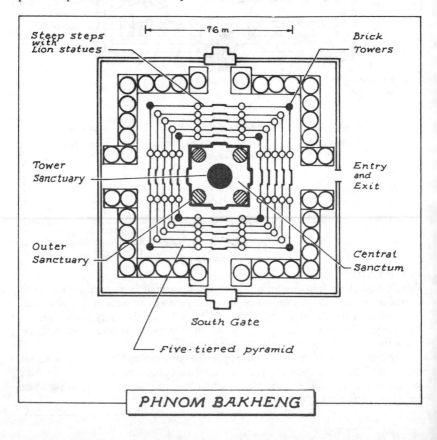

Steep steps with Lion statues

Brick Towers

Tower Sanctuary

Entry and Exit

Outer Sanctuary

Central Sanctum

South Gate

Five-tiered pyramid

76 m

PHNOM BAKHENG

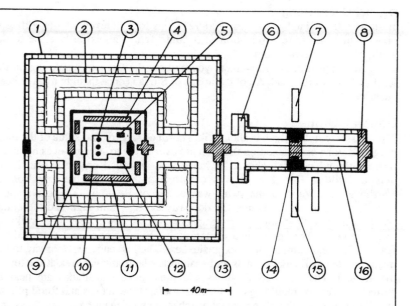

1. WALL. Surrounds first enclosure.
2. MOAT. Surrounded by laterite walls.
3. TOWERS on platform. Badly crumbled, each has a guardian with animal head and human body.
4. MEDITATION Building.
5. North east LIBRARY. East pediment depicts Indra on chariot drawn by Airávata, surrounded by animals. West pediment shows Krishna trying to kill King Kamsa.
6. PEDIMENT on the ground: Sita being abducted.
7. PEDIMENT. Vishnu as a man-lion (Avatáras).
8. ENTRY and EXIT tower.
9. WALL. Laterite.
10. WALL. Brick.
11. ANNEXE Building. (One of six.)
12. South east LIBRARY. East pediment depicts Rávana, the Rákshasa king, shaking Mount Kailása. Shiva sits on the mountain, with his wife Párvati. West pediment shows Káma attempting to kill Shiva.
13. ENTRY tower.
14. ENTRY tower.
15. BUILDING. Of unknown function.
16. CAUSEWAY: sandstone. Sandstone and laterite galleries either side.

BANTÉAY SREI

Baksei Chamkrong

Built in 920 by Harshavarman I (900-921), this four-storeyed laterite edifice is another more basic representation of Mount Meru. This is fairly close to the south gate of Angkor Thom.

As you approach this monument you will see the Baksei Chamkrong on the left hand side of the road. A golden image of Shiva is once thought to have been enshrined here.

Bantéay Srei

This classic temple, which is about 25km north of Angkor, has some of the most gorgeous stone ornamentation that you are ever likely to set your eyes upon. Its overall ground plan is believed to have been modelled on the Prasat Thom Temple built at Koh Ker. It was constructed in 967 by the grandson of Harshavarman, Yajnavaraha, who was a devout Brahmin. The Ishvarapura Temple was built in miniature, the doorway is only 1.3m high and the entire complex is only 200m long. Photographers walking down the central walkway won't know where to point their cameras next. Every portico and every gallery features Khmer sculpting at its exquisite best. The low entrance doorway to the main temple has flawless lintels and spandrels (the triangular area at the top of the arches). The traceried windows and their stone balustrades are near to perfection. Terrace mouldings, pediments, roofs, stone lattices and floral plinths are all outstanding. Prasats are lavishly enhanced by elegant *apsarās*, *devas* and *dvārapālas*. The complex is made even more appealing by the fact that pink sandstone was used as the construction material throughout. In front of the prasats you will see lively figures of monkeys, the Brahmani kite (*garuda*) and terrifying demons.

In the complex there is a triple enclosure. In front of the central tower is the prayer hall. To the right hand side of it is the south tower and to the left is the north tower. The gables over the entry gates are particularly impressive.

Some of the most notable features of the complex are the gable over the eastern entrance and the low relief sculpturing on the spandrel of the library which would take some beating. This shows Krishna in the process of murdering his uncle Kamsa. Many of the lintels feature scenes from the Rāmayăna; the most magnificent is the one where the god of the underworld, Rāvana, is transporting away Sita, the wife of Rāma. You will also be impressed by the geese sculptures, decorative door jambs, terraced pavilions on the roofs and chequer-board patterning on the prayer hall.

OTHER BRADT GUIDES TO ASIA

Guide to Vietnam by John R Jones
The companion guide to Laos and Cambodia, packed full of information for independent travellers and those on organised tours.

Guide to Burma by Nicholas Greenwood
The definitive guide to Burma (Myanmar), full of literary and historical detail and covering every part of the country accessible to visitors. Illustrated with 24 pages of colour photos.

Burma Then and Now by Nicholas Greenwood
The hardbook edition of the above, aimed at the armchair reader.

Thailand, Malaysia and Singapore by Rail by Brian McPhee
A user-friendly guide, written by a resident of Thailand, describing the 6,000km of railway and places easily reached by train.

India by Rail by Royston Ellis
A highly-praised guide detailing India's extensive railway network, full of practical information and evocative description.

Sri Lanka by Rail by Royston Ellis
A complete guide to the island with an emphasis on places accessible by train, written by a resident of Sri Lanka.

Guide to Maldives by Royston Ellis
A garland of over 1,200 coral islands south of Sri Lanka, providing almost perfect diving and snorkelling.

And then there's the rest of the world...

Send for a catalogue from Bradt Publications, 41 Nortoft Road, Chalfont St Peter, Bucks SL9 0LA, England. Tel/fax: 01494 873478

Appendix One

GLOSSARY

In Laos

Abhayamudra	Buddha 'attitude' which conveys giving protection.
baht	Thai currency commonly used in Laos.
ban	Laotian word meaning a village or a house.
Basi	Lao religious ceremony which is associated with a 'welcome' or 'goodbye' party. During the ceremony *khwan* (spirits) are called back to the body organs so as to restore courage to the person.
Bhumisparcamudra	Buddha 'attitude' which is associated with 'calling the earth goddess Thoranee to witness the Buddha's enlightenment'.
CDNI	Committee for the Defence of National Interests formed between 1958-1962 to introduce government reforms.
chedi	Buddhist stupa.
Chieng Mai	ancient Lao Kingdom which, during the reign of King Phothisarath in the 16th century, was also called Lan Na. It included parts of today's northern Thailand.
don	Laotian word meaning island.
Dharmacakramudra	Buddha 'attitude' known as 'spinning the Wheel of Law'. The Buddha is in teaching posture.
Dhyanamudra	meditation mudra or 'attitude'.
Free Lao	also known as Lao Issara, this movement, which was formed in 1945, ardently resisted a return to colonial status.
hùay	stream.
jumbo	also known in Thailand as *tùk túk*, a form of motorised transport used as a taxi.
karma	fate.
khào nio	glutinous rice which is very popular in Laos.
khùu baa	monk.
kip	Laotian currency.
làap	salad containing chicken, fish or other meats which are highly spiced.
Lan Xang	the Kingdom of a Million Elephants, founded in AD1353. Its capital was Muong Swa, built on the site of present day Luang Prabang.
lào-láo	Laotian rice liquor produced through the process of distillation.
Lao Lum	valley dwellers, the ethnic Lao.
Lao Sung	highlanders and include ethnic minorities such as H'mong and Yao.

Lao Thai	ethnic Thai found on the plateaux and upland valleys. They are non-Buddhists.
Lao Theung	people of the mountain slopes such as the Khmu who still practise slash and burn agriculture.
lam wong	traditional 'circle dance' performed at weddings and festivals.
mae nâam	Laotian word meaning river.
mùong	subdivision of a province or district.
NLHS	Neo Lak Hak Sat, the Lao Patriotic Front, which was formed in 1956. A political communist organisation.
Pathet Lao	the NLHS military.
pha	image of great religious significance such as a Buddha.
phi	Laotian spirits that inhabit all parts of the universe.
phuu	Laotian word for mountain or hill.
sàa-tòk	the life of Lord Buddha.
sala	Laotian word for a shelter.
samlor	three-wheeled pedicab used as a taxi.
Sangha	the Theravada Buddhist brotherhood.
se	southern Laotian word meaning a river. Can also be written *xe*.
sim	the main sanctuary in a Laotian Buddhist temple or monastery.
talàat	Laotian word for a market.
thâat	Laotian stupa, shaped like a hemispherical mound. It generally holds a Buddhist relic or the ashes of a famous person such as a Prime Minister.
thanon	Laotian word meaning a street.
Vajrasana	meditation posture where both soles of the feet are clearly seen.
Virasana	meditation posture where the legs are crossed but the right leg rests on top of the left.
Vitarkamudra	Buddha in the preaching attitude, either standing or seated.
Viet Minh	members of Vietnam's Workers Party who were ardently opposed to French domination.
wat	Buddhist temple complex enclosed by a wall and accessed through gateways.

In Cambodia

Agni	the God of Fire, usually with two heads and four arms.
Amitāba	Buddha in the seated posture in a state of meditation.
amrta	the elixir of life.
Angkar	another name for the Khmer Rouge or DK Party.
ANS	Armeé Nationale Sihanoukiste.
apsarā	heavenly maiden depicted in Khmer art as a dancer.
ASEAN	Association of Southeast Asia Nations.
asura	god-like demon.
balustre	short pillar arranged in a series to form a balustrade.
Bana	demon.
Bantéay	Khmer word meaning a fortified temple.
baray	large water mass created by an earth dam.
BDLP	Buddhist Liberal Democrats.
bodhisattva	term used in Mahayana Buddhism to describe a being with the compassion to become a Buddha.
Brahmā	husband of Sarasvati, who is usually depicted riding a sacred goose (*hamsa*). He has four faces which signify his dominance over all he created.
Buddha	an enlightened one who has reached the state of nirvana.
CGDK	Coalition Government of Democratic Kampuchea.
Champa	the Kingdom of the Cham minority which existed in South and Central Vietnam from the 2nd to the 15th century.
Chaul Chlam	Khmer New Year Festival.
Chenla	Chinese name for Cambodia, 6th to 8th centuries.
CMAC	Cambodian Mine Action Centre.
corbel arch	archway spanning a narrow opening.
CPAF	Cambodian People's Armed Forces.
CPP	Cambodian People's Party.
deva	female deity.
devarāja	cult which lifts the status of a king to that of a god.
Durgā	the wife of Shiva, depicted in bas-reliefs riding a tiger.
dvārapāla	temple guardian.
FUNCINPEC	Front un National pour un Cambodge Independent Neutre, Pacific et Cooperatif.
Funan	Indianised kingdom which occupied the lower Mekong basin between the 1st and 7th centuries.
Ganesá	God of Wisdom. He is depicted with the head of an elephant and a human's body. He usually rides on a rat and has either two or four arms. He is the son of Shiva and Părvatī.
Ganga	Shiva's second wife.

Garuda	half man and half bird, this mythical creature is Lord Vishnu's mount and the deadly enemy of *nāga* serpents.
gopura	elaborately sculpted entrance tower made out of sandstone or laterite.
HALO Trust	UK Mine Cleaning Agency.
Hanumān	demi-god with the head of a monkey. Frequently seen on bas-reliefs in stories taken from the Rāmāyana.
Hari-Hara	combination of the two Hindu deities, Vishnu represented by Hari and Shiva represented by Hara. Hari usually wears a tiara and Hara can be recognised by plaited hair.
HEKS	Humanitarian Aid group from Switzerland.
Hīnayāna Buddhism	Theravada or 'Lesser Vehicle' Buddhism, introduced into Cambodia from Ceylon in the 15th century.
Hinduism	Hindu religion which rose in prominence in Cambodia between 1st and 13th centuries.
IDP	Internally Displaced People.
Indra	God of the Sky. Usually depicted riding a white elephant with three heads. The god generally has a tiara on his head and holds a thunderbolt in his hand.
kāla	monster with no jaw. Lintels at Roluos depict him swallowing his own body.
Kāma	God of Love. Wife of Rati, he is usually depicted riding a parrot and holding a bow and floral arrows.
KNUFNS	Kampuchean National United Front of National Salvation.
KPNLF	Khmer People's National Liberation Front.
KPNLAF	KPNLP military.
Krishna	reincarnation form of Vishnu (Krishna).
Kubera	God of Wealth. Bas-reliefs show him sitting on a horse.
Laksmana	Rāma's brother.
Lamthon	Khymer classical dance.
Laksmī	Goddess of Beauty. Some bas reliefs depict her as Sita, Rāma's wife. Sometimes she sits on a lotus pedestal clasping a lotus flower.
laterite	red, porous material produced from decayed rocks.
LDP	Liberal Democratic Party.
linga	symbolises the creational power of Lord Shiva. It is depicted as a male sex organ.
Lokesvara	the Bodhisattva of Compassion.
MAG	Mines Advisory Group.
Mahabharata	the epic story of war in northern India.
Mahayana Buddhism	sometimes known as 'Greater Vehicle' Buddhism, it reached its zenith in Cambodia late in the 12th century and continued being popular during the 13th century.

makara	mythical water monster sporting an elephant's trunk, the scaly body of a crocodile and eagles' talons.
Maya	beautiful maiden, a reincarnation form of Vishnu.
MCTU	Mine Clearance Training Unit.
Meru	the mountain home of the gods in the centre of the universe.
mohon	all female orchestra.
mokot	Khymer mitre crown.
nāga	sacred snakes of Hindu mythology, often depicted supporting Vishnu on the cosmic ocean. This aquatic, multi-headed serpent is seen all over South-East Asia.
Nala	monkey soldier.
Nandi	Shiva's sacred bull on which he is frequently seen mounted.
nirvana	the state of blissful happiness reached after the final reincarnation.
NUFK	The National United Front of Kampuchea.
Pachom Bun	Remembrance festival held in September or October
Pārvatī	Shiva's chief wife. She is usually depicted riding a lion or mounted on a lotus pedestal. One of her main forms is Uma when she wears a chignon covered in a mass of curls.
pediment	triangular shaped portion of a wall above the portico.
phnom	Khmer word meaning hill or mountain.
pip-hat	all male orchestra.
prah	Khmer word meaning holy or sacred.
prasat	tower sanctuary.
PRK	People's Republic of Kampuchea.
quincunx	platform in the shape of a square which supports one tower on each corner and one in the middle.
Rāhu	demon with the head of a monster.
rākshasa	demon of the night.
Rāmāyana	the story of Rāma and Sita
Rati	goddess of sexual desire, wife of Kama.
Rāvana	important character in the Rāmāyana, Indian epic. Bas reliefs often show him with his evil band of rakhsasa demons in the process of abducting Sita, Rāma's wife.
rohat	Khmer word for wooden, hand driven irrigation wheel.
sampot	wrap around skirt-like garment worn by Khmer women.
Sangkum	national movement with considerable control over country's affairs.
Sarasvatī	Goddess of Fine Speech. She is often shown riding a peacock and holding a book. She is Brahma's wife.

Shiva	Shiva, the Destroyer. Often depicted with a third eye, four arms, holding a trident. He is often seen riding his sacred bull, *Nandi*. His wife is Pǎrvatī.
Singha	lion guardian, often at the entrance to temples.
Sita	Rāma's wife.
Skanda	God of War. Often depicted as an archer, he is the son of Shiva and Pǎrvatī.
SNC	Supreme National Council.
SOC	the State of Cambodia.
spean	Khmer word for a bridge.
srei	Khmer word for a woman.
Shrī	Goddess of Good Luck.
Sugriva	Monkey King.
Surya	God of the Sun. On bas-reliefs he often rides a war chariot pulled by seven wild stallions.
ta	Khmer word for ancestor.
Theravāda Buddhism	another word for Hīnayǎna Buddhism.
Tonlé Sap	Khmer word meaning sweet water. It forms the largest lake in Cambodia which is connected to the River Mekong by a river of the same name.
Umā	the gracious wife of Shiva.
UNAMIC	United Nations Advanced Mission in Cambodia.
UNDP	United Nations Development Programme.
UNHCR	United Nations High Commission for Refugees.
UNICEF	UN relief and development agency.
UNTAC	United National Transitional Authority in Cambodia.
Vāsuki	serpent which is usually depicted supporting Lord Vishnu. In the masterpiece 'The Churning of the Sea of Milk' its body is used to churn the ambrosia of life.
vihara	temple sanctuary.
Vishnu	the Preserver. He is usually depicted in a *sampot* riding a *Garuda*. He has four arms and sports a cylindrical head dress or a diadem. He has many incarnations (*avataras*) which include Buddha, a tortoise, a boar, Rāma, a fish, Krishna, a man-lion, a man-horse and a dwarf.
wat	word meaning temple in Thai.
Yama	God of the Underworld. Depicted riding a buffalo. In all his eight arms he carries the weapons of justice which enables him to perform judgement on the world.
yaksha	being with supernatural powers enabling him to be good or evil.

Appendix Two

SELECTED READING

Laos

Abhay, Nhouy *Buddhism in Laos* Ministry of Education Library Committee 1988.

Adams, Nina S and McCoy *War and Revolution* Harper and Row, NY 1970.

Barney, G Linwood *The Meo of Xieng Khouang Province* Princeton University Press 1967.

Berval, René *Kingdom of Laos* Saigon France Asil 1959.

Burns, Richard D *The Wars in Vietnam, Cambodia and Laos 1945-1982* Santa Barbara ABC-Clio 1984.

Cady, John Frank *Thailand Laos and Cambodia* N J Prentice-Hall 1966.

Dooley, T A *The Night They Burned the Mountain* Farrar-Strauss-Cudaby 1960.

Harvey, H *Travel in French Indochina* London Thornton 1928.

Hill, Lawrence *The Politics of Heroin* Chicago Review Press 1991.

Jain, O P *Economy of Laos* Indian Quarterly 28,3 1972.

Kemp, Peter *A Visit to Laos* Journal of the Royal Central Asian Society, January 1962.

Lebar, Frank *Ethnic Groups of Mainland Southeast Asia* New Haven Press 1964.

Meeker, O *The Little World of Laos* New York: Scribner's Sons 1959.

Menger, Matt J *In the Valley of the Mekong* St Anthony Guild Press 1971.

Phouvong Phimmasone *The That Luang of Vientiane* Asia 1953.

Piriya Krairiksh *Early Khmer Sculptures in Southern Laos* Asia 1980.

Rawson, P S *The Art of Southeast Asia* Thames and Hudson 1967.

Saveng Phinith *Contemporary Lao Literature* Asia 1963.

Stuart-Fox, Martin and Bucknell R S *Politicisation of the Buddhist Sangha in Laos* Scarecrow Press, London.

Stuart-Fox, Kooyman, May *Historical Dictionary of Laos* Scarecrow Press Inc. Metuchen, N J & London 1992.

Sweet, Norman L *Fact Book on Aid to Laos* Vientiane: USAID 1967.

Thompson, Virginia *French Indochina* Allen and Unwin, London 1973.

Whitaker, Donald P, Barth, A, Berman, Sylvan M, Heimann, Judith M, MacDonald, John E, Martindale, Kenneth W, Shinn, Rinn-Sup *Laos a country study* US Government Printing Office 1979.

Williams, Bradford *Classical Dances of Laos* Free World (Manila 1965).

Cambodia

Anderson, Jo Pronzine B *The Cambodian File* Sphere 1983.

Aymonier, E *Le Cambodge vol 1-111* Paris 1901-1904.

Bekaert, Jacques F8]*Selected Articles from Bangkok Post* D D Books 1989.

Boisselier, J *Trends in Khmer Art* Cornell University 1989.

Briggs, Palmer *The Ancient Khmer Empire* Philadelphia 1951.

Chandler, David P *When the War Was Over* Simon & Schuster 1991.

Coedes, G *Angkor An Introduction* Bangkok 1963.

Dagens, B *Angkor La Forêt de Pierre* Gallimard Paris 1989.

303

Davies, Paul *War of the Mines: Cambodia, Landmines and The Impoverishment of a Nation* Pluto Press 1995.

Freeman, M *A Golden Souvenir of Angkor* Pacific Rim Press HK 1992.

Fujioka, Michio *Angkor Wat* Kodansha International, Japan 1972.

Glaize, Maurice *Les Monuments du Groupe d'Angkor* A Portail, Saigon 1948.

Groslier, Bernard *The Art of Indochina* London 1962.

Groslier, George *Angkor* Laurens, Paris 1933.

Hildebrand, George and Porter Gareth *Starvation and Revolution* Monthly Review Press 1976.

Hoskin John, Hopkins Allen *The Mekong* Shell, Bangkok Post and Thai Nestles Company (combined publication), Bangkok 1992.

Igont, M *Then and Now* M Whitel Otus 1993.

Jackson, K *Cambodia 1975-1978* Princetown University Press 1989.

Jennar, Raoul *Cambodian Chronicles* Cereo, BP44, B1370, Jodoigne Belgium.

Jumsal, Manich *A History of Cambodia and Thailand* Chalermnit Press, Bangkok 1987.

Kiernan, Ben *How Pol Pot came to Power* Verso 1950.

Kiernan, Ben *Peasants and Politics in Kampuchea* Zed Press 1952.

Kiljunen, Kimmo *Kampuchea - Decade of the Genocide* Zed Books Ltd, London 1984.

MacDonald, Malcolm *Angkor and the Khmer* Oxford University Press, 1987.

Mekong Secretariat *Cambodia and the Mekong Project* Bangkok 1976.

Madsen, Axel *The Asia Adventures of Clara & André Malraux* IB Tauris, London 1990.

Mysliwiec, Eva *Punishing the Poor* Oxfam 1988.

National Geographic *The Temples of Angkor* May 1982.

Parmentier, Henri *Angkor Guide* Eklip/Albert Portail, PhnomnPenh 1959/60.

Pilger, John *Heroes* Pan Books 1989.

Pilger, John *Distant Voices* Vintage 1992.

Rawson, P *The Art of Southeast Asia* Thames & Hudson 1990.

Reynell, Josephine *Political Pawns* Oxford 1989.

Shawcross, W *Cambodia Year Zero* Penguin, London 1984.

Srivastava, K M *Angkor Wat and its Cultural History Ties with India* Books and Books, New Delhi 1985.

Stierlin, Henri *The Cultural History of Angkor* Aurum Press Ltd, London 1984.

Szymusiak, Molyda *The Stones Cry Out* Spere Books Ltd 1987.

Taing, Huong Vek *Ordeal in Cambodia* Life Publishers, San Bernardino, 1980.

Var Hong Ashe *From Phnom Penh to Paradise* Hodder and Stoughton, London 1975.

Vicery, M *Cambodia 1975-1982* George Allen and Unwin 1984.

Vincent, Frank *The Land of The White Elephant* 1871-1872 rep - Oxford University Press 1988.

304

Appendix Three

WORLDWIDE TRAVEL AGENCIES DEALING WITH LAOS AND CAMBODIA

UK
Abercrombie and Kent, Sloane Square House, Holbein Place, London
DW1W 8NS; tel: 0171 730 9600; fax: 0171 730 9376; telex: 8813352.
Asia Voyages, 230 Station Road, Addleston, Weybridge, Surrey;
tel: 01932 820050; fax: 01932 820633; telex: 266592.
Bales Tours Ltd, Bale House, Barrington Road, Dorking, Surrey RH4 3EJ;
tel: 01306 885991.
Exodus Discovery Holidays, 9 Weir Road, London SW12 0LT. Reservations -
tel: 0181 675 5550, Brochures and Dossiers; tel: 0181 673 0859 (24 hours);
fax: 0181 673 0779; telex: 8951700 EXODUS G.
Explore Worldwide Ltd, 1 Frederick Street, Aldershot, Hants GU11 1LQ.
Reservation/Information tel: 01252 319448. Brochures and Dossiers
tel: 01252 344161; fax: 01252 343170; telex: 858954 EXPLOR G.
Imaginative Traveller, 14 Barley Mow Passage, London W4 4PH. Information
tel: 0181 742 8612, Brochures and Dossiers tel: 0181 742 3049.
Progressive Tours Ltd, 12 Porchester Place, Marble Arch, London W2 2BS;
tel: 0171 262 1676; fax: 0171 724 6941; telex: 25135.
Regent Holidays (UK) Ltd, 15 John Street, Bristol BS1 2HR;
tel: 0117 921 1711 (24 hours); fax: 0117 925 4866.
Westeast Travel, 39B Wicoll Road, London NW10 9AX; tel: 0181 961 0117.

Other European Agencies
Austria
View Travel, Sankt Voitgasse 9, A-1130 Vienna; tel: 222 821532;
telex: 13667 MRD A.

Belgium
Boundless Adentures, Avenue Verdiliaan 23/15, 1080 Brussels, Ganshoren;
tel: 02 426 40 30; fax: 02 426 03 60.
Divantoura, Bagattemstraat 176, B-9000 Gent; tel: 09 223 0069;
fax: 09 223 04 35.
Divantoura, St Jacobsmarkt 5, 2000 Antwerpen; tel: 03 233 19 16;
fax: 03 233 21 39.

Bulgaria
Balkantourist Agency, 1 dai 10 Vitosha, Sofia; tel: 855039; telex: 22567/8.

Denmark
Albatros, Frederiksberggade 15, 1459 Copenhagen K; tel: 33 32 2488.
Inter-Travel, Frederiksholms Kanal 2, DK-1200 Copenhagen K;
tel: 33 150077; fax: 33 156018; telex: 16125.

France

Akiou et Planete, 2 Rue de la Paix, 75002 Paris; telex: 230970 F.

ET Voyage (Eurasie Travel France), 142 Boulevard Massena, 75013 Paris; tel:
45 83 11 22; fax: 45 83 22 66
and 5 Rue de Marseilles, 69007 Lyon; tel: 72 73 30 18; fax: 78 69 88 59.

Hit Voyages, 21 Rue des Bernadins, Paris 75005; tel: 43 52 99 04.

International Tourism, 26 Bd St Marcel, 75005 Paris; tel: 45 87 07 70;
telex: 201647 F.

KLV, 67 Boulevard de Belleville, 75011 Paris; tel: 48 1080; fax: 436 6918.

Locotour, Le jardin Tropical 3, Rue des Cgenes Poupres, 95000 Cergy;
telex: CESVLOC 607784 F.

Loisirs et Vacances de la Jeunesse, 4 & 6 Fue de Chateau-Landon,
75005 Paris; telex: LVJ 230G9748F.

Pacific Holidays, 34 Avenue du General Leclerc, 75014 Paris;
tel: 45 41 52 58.

Germany

Council Travel, Graf-Adolf-Str-18, 4000 Dusseldorf 1; tel: 0211 329 106.

Explorer, Huttenstrasse 17, 40215 Dusseldorf; tel: 0211 99 49 02;
fax: 0211 37 70 79.

Fremdenverkehrsamt Der Sr Indochina, Hamburger Strasse 132,
200 Hamburg 76, Postfach: 761163; tel: 040 295345; fax: 040 296705;
telex: 213968 HT-D.

Indo Culture Tours, Indoculture Reisedienst GmbH, Bismarkplatz 1,
D-7000 Stuttgart 1; tel: 0711/61 7057-58; telex: 0723368 ICLT D

Judendtourist, 1026 Berlin Alexanderplatz 5; tel: 2150;
telex: 114657 RSBJT DD.

Reisburo, Berlin; tel: 2150; telex: 114648, 114652 RSBODD.

Saratours, Sallstr, 21 D 3000, Hanover 1; tel: 0511 282353;
telex: 4170329 ASI VA 17. 6997263.

Ireland

Maxwells Travel, D'Olier Chambers, 1 Hawkins Street, Dublin 2;
tel: 677 9479; fax: 679 3948 or 307 237.

Italy

Imaginative Traveller, Rome CTS VIAGGI via Genova 15, 00184, Roma;
tel: 06 46791.

Going Tour, 10121 Torino, Italy; tel: 011 517475; telex: 2135589 GOING 1.

Malta

NSTS, 220 St Paul Street, Valletta; tel: 356 244 983.

Netherlands

Arke Rotterdam BV My Way, Rietbaan 10, 2908 LP Capelle A/D ljssel;
tel: 010 258 1260.

Norway

EVENTYRREISER AS, Hedgehougsveien 10 0167 Oslo; tel: 472 11 31 81.

Poland

Orbis Agency, 16 Bracka Street, 00—28 Warsaw; tel: 260271;
   telex: 817781 ABZTW PL.
Polish Tourism Cooperative, 23 UL Podwale, 00952 Warsaw; tel: 312135;
   telex: 312386 CROM PL.

Spain

ANOSLUZ, Rodriguez San Pedro 2, 28015 Madrid; tel: 445 11 45.
General Tours, Monteleen, 30-10 Madrid; tel: 4486963/12; telex: 42804 viju e.

Switzerland

Artou, 9 Rue de Rive, 1205 Geneve; tel: 4122 2184; telex: 427460 ARTU CH.
Eurotrek, Malzstrasse 17-21, CH 8036 Zurich; tel: 01 462 0203.
Exodus GSA Switzerland, Rain 35, POB 2226 5001 Aarau; tel: 064 22 76 63;
   fax: 064 23 10 84.
Exotissimo, 8 Ave Du Mail, 1205 Geneve; tel: 22 81 21 66; fax: 22 81 21 71;
   telex: 421358 EXOTCH.
Fer Nost-Reisen (Far East), Welchogasse 4, 8050 Zurich; tel: 01 312 4040.
MB Reisen Travel Agency, Limattal STR 200, CH 8049 Zurich-Hongg;
   telex: 823913 mbzh SBG Zurich-Hongg.
Suntrek Tours Ltd, Birmensdorferst 187, PO Box 8371, 8036 Zurich;
   tel: 01 462 6161; fax: 01 462 6565.

USA and Canada

Adventure Center, 3133 63rd Street, Suite 200, Emeryville, CA 94608;
   tel: 510 654 1879; toll Free 800 227 8747; fax: 510 654 4200.
Angkor Wat Adventures, 653 Mt Pleasant Road, Toronto, Ontario M4S 2N2;
   tel: 416 482 1223; fax: 416 486 4001.
Boulder Adventures, PO Box 1279, Boulder, CO80306, USA;
   tel: 800 642 2742; fax: 303 443 7078.
Budgetours International, 8907 Westminster Ave, Garden Grove, CA 92644;
   tel: 714 221 6539, 637 8229, 895 2528.
Club Voyages Berri, 1650 Berri, Suite 8, Montreal, quebec H2L 4E6;
   tel: 514 9826168/9; fax: 514 9820820; telex: 05561074.
Diva Worldwide, 123 Townsend Street, Suite 245, San Francisco, CA 94107;
   tel: 415 777 5351; fax: 415 334 6365.
Edmonton International Tours, 8412-109 Street, Edmonton T6G 1E2;
   tel: 403 439 9118; fax: 403 433 5494.
GAP Adventures, 227 Sterling Road, Suite 105, Toronto, Ontario;
tel: 416 535 6600; fax: 416 535 1197; toll free: 1 800 465 5600.
Go Worldwide Tours, San Francisco; tel: 415 781 3388.
Indochina Consulting Group, 844 Elda Lane, Westbury, New York 11590;
   tel: 516 333 6662 or 516 872 3885.
Lao-America, 338 S Hancock Avenue, South Elgin, IL 60177, USA;
   tel: 708 742 2159; fax: 708 742 432.
Marazul Tours, New York; tel: 212 582 9570.
Mekong Travel, 151 First Avenue, Suite 172, New York, NY 10003;
   tel: 212 420 1586.

New Asia Tours, Tour Nouvelle Asia Inc, 210 Quest Rue Chabanel, Que,
  Canada HZN 1G2; tel: 514 384 4180; fax: 514 384 7045.
Pacific Hemisphere International, 8942 Garden Grove Boulevard, Suite 220,
  Garden Grove, CA 92644.
Tours Connections, 8907 Westminster Avenue, GArden Grove, CA 92644;
  tel: 213 465 7315 or 714 895 2839.
Trek Holidays, Agents Reservations Cadana Wide (Toll Free);
  tel: 1 800 661 7265.
Trek Holidays, 8412-109 Street, Edmonton, Atla T6G 1E2;
  tel: 1 800 661 7265.
Trek Holidays, 336-14 Street NW, Calgary, Atla T2N 1Z7; tel: 403 283 6115;
  fax: 403 283 4166.
Trek Holidays, 1965 West 4th Avenue, Vancouver BC V6J 1M8;
  tel: 604 734 1066; fax: 604 734 2717.
Trek Holidays, 25 Bellair Street, Toronto, Ontario M5R 3L3;
  tel: 416 922 7584; fax: 416 922 8136.
USA Indochina Reconciliation Project, 5808 Green Street, Philadelphia,
  PA 19144; tel: 215 848 4200.
Westcan Treks, 336-14 Street NW, T2N 127, Calgary; tel: 403 283 6115;
  fax: 403 283 4166.
Westcan Treks, 1965 West 4th Avenue, Vancouver BC V6K 1M8;
  tel: 604 734 1066.

Thailand
Air People Tour and Travel, 307 Sa la Daeng Road, Bangkok 10500;
  tel: 2352668 9, 23333864; fax: 662 2409003; telex: 21131 GUETH.
Alternative Tour, 14/1 Soi Rajatapan, Rajaprarop Road, Bangkok;
  tel: 2452963; fax: 2467020.
Asian Holiday Tour, 294/8 Phayathai Road, Bangkok; tel: 2155749.
Asian Lines Travel, 755 Silom Road, Bangkok; tel: 2331510; fax: 233485
Aranya Tour, 105 Makkaeng Road (near Udon Hotel), Udon Thani;
  tel: 42 24 7320.
Banglamphu Tour Services, 17 Khaosan Road, Bangkok; tel: 2813122;
  fax: 2803642.
Cham Siam Tour Sercies, 288 Surawong Road, Bangkok; tel: 255 5570.
Dee Jai Tour, 2nd Floor, 491/29 Silom Plaza Building, Silom Road, Bangkok;
  tel: 234 1685; fax: 2374231.
Diethelm Travel, Kian Gwan Building 11, 140/1 Witthayu Road, Bangkok;
  tel: 2559150; fax: 2560248/9; telex: 8113, 21763, 22700, 22701 DIETRAV
  TH.
Dior Tours, 146-158 Khaosan Road, Bangkok; tel: 2829142.
East-West Travel, 46-1 Sukhumvit Soi 4, Bangkok; tel: 2530681.
Exotissimo Travel Service (Bolsa Travelart), 21/17 Sukumvit Soi 4,
  Bangkok 10110; tel: 2535240/1 or 2552747; fax: 2547683;
  telex: 20479 ASIAN TH.
Ferguson and Associates (USA), 426 1 Soi 10 Paholyothin Road,
  Bangkok 10400; tel: 271 3905; telex: 81070 FERGUSN.
Fortune Tours, 9 Captain Bush Lane, Charoen Krung 30, Bangkok;
  tel: 237 1050.

Guest House Tours, 46/1 Khaosan Road, Bangkok; tel: 2823849.

Inter Companion Group Tours, 86/4 Rambutri Road, Bangkok; tel: 282 9400.

Kannika Tour, 36/9 Sisattha Road, Udon Thani; tel: 42 241378.

Lam Son International Ltd, 23/1 Sukhumvit Soi 4 (Soi Nana Tai), Bangkok; tel: 2556692/3/4/5. 2522340; fax: 2558859.

M K Ways, 18/4 Sathorn Tai Soi 3, Bangkok; tel: 21221532.

Magic Tours, 59/63 Moon Mùang Road, Chiang Mai; tel: 214 572; fax: 214 749,

Nalum Tour, 824 Praisani Road, Nong Khai; tel: 42 512565.

Namthai Travel Company, Bangkok; tel: 2159003/10 or 2157339; fax: 2156240; telex: 22663 NAMTHAI TH.

Pawana Tour and Travel Company, 72/2 Khaosan Road, Bangkok; tel: 2678018.

Pangkaj Travel Services, 625 Sukhumvit Road, Soi 22 Bangkok 10110; tel: 2582240.

Red Carpet Service and Tour, 459 New Rama 7 Road, Phayathai, Bangkok 10400; tel: 2159951; fax: 662 2153331.

S I Tours, 288/2 Silom Road, Bangkok; tel: 2332631.

Siam Wings Travel Company, 173/1-3 Surawong Road, Bangkok; tel: 2534757; fax: 2366808.

Skyline Travel, 491/39-40 Silom Plaza (2nd Floor), Silom Road, Bangkok; tel: 2331864; fax: 2366585.

Spangle Tour Services, 205/1 Sathorn Tai Road, Bangkok; tel: 2121583; fax: 2867732.

Thai Indochina Tours, 4th Floor, 79 Pan Road, Bangkok; tel: 2335369; fax: 2364389.

Thai Travel Service, 119/4 Surawong Road, Bangkok; tel: 2349360.

Thaininee Trading Company, 1131/343 Terddumri Road, Dusit, Bangkok 10300.

Top Thailand Tour Company, 61 Khosan Road, Bangkok; tel: 2802251.

Tour East, Rajapark Buyilding, 10th Floor, 163 Soi Asoke, Bangkok; tel: 2593160; fax: 2583236.

Transindo Ltd, 9th Floor, Thasos Building, 1675 Chan Road, Bangkok; tel: 2873241; fax: 2873245.

Tri Virgo International Travel, 377 Charoen Krung Road, Bangkok 105000; tel: 234 4642; fax: 233 4776.

Udorn Travel, 447/10 Haisok Road, Nong Khai; tel: 411393.

Vikamla Tours, Room 401, Nana Condo, 23/11 Sukhumvit Soi 4 (Soi Nana Tai), Bangkok 10110; tel: 2522320; fax: 2558859.

Vista Travel Service, 24/4 Khao San Road, Banglumphoo, Bangkok; tel: 280 0348/281 0786; fax: 280 0348.

Western Union Travel Services, 78 Sukhumvit Road, Soi 2, Bangkok; tel: 2552151.

Hong Kong

Chu and Associates Co Ltd, Unit E, 5/F, 8 Thomson Road; tel: 5278828 or 5278841; telex: 61113 CHULE HK.

Fimoxy Nacs Ltd, 1801 Yue Xiu Building, 160-174 Lockhart Road, Wanchai, Hong Kong; tel: 511 8732; fax: 507 4991.

Indochina Tours, Friendship Travel, Houston Center, 63 Mody Road,
   Kowloon; tel: 36666862; telex: 31712 WHLTCHX.
Phoenix Services Agency (HK) Ltd, Rm B, 6/F Milton Mansion,
   96 Nathan Road, Kowloon, Hong Kong; tel: 7227378 (5 lines);
   fax: 852 3698884.
Skylion Ltd, Suite D, 11F Trust Tower, 68 Johnston Road, Wanchai;
   tel: 5 8650363; fax: 852 840 0428; telex: 66971 WSKYHX.
The Travel Advisers Ltd, Room 302 Leader Commercial Building,
   54 Hillwood Road, TST KLN; tel: 3682493/3676663; fax: 852 5766635;
   telex: 74237 TME HX.

Philippines
IMPEX International PHILS, Suite 201 Centrum Building, 104 Perea Street,
   Legasapi Village Makati MM; tel: 81648656667; telex: 66687 MBC PN
Indochina Tours, Ground Floor, Corinthian Plaza Building,
   Paseo de Roxas Makati, MM Philippines; tel: 810 4391 to 94;
   fax: 632 801 1010; telex: 54013 IMEXPM.

Japan
Disc Tours, 3rd Floor, Grandeur Yotsuya Buildings, 2-1 Samoncho,
   Shinjuku-ky, Tokyo 16; tel: 03 353 2246; fax: 03 353 6160;
   telex: DISC JJ2325172.
Japan-Indochina Travel Service, 5th Floor, Daihachi-Tanaka Buildings 5-1,
   Gobancho Chiyoda-ku, Tokyo; tel: 03 323 44101.
Rainbow Tours, 7th Floor Crystal Building. 1-2 Kanda,. awaji-Cho,
   Chiyoda-ku, Tokyo 101; tel: 03 253 5855; fax: 03 253 6819;
   telex: 2222611 IDITYOJ (Agents for Saigon Tourist).
Sai Travel Service, 2F Suzuki Daini Building 4-12-4, Shinbashi Minato-ku,
   Tokyo.

Australia and New Zealand
Adventure World, 73 Walker Street, North Sydney, NSW 2060; tel: 956 7766;
   toll free: 008 221 931; fax: 956 7707; telex: 22680.
Adventure World, 3rd Floor, 343 Little Collins Street, Melbourne Vic 3000;
   tel: 670 0125; toll free: 008 133 322; fax: 670 0505.
Adventure World, Level 3, 333 Adelaide Street, Brisbane Qld 4000;
   tel: 2290599; toll free: 008 177 508; fax 221 1399.
Adventure World Adelaide, 101 Currie Street, Adelaide SA 5000;
   tel: 231 6844; fax: 231 6792.
Adventure World Travel, 2nd Floor, 8 Victoria Avenue, Perth WA 6000;
   tel: 221 2300; fax: 221 2337.
Adventure World, 101 Great South Road, Remuera, PO Box 74008, Auckland;
   tel: 524 5118; toll free: 0800 652 954; fax: 520 6629; telex: NZ63125.
Destinations, 2nd Floor, Premier Building, 4 Durham Street, Auckland;
   tel: 09 390464.
Exodus Travels, Level 5, 95-99 York Street, Sydney; tel: 02 299 6355;
   fax: 02 299 6330.
Keyline Trading Co, 31 Pleasant Street, Onehunga, Auckland.

Orbitours, 3rd Floor, 73 Walker Street, North Sydney NSW Australia, 2060, PO Box 834 North Sydney NSW 2059; tel: 61 2 954 1399; fax: 61 2 954 1655; toll free: From USA - 1-800-235-5895; From Australia - 008-221-796. Orbit's general sales agents are Adventure World above.

Peregrine Adventures PTY Ltd, 258 Lonsdale Street, Melbourne VIC 3000; tel: 03 663 8611; fax: 03 663 8618.

Peregrine Adventures, 1st Floor, Scout Outdoor Centre, 132 Wickham Street, Fortitude Valley QLD 4006; tel: 07 854 1021; fax: 07 854 1079.

Peregrine Adventures, 192 Rundle Street, Adelaide SA 5000; tel: 08 223 5905; fax: 08 223 5347.

Peregrine Adventures, 165 Liverpool Street, Hobart 7000; tel: 002 310977; fax: 002 348219.

Peregrine Adventures, 1st Floor, 862 Hay Street, Perth WA 6000; tel: 09 324 1105; fax: 09 231 1259.

Peregrine Adventures, Cnr Marcus Clarke & Alinga Streets, Canberra City NSW 2601; tel: 06 247 6717; fax: 06 248 7250.

Prima Holidays Ltd, 1st Floor, 227 Flinders Lane, Melbourne, VIC 3000; tel: 03 654 4211; fax: 03 654 7204.

South Africa

Gentravel, 2nd Floor, Regent Place, Craddock Avenue, Rosebank 2196 Johannesburg; tel: 011 447 7007; fax: 022 447 7039.

Travel Vision, 2nd Floor, North City House, 28 Melle Street, Braamfontein 2001; tel: 011 403 5710; fax: 011 339 3804.

Appendix Four

TOUR PROGRAMMES

In this Appendix we summarise tours known to be available for 1996 and 1997. Clearly, a guide book of this kind has neither the scope nor the space for full listings and the information is given as a pointer only. But we would recommend the use of the agencies listed and suggest that it really is worth contacting as many agents as you can before settling on the deal that suits you. Please be aware that it can take an awfully long time to get answers from many companies in Laos and Cambodia. Allow as many months (yes, *months!*) as you can.

FOR LAOS

Tours available from Laotian agencies

ADDRESSES ARE GIVEN IN THE VIENTIANE DIRECTORY.

Some of the best deals can obviously be obtained by shopping around. If you first enter the country on a bare tourist package which includes three days in Vientiane, at the end of this period you will be free to extend. Your visa will be valid for 15 days. You will then be in a position to wander from agency to agency. With this flexibility, don't take the first good deal you are offered, bargain hard. Rather than lose your custom some agencies will be prepared to drop their prices by up to 10%. You may prefer to buy a flight/permit package which may work out cheaper still. Remember that Raja Tour are offering a visa authorisation permit for US$40.

Typical packages

Vientiane

3 days, 2 nights

Day 1   Transfer from Mittaphap Bridge to hotel. Morning tour- Arch of Triumph, Pa That Luang. Afternoon excursion to Wat Phra Kéo, Wat Si Saket, Sieng Khuan or Buddha Park.

Day 2   Full day excursion by road to Lake Nam Ngum. Boat trip on lake, picnic. Visit to small archaeological site of Vang Sang and the traditional salt mine of Ban Kheun.

Day 3   Transfer back to Mittaphap Bridge.

For the above package which includes meals and visa processing costs, agencies are charging (in US$):

Agency and Hotel Allocation	Number of Passengers				Single Supp't
	1	2	3	4-6	
Raja Tour Backpacker Hotel or Guest House	225	180	162	143	40
Diethelm Travel Laos Lanexang Hotel (First Class Hotel)	380	325	290	270	60
Sodetour (Second Class Hotel) e.g.: Saysana	300	265	230	200	50

Luang Prabang - 3 days, 2 nights

Day 1   Transfer from airport to hotel. Afternoon visit to various wats and Phu Si Mount.

Day .   Full day Mekong River cruise to Pak Ou Caves. Stops at Lao whiskey distillery and gold panning village.

Day 3   Visit to Royal Palace Museum (Haw Kham). Afternoon flight back to Vientiane.

The prices quoted below for the various agencies do not include the price of the return flight to Luang Prabang. Add US$132 for this.

Agency and Hotel Allocation	Number of Passengers				Single Supp't
	1	2	3	4-6	
Inter-Lao Tourisme Villa de la Princesse (First Class Hotel)	270	235	215	195	85
Diethelm Travel Laos Phu Vao Hotel (First Class Hotel)	255	225	205	185	80
Sodetour Phousy Hotel (Second Class Hotel)	240	180	150	110	60
That Luang Tour Co. Rama Hotel (Budget Hotel)	180	165	155	140	25

Since there are now many tourist companies in Luang Prabang, it is possible for tourists to purchase just a cheap flight/permit package in Vientiane. This would work out far cheaper because you would be free to choose your own hotel and itinerary. This offers some interesting options, including trekking and longer boat trips.

Itineraries offered by Luang Prabang agencies.

Itinerary 1 Walkabout tour to see all the historical and religious sites.
Itinerary 2 Boat trip to Pak Ou Holy Caves and stop-overs in several villages.
Itinerary 3 Trek lasting for four days and three nights. This includes visits and overnight at minority villages.
Itinerary 4 Three-day boat trip. First night you will stay at Muang Pakbéng in Oudomsay Province. This is reached by fast speedboat (*héua wái*). Next day you will proceed to Ban Houayxay in Bokeo Province. The third day you will return to Luang Prabang. Clients refusing to wear protective helmets will not be allowed to make this trip.

Guide prices (in US$) for the above.

Agency	Itinerary 1	Itinerary 2	Itinerary 3	Itinerary 4
Lanexang Travel Co.	8	20	95	65
Diethelm Travel	12	30	-	-
Luang Prabang Tourism	10	25	-	-

These prices are based on four people taking the tour. SODETOUR offers longer packages in this area.

The agencies above will also hire out guides to accompany travellers. Quotations are given by Lanexang for much longer treks and other boat trips. Itinerary 4 will only run as far as Muang Pakbéng if there is ethnic trouble beyond Muang Pakbéng. Inter-Lao Tourisme in Vientiane will also arrange this for US$70.

Extension to Plain of Jars in Xieng Khouang Province

Agency and Hotel Allocation	Number of Passengers				Single Supp't
	1	2	3	4-6	
Inter-Lao Tourisme Mittaphap Hotel (Basic)	320	255	232	190	30
Sodetour Auberge de Plaine de Jarres (Cabin accommodation)	280	245	222	205	35
Diethelm Travel Laos Hotel Plaine de Jarres (Basic)	295	250	215	190	30
That Luang Tour Co. Hay Hin Hotel (Very basic)	250	220	190	155	10

The above prices are quoted in US$ and include flights, accommodation in Phônsavan for one night and sightseeing excursion to the Plain of Jars. Extra nights can be arranged for between US$85-100/night. Sodetour will rent out cabins for longer periods at reduced rate.

Sodetour-FIMOXY, 114 QUA FA-NGUM, PO Box 70, Vientiane. Tel: 865 21 216313/21 5489, Fax: 856 21 216314, Telex: 4314 PACLAO LS

This company has considerable experience and offers an extensive range of tours. They are highly recommended. Contact Claude Vincent and/or Céline.

Vientiane, Xieng Khouang, Luang Prabang, Paksé and Không.
7 days-6 nights/Ref: STL-01

Day 1	Arrive Vientiane. Transfer to hotel. Sightseeing tour.
Day 2	Early morning, fly to Phônsavan (Xieng Khouang Province). Excursion to the Plain of Jars.
Day 3	Visit the market then return flight to Vientiane. Continuation to Luang Prabang. On arrival, excursion by boat on the Mekong River to the holy caves of Pak Ou.
Day 4	In the morning, visit the former royal palace, now the national museum, and the market. After lunch return flight to Vientiane.
Day 5	Leave Vientiane for Paksé. Proceed by boat for Wat Phou in Champassak. Continuation by road for Không Island in the afternoon.
Day 6	Full day excursion through the area of '4,000 islands' and the Mekong waterfalls.
Day 7	Return to Paksé, then transfer to the border at Chongmeck for departure to Udon Ratchathani.

Vientiane, Xieng Khouang, Luang Prabang, Paksé and Champassak.
7 days-6 nights/Ref: STL-01 BIS

SAT	Arrival by air or ferry. Tour of the Lao capital.
SUN	Fly early morning for Phônsavan. Balance of the day is exploring the Plain of Jars.
MON	This morning explore the local market then fly to Vientiane with direct connection to Luang Prabang.
TUE	Whole day excursion on the Mekong River to the Pak Ou caves where are found some of the most famous Buddhist sculptures in South-East Asia. Picnic lunch. On return, visit some villages.
WED	This morning visit the central market and then the palace of the Lao Kings which is now a museum open to the public, before returning to Vientiane.
THU	Depart early morning for Paksé by air, and then by boat down the Mekong River to Champassak to visit ancient Khmer ruins at Wat Phou. Picnic lunch and overnight at Champassak.
FRI	Travel by road to the Lao-Thai border of Chongmeck for Udon Ratchathani, or to Paksé airport for Vientiane or Phnom Penh.

Vientiane, Luang Prabang, Sayaboury, Paksé and Saravane
14 days-13 nights/Ref: STL-02

Day 1   Arrive Vientiane. After lunch, city tour.
Day 2   Full day excursion to the Nam Ngum lake with picnic lunch on an island. Visit on the way the archaeological site of Vang Sang.
Day 3   Flight to Phônsavan. Excursion by road to the Plain of Jars.
Day 4   Excursion through the mountainous area bordering Vietnam. Visit ethnic minority villages.
Day 5   In the morning return flight to Vientiane and continuation to Luang Prabang. City tour.
Day 6   Full day excursion to Kouang Si waterfall and then by boat on the Mekong river to the holy caves of Pak Ou. Picnic lunch by the river.
Day 7   Full day excursion to Sayaboury by boat and by car.
Day 8   In the morning visit the royal palace. Afternoon: fly to Vientiane.
Day 9   Depart early morning by air to Paksé with continuation by boat to Champassak, visit the Khmer ruins of Wat Phou. Picnic lunch, then proceed to Không Island. Overnight at Không.
Day 10 Excursion through the area of the '4000 islands' and to the Mekong waterfalls.
Day 11 Day of leisure to explore Không on bicycles or on foot.
Day 12 After breakfast return to Paksé by road. After lunch continuation by road to Saravane province. Overnight at Tad Lo Lodge.
Day 13 Full day trip through the Bolovens Plateau by car and on elephants.
Day 14 After breakfast, return to Paksé. Transfer to the border at Chongmeck for departure to Udon Ratchathani, or at airport for departure to Vientiane or Phnom Penh.

From the Golden Triangle to Yunnan
6 days-5 nights/Ref: HL 01

Day 1   Arrive Ban Houayxay in the Golden Triangle. Excursion to sapphire mines and a Lantene ethnic minority village. Overnight.
Day 2   Leave by boat for Luang Prabang. Visit Pak Ou.
Day 3   Luang Prabang. Visit the former royal capital.
Day 4   Leave Luang Prabang by boat for Nam Bak then by car for Oudomsay. Overnight.
Day 5   Oudomsay/Luang Nam Tha by road. Overnight.
Day 6   Leave Nam Tha for China by car.

The Upper Laos from Yunnan to Vientiane
8 days-7 nights/Ref: HL 02

Day 1   Arrive Botén (Lao-China border) from Muong La. Transfer to Luang Nam Tha. Overnight.
Day 2   Full day excursion to Muong Xing, the former capital of the Lao Sipsongpanna. Visit villages of different ethnic minorities. Return to Nam Tha late afternoon.
Day 3   Leave by car for Oudomsay. Overnight.
Day 4   Oudomsay Nam Bak by car then by boat down the Nam Ou River for Luang Prabang.
Day 5   Luang Prabang.

Day 6	Leave by plane for Phônsavan (Xieng Khouang Province). Excursion to the Plain of Jars.
Day 7	Leave for Vientiane in the morning. Sightseeing tour.
Day 8	Departure for your next destination.

Grand Tour of Laos

Day 1	Arrive Houayxay in the morning. In the afternoon, excursion to sapphire mine and to a village of Lantene ethnic minority.
Day 2	Leave by speed boat down the Mekong river. Visit several villages and the Pak Ou caves on the way. Arrive Luang Prabang late afternoon. Transfer to hotel.
Day 3	Morning sightseeing tour. Afternoon at leisure.
Day 4	Leave by boat down the Mekong river for the province of Sayaboury. Visit Kouang Si waterfalls on the way. Arrive late afternoon.
Day 5	Visit the market. See elephants at work then return by road to Luang Prabang. Overnight.
Day 6	Leave by boat for Nam Bak up the Mekong River then its subsidiary, the Nam Ou River. Overnight.
Day 7	Leave by mountainous road for Oudomsay. Visit villages of the Mekong ethnic minority up in the mountains. Arrive in the afternoon. Visit the market. Overnight.
Day 8	Leave by car for Nam Tha, visit different villages on the way. Arrive in the afternoon. Overnight.
Day 9	Full day excursion to the Chinese border and to the old city of Muong Sing and to see ethnic minority villages.
Day 10	Excursion to a Khmer village up in the mountain before leaving by plane, early afternoon, for Vientiane. Proceed for Vang Vieng by road with a stop at archaeological site of Van Xang. Overnight.
Day 11	Morning excursion on the River Nam Sone. After lunch leave by road then by boat for the Nam Ngum lake. Overnight.
Day 12	Return to Vientiane airport in the morning then fly to Phônsavan in the province of Xieng Khouang. Visit the Plain of Jars.
Day 13	Full day excursion to Muang Kham, near the Vietnamese border, to H'mong and Thai Dam ethnic minority villages.
Day 14	Morning at leisure. Early afternoon fly back to Vientiane.
Day 15	Morning sightseeing tour of the Lao capital.
Day 16	Leave by road for Thakhek. Visit on the way the famous temple of Buddha's print at Pha Bat, then continue to Paksane and Pakhadine. Arrive later afternoon. Overnight.
Day 17	Full day excursion through the fantastic landscape of limestone mountains to Mahasay.
Day 18	Leave by road for Savannakhét visiting on the way the traditional sale extraction site. Arrive in the afternoon. Visit the city. Overnight.
Day 19	Leave by road for Saravane Province. Visit the Khmer site of Huane Hine, the rapids of the Mekong at Khemmarat, then Saravane along the Se Done river road. Arrive Tad Lo late afternoon. Overnight.
Day 20	Morning elephant ride in the jungle. Afternoon, drive to Sékhong.
Day 21	Full day boat trip on the Se Kong River down to Attopeu. Arrive later afternoon. Overnight.

Day 22   Visit Attopeu surrounding then drive to Paksé through the mountains of the Bolovens area. Visit the ethnic minority villages, coffee and tea plantations; stop at Tad Fan waterfall. Arrive Paksé late afternoon.

Day 23   Visit the market before going by boat on the Mekong river to the Khmer ruins of Oup Mong. Excursion to the ancient fortress of Phon Assa. In the afternoon, drive to Không Island. Overnight.

Day 24   Full day tour by car and by boat through to '4000 islands' area up to the Mekong waterfalls. Return to hotel late afternoon. In the evening, traditional *Basi* ceremony.

Day 25   Morning drive to Champassak. Visit Wat Phou ruins and Ban That. Overnight at Champassak.

Day 26   Leave for Chongmeck, the border crossing point between Laos and Thailand, or to Paksé airport.

Travelling down the Mekong River

Floating down the most beautiful sections of the river Mekong on traditional sampans. These sampans are middle sized and will allow the tourist to have a real experience of travelling by boat in Laos as close to nature and the people as possible without any danger.

Day 1   Arrive Vientiane late morning. Afternoon sightseeing tour.

Day 2   Fly early morning to Ban Houayxay in the Golden Triangle. Full day excursion to sapphire mine and to a Lantene ethnic minority village.

Day 3   Leave early morning for Pakbéng down the Mekong River. Arrive in the afternoon. Overnight.

Day 4   Leave for Luang Prabang. Visit Pak Ou Caves on the way. Arrive Luang Prabang late afternoon.

Day 5   Visit the former royal capital.

Day 6   Leave for Sayaboury Province. Visit Kouang Si waterfalls on the way. Arrive Tha Deua in the afternoon. Proceed by car for Sayaboury. Overnight.

Day 7   Morning sightseeing tour of Sayaboury surroundings. Afternoon fly back to Vientiane. Overnight.

Day 8   Depart early morning for Savannakhét. Sightseeing tour of the city then down the Mekong to the Angkorian ruins of Huane Hine. From there, board a small pirogue type boat to see the rapids of Khemmarat. In the afternoon, continuation by car for Paksé.

Day 9   Visit Paksé market then proceed by boat for Oup Mong, a small Angkorian ruins lost in a dense forest of fromage trees. Continuation for Không Island. Overnight.

Day 10   Full day tour of the '4000 Islands' area.

Day 11   Tour of Không Island by bicycle or *túk-túk*.

Day 12   Leave Không by car for Champassak. On the way, elephant ride to the ancient citadel of Phon Assa at the top of a mountain overlooking the Mekong. Arrive late afternoon. Overnight.

Day 13   Full day excursion to Wat Phou ruins and its two main annexes of Nang Sida and Ban That.

Day 14   Depart for Chongmeck then proceed to Udon Ratchathani or fly back to Vientiane or Phnom Penh.

Prices Hotel First Category:

Ref: Tours/Nb/Pax	1	2	3	4-6	7-9	10-14	15 up	Sup Sgl	Sup F/Brd
STL01	1932	1129	953	891	767	749	705	159	155
STL01 bis	1713	1047	902	790	753	733	701	155	166
STL02	3250	1834	1516	1404	1174	1143	1129	345	324
HL 01	1563	788	579	557	425	388	375	117	106
HL 02	1831	1050	863	826	690	658	648	157	155
Grand Tour		3257	2454	2267	1646			430	419
Mekong River		2256	1783	1580	1233	1178	1063	304	287

Prices Hotel Category Standard

Ref: Tours/Nb/Pax	1	2	3	4-6	7-9	10-14	15 up	Sup Sgl	Sup F/Brd
STL01	1757	1023	843	787	663	644	596	99	110
STL01 bis	1523	955	818	764	664	642	620	103	113
STL02	2814	1598	1285	1188	957	928	875	183	247
HL 01	1397	710	512	498	369	333	314	61	66
HL 02	1535	891	713	671	539	501	480	88	95
Grand Tour		3048	2266	2030	1375			193	319
Mekong River		1991	1458	1271	913	853	726	121	193

Prices are in US$ per person. They include hotel accommodation, with American breakfast, all transfers and excursions included in the programme, entrance fees on site, assistance of an English or French speaking guide, domestic airport taxes, domestic flights. They don't include meals, drinks, international airport tax, personal expenses.

All these tours can also be booked through Becky Bale at Phoenix Services Agency (Hong Kong); tel: 7227378 (5 lines); fax: 852 369884. They have a very friendly service.

Lanexang Travel and Tour Co Ltd, Paingkham Road, PO Box 4452, Vientiane, offer the interesting Laos Adventure Tour.

Day 1   Enter Laos at Ban Houayxay; city tour; visit the temple Wat Chom Kao then proceed by car (truck or jeep) out of the city to visit the villages of Lao Lu Ban Phoung, Yao Ban Len Ten and Lu Ban Tom Lao minorities. Overnight at Manirat Hotel or similar.

Day 2	Boat trip down the Mekong River to Pakbéng.

Day 2   Boat trip down the Mekong River to Pakbéng.

Day 3   Leaving Pakbéng by car (truck or jeep) to Luang Nam Tha. Overnight at Houa Kong Cottage.

Day 4   Full day excursion by car (truck or jeep). Visit the minorities surroundings and the Lao-Chinese border at Botén.

Day 5   Leave for Pak Bak passing the villages of hill tribes and beautiful mountain scenery. Arrive Pak Bak in the evening.

Day 6   Leave Pak Bak by longboat down the Nam Ou River to Luang Prabang. Stop at Pak Ou Cave to visit the thousands of Buddha images and Ban Sang Hai where the people distil rice wine. Arrive Luang Prabang in late evening, overnight at Princess Hotel.

Day 7   Excursion by car (truck or jeep) to Kuang Si Waterfalls, visit the A'ka village of Ban Tha Paen, picnic lunch at waterfall site. Return to Luang Prabang in the afternoon. Visit Wat Xieng Maen, Wat Hath Siao, Wat Tham, Wat Chom Phet Bon, Ban Pha Nom.

Day 8   Excursion to Sayaboury Province, en route visit H'mong village of Ban Long Lao, and the ancient temple of Wat Sakarit. Return to Luang Prabang in late afternoon.

Day 9   Morning visit to the Museum (former king's palace) built in 1904, Wat Xieng Thong, the royal temple, Phousi Mount, and Wat Visoun where the biggest Buddha statue is housed. Visit silversmith shop where local people make silver ornaments. Fly back to Vientiane in the afternoon.

Day 10   Excursion by car to Nam Ngum Dam via Ban Hua Khua, Na Sone, Na Ngang, Dan Soung visiting the archaeological site of Vang Sang and Buddha statue at Dan Pha Dan Phone Hong. Boat tour on the Nam Ngum Lake and picnic lunch on the island Don Khoune Khan. Return to Vientiane on road No 10. Visit traditional salt manufacture plant at Ban Kuen.

Day 11   Excursion by car to Tha Bok to visit the foot print of the Buddha at Pha Bat Phone San, picnic lunch at Tad Lang Waterfall.

Day 12   Half day tour to the Garden of Xian Khouane. Afternoon free for shopping.

Day 13   Departure by plane to Xieng Khouane (Phônsavan Airport). Proceed by car to visit the Plain of Jars and Muang Khoune.

Day 14   Excursion by car to Lat Huang, Muang Sui, San Tio to visit temples.

Day 15   Departure by plane back to Vientiane. Free.

Day 16   Departure by plane to Paksé. Upon arrival at Paksé Airport, proceed by car to Tad Lo to visit the villages of Alak minority. On the way, visit Tha Teng, Kalum and Cotu. Overnight at Tad Lo Lodge.

Day 17   Leaving Tad Lo by car to Paksé, continue by boat down the Mekong River to Champassak. Visit Wat Phou. Overnight at Không Island.

Day 18   Full day to spend exploring the Không area. Just upriver from Không you will be able to view rare freshwater dolphins during the winter months. Known for natural beauty and memorable collection of colonial era buildings and bridges, this district was once a major transportation hub on the Mekong River.

Day 19   Return to Paksé and head for Lao/Thai border. Transfer to Ubol Airport for evening flight to Bangkok.

The price of the Laos Adventure Tour will be given on contacting Lanexang Travel Co Ltd. It will cost around US$3,000 for one person staying in budget accommodation. If an entry visa is not permitted by Lao Government, Lanexang Travel will fully refund the deposit of 50% to the passenger.

FROM WORLDWIDE TOURIST COMPANIES

In the UK
Regent Holiday (UK) Ltd
Itinerary 1. Vientiane/Luang Prabang/Vientiane
5 days, 4 nights.

Day 1	Transfer from Mittaphap Bridge or Wattay Airport. City tour.
Day 2	Flight to Luang Prabang. Temple tour on arrival.
Day 3	Full day boat trip to Pak Ou holy caves on Mekong River.
Day 4	Visit to former Royal Palace before flight to Vientiane.
Day 5	Visit central market before transfer to airport or Mittaphap Bridge.

	Number of Passengers				Single Supp't
	1	2	3	4-6	
Price in US$	815	574	521	471	70

Half board supplement US$27. Full board supplement US$65.

Itinerary 2. Vientiane/Luang Prabang/Vientiane/Phônsavan/Vientiane
8 days, 7 nights

Day 1-3	Same as for Itinerary 1.
Day 4	Visit former Royal Palace and market before flight to Vientiane. Afternoon excursion to weaving village.
Day 5	Flight to Xieng Khouane. Excursion to Muang Khoune and tour of Xieng Khouang.
Day 6	Excursion to Plain of Jars, Muang Khan and Tham Piou hot spring and ethnic village.
Day 7	Visit local market before flight to Vientiane.
Day 8	Transfer to airport or Mittaphap Bridge.

	Number of Passengers				Single Supp't
	1	2	3	4-6	
Price in US$	1190	815	791	666	110

Half board supplement US$50. Full board supplement US$110.

Itinerary 3. Vientiane/Luang Prabang/Vientiane/Paksé/Vientiane
8 days, 7 nights

Day 1-4	Same as Itinerary 1.
Day 5	Morning flight to Paksé with afternoon excursion to Bolovens Plateau.

Day 6   Full day boat/car excursion to the pre-Angkorian ruins of Wat Phou near Champassak City.
Day 7   Tour of central market before transfer to airport for Vientiane flight.
Day 8   Flight to Xieng Kouang Province, visit to H'mong village.
Day 9   Visit Plain of Jars before flight back to Vientiane.
Day 10   Transfer to Wattay airport or Tha Deua exit point.

	Number of Passengers				Single Supp't
	1	2	3	4-6	
Price in US$	1936	1348	1201	1126	145

Half board supplement US$75. Full board supplement US$163.

Explore Worldwide
This company offers Laos as part of an Indochina tour package (five days out of a total of 19) which takes in Vietnam and Cambodia as well. The cost is £1,789 and 1996 departure dates are 18th February and 24th March.

They also offer a Laos and Thailand package (seven days in Laos) for £1,239. Departure dates in 1996 are 4th February and 10th March.

In France
Eurasie Travel France (ET Voyage)
Programme 1   Vientiane/Houayxay. 3 days, 2 nights. For onward flight to Thailand.
Programme 2   Vientiane/Houayxay. 5 days, 4 nights.
Programme 3   Vientiane. 3 days, 2 nights.
Programme 4   Vientiane/Nam Ngum/Vientiane. 3 days, 2 nights.
Programme 5   Vientiane/Nam Ngum/Vientiane. 4 days, 3 nights.
Programme 6   Vientiane/Nam Ngum/Vientiane/Vang Vieng/Vientiane. 4 days, 3 nights.
Programme 7   Vientiane/Luang Prabang/Vientiane. 4 days, 3 nights.
Programme 8   Vientiane/Luang Prabang/Vientiane. 5 days, 4 nights.
Programme 9   Vientiane/Luang Prabang/Vientiane. 6 days, 5 nights.
Programme 10   Vientiane/Luang Prabang/Vientiane. 7 days, 6 nights.
Programme 11   Vientiane/Luang Prabang/Vientiane/Paksé/Vientiane. 8 days, 7 nights.

Programme	1 PAX	2 PAX	3 PAX	4-5 PAX	6-7 PAX	8-10 PAX	11-13 PAX	14-15 PAX	16+ PAX	Single Supp't
1	262	235	211	200	198	174	172	171	163	6
2	537-573	393-426	368-401	357-391	354-388	333-364	330-361	327-358	311-341	45-51
3	249-328	161-227	147-214	141-207	140-206	124-188	123-186	122-185	117-180	34-51
4	343-421	209-278	184-254	172-242	171-240	144-208	143-206	142-205	133-196	34-51
5	430-540	269-366	249-345	235-331	233-328	195-292	193-290	191-287	183-276	51-73
6	560-630	350-405	292-349	267-324	264-321	200-259	199-256	197-254	183-240	45-57
7	587-797	413-510	375-473	350-447	347-443	327-423	324-420	321-416	308-403	40-96
8	669-876	470-602	425-561	400-532	397-528	372-505	369-501	365-496	353-483	57-119
9	783-1043	544-708	495-660	478-641	473-635	435-596	431-591	427-585	409-569	73-153
10	1060-1415	763-972	694-899	658-858	652-851	588-782	583-775	578-768	557-712	79-175
11	1175-1549	838-1090	754-992	710-939	704-931	632-848	626-840	620-833	597-806	85-192

Price range: depends on accommodation standard selected. Prices (in US$) are to be held until October 1996.

In Thailand
Diethelm Travel, Bangkok.
Offer similar itineraries to Regent Holidays (UK) Ltd. Price is slightly cheaper if booked direct. Would recommend booking with Regent who will sort out everything for you before you leave the country.

In Australia
Orbitours, Sydney.
Vientiane visit. *3 days, 2 nights.*
Full tour of city included. Rates based on minimum of two passengers.

Hotel Class	Twin Share	Single Sup.	Extra Night	Single Sup.
Backpacker/Guest House No Meals.	A$254	A$20	A$15	A$10
Budget Hotel, B&B	A$301	A$30	A$25	A$16
Saysana Hotel. (Moderate - Full Board)	A$329	A$42	A$32	A$21
Lanexang Hotel (First Class - Full Board)	A$399	A$70	A$59	A$35
Belvedere Hotel (Superior Class)	A$459	A$98	A$80	A$49

Vientiane/Luang Prabang. *5 days/4 nights.*

This includes Vientiane tour, Luang Prabang tour, boat to Pak Ou Caves all transfers

Hotel Class	Twin Share	Single Sup.	Extra Night	Single Sup.
Vientiane Hotel/Rama Guest House, B&B	A$690	A$68	A$65	A$9
Saysana Hotel/ Phousi Hotel	A$799	A$79	A$103	A$20
Lanexang/ Phu Vao Hotel	A$948	A$165	A$136	A$49
Extension - Plain of Jars Guesthouse	A$401	A$39	A$188	A$201
Superior Hotel	A$368	A$16	A$149	A$16

This company will organise any individual itinerary you want, prices on application. Highly recommended.

In Vietnam
Saigon Tourist Saigon/Hanoi

They offer Laos programmes as extensions to their Vietnam programmes.

Programme 1   Vientiane. 4 days, 3 nights
Programme 2   Vientiane/Luang Prabang. 5 days, 4 nights.
Programme 3   Vientiane/Luang Prabang. 6 days, 5 nights.
Programme 4   Vientiane/Luang Prabang/Paksé/Champassak. 7 days, 6 nights.
Programme 5   Vientiane/Luang Prabang/Xieng Khouang. 8 days, 7 nights.

	1 PAX	2 PAX	3-6 PAX	7-10 PAX	11 PAX UP	Sgl Sup
Programme 1	1428	714	702	645	582	75
Programme 2	2172	1086	1074	1056	966	100
Programme 3	2520	1260	1236	1224	1116	125
Programme 4	3912	1956	1884	1842	1638	150
Programme 5	4536	2268	2040	2004	1860	175

All prices quoted in US$. Prices include accommodation in Vietnam, flights to/from Laos, all transfers, accommodation in best available hotels in Laos, all meals, visa fee, permit fees and services of interpreter/guide. Very expensive but prices include three days in Vietnam.

FOR CAMBODIA

The agencies in Phnom Penh we are able to recommend are Diethelm Travel, Phnom Penh Tourism, Aroon Tours and Apsara Tours. There may be others; let us know in plenty of time for the next edition, please ...

We also mention some of the worldwide agencies which, as for Laos, should be taken for the purpose of example only (ie not as an exclusive list). Prices are, again, given for two people travelling together.

Booking direct with Phnom Penh Tourism
By far the cheapest way to tour Cambodia is to organise a group of people yourself and then book directly with Phnom Penh Tourism.

Phnom Penh Tourism Travel Service offer the following for the 1995-6 period. They can be contacted at No 313 Vithei Karx, Phnom Penh, The State of Cambodia; tel: 24059; fax: 855 23 26043.

Make sure that you book with them at least three months before you intend to travel. This allows plenty of time for confirmations and bureaucratic hassle involved to be sorted out. Payment can be made by bankers draft once everything has been confirmed. Booking directly with Phnom Penh Tourism Travel Service will save you a lot of money. They are offering 13 package tour programmes for the 1995/96 period. All prices are in US$.

Itinerary 1 - *3 days/2 nights*
Day 1   Arrival at Pochentong airport, transfer to hotel. City Tour: Wat Phnom, Ounalom Pagoda, Independence Monument, Chadomuk, National Museum, Silver Pagoda.
Day 2   Fly to Siem Reap. Visit Angkor Wat and Angkor Thom. Lunch. 14.00: Transfer to airport for departure. PNH. Visit Tuol Sleng.
Day 3   Breakfast, morning at leisure. Transfer to airport.

Itinerary 1	Number of passengers					
	1	2	3-5	6-9	10-15	16 UP
Hotels Cambodiana & Ta Prohm	865	574	551	506	497	482
Le Royal or Ambassador & Grand Hotel	621	450	427	382	373	358
Pailin or similar & Bayon or similar	601	430	407	362	353	338
Monorom or Orchidee & Bayon or similar	551	404	381	336	327	312

Itinerary 3 - *4 days/3 nights*

Day 1　　Same as above.

Day 2　　AM - Visit Bayon Temple. Lunch.

　　　　　PM - Visit Angkor Wat Temple. Dinner and overnight.

Day 3　　AM - Visit Thommanon, Chau Say Tevoda, Ta Keo, Ta Prohm, Bantéay Kdei, Srah Srang.

　　　　　PM - Transfer to airport for departure.

Day 4　　AM - Visit to Tuol Sleng Museum and 'Killing Fields of Choeung Ek'.

　　　　　PM - Connecting flight to...

Itinerary 3	Number of passengers					
	1	2	3-5	6-9	10-15	16 UP
Hotels Cambodiana & Ta Prohm	1038	685	662	608	592	571
Le Royal or Ambassador & Grand Hotel	988	545	522	468	452	431
Pailin or similar & Bayon or similar	728	505	482	428	412	391
Monorom or Orchidee & Bayon or similar	679	479	456	402	386	365

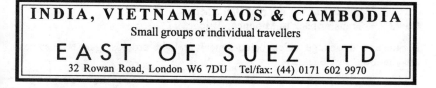

IItinerary 7 – *6 days, 5 nights*

Day 1   Same as above, tour of Phnom Penh.

Day 2   Visit Ta Prohm Temple and Tonlé Bati. In the afternoon a visit is made to Koh Dach, silk weaving village and Mekong Island.

Day 3   AM - Flight to Siem Reap. Visit to south gate of Angkor Thom, Bayon and Elephant terrace. Lunch.
PM - Visit to Angkor Wat. Dinner and overnight.

Day 4   AM - Visit to North Gate of Angkor Thom, Thommanon, Chau Say Tevoda, Ta Kéo, Ta Prohm. Lunch.
PM - Visit to Bantéay Kravan, Bantéay Kdei and Srah Srang. Dinner and overnight.

Day 5   AM - Flight back to Phnom Penh.
PM - Visit to Tuol Sleng Prison and 'Killing Fields of Choeung Ek'.

Day 6   At leisure until connection flight.

Itinerary 7	Number of passengers					
	1	2	3-5	6-9	10-15	16 UP
Hotels Cambodiana & Ta Prohm	1504	1027	969	902	868	840
Le Royal or Ambassador & Grand Hotel	1154	817	759	692	658	630
Pailin or similar & Bayon or similar	1074	782	724	657	623	595
Monorom or Orchidee & Bayon or similar	999	747	689	622	588	560

Itinerary 11 – *7 days/6 nights*

Day 1   Tour of Phnom Penh.

Day 2   AM - Flight to Siem Reap.

Day 3   Visit Angkor Thom, Thommanon, Chau Say Tevoda, Ta Kéo and Bantéay Kdei.

Day 4   Visit Preah Kô, Bakong, Lolei, the city and a crocodile farm.

Day 5   Visit to Preah Khan, Phimeanakas, Mébon, Pré Rup. Dinner and overnight.

Day 6   Excursion to Tonlé Sap Lake. Transfer to airport for flight.

Day 7   Flight back to Phnom Penh. Excursion to 'Killing Fields of Choeung Ek' and visit to Tuol Sleng Prison. Transfer to airport.

Itinerary 11	Number of passengers					
	1	2	3-5	6-9	10-15	16 UP
Hotels Cambodiana & Ta Prohm	1494	1036	1005	940	908	805
Le Royal or Ambassador & Grand Hotel	1144	846	815	750	718	675
Pailin or similar & Bayon or similar	1044	796	765	700	668	625
Monorom or Orchidee & Bayon or similar	1004	781	740	675	643	605

Itinerary 13 – *8 days/7 nights*

Day 1   Tour of Phnom Penh.
Day 2-7   Visits to all the temples in vicinity of Angkor including Angkor Wat and Bantéay Srei.
Day 7   Flight back to Phnom Penh, visit to 'Killing Fields of Choeung Ek' and Tuol Sleng Prison.
Day 8   At leisure until transfer to airport for flight to ...

Itinerary 13	Number of passengers					
	1	2	3-5	6-9	10-15	16 UP
Hotels Cambodiana & Ta Prohm	1594	1127	1102	1051	1010	962
Le Royal or Ambassador & Grand Hotel	1194	912	887	836	795	747
Pailin or similar & Bayon or similar	1054	842	817	766	725	682
Monorom or Orchidee & Bayon or similar	1004	817	792	741	700	657

Diethelm Travel (Cambodia) Ltd

8 Samdech Sothearos Boulevard, Phnom Penh, Kingdom of Cambodia;
tel:855 2326 648; fax: 855 2326 676.

The following tours are available with daily departures. Depending on the actual flights used, the schedules of Phnom Penh sightseeing tours may sometimes have to be adjusted.

Although Diethelm Travel offers a selection of accommodations at various hotels, it may not always be possible to confirm accommodations as requested, due to very limited capacity in Phnom Penh and Siem Reap. Alternative accommodations can in some cases be at substandard hotels which lack essential facilities. No refund can be made for any shortcomings related to accommodation in Siem Reap.

The Siem Reap tour programme is with the first flight to Siem Reap and with the last flight to Phnom Penh. The tour programme is subject to change according to the flight schedule.

All tours include airfares between Phnom Penh/Siem Reap/Phnom Penh, domestic airport tax, hotel accommodation, full board, all sightseeing as detailed in the programmes, air-conditioned cars/vans/buses and the services of English or French speaking local guides. Prices are valid through until July 1996.

Diethelm Travel will cater for group sizes up to 28 (for Phnom Penh) and 20 for Angkor region. All prices quoted are subject to 2% government tax. Payment can be made directly through their bank account number, which is 30.060.768, The Foreign Trade Bank, Phnom Penh. They have the usual liability conditions. They also accept bookings for individual hotels in Phnom Penh.

Cambodia tours
VC3   3-day Cambodia/Angkor Wat Tour (incl. day-trip to Angkor Wat).

Day 1   Transfer Phnom Penh Pochentong airport to hotel. Lunch. City tour.
Day 2   Flight to Siem Reap. Angkor Wat tour.
Day 3   Breakfast at hotel. Tuol Sleng and 'Killing Fields' tour. Transfer to Pochentong airport

Phnom Penh hotel	Number of passengers					Single Suppt	Total reduction for 16 pax
	1	2	3-5	6-14	15-29		
Sofitel Cambodiana	813	559	542	513	429	175	312
Juliana or Allson Star	589	435	418	393	368	75	250
Hawaii	507	396	379	354	329	32	218

All rates are per person, in US$.

VC5   5-day Cambodia/Angkor Wat Tour.

Day 1   Transfer to hotel. Lunch at hotel. City tour.
Day 2   Flight Phnom Penh/Siem Reap. Visits to the South Gate of Angkor Thom, Bayon, Baphuon, Elephant Terrace and Royal Palace. Visits to Angkor Wat and Phnom Bakheng.

Day 3   Visits to the Victory Gate, Thommanon, Chau Say Tevoda, Ta Kéo, Ta Prohm, Bantéay Kdei, Srah Srang and Kravan Temples. Visits to Tep Pronom, Preah Palilay, Preah Pithu Group, North and South Khleang, Prasat Suor Prat. Sunset at Angkor Wat.

Day 4   Visits to Preah Khan, Neak Pean, Ta Som, Eastern Mébon and Pré Rup Temple. Visit to the Rolous Group: Preah Kô and Bakong. Flight Siem Reap/Phnom Penh.

Day 5   Tuol Sleng and Killing Fields tour. Transfer to airport

Hotel	Number of passengers					Single Suppt	Total reduction for 16 pax
	1	2	3-5	6-14	15-29		
Sofitel Cambodiana (Phnom Penh) Ta Prohm or Grand (superior room) (Siem Reap)	1064	720	695	655	552	230	332
Juliana or Allson Star (PP) Banteay Srey or Diamond (SR)	841	600	575	535	500	132	313
Hawaii (PP) Grand (standard room) or similar (SR)	702	530	505	465	427	59	238

All rates are per person, in US$.

VC7   7-day Cambodia/Angkor Wat Tour.

Day 1   Transfer to hotel. Lunch at hotel. City tour.

Day 2   Flight Phnom Penh/Siem Reap. Visits to the South Gate of Angkor Thom and Bayon. Visit to Angkor Wat until sunset.

Day 3   Visits to Baphuon, Elephant Terrace, Leper King Terrace, Royal Palace, Tep Pronom and Preah Palilay. Visits to Preah Pithu Group, North and South Khleang, Group of Prasat Suor Prat and sunset on Phnom Bakheng.

Day 4   Visits to Victory Gate, Thommanon, Chau Say Tevoda, Ta Kéo and Ta Prohm. Visits to Bantéay Kdei, Srah Srang, Kravan Temple, Bat Chum and Pré-Rup Temple.

Day 5   Visits to Preah Khan, Neak Pean, Ta Som and Eastern Mébon. Boat trip on Tonlé Sap lake.

Day 6   Visit to the Roluos Group, Preah Kô and Bakong. Local market. Visit the Crocodile Farm and Western Baray. Flight Siem Reap/Phnom Penh and transfer to hotel.

Day 7   Tuol Sleng and Killing Fields tour. Transfer to Pochentong airport.

Hotel	Number of passengers					Single Suppt	Total reduction for 16 pax
	1	2	3-5	6-14	15-29		
Sofitel Cambodiana (Phnom Penh) Ta Prohm or Grand (superior room) (Siem Reap)	1322	890	856	799	681	285	352
Juliana or Allson Star (PP) Banteay Srey or Diamond (SR)	1100	772	737	682	635	188	377
Hawaii (PP) Grand (standard room) or similar (SR)	906	673	639	583	531	87	258

All rates are per person, in US$.

Angkor Tours
AK1   1 day trip.

Fly to Siem Reap. Visits to the South Gate of Angkor Thom, Bayon, Baphuon, Elephant Terrace and Royal Palace. Lunch. Visit to Angkor Wat. Flight Siem Reap/Phnom Penh.

Number of persons	1	2	3-5	6-14	15-29	Total reduction for 16 pax
	257	217	209	195	185	138

All rates are per person, in US$.

AK3   3 days and 2nights

Day 1   Flight to Siem Reap. Visits to the South Gate of Angkor Thom, Bayon, Baphuon, Elephant Terrace, Leper King Terrace and Royal Palace. Lunch. Visits to Angkor Wat and Phnom Bakheng.

Day 2   Visits to the Victory Gate, Thommanon-Chau Say Tevoda, Ta Kéo, Ta Prohm, Bantéay Kdei, Srah Srang and Kravan Temple. Lunch. Visits to Tep Pronom, Preah Palilay, Preah Pithu Group, North and South Khleang and Prasat Suor Preat. Sunset at Angkor Wat.

Day 3   Visits to Preah Khan, Neak Pean, Ta Som, Eastern Mébon and Pré Rup Temple. Lunch. Visit the Roluos Group, Preah Kô and Bakong. Flight Siem Reap/Phnom Penh.

Siem Reap hotel	Number of passengers					Single Suppt	Total reduction for 16 pax
	1	2	3-5	6-14	15-29		
Ta Prohm or Grand (superior room)	507	379	362	334	309	55	157
Banteay Srey or Diamond	509	383	366	337	317	57	201
Grand (standard room) or similar	452	352	335	306	284	28	157

AK5   5 days and 4 nights.

Day 1   Flight to Siem Reap. Visits to the South Gate of Angkor Thom and Bayon. Visits to Angkor Wat until sunset.

Day 2   Visits to Baphuon, Elephant Terrace, Leper King Terrace, Royal Palace, Tep Pronom and Preah Palilay. Visits to Preah Pithu Group, North and South Khleng Group of Prasat Suor Prat and sunset on Phnom Bakheng
Dinner and accommodation at hotel

Day 3   Visits to the Victory Gate, Thommanon, Chau Say Tevoda, Ta Kéo and Ta Prohm. Visits to Bantéay Kdei, Srah Srang, Kravan Temple, Bat Chum and Pré Rup Temple.

Day 4   Visits to Preah Khan, Neak Pean, Ta Som and Eastern Mébon. Boat trip on Tonlé Sap Lake.

Day 5   Visit the Roluos Group, Preah Kô and Bakong. Local market. Visit Crocodile Farm and Western Baray. Flight Siem Reap/Phnom Penh.

Siem Reap hotel	Number of passengers					Single Suppt	Total reduction for 16 pax
	1	2	3-5	6-14	15-29		
Ta Prohm or Grand (superior room)	766	549	524	479	437	110	177
Banteay Srey or Diamond	767	554	529	484	452	113	265
Grand (standard room) or similar	656	494	469	424	387	55	177

Aroon Tour Co Ltd

Another recommended tour operator in Phnom Penh is Aroon Tour Co Ltd, 201 Achar Mean Road, Sangkat Monorom Khan 7 Makara; tel/fax: 855 23 26 300 or No 2 Dusit Hotel, 120 Street, Khan Daun Penh, Phnom Penh; tel/fax: 855 23 64 397. You won't find friendlier tour guides anywhere. The company was formed recently by co-directors, Chith Pok and or Anthony (Yuthana). Until mid-1996 they are offering seven packages. The three examples given are nearly identical to those offered by Diethelm Travel (Cambodia) Ltd. Prices depend on which hotels are used in the package. All include accommodation, transfers and tours, admission fees, airfare Phnom Penh/Siem Reap/Phnom Penh, domestic airport tax, US$8/person, admission fees for National Museum and Angkor Wat/Bayon. All meals. International airport tax is not included.

First Class Hotel in Phnom Penh and in Siem Reap: Cambodiana Hotel (Phnom Penh), Ta Prohm, Grand, Apsara, Banteay Srey Hotel (Siem Reap).

DESCRIPTION	01 PAX	2-5 PAX	6-9 PAX	10 PAX UP
3 days/2 nights	755	623	588	505
5 days/4 nights	967	798	773	753
7 days/6 nights	1379	1058	1033	1018

All prices in US$
Single room supplements: Cambodiana US$75/night
Ta Prohm, Grand, Apsara, Banteay Srey US$50/night

Second Class Hotel in Phnom Penh and First Class Hotel in Siem Reap.
Diamond , Allson Star Hotel in Phnom Penh; Taprohm, Grand, Apsara, Banteay Srey Hotel (Siem Reap)

DESCRIPTION	01 PAX	2-5 PAX	6-9 PAX	10 PAX UP
3 days/2 nights	645	540	494	484
5 days/4 nights	907	786	761	741
7 days/6 nights	1079	1034	999	979

All prices in US$
Single room supplements: Diamond, Allson Star US$50/night
Ta Prohm, Grand, Apsara, Banteay Srey US$50/night

Second Class Hotel in Phnom Penh & Standard Class Hotel in Siem Reap.
Diamond , Allson Star Hotel in Phnom Penh; Bayon, Diamond, Bopear, Bopha (Siem Reap)

DESCRIPTION	01 PAX	2-5 PAX	6-9 PAX	10 PAX UP
3 days/2 nights	520	415	400	390
5 days/4 nights	818	711	673	658
7 days/6 nights	1058	865	830	794

All prices in US$
Single room supplements: Diamond, Allson Star US$50/night
Bayon, Diamond, Bo Phear, Bopha US$30/night

Standard Class Hotel in Phnom Penh & in Siem Reap.
Pailin, Paradise, Champs Elysess, Golf, Ramain in Phnom Penh; Bayon, Diamond, Bopear, Bopha (Siem Reap)

DESCRIPTION	01 PAX	2-5 PAX	6-9 PAX	10 PAX UP
3 days/2 nights	520	415	400	390
5 days/4 nights	730	623	585	570
7 days/6 nights	970	784	740	730

All prices in US$
Single room supplements: All hotels above US$30/Night

Alternatives

If you require an individual itinerary contact either **Orbitour** in Sydney or **Phoenix Services Agency,** in Hong Kong. They are at Toom B, 6/F, Milton Mansion, 96 Nathan Road, Kowloon, Hong Kong; tel:722 7378 (5 lines); fax:852 369 8884. Becky Bale will quote you a package which will suit your requirements, whatever your financial status. Phoenix Services Agency is thoroughly recommended. They can book most hotels in Cambodia.

Apsara Tours, No 8 Street, R.V. Senei Vinnavaut Oum, Norodom Boulevard Sangkat, Chaktomuk, Khan Daun Penh; tel: 855 15 911 634/914 199/914 073/914 194; fax: 855 23 26 705/855 23 27 835.
These are slightly on the expensive side but offer some interesting tours as well as the standard type offered by other tourist companies. These include:

1. Visits to the Province of Takeo

Day 1	Departure from Phnom Penh. Visits to the Ta Prohm Temple in Tonlé Bati, Neang Khmao Temple, Phnom Chisor. City sightseeing. Lunch, dinner and overnight at the Vimean Suor Hotel in Takeo.
Day 2	Excursion to Phnom Dar. Lunch at Angkor Borei. Return to Takeo, then to Phnom Penh

Price per PAX: 1 PAX   US$375
                   2-3 PAX   US$230 (Single Supplement: US$15)

2. Visits to Sihanoukville

Day 1 (Sat)	Flight Phnom Penh - Sihanoukville. City sightseeing. Sea cruise. Lunch, dinner and overnight at the Seaside Hotel
Day 2 (Sun)	Wat Loeu, Wat Krom, Port. Lunch, dinner and overnight at the Seaside Hotel
Day 3	Flight back to Phnom Penh

Price per PAX: 1 PAX   US$442
                   2-3 PAX   US$427 (Single Supplement: US$50)

3. Visits to Angkor

Day 1	Flight Phnom Penh/Siem Reap. City sightseeing. Visit to the Bayon and Angkor Wat temples.

Day 2	Visit to Chau Say Tevoda, Thommanon, Ta Kéo, Ta Prom, Bantéay Kdei, Kravan, Srah Srang.
Day 3	Visit to Bakong, Preah Kô, Lolei, Pré Rup, Neak Pean, Eastern Mébon, Ta Som and Neak Pean.
Day 4	Excursion to the Tonlé Sap Lake.
Day 5	Flight back to Phnom Penh

4. Visits to the remote Province of Rattanakiri

Day 1 (Sat)	Flight Phnom Penh/Rattanakiri. City sightseeing. Visits to the Isei Patamak Pagoda, the Falls of Kachanh.
Day 2	Visit to Yak Lom.
Day 3	Visit to tribal villages, the Kanseng and Kamsan lakes.
Day 4	Visit to the O Chum Dam, Rom Plao.
Day 5	Flight back to Phnom Penh

| Price per PAX: | 1 PAX | US$778 |
| | 2-3 PAX | US$750 (Single Supplement: US$80) |

FROM WORLD-WIDE TOURIST AGENCIES

In the United Kingdom

Contact **Regent Holidays (UK) Ltd**, 15 John Street, Bristol BS1 2HR; tel: (0117) 921 1711 (24 hours); fax: (0117) 925 4866. Regent, who have specialised in travel to Indochina since 1980, offer the following for the 1995/96 season.

Itinerary 1

Day 1	Airport transfer. Afternoon introductory tour of Phnom Penh including Wat Phnom, the Ounalom Pagoda and Victory Monument.
Day 2	Day trip to Siem Reap. Sightseeing to Angkor Wat, Bayon and South Gate of Angkor Thom.
Day 3	National Museum, Tuol Sleng, Tuol Tom Pong Market and the 'Killing Fields of Choeung Ek'.
Day 4	Transfer to Phnom Penh Airport.

Itinerary 2

Day 1	Airport transfer. Same as Day 1 above.
Day 2	Flight to Siem Reap. Afternoon visit to South Gate of Angkor Thom and Bayon.
Day 3	Further sightseeing at Angkor Thom and Angkor Wat.
Day 4	Same as Day 3 above.
Day 5	Airport transfer.

	Prices in US$		
	1 PAX	2 or more PAX	Single Suppl't
Itinerary 1	741.00	566.00	108.00
Itinerary 2	1062.00	751.00	142.00

Price includes: Accommodation on bed and breakfast basis in Phnom Penh and Siem Reap, transportation and transfers in Cambodia. Flight London-Phnom Penh return by Thai International (+ UK air passenger duty of £10) £710.

They also have a Vietnam, Cambodia and Laos tour (16 days) for US$3455 (1 PAX), US$2476 (2 PAX).

In Australia
Orbitours Pty Ltd, 3rd Floor, 73 Walker Street, North Sydney NSW 2060, PO Box 834, North Sydney NSW 2059, Australia; tel: 612 954 1399; fax: 612 954 1655. They have specialised in travel to Indochina since 1980.

Itinerary 1

Day 1　Airport transfer after arrival. Afternoon tour of Phnom Penh including Wat Phnom, Ounalom Pagoda, Royal Palace including Silver Pagoda and National Museum.

Day 2　Flight to Siem Reap. Tour to Angkor Wat, Bayon, South Gate of Angkor Thom, Elephant Terrace, Terrace of the Tightrope Walkers.

Day 3　Further sightseeing if time allows before return flight to Phnom Penh. Tour to Tuol Sleng, and 'Killing Fields of Choeung Ek'.

Day 4　Airport transfer.

Hotel Class	Twin Share	Single Sup	Extra n't Angkor	Single Sup	Tour Code
Standard Hotels e.g. Regent/de la Paix	A$819	A$82	A$111	A$12	AN4C
Superior Hotels e.g. Juliana/Grand	A$915	A$175	A$161	A$51	AN4B
Deluxe Hotels e.g. Cambodiana/ Ta Promh	A$1082	A$350	A$185	A$61	ANLA

Itinerary 2

Day 1　Arrive Phnom Penh. Half day introductory tour of Phnom Penh similar to Day 1 (Itinerary 1).

Day 2　Free morning to explore. Afternoon, Tuol Sleng, 'Killing Fields of Choeung Ek'. Visit to Tuol Tom Pong Market.

Day 3　Visit Tonlé Bati Temple, south of Phnom Penh. One hour cruise on Mekong and Tonlé Sap (visit to Tonlé Bati sometimes not available).

Day 4　Flight to Siem Reap. Visit South Gate of Angkor Thom, Bayon, Elephant Terraces, the Terrace of the Tightrope Walkers, sunset at Angkor Wat.

Day 5　East Gate Angkor Thom, Chau Say Tevoda, Thommanon, Ta Kéo, Preah Kravan, Bantéay Kdei, sacred pond of Srah Srang.

Day 6　Temples north of Angkor Thom. Complex of Preah Khan, Phimeanakas. Temples east of Angkor Thom. Roluos Group including Bakong and Lolei.

Day 7　Flight to Phnom Penh. Afternoon free.

Day 8　Transfer to airport for onward flight.

Hotel Class	Twin Share	Single Supplement
A. Cambodiana or Floating/Grand	A$2370 US$1588	A$863 US$578
B. Borey Thmei/Grand or Bophea	A$1912 US$1281	A$373 US$250

Prices are liable to change at short notice due to hotels changing their rates.

Both itineraries include air Phnom Penh/Siem Reap, accommodation, meals, transfer, sightseeing and guide, visa fee.

Other more extensive itineraries are available on request. They offer an extensive 21 day/20 night tour of Indochina for A$4809 (using superior hotels) and A$5934 (using deluxe hotels).

They also have an 18 day/17 night tour of Indochina for A$4343 (using superior hotels) and A$5468 (using deluxe hotels) and a 15 day/14 night tour for A$3583 (using superior hotels) and A$4495 (using deluxe hotels). All give 2 nights in Vientiane, 3 in Luang Prabang, 3 in Phnom Penh, 3 in Angkor, 2 in Hanoi and 2 in Saigon.

In Vietnam

Saigon Tourist Travel Service, 49 Le Thanh Ton, Ho Chi Minh City; tel: 848 298914/298129/230102; fax: 848 224987/225516; telex: 812745 SGTOUR-VT. Also at Hotel Saigon, 80 Ly Thuong Kiet Street, Hanoi; tel: 844 268501/268502//268503 ext 339; fax: 266631; telex: 411259 SGNHOT-VT.

For the 1995/96 season they are offering:
Itinerary 1   Phnom Penh-Siem Reap 4 days/3 nights.
Itinerary 2   Phnom Penh-Siem Reap 5 days/4 nights.
Itinerary 3   Phnom Penh-Siem Reap 5 days/5 nights.
Itinerary 4   Phnom Penh-Siem Reap 7 days/6 nights.
Itinerary 5   Phnom Penh-Siem Reap 8 days/7 nights.

Itinerary	Number of people					
	1	2	3-6	7-10	11 up	Sgl Sup
1	2484	1308	1308	1296	1296	240
2	2892	1536	1536	1524	1524	320
3	3360	1776	1776	1752	1752	400
4	4008	2136	2136	2112	2112	480
5	4476	2376	2376	2352	2352	560

Above prices include air transfers, accommodation in superior class hotels in Saigon and Phnom Penh/Siem Reap all tours including Saigon. Hanoi transfer extra.

Index